Planning and Conflict

Planning and Conflict discusses the reasons for conflicts around urban developments and analyzes their shape in contemporary cities. It offers an interdisciplinary framework for scholars to engage with the issue of planning conflicts, focusing on both empirical and theoretical inquiry.

By reviewing different perspectives for planners to engage with conflicts, and not simply mediate or avoid them, *Planning and Conflict* provides a theoretically informed look forward to the future of engaged, responsive city development that involves all its stakeholders.

Enrico Gualini is Professor of Planning Theory and Urban–Regional Policy Analysis at the Institute for Urban and Regional Planning of Technische Universität Berlin – Berlin University of Technology, Germany. Among his published books are *Planning and the Intelligence of Institutions* (Ashgate, 2001), *Multilevel Governance and Institutional Change* (Ashgate, 2004) and *Framing Strategic Urban Projects* (Routledge, 2007, co-edited with Willem Salet).

"To avoid conflict is to weaken planning's potential to contribute to a just society. But how should we think of conflict theoretically and in relation to planning practice? This book provides insightful answers and Enrico Gualini is to be lauded for organizing a significant contribution to the planning literature."

Robert A. Beauregard, Professor, Columbia University, USA

"This timely collection offers a much-needed, multidisciplinary rethinking of the consensus/conflict debates. A rich collection of cases critically enquires into the capacities of planning processes to frame and transform the role of conflict and to repoliticize planning and urban policy-making. This highly accessible book stimulates consideration of alternative ways of thinking and acting."

Jean Hillier, Professor Emeritus, RMIT University, Melbourne, Australia

"Finally a book that elevates the idea of conflict and dissensus to the forefront of planning theory and practice. This collection dispels the myth that planning is about seeking consensus by demonstrating that democratic and transformative planning requires nurturing dissensus and acknowledging conflict. A must-read for those who seek to lift planning theory and practice from the deadlock they are currently in."

Erik Swyngedouw, Professor of Geography, University of Manchester, UK

"In contemporary cities urban development often becomes a flashpoint of citizen disaffection, resulting in widespread protest, and confounding politicians and the media. The contributions in this important book explore, theoretically as well as empirically, the nature of such conflicts, and, more significantly, suggest how these can be handled to strengthen urban democracy and civic engagement, instead of creating political alienation, cynicism or worse."

Hendrik Wagenaar, University of Sheffield, UK

The RTPI Library Series

Editors: Robert Upton, *Infrastructure Planning Commission in England*
Jill Grant, *Dalhousie University, Canada*
Stephen Ward, *Oxford Brookes University, United Kingdom*

Published by Routledge in conjunction with the Royal Town Planning Institute, this series of leading-edge texts looks at all aspects of spatial planning theory and practice from a comparative and international perspective.

Planning in Postmodern Times
Philip Allmendinger

The Making of the European Spatial Development Perspective
Andreas Faludi and Bas Waterhout

Planning for Crime Prevention
Richard Schneider and Ted Kitchen

The Planning Polity
Mark Tewdwr-Jones

Shadows of Power
An Allegory of Prudence in Land-Use Planning
Jean Hillier

Urban Planning and Cultural Identity
William J.V. Neill

Place Identity, Participation and Planning
Edited by Cliff Hague and Paul Jenkins

Planning for Diversity
Dory Reeves

Planning the Good Community
New Urbanism in Theory and Practice
Jill Grant

Planning, Law and Economics
Barrie Needham

Planning and Conflict

Critical Perspectives on Contentious Urban Developments

Edited by Enrico Gualini

Routledge
Taylor & Francis Group

NEW YORK AND LONDON

First published 2015
by Routledge
711 Third Avenue, New York, NY 10017

and by Routledge
2 Park Square, Milton Park, Abingdon, Oxon OX14 4RN

Routledge is an imprint of the Taylor & Francis Group, an informa business

Library of Congress Cataloging in Publication Data
Planning and conflict : critical perspectives on contentious urban developments
/ edited by Enrico Gualini.
pages cm. -- (RTPI library series)
1. City planning. 2. Land use, Urban--Political aspects. 3. Urban policy. I.
Gualini, Enrico. II. Title: Planning, conflict.
HT166.P526 2015
307.1'216--dc23
2014031798

ISBN: 978-0-415-83584-8 (hbk)
ISBN: 978-0-415-83585-5 (pbk)
ISBN: 978-0-203-73493-3 (ebk)

Typeset in Goudy
by Saxon Graphics Ltd, Derby

MIX
Paper from
responsible sources
FSC
www.fsc.org   FSC® C013604

Printed and bound by CPI Group (UK) Ltd, Croydon, CR0 4YY

Contents

Illustrations

Figures

Tables

Contributors

Sophie Allain is Senior Researcher at the French National Institute for Agricultural Research. She conducts research in policy analysis on environmental governance and deliberative situations, through an interpretive approach relying on the negotiation concept and a mediative standpoint. Along these lines, she has created specific learning-training programs for deliberative practitioners and is engaged as a consultant in complex public environmental operations requiring dialogue and implying governance change.

Marco Allegra (MA Middle Eastern Politics, SOAS; PhD Political Science, University of Torino, Italy) is Research Fellow at the Centro de Investigação e Estudos de Sociologia (CIES), Instituto Universitàrio de Lisboa (IUL), Lisbon, Portugal. His main research interests are urban studies and political geography, Middle East politics and the Israeli–Palestinian conflict. His articles have appeared in, among others, *Citizenship Studies*, *Mediterranean Politics*, *The Geography Compass*, *Urban Studies* and *Environment and Planning A*.

Irene Bianchi is a Research Fellow in the Department of Design and Planning in Complex Environments at IUAV University of Venice, Italy. She received a Bachelor's Degree in Economics and Social Sciences from the Free University of Bolzano/Bozen, Italy, and a Joint Master's Degree in Urban and Environmental Planning from IUAV and the University of Girona, Spain. Her academic experience includes an internship at the Institute of Urban and Regional Planning at Technische Universität Berlin – Berlin University of Technology, Germany.

Giacomina Di Salvo is an architect and planner and holds a PhD in Urban and Territorial Planning from Sapienza Università di Roma, Italy, where she also was Post-doctoral Fellow in Local Development and Lecturer in Urban Planning and Design. She is currently working as a local councilor in Rome at the neighborhood level. Her competences in local development and planning have been developed through participating in EU projects and in her professional experience as a planner in the field of environmental risk, with a focus on seismic risk and climate change in urban and regional planning.

Anna Durnová is a Hertha-Firnberg Assistant Professor at the University of Vienna, Austria, and associated researcher at the Life-Science Governance Research Platform. A political scientist and a language theorist by training, she researches the role of emotions in politics. She was Visiting Professor at the Masaryk University of Brno, Czech Republic and a Researcher at the University of Lyon, France, as well as a Visiting Research Fellow at the Universities of Essex, Paris and Prague. Furthermore, she is an advisory board member of the Interpretive Policy Analysis Conference, editor of the Austrian *Journal for Political Science* and a Book Review Editor of *Critical Policy Studies*.

Nina Gribat is currently Interim Professor and Chair of International Urbanism at the University of Stuttgart, Germany. She has qualifications in architecture and planning and her PhD was on the topic of 'Governing the Future of a Shrinking City: Hoyerswerda, East Germany.' Her research interests include urban conflicts and protests, urban shrinkage, the 1960/1970s reforms and protests in German Faculties of Architecture, and the different waves of applied teaching methodologies in architecture and planning. She is part of the editorial collective of the open access and German language journal on critical urban studies *sub\urban*. She has published papers on translation and conflicting subjectivities of governing shrinkage.

Enrico Gualini is Professor of Planning Theory and Urban–Regional Policy Analysis at the Institute for Urban and Regional Planning of Technische Universität Berlin – Berlin University of Technology, Germany. He holds a PhD in Planning from Politecnico di Milano (1997) and was affiliated with Politecnico di Milano (1994–1997), the University of Dortmund (1997–2000), and the University of Amsterdam (2001–2006). His research interests are the social construction of space and the political dimension of socio-spatial practices, the analysis of spatial development policies, the emergence of governance practices and the resulting challenges for democratic politics and institutions, as well as current planning-theoretical reflections on such issues.

Patsy Healey is Professor Emeritus in the School of Architecture, Planning and Landscape at Newcastle University, UK. She has qualifications in geography and planning and is a specialist in planning theory and practice, with a particular interest in strategic spatial planning for city regions and in urban regeneration policies. She is also known for her work on planning theory. She is a past President of the Association of European Schools of Planning, and was awarded the OBE in 1999, and the RTPI's Gold Medal in 2007. In 2009, she was made a Fellow of the British Academy.

Margo Huxley has a PhD in geography and research interests in cultural, historical and post-colonial urban geography and planning. Before retirement, she was Senior Lecturer in Town and Regional Planning at the University of Sheffield, UK; she has held visiting posts in Canada, New Zealand and South Africa, and has worked in planning practice in Australia. She has published numerous papers on gender and the built environment, foreign property investment, and spatial aspects of Foucault's notion of governmentality. Ongoing interests include informal settlements and urban shrinkage as contrasting aspects of contemporary urban conditions, and archival research on nineteenth-century advocacy of domestic (UK) 'home colonies.'

Donald Leffers is currently a PhD candidate in the Department of Geography at York University, Toronto, Canada. He is interested in the power and politics of urban planning, development and environmentally based land-use policies. His current work focuses on property developers as institutional actors in the governance, planning and practice of urban–rural fringe development in the Toronto region.

Samuel Mössner holds a PhD in geography and is a Researcher at the Institute for Environmental Social Sciences and Geography at the University of Freiburg, Germany. He is the author of a book on urban social policy and governance and several papers on urban politics. His research has a focus on the post-politics of urban sustainability. Moreover, he is working on protests and conflicts in the context of urban regeneration projects in Europe. Currently, he is conducting a research project about protest movements in Barcelona, Frankfurt and Turin.

Carolina Pacchi is Assistant Professor in the Department of Architecture and Urban Studies at Politecnico di Milano, Italy, where she teaches Planning Theory and Practice and Local Conflict Management. Her research interests concern urban governance, social innovation at local level, and planning strategies based on stakeholder involvement. She has been involved in a number of EU-funded research projects on governance in urban, environmental and local development policies. She is the author of a number of papers and articles, and of the book *La macchina del tempo: Leggere la città europea contemporanea* (with E. Granata, Marinotti, 2001), which was translated into Spanish and also published in Latin America.

Gabriele Pasqui is Director of the Department of Architecture and Urban Studies at Politecnico di Milano, Italy, where he is Full Professor of Urban and Local Development Policies and past President of the Bachelor Course in Planning and of the Master's Course in Urban Planning and Policy Design. His key research interests include strategic planning in metropolitan regions, urban politics and policies, and local development policies. He is the author of the book *Strategic Planning for Contemporary Urban Regions* (with A. Balducci and V. Fedeli, Ashgate, 2011).

Barbara Pizzo is Researcher and Senior Lecturer in Urban Planning at Sapienza Università di Roma, Italy. She holds a PhD in Urban and Territorial Planning and is currently a member of the board of this PhD Program. She works mainly in the field of planning theory with a critical orientation. Her interests are in the processes of socio-spatial structuration and their links to socio-economic changes and to public policies. She has done work on the concept of landscape as an instrument to investigate the social construction of reality, on the importance of time and scale, and on the political meaning of nature and related environmental issues.

Paola Pucci is Associate Professor in Urban Planning at Politecnico di Milano, Italy, where she coordinates the PhD course in Urban Planning, Design and Policy. She holds a PhD in Regional Planning and has taught urban design and mobility policy during a fellowship at Institut d'Urbanisme de Grenoble, France, (2009–2010) and in the Master's Program at Politecnico di Milano. She has taken part in Italian and international research projects on infrastructures and mobility policy, on which she has published books and articles in Italian and international journals. Her latest publications include *Designing Open Spaces in a Valley* (Maggioli, 2013).

Jonathan Rokem is an urban researcher and planner. In 2013–2014, he was Erasmus Mundus Post-doctoral Research Fellow in the Department of Human Geography at Lund University, Sweden. He holds a PhD (2009–2014) from the Department of Politics and Government at Ben Gurion University of the Negev, Israel, and a Master's Degree from the 'Cities Program' at the London School of Economics and Political Science, UK. His research interests and publications focus on spatial and social critical analysis of urban planning, comparative urbanism, housing policy and urban segregation. He also works as an urban planning consultant specializing in community engagement with NGOs and the private and public sectors.

Luis del Romero Renau is Lecturer in Geography and Environment Studies in the Department of Geography at the University of Valencia, Spain. He has worked as a PhD researcher at the Universities of Quebec and Laval in Canada and as Visiting Professor at the University of Freiburg, Germany. His main research interests are the study of land-use conflicts in the city and the study of shrinking regions, in both cases to propose new planning tools. He has published articles and book chapters about these topics in Spanish, Catalan, English and French. He is currently responsible for the Spaces in Conflict and Crisis research group.

Nanke Verloo is a PhD candidate and Lecturer in the Department of Political Science at the University of Amsterdam, the Netherlands. She is a political ethnographer who is interested in the interactions between policy-practitioners, citizens and street-level bureaucrats in the urban environment. Her PhD research reveals how urban conflicts can be understood as an opportunity for democratic governance. She writes about the ways in which informal performances of citizenship are often excluded from formal political repertoires of citizen participation. Her research takes place on the boundary between theory and practice.

PART I
INTRODUCTION TO
THE VOLUME

1

Conflict in the City: Democratic, Emancipatory—and Transformative? In Search of the Political in Planning Conflicts

Enrico Gualini

Introduction

This volume addresses the issue of conflict in urban development in two dimensions: as a key to regaining meaning for the political in urban policy contexts, and as a potential resource for transformation in local policy.

Understanding conflict as a constitutive element of social relations and as a source of their strength and ability to innovate has an important tradition in policy analysis and planning. Authors who have significantly influenced thinking about urban policy and planning in pluralist and contentious societies (e.g., Lindblom 1965; Friedmann 1987; Hirschman 1994; Dahl 2000) have addressed the question of the conditions under which conflict and antagonism can be turned from disruptive social phenomena into transformative potentials. There is no doubt that this can be seen as an important thread in critical and progressive planning theory.

The issue gains a new meaning today, however, in relation to 'post-democratic' and 'post-political' practices that tend to fence off contestation and conflict from the domain of urban politics—only to see them emerge in new, 'insurgent' forms at the core of contested urban development practices.

The contributions in this volume address contemporary issues of conflict in urban development and planning in a plurality of perspectives. In doing so, they move from three assumptions that together define the scope and intention of the volume: they see contention and conflict as key dimensions for understanding and conferring meaning to politics and to 'the political' in cities; they aim to (re)politicize urban policy and planning as well as planning theory debates; and they do so by intersecting relevant contributions and debates in the social sciences, political theory and policy analysis, and planning theory.

The latter point is crucial, as different understandings of the political and of the role of conflict as a potential resource for political emancipation and democratic transformation—and different conceptual frames of reference—appear today as a reason for a divide among scholars in the fields of urban theory and research on one side, and of planning theory and research on the other side. As will be argued in this volume, there is, however, much scope for exchange in a mutual focus on understanding processes of formation and potentials for social and political transformation of insurgent practices of contestation in urban development and planning.

Planning, Conflict and Pluralist Society: Which Democratic Politics?

A first conceptual node to be addressed, as we approach a discussion of conflict and the political, is represented by conceptions of democratic politics in a pluralist society that frame their understanding.

A key tenet of liberal–pluralist conceptions of democracy is acknowledging conflict as a constitutive reality and as a challenge for democratic politics. Accordingly, in light of an understanding of planning as a public task, embedded in liberal-democratic societies and institutions, acknowledging conflict and the responsibility and role of planning in the face of conflict has represented something like a political coming of age.

Behind references to democracy, however, stand different models of democratic politics, with different implications for understanding and, above all, dealing with conflict. This is apparent both in the historical development of planning theory's engagement with social conflict and in current debates—with significant potentials for division. As a matter of fact, the issue of conflict still marks significant differences in worldviews in planning theory and practice. The aim in this brief overview is not to single out theoretical models of democracy per se but to assess how these have framed planning debates and practices in a complex interplay with a variety of cultural influences. The idea is that we need to bridge theoretical debates on democratic politics and debates in relevant areas of empirical social research—in particular research on contentious politics and social movements in urban policy (cf. Della Porta 2013)—in order to critically engage with planning conflicts in a cross-disciplinary dialogue.

The rise of planning as a public task increasingly embedded in state bureaucracies and supported by the development of an integrated planning system relied on a dominant *aggregative-representative* model of democracy. The statist-technocratic model embodied by the 'rational-comprehensive planning ideal' supported the claims for institutional recognition and the rise of an institutionalized 'politics of expertise,' as it fitted the process of consolidation of the dominant Eastonian model of a democratic state-centered politics (cf. Easton 1965).

The assumption underlying the 'democratic moment' (Crouch 2004: 6–11)—occurring in most Western-capitalist countries at the outset of the Keynesian–Fordist post-war era—was that, with expanding mass democracy, popular sovereignty (as understood by the classical model of democracy) was increasingly becoming inadequate to deal with complex, development-oriented public tasks in the areas of the economy and welfare. While notions of the 'common good' and the 'public interest' became part of the mythology of modern liberal democracies, their pursuit was hence only conceivable as an aggregation of interests and preferences and no longer as an object of a 'rational' political consensus. Hence the emphasis on democratic procedures of the aggregation of preferences, in the first place, through political representation by parties and a political apparatus legitimated by popular vote but, even more significantly, through administrative 'expert' practices. Democratic politics is therefore primarily viewed from an instrumentalist-procedural viewpoint; it is a set of political procedures for the treatment of interest-groups pluralism, but also—and increasingly so in the view of planners—as a procedural 'expert' rationality for bringing to a synthesis and for achieving the public interest. Significantly, a procedural understanding of systems planning based on the act of making decisions by design—against the arbitrariness of political behavior— as "a set of procedures" with "exercise of choice as its characteristic intellectual act" (Davidoff and Reiner 1962: 103) or, as in Faludi (1973), as a general approach to decision-making intended as application of scientific method to decision-making, highly relied on assumptions on the availability and legitimacy of means for interests aggregation, through the public function of 'embedded' technical expertise.

The *aggregative-representative* democratic model is thus premised on the assumption of a 'tacit consensus' on the political validity of technocratic choice—one that could only be validated, self-referentially, through technical-instrumental verification. In light of such assumption, conflict is bound to be viewed as either expression of political arbitrariness or 'systemic noise.' Conflict is seen as a disruptive force that causes an imbalance in a system of interrelated parties—an imbalance that needs to be institutionally resolved through legitimate modes of representation and aggregation of interests.

The belief in a tacit consensus underlying liberal democracy was soon to be shaken, as we know, on both theoretical and socio-political grounds—with the discovery of social conflict playing a key role. The emergence of civil rights movements and social contention in cities highlighted—from the grassroots— the political dimension of planning processes that was being uncovered, among others, by Banfield's analysis (1959) of the urban policy process, by Altshuler's and Schön's inquiries into planners' 'espoused theories' (Altshuler 1965a, 1965b; Schön 1983) and by Wildavsky's critique (1973) of planners' false consciousness vis-à-vis politics. Simon's arguments about 'bounded rationality' (1957), the discovery of the dilemmas of decision-making (Rittel and Webber 1973) and Lindblom's and Dahl's 'incremental rationality' (Lindblom 1959, 1965; Dahl 1961; Polsby 1980) contributed to theoretically delegitimize the idea of a technocratic pursuit of the public interest on grounds of a different ontology and epistemology of policy processes, in which the idea of the political was strictly tied to the capacity of mutual adjustment in an environment characterized by potential non-mediated conflicts of interest. While the incrementalists' and pluralists' ideas of an 'intelligence of democracy' and of a polyarchic social order (Dahl 1971) was premised on a conception of embedded liberalism, their influence was crucial in reassessing conflicts of interest and strategically oriented negotiating practices as social forces. Conflicts are seen here as a potentially positive force that can promote change, integration and adaptability. Meanwhile, social activism and progressive planning opened to understanding the role of contention and of struggles for values—and of the role of planning in facilitating their treatment—in a public domain that proved ever more contested (e.g., Davidoff 1965; Webber 1969; Forester 1982).

Critique of the practice of Western democracies highlighted the perverse combination of rational actor assumptions, reliance on institutionalized representation and belief in the neutrality of a 'politics of expertise' under-lying the aggregative-representative model of democracy. The effects of this combination originated diffuse disaffection with democratic institutions, the emerging legitimacy crisis of institutionalized democratic apparatuses (e.g., Habermas 1975; Offe 1984), and a spread of democratic experiments—in order to change, but also extend beyond, liberal institutions.

The *participatory-deliberative* model of democracy emerges as an alternative throughout a variety of local experimental practices, backed by a significant renewal in theoretical frameworks. Its key underlying assumption is that, in a democratic system, political decisions should be reached through a process of deliberation among free and equal citizens, endowed with the rationality of argumentation and adequate means of communication. Under this conception of democratic politics, the reality of pluralism and of the co-presence of many different conceptions of the good—including their contested nature and their conflictual potential—is a premise that needs to be acknowledged and accepted as a normative requisite; at the same, a normative idea of the 'public' and of the 'public interest' is revived in the form of the pursuit of a consensus on normatively and ethically defined political issues. A participatory-deliberative democratic politics pursues therefore a normative and ethical rationality which is premised, first of all, on the existence of liberal-democratic institutions that, second, enable the embedment of democratic sovereignty to be actively exercised. The embedment of democratic practices in liberal institutions is therefore only a precondition for a practice of democracy that needs to be exercised through adequate procedures of deliberation. Through deliberation, it is possible to reach forms of agreement that would satisfy both rationality—understood as defense of liberal rights—and democratic legitimacy—as represented by popular sovereignty.

Particularly significant for planning theory and practice—and a key inspiration for redefining its progressive mission—is the fact that the exercise of democracy in this model is no longer premised on general systems of representation but on a renewal of popular sovereignty as 'communicatively generated power' through "free public reasoning among equals who are governed by the decisions" (Cohen 1988: 186). This implies the need to reconstruct democracy and conditions for sovereignty at the local level, in the context and in adherence to the situation in which a public issue is raised and is contested. Accordingly, the practice of deliberation is seen as both legitimate and effective when practiced within a political community that is identifiable inasmuch as it shares a public issue or concern—even if controversially or contentiously.

The idea of a deliberatively enacted popular sovereignty is significantly inspired by the tradition of philosophical pragmatism, particularly influential in progressive planning (Healey 2008), as well as by a conception of a communicative rationality and political ethics influenced by the renewal of liberal philosophy represented paradigmatically by the work of Rawls (1971) and Habermas (1984).

The prospects of political emancipation are no longer tied to the pursuit of a public interest directed toward an ideal of progress based on abstract—and increasingly contested—goals, but to dealing with pluralism and differences within 'communities of fate' that take their own responsibility in defining the directions of public action. This includes a more politically responsible as well as socially effective way of dealing with conflicts.

Planning inspired by a participatory and deliberative model of democratic politics develops therefore from the initial adversarial model inspired by the idea of reconstructing community representation through advocacy (e.g., Davidoff 1965) to the development of collaborative approaches based on communicative ethics and argumentative rationality (e.g., Healey 1993, 1997: Innes 1995, 1996; Innes and Booher 1999) and on an engagement with relations of power and the reality of conflict (Forester 1982, 1989; Innes et al. 1994). Along with the idea of a 'critical pragmatism,' planning intended as a pragmatic-communicative practice (Forester 1989) is increasingly seen as a contribution to (re)constructing democratic communities. This ties in with the development of 'alternative,' i.e., integrative approaches to conflict resolution, in which the conduct of negotiation capable of overcoming deadlock and of producing 'positive-sum games' is premised upon the realization of conditions for a transparent deliberation on interests (cf. Susskind and Cruikshank 1987; Bryson and Crosby 1992; Susskind et al. 1999). Moving beyond this, however, practices of consensus-building in local planning processes are conceived not only as a way of anticipating or resolving conflicts in spatial and environmental development, but as a means for democratization and community-building. Hence, planning comes to be related to notions like the building of social, intellectual and political capital (Innes et al. 1994), institutional capacity-building (Healey 1997; Cars et al. 2002), the contribution to a political economy of attention and argumentation (Forester 1989) and to 'political alphabetization' (Forester and Krumholz 1990). Conflict is seen not only as a necessary starting point that reveals social power relations and demands to be acknowledged, but as a potential resource for change and social innovation if inscribed in a participatory and deliberative design, of which the planner is a key facilitator.

The intensified exchange with theories and applications of a deliberative-participatory model of democratic politics (e.g., Elster 1988; Dryzek 1990; Hirst 1994; Wright 1995; Fung and Wright 2003; Fung 2004) along with developments in critical and interpretive policy analysis and the argumentative turn (cf. Majone 1989; Fischer and Forester 1993; Hajer and Wagenaar 2003) give a crucial theoretical backing to this emergent paradigm of planning. To this must be added two major lines of contribution to dealing with conflict in public policy and planning: Rein and Schön's both individual and joint explorations of policy controversy and its connection to frame analysis (cf. Rein and Schön 1993; Schön and Rein 1994; Rein and Laws 2000), and Roe's narrative analysis approach to overcoming policy controversies (Roe 1994). Although not explicitly framed in terms of a theory of deliberative democracy, both Rein and Schön's idea of the reframing of controversies—through a design rationality based on the shared processes of de- and reconstruction of cognitive and action frames—and Roe's idea of building meta-narratives (as a means for overcoming power differentials by shared narrative exercise) imply participatory settings and conditions for public argumentation and communication typical of deliberative approaches (on this aspect, see also: Fischer 2003: 179; Wagenaar 2011: 88–90).

Deliberative ideas and practices of democracy have become a matter of theoretical contestation, and so have planning practices inspired by the 'collaborative planning' paradigm. This has originated in planning theory a wealth of critical contributions (e.g., Flyvbjerg 1998; Yiftachel and Huxley 2000; Flyvbjerg and Richardson 2002; Harris 2002), delineating—in an often schematic way—a confrontation between two camps with incompatible theoretical references: Habermas's ethics of communicative action on the one side and Foucault's analysis of discursive formation and the 'micropolitics' of power on the other. A key dilemma facing the participatory-deliberative model of democracy lies not only in its practical challenges—on which a wealth of applied and often barely critical literature has developed—but in its inherently political implications, and actually in the idea of the political it involves. A participatory-deliberative model of democratic politics assumes that social inclusion and social objectivity—if local and contingent—can be realized through and in the form of a rational argumentation; this, however, stands at odds with an alternative interpretation of one key assumption of the model, the fact that sovereignty and political subjectivity are exercised through such a rational argumentation, and that this represents the means for realizing an equal public. From a post-structuralist and post-foundational critical perspective, however, argumentation is constituted through relations of power and through hegemonic practices, in which what is defined as a consensus may be disguised through forms of 'objectivation.' The converse assumption, therefore, is not that rationality, or rational argumentation à la Habermas, can overcome power, but that power has a rationality of its own (cf. Flyvbjerg 1998).

According to the *radical-agonistic* model of democracy, the institutions and practices of politics' liberal democracy, rather than a necessary frame for deliberative emancipation, tend to reproduce relations of power and hegemony that impede a 'free public reasoning among equals'; particularly when geared toward realizing a 'consensus society,' deliberative practices therefore tend to contribute to building a 'post-democratic trap.' On the contrary, a radical-agonistic conception of democracy assumes that the formation of political subjectivity is truly only possible in a struggle for diversity and inclusion and in a struggle over hegemony. Beyond a rational consensus, therefore, the passions and emotions that are at play in politics are struggles for interpretation in a hegemonic field of practices that cannot pragmatically be reduced to a common interest. Politics is therefore, in its essence, made of practices which give expression to this struggle.

Whereas the participatory-deliberative model of democracy emphasizes consensus without exclusion and free dialogue among equals, the public sphere as a domain for settling differences and the possibility of integrative conflict resolution within a framework of liberal institutions, radical-agonistic thinkers of democracy emphasize 'radical negativity' and antagonism as the essence of politics, relating to a 'constitutive outside' as a condition for political subjectivity, the public sphere as a domain for dissent and resistance, and a condition of 'radical' or 'deep' pluralism that challenges the legitimacy of the liberal order. When contention and conflict arise, their innovative potential lies in producing insurgent practices at the disjunctions of liberal-democratic institutional practices (cf. Holston 1999, 2009; Harvey 2009, 2012). This has obviously a crucial significance for the way of understanding conflict. It is from here—from these alternative understandings of a democratic politics—that we now move on to discuss the current divide in dealing with conflicts in planning theory and urban studies.

Redefining 'the Political': Planning as Agonistic Pluralism?

The debate on the political in urban policy and planning has been enlivened by the influence exerted by post-foundational political thinking and by radical theories of democracy by authors such as Claude Lefort (1988), Jacques Rancière (1995, 1999, 2001, 2006), Ernesto Laclau (Laclau and Mouffe 1985; Laclau 1996), Chantal Mouffe (1993, 2000, 2005, 2013), Alain Badiou (2001) and others (e.g., Donolo 1992; Norval 2007). Moving beyond the Habermas–Foucault divide that dominated debate on collaborative planning, this line of theorizing has exerted a powerful impact as it challenges the conception of the political represented by planning theory affiliated to traditional models of democracy.

A radical-agonistic conception of democratic politics inserts a disruptive wedge between the classical liberal model of aggregative-representative democracy, on the one hand, and the model of participatory-deliberative democracy, embedded in a framework of liberal institutions, on the other hand. To adopt an expression by Rancière, the former model appears to realize a "reduction of the political by the social" (1995: 11) insofar as what is 'political' is reduced to a technically and institutionally appropriate calculus of the aggregation of social preferences. The latter, conversely, appears to realize a "reduction of the social by the political" (ibid.), insofar as societal pluralism and its differences seem amenable to be captured by the procedural rationality of a politics of deliberation. The relationship between the social and the political, to the contrary, is what radical democratic thinking assumes to be ever open, and not amenable to closure.

By 'the political,' reference is here to the meaning that authors like Mouffe and Rancière—despite their differences—attach to the terms, respectively, 'the political' and 'politics.' Given the theoretical significance of distinctions made by radical thinkers in defining politics, it is useful to sort out ambiguities by clarifying terms and, by this, to clarify our position. As is known, several of these authors place emphasis on a definition of politics that entails a dualistic distinction, but this precise distinction is terminological, not consistent across them despite theoretical similarities. The most notable cases discussed here are Badiou, Mouffe and Rancière. In his work on the ethics of political experience, Badiou defines *le politique* (i.e., 'the political') as the tradition of political philosophy—in a way akin to the critique of political philosophy and to its longing to 'dissolve' politics conducted by Rancière (1995, 1999). On the other hand, he defines *la politique* (i.e., 'politics') as an experiential identification with the truth of an event which is 'political' and confers political meaning in this experience, as it represents an interruption of the order of the real: a truth as "the real process of a fidelity to an event: that which fidelity *produces* in the situation" (Badiou 2001: 42, cit. in Mouffe 2013: 16). Political action is seen as ethical adherence to such an event. Mouffe on her part has conducted and articulated since her early work (Mouffe 1993, 2000, 2005) a critique of political theory and practice based upon a distinction between 'politics' and 'the political.' For Mouffe, 'politics' "refers to the ensemble of practices, discourses and institutions that seeks to establish a certain order and to organize human coexistence in conditions which are always potentially conflicting, since they are affected by the dimension of 'the political'"; this is, in turn, the dimension of antagonism that is ever present and never fully suppressed in the sphere of social relations (Mouffe 2013: 2–3). In a similar vein to Rancière (1995), it is the constitutive dimension of antagonism in social relations that defies attempts to reduce the political to the social, and that confers on social relations their political meaning.

More radically, Rancière identifies in the sphere of political organization a counterpart—if not a counterproject—to politics as lived experience; hence his well-known distinction between 'police' (*police*) and 'politics' (*politique*) (Rancière 1999: 28–42, 2004: 6). For Rancière, 'police' is "the set of procedures whereby the aggregation and consent of collectivities is achieved, the organization of powers, the distribution of places and roles, and the systems for legitimizing this distribution" (Rancière 1999: 28). 'Police' is not the same as state apparatus, but rather the ensemble of *dispositifs* that define "the configuration of the perceptible in which one or the other is inscribed" (ibid.: 29). The following quotation from his major work, *La mésentente* (1999, orig. 1995), expresses this in a powerful way:

> The police is thus first an order of bodies that defines the allocation of ways of doing, ways of being, and ways of saying, and sees that those bodies are assigned by name to a particular place and task; it is an order of the visible and the sayable that sees that a particular activity is visible and another is not, that this speech is understood as discourse and another as noise. (Rancière 1999: 29)

This quotation hints at the proximity of Rancière's approach to sociological new institutionalism and governmentality studies in understanding 'police' as a quasi-natural order of things and as an institutionalized domain of discursive and material practices realizing effects of the 'conduct of conduct.' 'Police' and 'policing' are not the 'essence' or the mode of agency or intentionality of institutions, and should not be identified with them or with their disciplining rationale or intentionality; rather, their institutional intentionality is mediated through discursive practices of meaning-making that may realize disciplining effects. Accordingly, 'police' is not necessarily the expression of a disciplinary intentionality, and "[p]olicing is not so much a 'disciplining' of bodies as a rule of governing their appearing, a configuration of *occupations* and the properties of the spaces where these occupations are distributed" (ibid., italics in orig.).

Police realizes a quasi-natural order of things, an articulation of relations in the sphere of the social that suppresses the sphere of the political—the *dispositifs* of police being actively involved in reproducing this policing order.

Politics, however, emerges whenever this quasi-natural order of things is challenged. Politics emerges when the contingency and the constructed character of a given order of things is revealed; and, according to Rancière, this occurs whenever a subject brings about the perception of a 'wrong.' Rancière, however, is wary of defining the nature of such a wrong in foundational ontological or deontological terms. Here, again, the possibility of asserting a 'fundamental wrong,' and the insurgence of the political in the domain of 'police,' is not premised on an ethics of democracy, but on understanding democracy as a never-ending political project—as one which can reach a contingent closure only in the forms of its contingent suppression, as 'police.' A 'democratic paradox' (see also: Mouffe 2000) is at play here which is largely discussed throughout Rancière's work: the fact that democracy can be identified with neither a form of society nor a regime of government, neither with representation nor with a juridico-political form. The "scandal of democracy" (Rancière 2006: 47) is precisely that it can only be realized as a never fully closed and never fully legitimized or uncontested interplay between inclusion and exclusion, as an ongoing practice of drawing borders and of contesting and pushing borders between inclusion and exclusion: "[d]emocracy is first this paradoxical condition of politics, the point where every legitimization is confronted with its ultimate lack of legitimacy, confronted with the egalitarian contingency that underpins the inegalitarian contingency itself" (Rancière 2006: 94).

The 'wrong' referred to by Rancière is not premised on an ethical principle (for a critique of the ethical reduction of politics, see: Rancière 1999: 135–136), but is perceived and acted upon, the moment in which a political subject breaks with a presupposition of 'policing' as a partition of society, with a configuration of democracy in which inclusion borders with exclusion. This is what Rancière means by stating that "politics exists wherever the count of parts and parties of society is disturbed by the inscription of a part of those who have no part" (Rancière 1999: 123). And this is what he intends by defining politics as "an extremely determined activity antagonistic to policing" (ibid.: 29).

The critique radical democratic thinkers express regarding consensual politics and deliberative approaches to dealing with conflicts has exerted significant influence on critical urban studies and planning theory (cf. Swyngedouw 2007, 2009; Purcell 2009, 2013). Their thinking on democratic politics has obviously important consequences for the way conflict is conceived. At same time, it is not unproblematic in many respects, and some of its key tenets deserve critical attention on their own terms. They may represent, at the same time, elements for a renewal.

What representatives of post-foundational political thinking share is, first of all, a rejection of essentialism and foundationalism (ontological or ethical) in understanding democracy. Their conception of the political is premised on the intrinsic fallibility of democracy, on the undecidability of democratic practices (Laclau and Mouffe 1985) and on the idea of 'democratic indetermination' (Lefort 1988). Furthermore, they share "a focus on identity, discourse, difference, struggle, and power as central forces in politics, a radically pluralistic conception of society, and a critical stance that is rooted in an ethics of pluralism" (Wagenaar 2011: 137). In particular, their conception of 'radical' or 'deep' pluralism represents an alternative to classic pluralist thinking in political theory and policy analysis, as their understanding of deep pluralism as a basic characteristic of the political underscores an inescapable political nature of social relations that cannot be reduced to representative or negotiated forms of the representation of interests (cf. Mouffe 2000, 2005). Deep pluralism represents a condition in which no common ground is given for settling political conflict (Mouffe 2000: 143). Deep pluralism, radical contingency, and the crisis of representation, combined with the fact that "the domain of politics [...] is not a neutral terrain that could be insulated from the pluralism of values" (Mouffe 2000: 92), but rather the domain in which this pluralism is potentially played out in its radicality, consequently lead the centrality of antagonism in the political. In authors like Laclau (1996), Mouffe and Rancière, the centrality attributed to antagonism is not dependent on a normativism of values. Rather, normativity is primarily defined in the negative, as it is the negation or suppression of antagonism that curtails the political and its emancipatory potential; hence, the centrality taken by "the dimension of antagonism that the pluralism of values entails and its ineradicable character" in conceiving the political (Mouffe 2000: 99). Antagonism is a category of the political related to the impossibility of any definite closure of political identities or social structures and of any overcoming of differences. There are therefore no a priori principles or criteria—no teleology, no eschatology—for overcoming difference, antagonism and conflict. 'The political' is a political ontology rooted in difference and conflict.

As the antagonistic moment is the defining element of the political, conflict is seen as a necessary dimension of democracy. And it is the terrain in which hegemonic and counter-hegemonic practices are played out, and through which the formation of political subjectivities may occur. This notion of political subjects being formed through the antagonistic moment is again premised on a non-essentialist rejection of a priori assumptions of individual subjectivism and collective identities. Political identities or subjectivities are intended as differential and as being constituted through antagonistic and counter-hegemonic practices. Thus, political identity is enacted in the constitution of a 'subject position' (cf. Laclau and Mouffe 1985: 115–122), always as a result of context and process. Identity and 'subject positions' are hence the expression of the relational, differential and contested nature of the political. They represent processes of 'subjectification' (Rancière 1999: 35–36) that question the effects of 'identifications' realized by a police order. In Rancière's words (Rancière 1999: 36), "[p]olitical subjectification produces a multiple" which contradicts the police logic: it does so not ex nihilo, but by transforming identities defined in the 'natural order' of police into "instances of experience of a dispute":

> Any subjectification is a disidentification, removal from the naturalness of a place, the opening up of a subject space where anyone can be counted since it is the space where those of no account are counted, where a connection is made between having a part and having no part. (Rancière 1999: 36)

From a planning theory perspective, what appear problematic are the consequences this conception may bring to bear on the possibility of agreement. Far from simply acknowledging the importance of disagreement as a source of social justice and innovation, defining antagonism and conflict as central moments of the political puts in question the political status of consensus. The way authors like Mouffe and Rancière conceive it appears in fact to admit it only from a perspective of radical negativity, apparently excluding any pragmatic—if critical—perspective of achieving a 'working consensus.' This obviously does not rule out the fact that the political takes place in a communicative and argumentative domain and is defined by discursive practices—this rather being a common concern of argumentative policy analysis, communicative planning theory and post-structuralist political thinking (e.g., Laclau and Mouffe 1985; Fischer and Forester 1993; Fischer and Gottweis 2012). The difference consists in the normative assumption of (dis)agreement. For Rancière, the possibility of 'agreement' consists not in finding a common ground, but in recognizing the subversive outside that challenges intrinsically contingent political identities. It expresses a rationality and a logic of communication that is radically different from that of Habermasian 'rational argumentation' (cf. Rancière 1999: 43–60). Similarly, agonistic public space is understood as a space of confrontation of diverse positions "without any possibility of a final reconciliation" (Mouffe 2013: 92). Consensus therefore is possible only as an outcome of articulation, not in the disappearance or overcoming of differences; according to Mouffe (2000: 33), non-coercive consensus is an impossibility, and consensus only politically conceivable as an ongoing dispute over the conditions for agreement. In a domain of the political defined by antagonism and radical negativity, consensus can be only the expression of an agonism as adversarial confrontation: a "conflictual consensus" (Mouffe 2013: xii).

We are obviously at a point here that highlights the reasons for the influence of radical democratic thinking on critical urban research vis-à-vis trends toward the post-democratic depoliticization and neoliberal instrumentalization of planning to a policing function (cf. Purcell 2008, 2009; Swyngedouw 2009; Gunder 2010), but also the difficulties they pose to a critical-pragmatic engagement with planning as progressive agency. The result is, all too apparently, the emergence of a new divide.

In the first place, it appears that the difficulties resulting from combining radical democratic thinking with planning resides in a dualism between thinking about agency in either 'policing' or antagonistic ways. The result is an undeniably important provocation—that planning cannot be 'democratic' (cf. Swyngedouw 2007, 2009, 2011). However, it is fair to say that, in the work of these thinkers, there seems to be a significant lack of theoretical elaboration on the mediation between the dualistic poles of 'police' and 'politics,' of 'democracy without agonism' and 'antagonism.' One reason for this may be a lack of engagement with the 'micropolitics' of social agency—something that has been precisely a core interest of a critical-pragmatic planning theory inspired by interpretive policy analysis. The result is often the reproduction of dichotomic and, ultimately, sterile interpretations. There has been a significant acknowledgment of this problem by authors who, while acknowledging the importance of these sources of critical political thinking, argue against adopting too rigid and unconciliatory oppositions (in planning theory, see: Sandercock 1998, 2000; Hillier 2002; Bond 2011; in urban studies, see: Beaumont and Nicholls 2008; Beaumont and Loopmans 2008). Uitermark et al. (2012: 2547–2548) also express their critique of the pervasive tendency to treat the thinking of authors of paradigmatic influence such as Habermas and Mouffe as epistemologically distinct and, above all, concerned with incommensurable conceptions of social agency and power. The suggestion is rather to adopt a perspective that enables us to capture their dialectics and co-evolution. These dimensions are not absent in the authors of reference, but their inherent difficulties need to be taken seriously.

Rancière, for instance, is well aware of this tension—even if expanding on it is not a core interest of his work. In his view, the political moment enacts a reconfiguration of the order of things, as politics "makes visible what had no business being seen, and makes heard a discourse where once there was only place for noise; it makes understood as discourse what was once only heard as noise." Thus, "political activity is always a mode of expression that undoes the perceptible divisions of the police order" by demonstrating "the sheer contingency of the order" (Rancière 1999: 29–30). However, "if politics implements a logic entirely heterogeneous to that of the police, it is always bound up with the latter. The reason for this is simple: politics has no objects or issues of its own" (ibid.: 31). The space of politics therefore is not a homogeneous and autonomous space; it is a configuration "determined by the state of relations between political logic and police logic," as well as a privileged space for its dissimulation (ibid.: 33). This is why la mésentente—"a term untranslatable into English"—ties up the parties to a conflict as it means "both 'the fact of not hearing, of not understanding' and 'quarrel, disagreement'," the rise of the politics against an established police order (Rancière 2004: 5). The dialectics of police and politics hence emphasizes the role of antagonism and resistance as constitutive of the political, but also urges caution against their romanticization, as political practice is always co-defined by the constitutive and co-evolutive conditions of its emergence (see also Laclau and Mouffe 1985: 111–114).

Antagonism is relational and can become a productive force only in and through interaction. This is obviously at the core of understanding the political in a logic of hegemony (Laclau and Mouffe 1985; Mouffe 2013). Differently than in Rancière, in Mouffe's work this represents therefore the core challenge for a normative reconstruction of democracy.

A full appraisal of Mouffe's contribution is made difficult by the ambiguities— if not contradictions—in her articulated discussion of the prospects of 'agonistic pluralism' and her dismissal of deliberative practices. According to her reading, the Habermasian model of a public space for the reconciliation of difference through rational argumentation "presupposes the availability of a consensus without exclusion, which is precisely what the hegemonic approach reveals to be impossible" (Mouffe 2013: 92).

For Mouffe, the horizon for constituting social power in forms compatible with the values of a democratic ethos is what she calls 'agonistic pluralism': that is, a set of practices and institutions that acknowledges the constitutive antagonistic nature of the political, but is capable of transforming the politics of antagonism into a politics of agonism, based on the recognition of differences but in a setting that transforms antagonism from a relationship between 'enemies' to a relationship between adversaries (Mouffe 2000: 101–105). Agonistic pluralism is an embodiment of democracy as an ongoing negotiation of conceptions of citizenship through adversarial engagement. Problematic is the fact that, in her polemic toward post-democratic consensus-seeking political-institutional orders, her dismissal of deliberative practices and of the everyday negotiation of meanings and pragmatic agreements—the micropolitics of democracy—Mouffe seems not to leave much room, or to be little interested, for forms of agency in between the above-mentioned dualism. As a consequence, any practice geared toward the realization of a local consensus in public matters—be it, for instance, in the form of 'mini-publics' (e.g., Fung 2006; Goodin and Dryzek 2006; Dryzek and Hendriks 2012)—implies in her view a drift toward "agonism without antagonism" (Mouffe 2013: xv). In a similar vein, but with more sensibility for the dimension of agency, Norval (2007) understands the exercise of democracy—between governance as 'policing' and antagonism as 'disturbance'—as an experience of contingency and of always possible disruption, but also as an experience in constituting the medium for developing and enacting alternatives.

On the other hand, the theoretical difficulty of the issue is highlighted by approaches to combining and, in a way, 'harmonizing' the requirements for dissent and antagonism with the requirements of public policy pragmatism. Moving from a critical consideration of shortcomings of participatory and deliberative practices leading frequently to the defiance of consensus-building, several authors have recently advanced an approach based on the idea of moving 'beyond consensus-building' and toward constituting the conditions for a dialogue in an agonistic space (see: Balducci and Mäntysalo 2013). The idea is that substantive consensus on policy issues and the overcoming of differences may not be necessary for cooperation in the domain of contested public policies, provided that a neutral space is created that allows the inclusion of a diversity of viewpoints and allows these viewpoints to be discussed in an interactive process. The possibility of establishing such a 'trading zone' is attached to the identification of 'boundary objects,' intended as deliberative devices that allow the realization of a shift from contention over the solution to a discussion—even if from different perspectives—on the problem and on possible commonalities in its definition as a public task.

Without denying the inspirational potential this idea may have for policy practice, it appears problematic against the background of our discussion. While it is difficult to recognize the conceptual innovation of the proposal— given that it shares key assumptions of the tradition of planning theory in which consensus-building has been articulated as a critical-pragmatic approach to dealing with local contention and conflict—it is precisely reference to philosophical pragmatism in combination with classical pluralism in the Lindblomean tradition that seems to defy the capacity of the notion of a 'trading zone' to grasp the nature of antagonism under conditions of deep pluralism. It may of course well be that social agency has different registers, and it is certainly possible to conceive of a coexistence of conflict and cooperation, of agonism and cooperation in a given public policy situation. But this obviously cannot equal eliminating the antagonistic dimension of related practices by means of a necessarily selective definition of issues for cooperation ('boundary objects'). Besides all considerations on the symbolic-cognitive dimension involved in such a selection—an issue of power in itself—a critical approach to such practices would require understanding, first, where and under what conditions integrative and transformative potentials are expressed, if ever, by agreeing on cooperation around 'boundary objects,' and, second, how this would displace and transform the nature and sites of antagonism. If a 'boundary object' is to be seen as a 'translation tool' between heterogeneous viewpoints and the communities who hold them (cf. Star and Griesemer 1989), then it is fair to counter that translation cannot be seen as independent of actors' relational settings; identifying 'boundary objects' cannot be separated from 'trials of strength' (Latour 1987). In this respect, the proposal seems to fit into the domain of practices of "agonism without antagonism" (Mouffe 2013: xv).

These explorations of the meanings—implicit or explicit—of 'the political,' and of their democratic, emancipatory and transformative potentials, make clear that there is a potential for even stronger cleavages between critical urban studies, conflicts and social movements research, and critical-pragmatic planning theory. This does not need to be the case, however. A possible way to turn these cleavages into something productive is to share concerns among these areas of research and to take hold of their respective insights. The following section outlines a few possible directions for this.

Conflicts, Democracy and the Political: Toward a Heuristic Framework

We need to take radical thinking on the political seriously, but this—in the first instance—appears to define even stronger divides. It faces us with the contradictions—not only theoretical, but empirical—of dealing with conflicts in terms of one-off moments of 'conflict resolution' and of the staging of 'democratization' events. How is it possible to engage critically in argumentative, participatory and deliberative practices in a post-political urban environment that aspires at "a world of self-pacified multiplicity," in which they tend to be reduced to "the mere filling of spaces left empty by power," to means for "depoliticizing conflicts in order to settle them" (Rancière 1995: 22, 60, 105)?

Urban policy and planning practices are part of policy regimes that comprise the general formal-institutional and legal guarantees of a liberal democracy. They are expressions of the dimension of 'politics' (Mouffe 2000) or 'police' (Rancière 1999), intended as "the ensemble of practices, discourses and institutions which seek to establish a certain order and organize human coexistence in conditions that are always potentially conflictual" (Mouffe 2000: 101). Contestation and conflict, on the other hand, are expressions of 'the political,' of the insurgence of the radical ineluctability of pluralism, of "the dimension of antagonism that the pluralism of values entails and its ineradicable character" (Mouffe 2000: 99).

Urban politics is therefore set in a fundamental tension. On the one hand, its practices, discourses and institutions define a repertoire of instruments and techniques, of *dispositifs* for defusing, domesticating and disciplining potentials for antagonism. On the other hand, antagonism may develop at the margins of its practices, discourses and institutions, as it emerges through the constitution of subject positions and collective identities in contestation of 'politics.' Urban politics hence does not only 'frame' conflicts, but also defines its conditions of emergence, and defines the political opportunity structures for contentious actions and collective mobilization.

The proposal I advance here is to address our expectations for democratization and change, with regard to contention and conflict in urban policy and planning, in heuristic terms. This heuristics should, in the first place, be concerned with the dynamics and the co-evolutive dimension of contention and conflict; in the second place, it should address this dynamics and co-evolution as it delineates in the interaction and interplay between different domains of practice. The latter is a key condition for overcoming scholarly divides and, on the contrary, to include and mutually fertilize their insights in a multifaceted perspective of inquiry. In this respect, this heuristics shares in the idea of a 'multiple ontology' of our object of inquiry.

Addressing the dynamics and co-evolution of planning conflicts means adopting a focus on processes of formation and of potential transformation of the practices involved. The underlying hypotheses are:

- that the features of policy and planning processes at the center of contention are also determinant in shaping the nature of social mobilizations and their co-evolutive trajectories;
- that the co-evolution of planning processes and social movements in a contentious situation depends upon the forms of strategic reflexivity that are developed on either side and on how these mutually interact; and
- that a more developed awareness of dynamics of contention and social mobilization in planning processes is essential for developing a strategic reflexivity of public policy that may make co-evolution toward integrative outcomes possible.

These hypotheses, however, gain a particular meaning in light of a series of heuristic assumptions—with implications of both an ontological and epistemological nature. These assumptions are in line with post-foundational political theory and radical democratic theory, the first being, however, somehow 'radicalized.'

First, for heuristic purposes, I propose to assume no single ontology and no normative epistemology of democracy. Democracy is neither represented nor accomplished by one of its 'models,' by playing the practices inspired by one model against those of the others. Rather, democratic politics is the ever-open exchange and interplay of different democratic practices in a hegemonic struggle for recognition and affirmation—even, of course, against what is respectively seen as 'un-democratic.'

Second, *antagonism* and *hegemony* are necessary and dialectically interrelated dimensions of the political. As a correlate to this, urban policy and planning should be seen as practices of *policing* and as practices producing *policing effects*. Urban policy and planning as practices of policing articulate responses to the inherent or overt antagonistic nature of social relations in the city and, in doing so, constitutively partake in a field of hegemonic practices. I understand here hegemonic practices in line with Laclau and Mouffe's critical analysis of discursive practices in constituting hegemony. 'Hegemonic practices' are "the practices of articulation through which a given order is created and the meaning of social institutions is fixed" (Mouffe 2013: 2; on 'articulation,' see: Laclau and Mouffe 1985: 105–113). According to this understanding, the order that confers a disciplining frame on urban policy and governance, that constitutes them as a policing effect, constitutes "the temporary and precarious articulation of contingent practices" (Mouffe 2013: 2) that are always potentially subject to challenge by antagonistic practice.

This conception is complementary to an anti-foundational understanding of governance and planning practices; in line with Bevir and Rhodes (Bevir 2003; Bevir and Rhodes 2003, 2006) and with Rancière's notion of 'police' (Rancière 1999), I understand governance and planning as an *emergent policing order*. Against a reified conception of institutions as 'fixing' frameworks for agency, this requires an agency-centered analysis of governance practices in a context of 'decenteredness' and indeterminacy, whereby governance and planning is constituted by assemblages of practices, narratives and beliefs by which actors attempt to constitute meanings, and alliances that sustain these meanings, in response to arising challenges and dilemmas.

Third, hegemonic practices are defined by a dialectics of articulation defined by recurrent practices of *dis-articulation* and *re-articulation*. The capacity of political subjects to dis- and re-articulate a given situation and to transform it into a new configuration is crucial to hegemonic struggles. The articulation of the urban order expressed by hegemonic practices is always subject to the possibility of dis-articulation as the result of challenges by antagonistic and/or counter-hegemonic practices. Conversely, there is always the possibility of a re-articulation of an order as result of the reappropriation of elements of social antagonism within hegemonic practices. This is, from this perspective, the nature of hegemonic practices: that of a discursive struggle for meaning and for its social validation, for the establishment of "an order of the visible and the sayable" (Rancière 1999: 29) in a field of differently constituted subject positions.

An exemplification of this, for instance, is the way neoliberalism can be interpreted as "a process of discursive re-articulation of existing discourses and practices" (Mouffe 2013: 73), capable of realizing a 'transition' in terms of an outcome of hegemonic intervention (see also: Boltanski and Chiappello 2005). In Gramscian terms, such practices of 'hegemony through neutralization' realize "a situation where demands which challenge the hegemonic order are appropriated by the existing system so as to satisfy them in a way that neutralizes their subversive potential" (Mouffe 2013: 73). Accordingly, innovative practices of dis-articulation are required in order to push the dialectics of hegemonic articulation further.

Fourth, the pathways and trajectories of a hegemonic struggle are in this respect dependent on the emergence of subject positions capable of developing processes of identification based on elements of dis-articulation of a given order, as well as on the capacity of given subject positions to realize a transition from elements of dis-articulation to elements of re-articulation of a new order. Related social practices are theoretically framed by critical theories of hegemony and discourse and are, moreover, at the core of empirical explanations of dynamics of contention and social mobilization in social research.

Finally, a reprise of my heuristic assumption about renouncing to a priori ontological or normative understandings of democracy. This assumption is by no means intended to imply some sort of 'value neutrality'; however, it does imply a choice for abductive reasoning (cf. Schwartz-Shea and Yanow 2012) where deductive reasoning may show its shortcomings. This is the case, for instance, of the ideal of 'agonistic pluralism.' Provided we agree that there is no proven 'design' for realizing it, we need to devote our attention to what are its possibilities and threats in practice; "from the perspective of 'agonistic pluralism' the aim of democratic politics is to transform *antagonism* into *agonism*" (Mouffe 2000: 103), and this occurs when the dialectics of hegemonic dis-articulations and re-articulations is kept open. Agonistic pluralism is, therefore, inherently transformative. The issue for politics and research, then, is under which situational conditions and along which trajectories—and by which subjects—it is enacted.

Conflict in Urban Development and Planning: Dynamics of Contention and the Prospects of 'Agonistic Pluralism'

This section finally presents some observations on a specific, but crucial, perspective for a conflict- and antagonism-sensitive planning theory. It is also intended as an exploration of the potentials of cross-fertilization discussed above. Social movement research has often been seen, with a few exceptions—most notably seminal works by Castells (1983) and Fainstein and Fainstein (1985)—as detached from critical urban studies (cf. Nicholls 2008). This has contributed in a way to rendering the research field of urban social movements somehow under-theorized or, rather, as theoretically split between barely communicating areas of inquiry. This is even more the case for planning theory, despite significant awareness of the literature in authors concerned with the prospects of collective action in planning processes, such as Healey (2006) and Innes and Booher (2010). Recently, there have been significant contributions to overcoming these gaps, particularly in line with engagement with contradictions generated by neoliberalization and the 'urbanization of injustice' (e.g., Merrifield and Swyngedouw 1996; Mitchell 2003; Nicholls and Beaumont 2004a, 2004b; Leitner et al. 2007) and in connection with urban contentious practices related to the framework of the 'right to the city' (e.g., Friedmann 1995; Harvey 2000, 2003; Dikeç 2001; Purcell 2003, 2006; Brenner et al. 2009; Routledge 2010). A few contributions have, however, also addressed the theoretical underpinning of reference to the urban (e.g., Leitner et al. 2008; see also: Nicholls et al. 2014). Exemplary in these terms is Nicholls' engagement with the relevance of urban space in defining social movements. Nicholls (2008) advances important theoretical considerations of the city as a generative space, introducing references to research on social movements as networked relations (Della Porta and Diani 1999; Diani and McAdam 2003) and expanding on networking-relational concepts of social agency in connection with the idea—borrowed from Sennett (1971)—of the city as a dialectical field of relational diversity and institutional control, defining trajectories of both generative and disciplinary nature. The direction delineated by Nicholls' contribution is of great importance; the argument made here, however, is that it should be integrated with similar and complementary theorizing on the way forms of agency in interaction between urban social movements and policy and planning practices define trajectories of 'the political.' The following paragraphs are an initial exploration conducted through research on contentious politics and social mobilization.

Contention and Social Mobilization as Emergent, Interactive-Relational and Co-Evolutive Phenomena

Research on contentious politics and social mobilization shows that contention and protest is an indispensable source for democratization and may represent a potential for innovating planning and governance practices, provided policy processes define 'opportunity structures' that allow agonistic pluralism to be expressed and to develop constructive and transformative potentials. From the perspective of urban governance and planning research, this raises the question of how far urban transformations represent an interface not only for the emergence of antagonism, but also for developing—from a perspective of 'agonistic pluralism'—reflexive and potentially transformative processes.

Despite obvious differences in theoretical derivation, there are arguably significant consistencies and complementarities between radical political theory and research that emphasizes the *emergent, interactive-relational* and *co-evolutive* nature of contention and social mobilization.

Contention and social mobilization are, first of all, *emergent* phenomena. Forms and dynamics of contention are a function of the specific political-institutional, social and economic conditions under which they emerge; it is in their shadow that a 'political opportunity structure' for collective action may emerge:

> contentious politics is triggered when changing political opportunities and constraints create incentives for social actors who lack resources of their own. They contend through known repertoires of contention and expand them by creating innovations at their margin. When backed by dense social networks and galvanized by culturally resonant, action-oriented symbols, contentious politics leads to sustained interaction with opponents. The result is the social movement. (Tarrow 1998: 2)

These observations bear two consequences. First, planning practices can be seen as constituting a 'policy regime,' i.e., an action situation not only shaped by political-institutional, social and economic framework conditions, but by a specific policy rationale orienting its courses of action and by a potential for selective regulation of modes of collective action. Second, the selectivity of forms of social-political regulation and discipline expressed by planning as 'policy regime' may turn into occasions for forms of mutual identification, leading to the emergence of a 'political opportunity structure' for collective mobilization. In Nicholls' terms (2008), a dialectics of constraining and enabling is at play in the way urban policy and planning define the possibility for protest and mobilization to emerge.

Contention and social mobilization are, moreover, *interactive-relational* phenomena. This is important in relationship with the insurgent, constructed, anything but 'natural' features of social movements. Contrary to approaches that emphasize factors for individual mobilization—material interests and resources as well as subjective and voluntaristic variables—over the symbolic-cognitive and interpretive aspects of social experience, social movements scholars like Melucci (1988: 330, 1989, 1996), Snow (et al. 1980, et al.

1986), Tarrow (1998) and Tilly (2004; Tilly and Tarrow 2007) emphasize the emergent and constructed character of collective mobilizations, warning against an 'ontologization' of their outcomes. Motivation to enter a context of interaction—like a form of collective mobilization—is rarely given per se, a priori of interaction itself; conversely, with the varying of activities and modes of involvement, interests and modes of participation also tend to vary: "the 'motives' for joining or continued participation are generally emergent and interactional rather than pre-structured" (Snow et al. 1980: 795). Motivation to participate cannot be seen as an exclusively individual or discrete variable; it is rather constructed and consolidated through interactions (Melucci 1988).

From a process perspective, "rationales for participation are both collective and ongoing phenomena" (Snow et al. 1986: 467). Actors 'produce' collective action when they are able to define themselves and their relationships with the environment—other actors, available resources, opportunities and obstacles—in terms of a collectively shared identification of issues and issue-boundaries, in relation to which they feel their interests involved and their resources worth being mobilized. Identities thus formed are 'social products' of the events that occurred in a particular time-space conjuncture (Melucci 1988, 1996).

Contrary to conceptions that see the outcome of a social movement as a function of the group's objectives or ideology—and thus of the sharing of defined 'values'—this conception understands processes of collective mobilization as phenomena subject to significant variability according to differences in relational structures. In this sense, the relational settings of interaction constitute at least as important factors in defining paths of participation and cooperation as dispositions or value assumptions. This is relevant in relationship with the fragmentation that characterizes societies in late modernity (Melucci 1989, 1996) and the way this affects social movements in urban contexts. It hints at a recognizable change in features in contemporary urban movements, whereby 'neoliberal' and globalized urban development policies and practices have contributed to a progressive erosion of cycles of urban movements based on established local groupings and interests based on traditional forms of affiliation and mutual—be they corporatist, class or community based—and on their social movement infrastructure (cf. Mayer 2000, 2007; Della Porta and Tarrow 2004; Tilly and Wood 2009). While moving away from conflicts grounded in basic social cleavages, urban conflicts reveal the emergence of a multiplicity of conflict potentials dwelling on the diversity of local societies and the emergent character of shared identities. The cross-sectional social visibility and impact of the 'neoliberal project' in cities and the unprecedented level of local and trans-local mediatization of urban struggles add to this complexity.

This supports the observation that contemporary social movements often take the form of "multiform movements" (Tarrow 1998: 103), flexibly and pluralistically combining different forms of collective action and tactics. It also supports the observation that often, in contemporary social movements, "heterogeneity and interdependence are greater spurs to collective action than homogeneity and discipline," and that mobilization often takes the form of democratically decentralized movements, i.e., of "decentralized, segmented, and reticulated" groups that capitalize on diversity and pluralism (ibid.: 137, 129).

Two interrelated conditions are hence crucial for collective mobilization to occur. The first is the enactment of opportunities for involvement through the development of a repertoire of actions; "contentious collective action demonstrates the possibilities of collective action to others and offers even resource-poor groups the opportunity that their lack of resources would deny them," and thus "it can pry open institutional barriers through which the demands of others can pour" (Tarrow 1998: 87). This aspect points to the importance of the 'public performance' of contention and of the development of itineraries of repertoire change in response to changing opportunity structures. The second is the importance of symbolic mobilization in order to define alternative belief systems that may constitute interfaces for mutual identification and support collective action. In fact, "it is participants' recognition of their common interests that translates the potential for a movement into action" (ibid: 6); but this recognition is an interpretive endeavor that implies developing frames of identification allowing the bridging of differences in positions and preferences and the creation of new symbolic-cognitive bonds. This explains the importance of collective action frames and of co-evolutive processes of 'framing' in the development of social movements.

Framing results from practices of consensus mobilization, intended as practices that involve constructing symbols of consensus; these, however, are not only drawn from "categorical identity" (Tarrow 1998: 119–120), but increasingly involve mobilizing emotional commitments that contribute to bridging categorical differences. Thus, "most of the work of 'framing' is cognitive and evaluative—that is, it identifies grievances and translates them into broader claims against significant others" but, to a significant extent, it involves "tapping or creating emotional energy" (ibid.: 111). This can occur through different processes of framing—like frame bridging, frame amplification and frame extension—and ultimately lead to frame alignment, i.e., to the alignment between individuals' or groups' frames and collective ones (Snow et al. 1986). Framing is anything but a purely intentional process; it is an interactional outcome—what Tarrow (1998: 121) calls "framing through contention"—and at the same time a condition for reproduction and co-evolution of interaction (Gamson and Meyer 1996).

Cycles of Contention, Modes of Mobilization and Their Co-Evolutive Dynamics

This leads to two crucial aspects for assessing contentious movements in the context of urban policy and planning and, in particular, their prospects of developing toward reflexive-integrative rather than polarizing-disruptive social-political outcomes: the nature of their 'framing,' and their intertemporal co-evolutive dimension.

Contention and social mobilization are, in fact, *co-evolutive* phenomena. This aspect will be discussed by reference to the ideal-types identified by scholars like Pizzorno (1993), Melucci (1996) and McAdam, Tarrow and Tilly (McAdam et al. 2001; Tilly and Tarrow 2007; Tilly and Wood 2009).

A caveat is in place here: the typologies adopted by these authors are not directly comparable, as they refer to different notions—respectively, to types of conflict, types of social mobilization and types of claims involved in contentious politics. However, it is safe to say that the lines of arguments of these authors stand virtually in a mutual dialogue as they share a contention and social mobilization as emergent, interactive-relational and co-evolutive phenomena. Moreover, this observation helps to underline an even more important aspect. The aim of these typologies—and the meaning they bear in our arguments—is not to capture the nature of such phenomena in an essentialist way, but rather to thematize their co-evolution. As such, these typologies may serve as a heuristic device for understanding the dynamics of contention and social mobilization in its relationality and co-evolution with the contextual features of the institutional and policy environment and of forms of political agency.

Pizzorno (1993) proposes a typology that distinguishes between 'recognition,' 'interest' and 'ideological (or value)' conflicts. *Interest conflicts* typically concern the distribution of scarce resources—e.g., land and its uses—by public policies. In planning arenas, they are often—if not necessarily—related to the preferences, positions and roles of defined actors with a defined identity, among which the bargaining of relative interests is at stake. They are typical for parties who share the same values and the same systems of relations in a pluralist environment in which they struggle for their relative distribution of benefits. Obviously, conflicts of interest can be radical and can entail radical opposition, but they usually are framed as a distributive game, in which what is at stake is typically a comparative benefit gain.

Recognition conflicts are conflicts that are promoted around actors' claims for recognition of their identity. They focus on claims by social groups that often identify themselves as 'local,' but struggle to gain recognition in a certain 'supra-local' policy or planning context. Examples are struggles in defense of 'local' values (environmental, cultural, communitarian) against superimposed, 'top-down' planning rationales. 'Identity,' however, is anything but a given, being often rather defined in opposition to other parties, and involving struggles for mutual identification in which a new identity is itself a possible outcome of the conflict.

Ideological (or value) conflicts, finally, involve clashes among (ontological) worldviews and among systems of values and beliefs claiming universal validity. When conflicts become 'ideological'—in Pizzorno's understanding—the matter of contention tends to focus on radically different interpretations of the policy situation in terms of both the knowledge and values involved. As Pacchi and Pasqui (Chapter 4 this volume: 82) point out, in this kind of conflict

> there is no shared framework of reference between the parts; the framework itself is the object of conflict. Radical ecological conflicts, for example, can be considered ideological, because the parts want to produce (different) universal systems of values and meanings.

The relation to concrete interests is often not transparent, if not irrelevant, and different interests can be bridged and conveyed within a movement, while becoming incommensurable to those held outside of it.

The distinction between *claimant, political* and *antagonistic movements* advanced by Melucci (1996) resembles Pizzorno's by stressing the importance of shifting frames as a factor for both external positioning and internal cohesion of social movements; moving from one type of mobilization to another may represent a crucial opportunity for collective identification and action but, as a possible consequence, also introduce factors for polarization and increasing radicalization.

Combining Pizzorno's typology of conflicts with the typology of social movements by Melucci, we gain elements for interpreting the potential trajectories of evolution involved. As Melucci underlines, new social movements increasingly involve practices of mutual identification and recognition that tend to stress the limits of social representation within which traditional class or corporatist struggles were played out. This argument is further supported by the analysis of the nature of claims raised in contentious politics conducted in various contributions by McAdam, Tarrow and Tilly. The distinction they advance is between what they define as *program claims* (or *programmatic politics*), *standing claims* (or *politics of standing*) and *identity claims* (or *identity politics*) (McAdam et al. 2001; Tilly and Tarrow 2007; Tilly and Wood 2009).

Program claims "involve stated support for or opposition to actual or proposed actions by the objects of movement claims" (Tilly and Tarrow 2007: 86). Their effectiveness is often premised on that of other claims (for instance, it may depend on the presence of and relationships to credible, recognizable actors, endowed with recognition within a system of representation of interests); if these conditions are given, the struggle may begin and take the form of contentious negotiations (Tilly and Wood 2009: 12).

Standing claims, on the other hand, are mainly concerned with the differential standing of claimants relative to other political actors; hence, they "assert ties and similarities to other political actors, for example, excluded minorities, properly constituted citizens' groups, or loyal supporters of the regime" (Tilly and Wood 2009: 12). Standing claims generally produce effects on a small number of actors who have power to certify them and to act to support them (Tilly and Tarrow 2007: 86). They may gain polarizing effects, however, particularly when defined or perceived in exclusionary terms.

The result can be the development of *identity claims*, which "consist of assertions that 'we'—the claimants—constitute a unified force to be reckoned with" vis-à-vis the objects of claims (Tilly and Wood 2009: 12). As a consequence, identity claims produce effects primarily by setting boundaries: by "announc[ing] a boundary, a set of relations within a boundary, a set of relations across the boundary, plus some meanings attributed to relations and boundaries" (Tilly and Tarrow 2007: 85–86). Contention then often focuses on redefining these boundaries through identity building, often with identity re-assessments and shifts as outcomes of contentious interactions.

As Tilly and Tarrow underline, "[t]he relative salience of program, identity, and standing claims varies significantly among social movements, among claimants within movements, and among phases of movements." Hence also the importance of shifting claims as a factor for both external positioning and internal cohesion of social movements: "[c]laims and counterclaims do not occur randomly; they take their shape from surrounding regimes, cultures, and institutions. They respond to a regime's opportunities, threats, and constraints" (Tilly and Tarrow 2007: 83). Accordingly, internal negotiations within movements focus a great deal "on the relative prominence the different claims will receive" (Tilly and Wood 2009: 12).

Such interpretation is consistent with the assumption of interpretive policy analysis (e.g., Yanow 1996; Fischer 2003; Wagenaar 2011) that how the meanings of a policy are constituted and collectively performed reflects a plurality of values and cognitive repertoires; these may be co-present, while situated on different, non-consistent levels of political argumentation (Fischer 1995, 2003: 191–198), possibly leading to ultimately incommensurable positions among policy actors. On a different theoretical ground, such dynamics mirrors what Laclau and Mouffe (1985: 128–129) call an *antagonistic* moment, the constitution of a 'counter-hegemonic' subject position characterized by a form of collective identification negatively defined by difference to an 'enemy' conceived as external threat to it. An antagonistic moment may play a crucial role in overcoming difference and joining collective forces. It can represent a critical juncture in certain forms of protest and mobilization; however, it may also entail a reduction of internal differences and pluralism. The resulting struggles tend to imply a division into two camps, in contrast to democratic struggles developing across a plurality of political spaces (ibid.: 131–134) and thus enhancing what Mouffe (2000: 101–105) calls *agonistic pluralism*.

This calls for considering the intertemporal dimension of social mobilization: the way trajectories and cycles of contention, through their evolution (Tarrow 1998: 142–150), may affect the reflexive prospects and outcomes of contentious policy processes. The nature of social movements around contentious projects depends upon the strategic selectivity of 'policy regimes' and the way emergent opportunity structures are recognized and appropriated by collective actors in response. The trajectory taken by this dynamic interplay, however, may define the prospects for reflexive and 'integrative' outcomes of conflicts. For instance, shifts from claimant to political and to antagonistic movements may imply a higher symbolic loading and conversely a reduction of the scope for negotiation of issues; this may imply the risk of escalation and polarization, resulting in a (selective) radicalization of the movement and an irreversible confrontation without prospects of 'integrative' public outcomes. Both aspects highlight the interpretive responsibility of policy analysts in addressing a critical understanding of their co-evolution. In particular, research should focus on the mutual interplay and varying co-evolutive effects between:

- processes of the constitution of political subjectivity and collective action through forms of collective mobilization and in interaction with policy and planning processes;
- strategies of dealing with conflict—in terms of prevention, diffusion, reduction, 'polymerization' or selective conventionalization; and
- strategies of upholding conflict through shifts in contention and mobilization.

This leads to a three-part research hypothesis:

1. As they contribute to defining the political opportunity structures for contention and collective mobilization, planning processes and the 'policy regimes' in which they are embedded are also determinant in shaping the nature of social movements and their co-evolutive trajectories.
2. The co-evolution of planning processes and social mobilization in a defined contentious situation depends upon the way forms of strategic reflexivity are developed on either side and on how these mutually interact.
3. A more developed awareness of dynamics of contention and social mobilization in urban development planning processes is of key importance for developing a strategic reflexivity of public policy that may make co-evolution toward transformative outcomes possible.

Conclusions: Agonistic Pluralism and Reflexivity in Planning

A subtext of this introduction is the question of how situated policy practices can contribute to redefining democracy in 'post-political' or 'post-democratic' times. The reflexive potential of participatory and deliberative planning practices may be a significant contribution. This rests upon one condition, however: recognizing the political salience of interplays between the macro-determinants of urban governance and planning and the micro-dynamics of social practices. Doing so requires taking antagonism as a dimension of the political seriously. It requires, furthermore, understanding planning as a set of practices developing in a hegemonic field, as constitutive of hegemonic practices.

The potential for social mobilization to develop forms of agonistic pluralism relies on the way it contributes to repoliticizing urban governance and planning; and this also depends on the establishment of reflexive interfaces with policy and planning practices. This appears essential in order to contribute to a transformative reframing of contentious issues. Such interfaces are highly dependent on situated, context- and policy-specific forms of agency, and can only to a limited extent be formalized and institutionalized. They depend, moreover, on the co-evolution of their relationships. What emerges, from this perspective, is the need not only to avoid 'romantic' views of social involvement and mobilization, but also to recognize the insufficiency of institutionalized approaches to dealing with them in transformative terms. This highlights the importance and responsibility, from a democratization perspective, for governance and planning actors to take agonistic pluralism seriously, as it is performed in situated processes of political contention and social mobilization. Agonistic pluralism is not intended here as an abstract, ideal principle, but as a practical exercise of engaging with the nature and evolution of forms of social contention as they arise in the field of urban policy and planning. This requires developing an embedded capacity of meta-reflexivity, of exploring the chances, the 'windows of opportunity' that forms of antagonism and their evolutive trajectories may offer for realizing reflexive openings at critical junctures of the urban policy and planning process.

References

Altshuler, A. (1965a) *The City Planning Process*, Ithaca, NY: Cornell University Press.
Altshuler, A. (1965b) "The Goals of Comprehensive Planning," *Journal of the American Institute of Planners*, 31(3): 186–197.
Badiou, A. (2001) *Ethics*, London, UK: Verso.
Balducci, A. and Mäntysalo, R. (eds.) (2013) *Urban Planning as a Trading Zone*, Dordrecht, Netherlands: Springer.

Banfield, E. C. (1959) "Ends and Means in Planning," *International Social Science Journal*, 9(3): 361–368.

Beaumont, J. R. and Loopmans, M. (2008) "Towards Radicalized Communicative Rationality: Resident Involvement and Urban Democracy in Rotterdam and Antwerp," *International Journal of Urban and Regional Research*, 32(1): 95–113.

Beaumont, J. R. and Nicholls, W. J. (2008) "Plural Governance, Participation and Democracy in Cities," *International Journal of Urban and Regional Research*, 32(1): 87–94.

Bevir, M. (2003) "A Decentered Theory of Governance," in H. H. Bang (ed.), *Governance as Social and Political Communication*, Manchester, UK: Manchester University Press: 200–222.

Bevir, M. and Rhodes, R. A. W. (2003) *Interpreting British Governance*, London, UK: Routledge.

Bevir, M. and Rhodes, R. A. W. (2006) *Governance Stories*, London, UK: Routledge.

Boltanski, L. and Chiappello, E. (2005) *The New Spirit of Capitalism*, London, UK: Verso.

Bond, S. (2011) "Negotiating a 'Democratic Ethos': Moving Beyond the Agonistic–Communicative Divide," *Planning Theory*, 10(2): 161–186.

Brenner, N., Marcuse, P. and Mayer, M. (2009) "Cities for People, Not for Profit," *City*, 13(2): 176–184.

Bryson, J. M. and Crosby, B. C. (1992) *Leadership for the Common Good: Tackling Public Problems in a Shared-Power World*, San Francisco, CA: Jossey-Bass.

Cars, G., Healey, P., Madanipour, A. and de Magalhaes, C. (eds.) (2002) *Urban Governance, Institutional Capacity and Social Milieux*, Aldershot, UK: Ashgate.

Castells, M. (1983) *The City and the Grassroots: A Cross-Cultural Theory of Urban Social Movements*, London, UK: Arnold.

Cohen, J. (1988) "Democracy and Liberty," in J. Elster (ed.), *Deliberative Democracy*, Cambridge, UK: Cambridge University Press: 185–231.

Crouch, C. (2004) *Post-Democracy*, Cambridge, UK: Polity Press.

Dahl, R. A. (1961) *Who Governs? Democracy and Power in an American City*, New Haven, CT: Yale University Press.

Dahl, R. A. (1971) *Polyarchy: Participation and Opposition*, New Haven, CT: Yale University Press.

Dahl, R. A. (2000) *On Democracy*, New Haven, CT: Yale University Press.

Davidoff, P. (1965) "Advocacy and Pluralism in Planning," *Journal of the American Institute of Planners*, 31(4): 331–338.

Davidoff, P. and Reiner, T. A. (1962) "A Choice Theory of Planning," *Journal of the American Institute of Planners*, 28(2): 103–115.

Della Porta, D. (2013) *Can Democracy Be Saved? Participation, Deliberation and Social Movements*, Cambridge, UK: Polity Press.

Della Porta, D. and Diani, M. (1999) *Social Movements: An Introduction*, Oxford, UK: Blackwell.

Della Porta, D. and Tarrow, S. (eds.) (2004) *Transnational Protest and Global Activism*, Lanham, MD: Rowman and Littlefield.

Diani, M. and McAdam, D. (eds.) (2003) *Social Movements and Networks: Relational Approaches to Collective Action*, Oxford, UK: Oxford University Press.

Dikeç, M. (2001) "Justice and the Spatial Imagination," *Environment and Planning A*, 33(10): 1785–1805.

Donolo, C. (1992) *Il sogno del buon governo*, Milan, Italy: Anabasi.

Dryzek, J. S. (1990) *Discursive Democracy: Politics, Policy and Political Science*, Cambridge, UK: Cambridge University Press.

Dryzek, J. S. and Hendriks, C. M. (2012) "Fostering Deliberation in the Forum," in F. Fischer and H. Gottweis (eds.), *The Argumentative Turn Revisited: Public Policy as Communicative Practice*, Durham, NC: Duke University Press: 31–57.

Easton, D. (1965) *A Systems Analysis of Political Life*, New York, NY: Wiley.

Elster, J. (ed.) (1988) *Deliberative Democracy*, Cambridge, UK: Cambridge University Press.

Fainstein, S. S. and Fainstein, N. I. (1985) "Economic Restructuring and the Rise of Urban Social Movements," *Urban Affairs Quarterly*, 21(3): 187–206.

Faludi, A. (1973) *Planning Theory*, Oxford, UK: Pergamon Press.

Fischer, F. (1995) *Evaluating Public Policy*, Belmont, CA: Wadsworth.

Fischer, F. (2003) *Reframing Public Policy: Discursive Politics and Deliberative Practices*, Oxford, UK: Oxford University Press.

Fischer, F. and Forester, J. (eds.) (1993) *The Argumentative Turn in Policy Analysis and Planning*, Durham, NC: Duke University Press.

Fischer, F. and Gottweis, H. (eds.) (2012) *The Argumentative Turn Revisited: Public Policy as Communicative Practice*, Durham, NC: Duke University Press.

Flyvbjerg, B. (1998) *Rationality and Power: Democracy in Practice*, Chicago, IL: Chicago University Press.

Flyvbjerg, B. and Richardson, T. (2002) "Planning and Foucault: In Search of the Dark Side of Planning Theory," in P. Allmendinger and M. Tewdwr-Jones (eds.), *Planning Futures: New Directions for Planning Theory*, London, UK: Routledge: 44–62.

Forester, J. (1982) "Planning in the Face of Power," *Journal of the American Planning Association*, 48(1): 67–80.

Forester, J. (1989) *Planning in the Face of Power*, Berkeley, CA: University of California Press.

Forester, J. and Krumholz, N. (1990) *Making Equity Planning Work: Leadership in the Public Sector*, Philadelphia, PA: Temple University Press.

Friedmann, J. (1987) *Planning in the Public Domain: From Knowledge to Action*, Princeton, NJ: Princeton University Press.

Friedmann, J. (1995) "The Right to the City," *Society and Nature*, 1(1): 71–84.

Fung, A. (2004) *Empowered Participation: Reinventing Urban Democracy*, Princeton, NJ: Princeton University Press.

Fung, A. (2006) "Varieties of Participation in Complex Governance," *Public Administration Review*, 66(Suppl. 1): 66–75.

Fung, A. and Wright, E. O. (eds.) (2003) *Deepening Democracy: Institutional Innovations in Empowered Participatory Governance*, London, UK: Verso.

Gamson, D. and Meyer, D. S. (1996) "Framing Political Opportunity," in D. McAdam, J. D. McCarthy and M. N. Zald (eds.), *Comparative Perspectives on Social Movements*, Cambridge, UK: Cambridge University Press: 275–290.

Goodin, R. E. and Dryzek, J. S. (2006) "Deliberative Impacts: The Macro-Political Uptake of Mini-Publics," *Politics & Society*, 34(2): 219–244.

Gunder, M. (2010) "Planning as the Ideology of (Neoliberal) Space," *Planning Theory*, 9(4): 298–314.

Habermas, J. (1975) *Legitimation Crisis*, Boston, MA: Beacon Press.

Habermas, J. (1984) *The Theory of Communicative Action*, Boston, MA: Beacon Press.

Hajer, M. and Wagenaar, H. (eds.) (2003) *Deliberative Policy Analysis*, Cambridge, UK: Cambridge University Press.

Harris, N. (2002) "Collaborative Planning: From Theoretical Foundations to Practice Forms," in P. Allmendinger and M. Tewdwr-Jones (eds.), *Planning Futures: New Directions for Planning Theory*, London, UK: Routledge: 21–43.

Harvey, D. (2000) *Spaces of Hope*, Berkeley, CA: University of California Press.

Harvey, D. (2003) "The Right to the City," *International Journal of Urban and Regional Research*, 27(4): 939–941.

Harvey, D. (2009 [1973]) *Social Justice and the City*, revised edition, Athens, GA: University of Georgia Press.

Harvey, D. (2012) *Rebel Cities*, London, UK: Verso.

Healey, P. (1993) "Planning Through Debate: The Communicative Turn in Planning Theory," in F. Fischer and J. Forester (eds.), *The Argumentative Turn in Policy Analysis and Planning*, Durham, NC: Duke University Press: 233–253.

Healey, P. (1997) *Collaborative Planning: Shaping Places in Fragmented Societies*, Basingstoke, UK: Macmillan.

Healey, P. (2006) *Collaborative Planning: Shaping Places in Fragmented Societies*, second edition, Basingstoke, UK: Palgrave Macmillan.

Healey, P. (2008) "The Pragmatic Tradition in Planning Thought," *Journal of Planning Education and Research*, 28(3): 277–292.

Hillier, J. (2002) "Direct Action and Agonism in Democratic Planning Practice," in P. Allmendinger and M. Tewdwr-Jones (eds.), *Planning Futures: New Directions for Planning Theory*, London, UK: Routledge: 110–135.

Hirschman, A. O. (1994) "Social Conflicts as Pillars of Democratic Market Society," *Political Theory*, 22(2): 203–218.

Hirst, P. (1994) *Associative Democracy: New Forms of Economic and Social Governance*, Cambridge, UK: Polity Press.

Holston, J. (1999) "Spaces of Insurgent Citizenship," in J. Holston (ed.), *Cities and Citizenship*, Durham, NC: Duke University Press: 155–173.

Holston, J. (2009) *Insurgent Citizenship: Disjunctions of Democracy and Modernity in Brazil*, Princeton, NJ: Princeton University Press.

Innes, J. E. (1995) "Planning Theory's Emerging Paradigm: Communicative Action and Interactive Practice," *Journal of Planning Education and Research*, 14(3): 183–189.

Innes, J. E. (1996) "Planning Through Consensus Building: A New View of the Comprehensive Planning Ideal," *Journal of the American Planning Association*, 62(4): 460–472.

Innes, J. E. and Booher, D. E. (1999) "Consensus Building as Role Playing and Bricolage: Toward a Theory of Collaborative Planning," *Journal of the American Planning Association*, 65(1): 9–26.

Innes, J. E. and Booher, D. E. (2010) *Planning with Complexity: An Introduction to Collaborative Rationality for Public Policy*, London, UK: Routledge.

Innes, J. E., Gruber, J., Neuman, M. and Thompson, R. (1994) *Coordinating Growth and Environmental Management Through Consensus Building*, Berkeley, CA: California Policy Seminar, University of California.

Laclau, E. (1996) *Emancipation(s)*, London, UK: Verso.

Laclau, E. and Mouffe, C. (1985) *Hegemony and Socialist Strategy: Towards a Radical Democratic Politics*, London, UK: Verso.

Latour, B. (1987) *Science in Action*, Cambridge, MA: Harvard University Press.

Lefort, C. (1988) *Democracy and Political Theory*, Cambridge, UK: Polity Press.

Leitner, H., Peck, J. and Sheppard, E. S. (eds.) (2007) *Contesting Neoliberalism: Urban Frontiers*, New York, NY: Guilford Press.

Leitner, H., Sheppard, E. S. and Sziarto, K. M. (2008) "The Spatialities of Contentious Politics," *Transactions of the Institute of British Geographers*, 33(2): 157–172.

Lindblom C. E. (1959) "The Science of 'Muddling Through'," *Public Administration Review*, 19(2): 79–88.

Lindblom C. E. (1965) *The Intelligence of Democracy*, New York, NY: The Free Press.

Majone, G. (1989) *Evidence, Argument, and Persuasion in the Policy Process*, New Haven, CT: Yale University Press.

Mayer, M. (2000) "Urban Social Movements in an Era of Globalization," in P. Hamel, H. Lustiger-Tahler and M. Mayer (eds.), *Urban Movements in a Globalizing World*, London, UK: Routledge: 141–157.

Mayer, M. (2007) "Contesting the Neoliberalization of Urban Governance," in H. Leitner, J. Peck and E. S. Sheppard (eds.), *Contesting Neoliberalism: Urban Frontiers*, New York, NY: Guilford Press: 90–115.

McAdam, D., Tarrow, S. and Tilly, C. (2001) *Dynamics of Contention*, Cambridge, UK: Cambridge University Press.

Melucci, A. (1988) "Getting Involved: Identity and Mobilization in Social Movements," *International Social Movement Research*, 1: 329–348.

Melucci, A. (1989) *Nomads of the Present: Social Movements and Individual Needs in Contemporary Society*, Philadelphia, PA: Temple University Press.

Melucci, A. (1996) *The Playing Self*, Cambridge, UK: Cambridge University Press.

Merrifield, A. and Swyngedouw, E. (eds.) (1996) *The Urbanization of Injustice*, London, UK: Lawrence and Wishart.

Mitchell, D. (2003) *The Right to the City: Social Justice and the Fight for Public Space*, New York, NY: Guilford Press.

Mouffe, C. (1993) *The Return of the Political*, London, UK: Verso.

Mouffe, C. (2000) *The Democratic Paradox*, London, UK: Verso.

Mouffe, C. (2005) *On the Political*, London, UK: Verso.

Mouffe, C. (2013) *Agonistics: Thinking the World Politically*, London, UK: Verso.

Nicholls, W. J. (2008) "The Urban Question Revisited: The Importance of Cities for Social Movements," *International Journal of Urban and Regional Research*, 32(4): 841–859.

Nicholls, W. J. and Beaumont, J. R. (2004a) "Guest Editorial: The Urbanisation of Justice Movements?" *Space and Polity*, 8(2): 107–117.

Nicholls, W. J. and Beaumont, J. R. (2004b) "The Urbanisation of Justice Movements? Possibilities and Constraints for the City as a Space of Contentious Struggle," *Space and Polity*, 8(2): 119–135.

Nicholls, W. J., Miller, B. and Beaumont, J. R. (eds.) (2014) *Spaces of Contention*, Aldershot, UK: Ashgate.

Norval, A. (2007) *Aversive Democracy: Inheritance and Originality in the Democratic Tradition*, Cambridge, UK: Cambridge University Press.

Offe, C. (1984) *Contradictions of the Welfare State*, Cambridge, MA: MIT Press.

Pizzorno, A. (1993) *Le radici della politica assoluta e altri saggi*, Milan, Italy: Feltrinelli.

Polsby, N. (1980) *Community Power and Democratic Theory*, second edition, New Haven, CT: Yale University Press.

Purcell, M. (2003) "Citizenship and the Right to the Global City: Reimagining the Capitalist World Order," *International Journal of Urban and Regional Research*, 27(3): 564–590.

Purcell, M. (2006) "Urban Democracy and the Local Trap," *Urban Studies*, 43(11): 1921–1941.

Purcell, M. (2008) *Recapturing Democracy: Neoliberalism and the Struggle for Alternative Urban Futures*, London, UK: Routledge.

Purcell, M. (2009) "Resisting Neoliberalization: Communicative Planning or Radical Democratic Movements?" *Planning Theory*, 8(2): 140–165.

Purcell, M. (2013) *The Down-Deep Delight of Democracy*, Oxford, UK: Wiley-Blackwell.

Rancière, J. (1995) *On the Shores of Politics*, London, UK: Verso.

Rancière, J. (1999) *Disagreement: Politics and Philosophy*, Minneapolis, MN: Minnesota University Press.

Rancière, J. (2001) "Ten Theses on Politics," *Theory and Event*, 5(3): 1–6.

Rancière, J. (2004) "Introducing Disagreement," *Angelaki*, 9(3): 3–9.

Rancière, J. (2006) *Hatred of Democracy*, London, UK: Verso.

Rawls, J. (1971) *A Theory of Justice*, Stanford, CA: Stanford University Press.

Rein, M. and Laws, D. (2000) "Controversy, Reframing and Reflection," in W. Salet and A. Faludi (eds.), *The Revival of Strategic Spatial Planning*, Amsterdam, Netherlands: Royal Netherlands Academy of Arts and Sciences: 93–108.

Rein, M. and Schön, D. (1993) "Reframing Policy Discourse," in F. Fischer and J. Forester (eds.), *The Argumentative Turn in Policy Analysis and Planning*, Durham, NC: Duke University Press: 145–166.

Rittel, H. W. J. and Webber, M. M. (1973) "Dilemmas in a General Theory of Planning," *Policy Sciences*, 4(2): 155–169.

Roe, E. (1994) "Stories, Nonstories, and Their Metanarrative in the 1982 California Medfly Controversy," *Narrative Policy Analysis: Theory and Practice*, Durham, NC: Duke University Press: 52–75.

Routledge, P. (2010) "Introduction: Cities, Justice and Conflict," *Urban Studies*, 47(6): 1165–1177.

Sandercock, L. (ed.) (1998) *Making the Invisible Visible: A Multicultural Planning History*, Berkeley, CA: University of California Press.

Sandercock, L. (2000) "When Strangers Become Neighbours: Managing Cities of Difference," *Planning Theory & Practice*, 1(1): 13–30.

Schön, D. A. (1983) *The Reflective Practitioner: How Professionals Think in Action*, New York, NY: Basic Books.

Schön, D. and Rein, M. (1994) *Frame Reflection: Toward the Resolution of Intractable Policy Controversies*, New York, NY: Basic Books.

Schwartz-Shea, P. and Yanow, D. (2012) *Interpretive Research Design: Concepts and Processes*, London, UK: Routledge.

Sennett, R. (1971) *The Uses of Disorder: Personal Identity and City Life*, New York, NY: Knopf.

Simon, H. A. (1957) *Models of Man, Social and Rational: Mathematical Essays on Rational Human Behavior in a Social Setting*, New York, NY: Wiley.

Snow, D. A., Burke Rochford, E. Jr., Worden, S. K. and Benford, R. D. (1986) "Frame Alignment Processes, Micromobilization, and Movement Participation," *American Sociological Review*, 51(3): 446–481.

Snow, D. A., Zurcher, L. A. and Ekland-Olson, S. (1980) "Social Networks and Social Movements: A Microstructural Approach to Differential Recruitment," *American Sociological Review*, 45(4): 787–801.

Star, S. L. and Griesemer, J. R. (1989) "Institutional Ecology, Translations and Boundary Objects: Amateurs and Professionals in Berkeley's Museum of Vertebrate Zoology," *Social Studies of Sciences*, 19(3): 387–420.

Susskind, L. and Cruikshank, J. (1987) *Breaking the Impasse: Consensual Approaches to Resolving Public Disputes*, New York, NY: Basic Books.

Susskind, L., McKearnan, S. and Larmer, J. (eds.) (1999) *The Consensus Building Handbook: A Comprehensive Guide to Reaching Agreement*, Thousand Oaks, CA: Sage.

Swyngedouw, E. (2007) "The Post-Political City," in BAVO (ed.), *Urban Politics Now: Reimagining Democracy in the Neoliberal City*, Rotterdam, Netherlands: NAI Publishers: 58–76.

Swyngedouw, E. (2009) "The Antinomies of the Postpolitical City: In Search of a Democratic Politics of Environmental Production," *International Journal of Urban and Regional Research*, 33(3): 601–620.

Swyngedouw, E. (2011) *Designing the Post-Political City and the Insurgent Polis*, London, UK: Bedford Press.

Tarrow, S. (1998) *Power in Movement*, Cambridge, UK: Cambridge University Press.

Tilly, C. (2004) *Social Movements, 1768–2004*, Boulder, CO: Paradigm.

Tilly, C. and Tarrow, S. (2007) *Contentious Politics*, Boulder, CO: Paradigm.

Tilly, C. and Wood, L. J. (2009) *Social Movements, 1768–2008*, Boulder, CO: Paradigm.

Uitermark, J., Nicholls, W. J. and Loopmans, P. (2012) "Cities and Social Movements: Theorizing Beyond the Right to the City," *Environment and Planning A*, 44(11): 2546–2554.

Wagenaar, H. (2011) *Meaning in Action: Interpretation and Dialogue in Policy Analysis*, Armonk, NY: Sharpe.

Webber, M. M. (1969) "Planning in an Environment of Change, Part II: Permissive Planning," *Town Planning Review*, 39(4): 277–295.

Wildavsky, A. (1973) "If Planning is Everything, Maybe It's Nothing," *Policy Science*, 4(2): 127–153.

Wright, E. O. (ed.) (1995) *Associations and Democracy*, London, UK: Verso.

Yanow, D. (1996) *How Does a Policy Mean? Interpreting Policy and Organizational Actions*, Washington, DC: Georgetown University Press.

Yiftachel, O. and Huxley, M. (2000) "Debating Dominance and Relevance: Notes on the 'Communicative Turn' in Planning Theory," *International Journal of Urban and Regional Research*, 24(4): 907–913.

2

Space, Politics and Conflicts: A Review of Contemporary Debates in Urban Research and Planning Theory

Enrico Gualini and Irene Bianchi

This chapter consists of a review of the main contributions to urban research and planning theory that have emerged in the last decade with respect to urban conflicts. As a review, it is not intended to be exhaustive, but rather to identify some important cornerstones of current debates that are deemed relevant for a further engagement in research and practice. The first section briefly introduces the conflictive dimension of spatial politics, considering in particular recent theoretical trends that have emerged in planning literature. The second section presents the ongoing debate on urban and planning conflicts. It focuses on the theoretical conceptualization and understanding of urban conflicts, as well as on the concrete management and resolution strategies proposed by different planning approaches, assessing also different interpretations provided for the underlying notions of dissent, participation and representation. Then, debates among the main theoretical frameworks are presented, and the role of planning in complex socio-spatial and conflictive contexts is briefly discussed. Finally, the potential role of the ongoing debate on conflicts for planning theoretical developments is considered.

Planning Theory and Urban Space: Introducing the Conflictual Dimension of Spatial Politics

The last twenty years of planning theory have been characterized by the rise of a number of issues that have called into question the theoretical basis of the discipline, the objectives to be achieved and the methodologies to be used in spatial management. The emergence of new interpretive schemes is primarily due to actual changes in the political, physical and even symbolic configuration of socio-spatial dynamics. This has been triggered by a multiplicity of factors including rapid socio-economic processes connected to globalization and to the (post-Fordist) restructuring of urban organizational patterns, as well as by a calling into question of contemporary participation and representation schemes. In this context, urban politics is required both to adapt to a multi-scalar context, characterized by territorial complexity, global–local interactions and interdependence among involved actors, and to provide planning models and methods capable of better facing contemporary dynamics. The necessity of redefining planning theories and practices in the attempt to overcome the traditional regulatory 'command and control' conception of spatial politics has therefore emerged in urban studies, also fostered by developments in other disciplinary fields, such as sub-national and regional economics, cultural geography and environmental sciences.

Urban conflicts are at the center of the complex debate on the redefinition of socio-spatial planning frameworks. This is grounded in the relation between individuals and space and it entails a questioning both of democratic models in urban politics and of the underlying notions of representation and participation (see: Gualini, Chapter 1, this volume). Within this debate, planning theory has been called to foster a proper understanding of the contradictions and conflictual tensions that emerge in the city and that are exacerbated by the new structuring of urban spaces while, at the same time, providing viable conflict resolution and management strategies. Although the foundation of these discourses had already been laid in the 1980s and 1990s, a review of the planning theoretical literature of the last decade shows the strengthening of specific trends in socio-spatial politics, such as, amongst others, an increasing attention to the relational character of space, a demand for the repoliticization of urban politics and a growing concern for local development paths.

With regard to the first, it can be stated that space is no longer conceived as a neutral basis, passively subject to policies, but rather as a *political space*. The interactions among the notion of space, social issues and political actions—which constitute the foundations of the discourse about planning conflicts—are, however, differently conceived. On the one hand, space can be defined, as argued by Hannah Arendt (2006, 2007), as the element that puts individuals into a political relation. This conception of space, which has been defined as *associative* (Marchart 2007), is embedded in a pluralist understanding of society, in which issues of public concern emerge and are debated (Dikeç 2012: 672) and where individuals act together, thus producing their own political space. On the other hand, space can be defined in *dissociative* terms, i.e., as the basis of antagonistic politics. Within space, indeed, friend/enemy divide relations are created (Schmitt et al. 2005 [1985]; Schmitt 2007 [1996]) in which one political identity is affirmed by acknowledging the non-belonging to the adversary field.

The second trend concerns the need for a repoliticization of the urban space. It partially emerges as a response to the crisis of representative democratic schemes that, according to a growing number of political and planning theorists, are no longer able to efficiently address complex social and spatial conflicts. The politicization of the spatial dimension has to be achieved through the "reconstruction of the city as a terrain of spatially informed politics" (Dikeç 2002: 94, see also: Swyngedouw 2009), where citizens have the possibility of engaging in order to build their own shared spaces and to create more livable places. These claims can be subsumed under the Lefebvrean notion of the 'right to the city' (see: Lefebvre 1977, 2005 [1992]), which has been redefined and included in the contemporary approach to urban and local-scale politics. Claims to the right to the city have been transversally supported by planning theorists (see, among the others: Purcell 2002; Hamelink 2008; Harvey 2008; Brenner et al. 2009; Routledge 2010). Notably, they have been conceived not only as "a formulation of certain rights and the cultivation of the political among city habitants," but also as a "reconsideration of the spatial dynamics that make the city" (Dikeç 2001: 1801).

The third element consists of a rediscovery of the local dimension of urban and regional politics, expressed through a reaffirmation of local identities in the globalized context (cf. Nel·lo 2003) and through the increasing demand for a "strategic, place-conscious evolution in sub-national governance" (Healey 1999: 112). This trend emerged in particular with regard to planning conflicts; in the last decade a great number of local mobilizations have appeared in response to controversial spatial interventions and projects, both when they were determined by local decision-making and planning and by supra-local initiatives.

A relational-based approach to space and the claims for a political reformulation of the conceptual and physical dimensions of urban politics—also at the local level—constitute the basis for the development of a new discourse on socio-spatial conflicts, grounded exactly in this renewed understanding of socio-spatial relations and their political significance. In the next section, the main responses to this demand for change will be discussed, with particular reference to collaborative and critical planning approaches.

Urban Conflicts in Planning Theories

Conceptualizing Urban Conflicts within the Main Theoretical Frameworks: Origins and Definitions

A first level of the ongoing debate on urban development and planning conflicts deals with their conceptualization, which has been widely discussed and redefined. The political and symbolic meaning of conflicts has been questioned, together with their origins and the mechanisms through which they develop.

A first understanding of urban conflicts is gathered under the label of *collaborative planning*. Before inquiring into the collaborative conception of spatial and planning conflicts, it is necessary to point out that this definition does not correspond to a consistent planning framework, but that it encompasses a variety of theoretical approaches, including communicative (Healey 1997), deliberative (Forester 1999) and argumentative/discursive politics (Dryzek 1994; Fischer 2000) (for an insightful discussion, see: Harris 2002). The theoretical foundations of collaborative planning are also heterogeneous, and can be attributed to structuration theory (Giddens 1986 [1984]) and the theory of communicative action (Habermas 1984), as well as to post-structuralist developments in social thought and post-modern perspectives on the increasing complexity of contemporary cultural and socio-economic schemes. From a democratic theoretical perspective, the redefinition of planning in collaborative terms is, first, grounded in an extensive definition of democracy that encompasses the double dimension of the concept, i.e., government *for* and *by* the people. The intrinsically communicative attitude of democracy is grounded in the dialectic relation that exists between these two dimensions.

In collaborative planning approaches, conflicts are conceived of as *creative tensions* among the different spheres of a pluralist society, and their emergence is attributed to the fact that "people confront each other from often very different relational positions, without any past history of actual encounters, even when they are neighbors in space" (Healey 1999: 115). Conflicts originate within the complex organizational patterns of the city and are inescapably connected to the relational structure of space. They are "inherent to urban life" (Hamelink 2008: 291), insofar as they are embedded in the pluralist nature of democratic society.

A second approach assumes an antagonistic and anti-neoliberal interpretation of urban dynamics, and inscribes them within a wider critique of contemporary social and political schemes. This perspective—which can be referred to as *critical planning theory*—derives from the historical materialist tradition, and is grounded in a dissociative interpretation of socio-spatial relations. As for collaborative planning, this approach, too, is not homogeneous; critical perspectives in spatial politics have been adopted by a number of scholars coming from different disciplinary fields, including planning, geography, environmental politics, urban sociology and so on. The discourses they develop with regard to planning conflicts vary in terms of degree of abstraction, dynamics analyzed, actors involved and so on, but they all follow (more or less explicitly) a post-Marxian approach, focusing in particular on the role played by neoliberal and capitalist processes in shaping the urban space. The basic (Marxian) assumption is that capital investments are always geographically uneven. Critical planners, and in particular critical geographers, highlight how urban boundaries result from the interaction among economic-political interests and power relations (e.g., Amin 2004; Harvey 1989, 2006, 2009 [1973]; Brenner et al. 2009; Peck et al. 2009; for a review of literature on neoliberal planning policies, see: Sager 2011), and state that urban configurations reflect a hegemonic and market-led development. Such an understanding of ongoing processes assumes that, as argued by Harvey, "processes do not occur *in* space but define their own spatial frame" (Harvey 2006: 274).

According to critical theorists, therefore, urban conflicts are generated and reproduced within this process of social and spatial construction, and particularly in the structural organization of the capitalist city, which is based on the exploitation of the many by the few (Harvey 2009 [1973]: 314). The origin of planning conflicts is indeed attributed first to the unjust opportunity structures of urban space, where opportunities are provided only to certain elites (e.g., the corporate sector, see: Swyngedouw 2005), while vulnerable social groups are marginalized and segregated. Critical planning theory, therefore, mainly focuses on contested spaces and socio-spatial inequalities, thus paying particular attention to global–local processes such as gentrification, urban commodification, aesthetization and profit-driven urbanization and to dynamics connected with segregation and displacement. (From a case-studies perspective, interesting examples are provided by recent literature, as it will be shown later in this chapter.)

As emerges from the different understandings of space and social relation, the debate on democratic structures and functioning upon which planning theories are inscribed does not provide fixed interpretive frames, but it rather allows the emergence of alternative understandings of the role played by conflicts in contemporary democratic discourse.

An important and highly influential contribution to the debate is provided by Mouffe (1993, 2000a, 2000b, 2005), who introduces the concept of 'agonistic pluralism.' Based on acknowledging the intrinsically conflictive nature of spatial politics, in which identity results from the delineation of antagonistic camps (see also: Dikeç 2012: 675), and on a conception of the public sphere as an 'agonistic arena' (see: Mouffe 2013), she argues in favor of a re-description of the basic understanding of relational space in liberal democratic regimes, stating that it should not be conceived as the arena of a friend/enemy divide, but rather as the field where strife between adversaries takes place.

The notion of agonism, developed by Mouffe in political-theoretical terms, has been applied to urban studies and planning conflicts by a number of authors, such as Pløger (2004), Beaumont and Loopmans (2008), Beaumont and Nicholls (2008), Collins (2010) and others. A more extensive analysis of the contribution provided by the notion of agonism for the understanding of concrete conflicts is provided in the following sections in relation to these debates.

Conflict Management and Resolution Strategies

A further dimension of the ongoing discourse on planning conflicts refers to management and resolution strategies. The planning theoretical debate about conflicts raises, indeed, some fundamental questions with respect to both planning objectives and strategies within urban conflicts. The appropriate level of political inclusion of the involved stakeholders, the degree of institutionalization of social mobilization, and the objectives to pursue in the development of participative and relational urban management processes are among the most controversial and debated issues, both from a theoretical and from a more concrete perspective.

On the one hand, an institutional and inclusive approach is followed, in particular, in the area of approaches broadly defined as 'collaborative.' A great number of collaborative practices for conflict resolution—such as deliberative forums, public consultations, focus groups, public debate and so on—have emerged in the last decade, also supported by legal frameworks increasingly oriented to sustainable development and urban governance (Fung and Wright 2003; Fung 2004, 2006; Goodin and Dryzek 2006; Dryzek and Hendriks 2012; Grönlund et al. 2014; for a critical review, see also: Fischer 2003). They are mostly developed at a neighborhood level, where face-to-face communication enables the emergence of shared imaginaries, thus strengthening collective identity (Sorensen and Sagaris 2010: 301). Collaborative practices in urban planning are normally used to face urban problems or to discuss specific projects to be implemented, and are mainly aimed at the resolution of conflict or, at least, at the definition of a compromise solution.[1]

By referring to the concept of relational space mentioned above, it can be stated that the collaborative practice is grounded in an *associative* understanding of urban politics, insofar as it is assumed that it is only in the contingent dimension of relational space that proper collective approaches to conflict resolution may emerge, and place-based governance schemes can be (socially) constructed. Furthermore, collaborative politics assumes a specific understanding of the role of citizens in the political discourse; they are not only "bearers of rights and beneficiaries of protection," but also active agents of the democratic system, from which the political power "borrows its normative legitimacy" (Warren 2008: 388). Management practices aimed at conflict resolution have therefore to be understood as part of a broader interpretive framework, which adopts "an inclusive dialogic approach to shaping social space" (Andres 2013: 760) and in which planning is basically conceived as an interactive bottom-up process aimed at the enhancement of spatial and territorial quality through community-focused participatory governance (Healey 2003).

Although collaborative and deliberative practices vary significantly in terms of scale, degree of institutionalization and level of inclusion, they are basically grounded in the notion of *reflexive dialogue*, through which—according to Habermas—it is possible to achieve a shared, collectively imagined, and context-related understanding of what is 'true' and what is 'right' and socially valid. Within this dialogic dimension a significant relevance is assumed by symbolic and linguistic discourses that develop in the public sphere (cf. Alfasi and Portugali 2007: 168). The optimal result of conflict resolution strategies (i.e., an unforced ex ante agreement among actors involved in the process) should be achieved—according to most authors—through consensus-oriented deliberative processes (Innes 1996, 2004; Innes and Booher 1999). The creation of a non-hostile communicative discourse is indeed a prerequisite for successful conflict resolution strategies, insofar as it provides a platform

> where value systems can be articulated, where shared strategic conviction can grow, where conflicts are re-framed in a less antagonistic manner and where the discourse shifts from the competitive bargaining of fixed interests to a mode of negotiated problem definition and consensus-building. (Brand and Gaffikin 2007: 290)

From a collaborative planning perspective, the advantages of assuming a communicative approach aimed at conflict resolution are significant. First, according to supporters of sustainable urban governance, collaborative practices not only enable the internalization of dissent (see the next sections for further discussion of the notion of dissent in planning theories) within a shared institutional framework, but they also foster a greater inclusion of the involved stakeholders in the decision-making process at different levels, from the agenda-setting to the ultimate decision-making. Second, they promote the accumulation of local knowledge, thus making possible a reshaping of the expert–citizen relationships in the governance context, the enhancement of political and cultural awareness among the involved stakeholders, and a general improvement of social learning. Furthermore, reflexive dialogue enables stakeholders to interact with each other in a "disarming conversation" (Hamelink 2008: 297), where they can effectively communicate, thus preventing the violent escalation of conflicts. This "preventive action" (ibid.: 296) helps citizens to reframe problems in non-threatening terms and to look at conflicts as an opportunity for change. In addition, communicative schemes can mitigate power differentials (Bond 2011: 164), which are not insurmountable if properly framed in a dialectic dimension. Finally, with regard to democratic theory, collaborative practices would contribute to decreasing the democratic deficit by reducing the gap between institutions and civil society (Habermas 1993; Dryzek 1994; Healey 1999: 119), thus improving the overall democratic legitimacy of the process.

The rise of collaborative conflict resolution schemes has been strongly criticized (e.g., Flyvbjerg 1998; Yiftachel and Huxley 2000; Flyvbjerg and Richardson 2002; McGuirk 2001; Bickerstaff and Walker 2005; Purcell 2006; Brand and Gaffikin 2007; Gunder 2010; Matthews 2013) and has raised a number of questions that concern their theoretical foundations, as well as their practical effectiveness. Are collaborative resolution strategies viable? Do they really resolve conflicts or do they only provide compromise solutions? Is it possible to overcome power differentials through dialogue? Who has the right to take decisions when policies and measures affect also non-directly involved stakeholders? To what extent do communicative practices enhance democratic legitimacy? Is it possible, as asked by Brand and Gaffikin (2007), to have "collaborative planning in an uncollaborative world"?

Critiques of consensus-oriented conflict resolution strategies and of 'collaborative' urban governance schemes have been advanced both by theorists belonging to the communicative democratic tradition and by authors embracing a more radical anti-neoliberal approach. With regard to the former, the main point deals with the as-unrealistic perceived and ideological nature of the Habermasian notion of consensus. Accordingly, adepts of deliberative democracy have developed approaches that try to overcome such theoretical difficulties by a pragmatics in which the idea of consensus-steering and consensus management is explicitly substituted by the idea of consensus-building as the deliberative construction of local agreements based on sharing problem definitions and on negotiating interest differentials (Innes et al. 1994; Innes 1996; Melo and Baiocchi 2006; Dryzek and Hendriks 2012: 36). From a critical perspective, consensus-steering as a conflict management strategy has even been accused of facilitating the neoliberal project, which "requires decision-making practices that are widely accepted as *democratic* but that do not (or cannot) fundamentally challenge existing relations of power" (Purcell 2009: 141). Questions about the authoritative power and the democratic legitimacy of deliberative pooling and collaborative forums also arise in the theoretical political literature. According to Nadia Urbinati, for example, deliberative assemblies risk being subject to external manipulation and "may become tools that elites can use to legitimate their policies while bypassing electoral accountability, or substituting for broader citizen judgment and participation" (Urbinati 2009: 74).

Communicative planning and participatory practices based on Habermasian discursive principles have been further interpreted "as part of a system of domination rather than [one of] emancipation" (Bickerstaff and Walker 2005: 2140), insofar as they allegedly ignore power structures (McGuirk 2001; Matthews 2013: 144) and marginalize antagonism and strife (Mouffe 2000b;

Pløger 2004; Gunder 2010), de facto flattening the political discourse and protecting the interests of capital investments (Falk 2000; Goodhart 2001). From a critical perspective, the main problem of the communicative approach in urban governance is to draw attention away from the underlying material and political processes that so significantly contribute to shape the city (Yiftachel and Huxley 2000: 907).

Critical geographers and planners state the necessity of building a new imaginary of the city and a new vision of urban life, where capitalism is no longer the structuring principle in the political and spatial organization of the city, and where the satisfaction of social needs is acknowledged as a priority (Brenner et al. 2009: 176). In this view, conflict management is inescapably related to the redefinition of power relations and to the questioning of neoliberal urban schemes, and therefore cannot be based on practices grounded in negotiation or consensus (for a comprehensive review of the obstacles to consensus-building, see: Margerum 2002: 244). Urban conflicts can only be solved through a proper reorganization of power relations, which would allow the achievement of higher degrees of social and spatial justice in contemporary urban patterns. This way, critique of consensus-oriented planning practices ties in with debates on the notion of the *just city* (see, among others: Marcuse 2009; Brenner et al. 2009; Fainstein 2010).

Understanding Dissent and Participation

One of the main contested issues in the ongoing debate on urban conflicts concerns the notion of dissent, the role it plays or should play within urban politics, and its relationship with democratic representative and institutional patterns. Divergent views about the articulation of disagreement and of oppositional practices are at the basis of the different conflict management and resolution strategies mentioned above, and are inscribed in a context increasingly defined by claims for political participation and bottom-up policy-making.

On the one hand, dissent is conceived as part of democratic schemes, i.e., as an expression of the tensions embedded in the pluralist nature of society. According to this interpretation, generally ascribed to collaborative and communicative planning schemes, disagreement and dissent have a potentially positive role in the articulation of urban discourse, insofar as they provide an opportunity to reframe it through a dialogic approach (Innes 1996, 2004; Forester 1997, 1999, 2006; Innes and Booher 1999, 2003, 2010; Fischer 2009; Fischer and Gottweis 2012). In this context, dissent can be successfully faced through participatory and discursive practices. The notion of participation is itself redefined in more inclusive terms, insofar as, as argued by Raniolo (2001), it assumes a double meaning: on the one hand, to *be part*, i.e., to belong to a certain community, and on the other hand, to *take part*, i.e., to be actively involved in the decision-making process. This understanding of participation assumes a particular relevance in urban planning and politics, where specific policies and measures directly affect local communities.

With respect to participation patterns in conflict resolution strategies, therefore, the focus is mostly on those actors who have an interest or stake, such as for example representatives of the government, politicians, interest groups, committees, citizens associations, NGOs and so on (Margerum 2002: 238). The definition of the interested actors is particularly important in collaborative planning, since normally only the involved stakeholders can take part in participatory practices aimed at conflict resolution. In this regard it is necessary to point out that, in opposition to conventional planning schemes, interests are not fixed nor exogenously determined, but they are rather constructed through dialogue within the process, i.e., following a co-evolutive approach.

On the other hand, from a critical perspective, the understanding of dissent is grounded in the unequal character of power structures and systems of domination that shape the political urban domain. In this view, social dissent emerges generally when individuals become aware of the socio-spatial injustices entailed in urban practices. Following such a raise of consciousness, actors can decide to act collectively, i.e., to engage in a (more or less antagonistic) spatial mobilization. The main focus is, in this case, on urban social movements (cf. Mayer 2013). Urban social movements were first defined in the 1980s, notably by Castells (1983: 305) as "urban-orientated mobilizations that influence structural social change and transform the urban meanings," and by Fainstein and Fainstein (1985: 189) as "a type of social movement rooted in collectivities with a communal base and/or with the local state as their target of action." Castells (1983) in particular, in revision of his previous structuralist Marxian conceptualization, introduced a distinction of movements that served to characterize forms of political activism typical of mobilization in the urban context:

- movements focusing on issues of collective consumption, i.e., struggles around social provision of and access to collectively managed services financed by the State;
- movements defending cultural and social identities in relation to a particular place; and
- movements seeking to achieve control and management of local spaces, institutions or assets.

These movements arise precisely to question power dynamics and to express the claim to the empowerment of citizens with respect to the choices that produce the urban space (Purcell 2006). Critical analytical contributions on social movements and their interaction with contemporary urban dynamics have been provided by a number of scholars in the last decade (see, among the others: Leitner et al. 2006; Leontidou 2006; Leitner et al. 2008; Nicholls 2008; DeFilippis et al. 2010; Künkel and Mayer 2012; Harvey 2012; Somerville 2012; Uitermark et al. 2012; Rutland 2013; Nicholls et al. 2014).

Antagonistic social movements, in contrast to institutional actors, do not share the political, symbolic and interpretive framework of spatial politics, and they generally refuse representative democratic schemes. When mobilizing against certain planning projects or measures, they not only oppose a determinate planning policy, but the whole context in which such a policy is embedded. Anti-neoliberal planning therefore critically assesses the political significance of institutionalized action, and—in most of the cases—does not accept any form of institutional intermediation within the development of its political discourse. This would entail not only a loss of identity for social movements (Castells 1983), but also a turn to conventional and formalized action strategies. An institutionalized understanding of dissent would necessarily imply the abandonment of any form of antagonistic practice and strife (Pruijt 2003), thus de facto excluding grassroots (antagonistic) urban and environmental movements from the political discourse (Beal 2012).

Revising the Role of Planning

Planning theoretical discourses on urban conflicts are wide, complex and controversial. Different theories are rooted in different understandings of socio-spatial relation, of the political dimension of the city and, ultimately, of democratic dynamics. Divergent perspectives are reflected in the current approaches toward urban and planning conflicts.

The ongoing debate on socio-spatial conflicts calls for a redefinition of the role of spatial planning in urban politics. Notwithstanding different ideological backgrounds and approaches to conflict management and resolution, a political turn in urban planning is requested. From the debate, it emerges that planners have to transcend the regulatory dimension to which their actions are traditionally relegated, and contribute both to a reconceptualization of urban politics and to a transformation of the physical and symbolical dimension of the space. The way in which this contribution should be provided depends on normative frameworks and on different understandings of conflicts and of planning schemes.

By referring to the approaches described in the previous sections, it can be considered how collaborative and communicative planning theories acknowledge the potential of urban conflicts in terms of increasing political legitimacy and overall democratization. Collaborative conflict resolution strategies, indeed, pursue a shift to value-driven and proactive spatial planning aimed at the creation of sustainable places, to be achieved through participative and inclusive planning and policy-making processes (Albrechts 2004). These can, in their supporters' view, enhance citizens' involvement through a discursive approach, thus helping to overcome democratic deficits at the national and sub-national level. Collaborative arenas, deliberative forums, public consultation and similar practices allow citizens to participate in the agenda-setting and decision-making processes, thus increasing their political influence in managing existing socio-spatial relations and also, as argued by Healey, "imagining and opening up future potentialities" (Healey 2008: 277). From a collaborative perspective, planning should provide the theoretical and analytical framework necessary for the proper development of collaborative practices. Furthermore, at the operational level, a demand for more *communicative planners* emerges; they should mediate between local and expert knowledge, thus promoting social learning while including the results of participatory and bottom-up processes within a wider framework that includes the analysis of contingent and placed-based dynamics.

According to critical theorists and planners, instead, the role of planning in urban politics should not be aimed at the resolution of conflicts, but it should "act to politicize the contradictions of capitalist restructuring, to challenge the discursive and institutional terrains of urban politics" (Routledge 2010: 1166). Critical and anti-neoliberal planning focuses basically on the transformative power that conflicts have over urban and territorial dynamics, both at the local and at the global level. Planners should actively participate in the process of urban restructuring, by triggering a self-conscious and socially inclusive transformation of urban dynamics, by identifying socio-spatial injustices and by contributing to the overall redefinition of the structural organization of the city.

New Developments in Urban Conflict Research

Looking at the urban-conflict-related literature of the last ten years, it appears clear that, notwithstanding the different theoretical approaches mentioned in the previous section, real conflicts and concrete problems are hard to define following collaborative or critical perspectives, insofar as theoretical and interpretive frames blur in the everyday practice of urban politics.

One first trend that can be identified with respect to possible development in urban conflict research concerns the attempt to establish an alternative theoretical framework, capable of acknowledging the conflictive nature of contemporary urban society, while providing at the same time viable solutions.

This *third way* has been proposed, from a democratic theoretical perspective, by Mouffe and by her notion of 'agonistic pluralism.' In opposition to more anti-neoliberal critical planners, she does not consider conflicts as related to complex socio-economic variables that cannot be successfully addressed at the local level, but rather she states the necessity to overcome not "this us/them opposition—which is an impossibility—but the different way in which it is established" (Mouffe 2000b: 14–15). Although assuming a critical interpretive approach, she argues for a redefinition of this us/them discrimination "in a way that is compatible with pluralist society" (ibid.). A development in this sense is proposed by Beaumont and Loopmans (2008), who develop their notion of *radicalized communicative rationality*—applied to conflict analysis—on a critical re-elaboration of theoretical foundations laid by Mouffe. Their aim is to combine the "ideals of the Habermasian ideal speech act and communicative rationality with grassroots empowerment and bottom-up processes of participation closer to the agonistic pluralism of Mouffe" (Beaumont and Loopmans 2008: 96).

A second trend developing in recent years in urban policy and planning literature, one which requires further developments in terms of research, concerns the increasing interdependence between global and local conflicts and mobilizations and the rise of antagonistic urban social movements connected by a critical understanding of urban dynamics. Local, urban social movements are emerging all over the world to protest not only against local policies and measures, but also against the global dynamics in which specific policies are grounded. Placed-based social movements are not only concerned with the local dynamics in which they are directly involved, but they also challenge the neoliberal structuring of the city (see: Smith 2002; Swyngedouw et al. 2002; Kohler and Wissen 2003; Hou 2010). Urban social movements are increasingly engaged in striving for the production of a more just urban space. One important claim concerns the reappropriation of urban spaces (for a critical analysis on squatting movements in different urban and socio-economic contexts, see: Bieri 2002; Pruijt 2003; Leontidou 2010; Holm and Kuhn 2011; for an analysis of case studies related to segregation and displacement processes connected to urban renewal, see: Musterd 2006; Musterd et al. 2006; Scharenberg and Bader 2009; Balaban 2011; Uysal 2012). This trend solicits a redefinition of urban planning theory and of the related urban decision-making structures. This should be based on the assumption that a formally inclusive approach to decision-making is not sufficient in order to effectively cope with conflicts, insofar as—as argued by Rancière—"the democratic theme is *not* the inclusion of the excluded: it is the posture of the redefinition of the whole and its modes of governance and partitioning" (in Dikeç 2002: 94).

Finally, a trend is developing concerning the increasing relevance assumed in defining the normative dimension of urban politics by the symbolic potentials of conflicts. Urban protests and strife are always multidimensional phenomena, and the reasons in which they are grounded are social, economic, spatial as well as symbolic. The increasingly symbolic value assumed by urban conflicts calls for more attention in conflict research to the narrative dimension of conflicts, the imaginaries in which they are grounded, the concrete language used to describe and manage them, and their traveling across space.

Note

1. Communicative and collaborative practices have been widely analyzed by scholars in the last decade, in terms of both democratic legitimacy and effectiveness. From a case-study perspective, some interesting (critical or descriptive) analysis deals with participatory schemes and consultative procedures promoted at different scales in relation to the location of infrastructures (see for example the literature on the French *débat public*, in particular Subra and Newman 2008); to the development of large-scale urban projects (see, among the others: Ahlfeldt and Maennig 2012 about the referendum for the Allianz Arena in Munich); and to the development of the related plans (see Bickerstaff and Walker 2005 on the development of local transport plans). The local political frameworks in which participatory practices take place are also considered, in order to assess their capacity to effectively include participatory practices (see: Majoor 2011, who considers the institutional and political framework in the case of the Universal Forum of Culture in Barcelona, or Jun and Musso 2012, who focus on the community mediation processes in neighborhood councils in San Francisco).

References

Ahlfeldt, G. and Maennig, W. (2012) "Voting on a NIMBY Facility: Proximity Cost of an 'Iconic' Stadium," *Urban Affairs Review*, 48(2): 205–237.

Albrechts, L. (2004) "Strategic (Spatial) Planning Reexamined," *Environment and Planning B*, 31(5): 743–758.

Alfasi, N. and Portugali, J. (2007) "Planning Rules for a Self-Planned City," *Planning Theory*, 6(2): 164–182.

Amin, A. (2004) "Regions Unbound: Towards a New Politics of Place," *Geografiska Annaler B*, 86(1): 33–44.

Andres, L. (2013) "Differential Spaces, Power Hierarchy and Collaborative Planning: A Critique of the Role of Temporary Uses in Shaping and Making Places," *Urban Studies*, 50(4): 759–775.

Arendt, H. (2006) *Between Past and Future: Eight Exercises in Political Thought*, New York, NY: Penguin Books.

Arendt, H. (2007) *The Promise of Politics*, ed. J. Kohn, New York, NY: Schocken Books.

Balaban, U. (2011) "The Enclosure of Urban Space and Consolidation of the Capitalist Land Regime in Turkish Cities," *Urban Studies*, 48(10): 2162–2179.

Beal, V. (2012) "Urban Governance, Sustainability and Environmental Movements: Post-Democracy in French and British Cities," *European Urban and Regional Studies*, 19(4): 404–419.

Beaumont, J. and Loopmans, M. (2008) "Towards Radicalized Communicative Rationality: Resident Involvement and Urban Democracy in Rotterdam and Antwerp," *International Journal of Urban and Regional Research*, 32(1): 95–113.

Beaumont, J. R. and Nicholls, W. (2008) "Plural Governance, Participation and Democracy in Cities," *International Journal of Urban and Regional Research*, 32(1): 87–94.

Bickerstaff, K. and Walker, G. (2005) "Shared Visions, Unholy Alliances: Power, Governance and Deliberative Processes in Local Transport Planning," *Urban Studies*, 42(12): 2123–2144.

Bieri, S. (2002) "Contested Places: Squatting and the Construction of 'the Urban' in Swiss Cities," *GeoJournal*, 58(2/3): 205–217.

Bond, S. (2011) "Negotiating a 'Democratic Ethos': Moving Beyond the Agonistic–Communicative Divide," *Planning Theory*, 10(2): 161–186.

Brand, R. and Gaffikin, F. (2007) "Collaborative Planning in an Uncollaborative World," *Planning Theory*, 6(3): 282–313.

Brenner, N., Marcuse, P. and Mayer, M. (2009) "Cities for People, Not for Profit," *City*, 13(2): 176–184.

Castells, M. (1983) *The City and the Grassroots: A Cross-Cultural Theory of Urban Social Movements*, Berkeley, CA: University of California Press.

Collins, M. (2010) "Conflict and Contact: The 'Humane' City, Agonistic Politics, and the Phenomenological Body," *Environment and Planning D*, 28(5): 913–930.

DeFilippis, J., Shragge, E. and Fischer, R. (2010) *Contesting Community*, New Brunswick, NJ: Rutgers University Press.

Dikeç, M. (2001) "Justice and the Spatial Imagination," *Environment and Planning A*, 33(10): 1785–1805.

Dikeç, M. (2002) "Police, Politics, and the Right to the City," *GeoJournal*, 58(2–3): 91–98.

Dikeç, M. (2012) "Space as a Mode of Political Thinking," *Geoforum*, 43(4): 669–676.

Dryzek, J. S. (1994) *Discursive Democracy: Politics, Policy, and Political Science*, Cambridge, UK: Cambridge University Press.

Dryzek, J. S. and Hendriks, C. M. (2012) "Fostering Deliberation in the Forum," in F. Fischer and H. Gottweis (eds.), *The Argumentative Turn Revisited: Public Policy as Communicative Practice*, Durham, NC: Duke University Press: 31–57.

Fainstein, S. (2010) *The Just City*, Ithaca, NY: Cornell University Press.

Fainstein, S. S. and Fainstein, N. I. (1985) "Economic Restructuring and the Rise of Urban Social Movements," *Urban Affairs Quarterly*, 21: 187–206.

Falk, R. (2000) "The Decline of Citizenship in an Era of Globalization," *Citizenship Studies*, 4(1): 5–18.

Fischer, F. (ed.) (2000) *Citizens, Experts, and the Environment: The Politics of Local Knowledge*, Durham, NC: Duke University Press.

Fischer, F. (2003) *Reframing Public Policy: Discursive Politics and Deliberative Practices*, Oxford, UK: Oxford University Press.

Fischer, F. (2009) "Discursive Planning: Social Justice as Discourse," in P. Marcuse, J. Connolly, J. Novy, I. Olivo, C. Potter and J. Steil (eds.), *Searching for the Just City: Debates in Urban Theory and Practice*, London, UK: Routledge: 52–70.

Fischer, F. and Gottweis, H. (eds.) (2012) *The Argumentative Turn Revisited: Public Policy as Communicative Practice*, Durham, NC: Duke University Press.

Flyvbjerg, B. (1998) *Rationality and Power: Democracy in Practice*, Chicago, IL: Chicago University Press.

Flyvbjerg, B. and Richardson, T. (2002) "Planning and Foucault: In Search of the Dark Side of Planning Theory," in P. Allmendinger and M. Tewdwr-Jones (eds.), *Planning Futures: New Directions for Planning Theory*, London, UK: Routledge: 44–62.

Forester, J. (1997) "Beyond Dialogue to Transformative Learning: How Deliberative Rituals Encourage Political Judgment in Community Planning Processes," in D. Borri, A. Khakee and C. Lacirignola (eds.), *Evaluating Theory-Practice and Urban-Rural Interplay in Planning*, Dordrecht: Kluwer: 81–103.

Forester, J. (1999) *The Deliberative Practitioner: Encouraging Participatory Planning Processes*, Cambridge, MA: MIT Press.

Forester, J. (2006) "Making Participation Work When Interests Conflict: Moving from Facilitating Dialogue and Moderating Debate to Mediating Negotiations," *Journal of the American Planning Association*, 72(4): 447–456.

Fung, A. (2004) *Empowered Participation: Reinventing Urban Democracy*, Princeton, NJ: Princeton University Press.

Fung, A. (2006) "Varieties of Participation in Complex Governance," *Public Administration Review*, 66(Suppl.1): 66–75.

Fung, A. and Wright, E. O. (eds.) (2003) *Deepening Democracy: Institutional Innovations in Empowered Participatory Governance*, London, UK: Verso.

Giddens, A. (1986 [1984]) *The Constitution of Society: Outline of the Theory of Structuration*, Berkeley, CA: University of California Press.

Goodhart, M. (2001) "Democracy, Globalization, and the Problem of the State," *Polity*, 33(4): 527–546.

Goodin, R. E. and Dryzek, J. S. (2006) "Deliberative Impacts: The Macro-Political Uptake of Mini-Publics," *Politics & Society*, 34(2): 219–244.

Grönlund, K., Bächtiger, A. and Setälä, M. (eds.) (2014) *Deliberative Mini-Publics: Involving Citizens in the Democratic Process*, Colchester, UK: ECPR Press.

Gunder, M. (2010) "Planning as the Ideology of (Neoliberal) Space," *Planning Theory*, 9(4): 298–314.

Habermas, J. (1984) *The Theory of Communicative Action*, Boston, MA: Beacon Press.

Habermas, J. (1993) *Justification and Application: Remarks on Discourse Ethics*, Cambridge, MA: MIT Press.

Hamelink, C. J. (2008) "Urban Conflict and Communication," *International Communication Gazette*, 70(3/4): 291–301.

Harris, N. (2002) "Collaborative Planning: From Theoretical Foundations to Practice Forms," in P. Allmendinger and M. Tewdwr-Jones (eds.), *Planning Futures: New Directions for Planning Theory*, London, UK: Routledge: 21–43.

Harvey, D. (1989) *The Urban Experience*, Baltimore, MD: Johns Hopkins University Press.

Harvey, D. (2006) "Space as a Keyword," in N. Castree and D. Gregory (eds.), *David Harvey: A Critical Reader*, Oxford, UK: Blackwell: 270–293.

Harvey, D. (2008) "The Right to the City," *New Left Review*, 53: 23–40.

Harvey, D. (2009 [1973]) *Social Justice and the City*, revised edition, Athens, GA: University of Georgia Press.

Harvey, D. (2012) *Rebel Cities*, London, UK: Verso.

Healey, P. (1997) *Collaborative Planning: Shaping Places in Fragmented Societies*, Vancouver, Canada: UBC Press.

Healey, P. (1999) "Institutionalist Analysis, Communicative Planning, and Shaping Places," *Journal of Planning Education and Research*, 19(2): 111–121.

Healey, P. (2003) "Collaborative Planning in Perspective," *Planning Theory*, 2(2): 101–123.

Healey, P. (2008) "The Pragmatic Tradition in Planning Thought," *Journal of Planning Education and Research*, 28(3): 277–292.

Holm, A. and Kuhn, A. (2011) "Squatting and Urban Renewal: The Interaction of Squatter Movements and Strategies of Urban Restructuring in Berlin," *International Journal of Urban and Regional Research*, 35(3): 644–658.

Hou, J. (2010) *Insurgent Public Space: Guerilla Urbanism and the Remaking of Contemporary Cities*, London, UK: Routledge.

Innes, J. E. (1996) "Planning Through Consensus Building: A New View of the Comprehensive Planning Ideal," *Journal of the American Planning Association*, 62(4): 460–472.

Innes, J. E. (2004) "Consensus Building: Clarifications for the Critics," *Planning Theory*, 3(1): 5–20.

Innes, J. E. and Booher, D. E. (1999) "Consensus Building as Role Playing and Bricolage Toward as Theory of Collaborative Planning," *Journal of the American Planning Association*, 65(1): 9–26.

Innes, J. E. and Booher, D. E. (2003) *The Impact of Collaborative Planning on Governance Capacity*, Institute of Urban and Regional Development, Berkeley, CA: Institute of Urban and Regional Development, available at: www.escholarship.org/uc/item/98k72547 (accessed September 22, 2014).

Innes, J. E. and Booher, D. E. (2010) *Planning with Complexity: An Introduction to Collaborative Rationality for Public Policy*, London, UK: Routledge.

Innes, J. E., Gruber, J., Neuman, M. and Thompson, R. (1994) *Coordinating Growth and Environmental Management Through Consensus Building*, Berkeley, CA: California Policy Seminar, University of California.

Jun, K. N. and Musso, J. (2012) "Participatory Governance and the Spatial Representation of Neighborhood Issues," *Urban Affairs Review*, 49(1): 71–110.

Kohler, B. and Wissen, M. (2003) "Glocalizing Protest: Urban Conflicts and the Global Social Movements," *International Journal of Urban and Regional Research*, 27(4): 942–951.

Künkel, J. and Mayer, M. (2012) "Neoliberal Urbanism and Its Contestations: Crossing Theoretical Boundaries," *International Journal of Urban and Regional Research*, 37(4): 1493–1496.

Lefebvre H. (1977) "Reflections on the Politics of Space," in R. Peet (ed.), *Radical Geography: Alternative Viewpoints on Contemporary Social Issues*, Chicago, IL: Maaroufa Press: 339–352.

Lefebvre, H. (2005 [1992]) *The Production of Space*, Oxford, UK: Blackwell.

Leitner, H., Peck, J. and Sheppard, E. S. (2006) *Contesting Neoliberalism*, New York, NY: Guilford Press.

Leitner, H., Sheppard, E. S. and Sziarto, K. M. (2008) "The Spatialities of Contentious Politics," *Transactions of the Institute of British Geographers*, 33(2): 157–172.

Leontidou, L. (2006) "Urban Social Movements: From the 'Right to the City' to Transnational Spatialities and Flaneur Activists," *City*, 10(3): 259–268.

Leontidou, L. (2010) "Urban Social Movements in 'Weak' Civil Societies: The Right to the City and Cosmopolitan Activism in Southern Europe," *Urban Studies*, 47(6): 1179–1203.

McGuirk, P. M. (2001) "Situating Communicative Planning Theory: Context, Power, and Knowledge," *Environment and Planning A*, 33(2): 195–217.

Majoor, S. (2011) "Framing Large-Scale Projects: Barcelona Forum and the Challenge of Balancing Local and Global Needs," *Journal of Planning Education and Research*, 31(2): 143–156.

Marchart, O. (2007) *Post-Foundational Political Thought: Political Difference in Nancy, Lefort, Badiou and Laclau*, Edinburgh, UK: Edinburgh University Press.

Marcuse, P. (ed.) (2009) *Searching for the Just City: Debates in Urban Theory and Practice*, London, UK: Routledge.

Margerum, R. D. (2002) "Collaborative Planning: Building Consensus and Building a Distinct Model for Practice," *Journal of Planning Education and Research*, 21(3): 237–253.

Matthews, P. (2013) "The Longue Durée of Community Engagement: New Applications of Critical Theory in Planning Research," *Planning Theory*, 12(2): 139–157.

Mayer, M. (2013) "First World Urban Activism," *City*, 17(1): 5–19.

Melo, M. and Baiocchi, G. (2006) "Deliberative Democracy and Local Governance: Towards a New Agenda," *International Journal of Urban and Regional Research*, 30(3): 587–600.

Mouffe, C. (1993) *The Return of the Political*, London, UK: Verso.

Mouffe, C. (2000a) *The Democratic Paradox*, London, UK: Verso.

Mouffe, C. (2000b) *Deliberative Democracy and Agonistic Pluralism*, Vienna, Austria: Institut für Höhere Studien, available at: www.ihs.ac.at/publications/pol/pw_72.pdf (accessed May 6, 2013).

Mouffe, C. (2005) *On the Political*, London, UK: Verso.

Mouffe, C. (2013) *Agonistics: Thinking the World Politically*, London, UK: Verso.

Musterd, S. (2006) "Segregation, Urban Space and the Resurgent City," *Urban Studies*, 43(8): 1325–1340.

Musterd, S., Murie, A. and Kesteloot, C. (2006) *Neighbourhoods of Poverty*, Basingstoke, UK: Palgrave Macmillan.

Nel·lo, O. (ed.) (2003) *Aquí, no! Els conflictes territorials a Catalunya*, Barcelona, Spain: Empúries.

Nicholls, W. J. (2008) "The Urban Question Revisited: The Importance of Cities for Social Movements," *International Journal of Urban and Regional Research*, 32(4): 841–859.

Nicholls, W. J., Miller, B. and Beaumont, J. R. (eds.) (2014) *Spaces of Contention*, Aldershot, UK: Ashgate.

Peck, J., Theodore, N. and Brenner, N. (2009) "Neoliberal Urbanism: Models, Moments, Mutations," *SAIS Review*, 29(1): 49–66.

Pløger, J. (2004) "Strife: Urban Planning and Agonism," *Planning Theory*, 3(1): 71–92.

Pruijt, H. (2003) "Is the Institutionalization of Urban Movements Inevitable? A Comparison of the Opportunities for Sustained Squatting in New York City and Amsterdam," *International Journal of Urban and Regional Research*, 27(1): 133–157.

Purcell, M. (2002) "Excavating Lefebvre: The Right to the City and Its Urban Politics of Inhabitant," *GeoJournal*, 58(2–3): 99–108.

Purcell, M. (2006) "Urban Democracy and the Local Trap," *Urban Studies*, 43(11): 1921–1941.

Purcell, M. (2009) "Resisting Neoliberalization: Communicative Planning or Radical Democratic Movements?" *Planning Theory*, 8(2): 140–165.

Raniolo, F. (2001) *La partecipazione politica*, Bologna, Italy: Il Mulino.

Routledge, P. (2010) "Introduction: Cities, Justice and Conflict," *Urban Studies*, 47(6): 1165–1177.

Rutland, T. (2013) "Activists in the Making: Urban Movements, Political Processes and the Creation of Political Subjects," *International Journal of Urban and Regional Research*, 37(3): 989–1011.

Sager, T. (2011) "Neo-Liberal Urban Planning Policies: A Literature Survey 1990–2010," *Progress in Planning*, 76(4): 144–190.

Scharenberg, A. and Bader, I. (2009) "Berlin's Waterfront Site Struggle," *City*, 13(2/3): 325–335.

Schmitt, C. (2007 [1996]) *The Concept of the Political*, Chicago, IL: University of Chicago Press.

Schmitt, C., Schwab, G. and Strong, T. B. (2005 [1985]) *Political Theology*, Chicago, IL: University of Chicago Press.

Smith, N. (2002) "New Globalism, New Urbanism: Gentrification as Global Urban Strategy," *Antipode*, 34(3): 427–450.

Somerville, P. (2012) "Resident and Neighbourhood Movements," in S. J. Smith (ed.), *International Encyclopedia of Housing and Home*, London, UK: Elsevier.

Sorensen, A. and Sagaris, L. (2010) "From Participation to the Right to the City: Democratic Place Management at the Neighbourhood Scale in Comparative Perspective," *Planning Practice and Research*, 25(3): 297–316.

Subra, P. and Newman, P. (2008) "Governing Paris: Planning and Political Conflict in Ile-de-France," *European Planning Studies*, 16(4): 521–535.

Swyngedouw, E. (2005) "Governance Innovation and the Citizen: The Janus Face of Governance-Beyond-the-State," *Urban Studies*, 42(11): 1991–2006.

Swyngedouw, E. (2009) "The Antinomies of the Postpolitical City: In Search of a Democratic Politics of Environmental Production," *International Journal of Urban and Regional Research*, 33(3): 601–620.

Swyngedouw, E., Moulaert, F. and Rodriguez, A. (2002) "Neoliberal Urbanization in Europe: Large-Scale Urban Development Projects and the New Urban Policy," *Antipode*, 34(3): 542–577.

Uitermark, J., Nicholls, W. and Loopmans, P. (2012) "Cities and Social Movements: Theorizing Beyond the Right to the City," *Environment and Planning A*, 44(11): 2546–2554.

Urbinati, N. (2009) "Unpolitical Democracy," *Political Theory*, 38(1): 65–92.

Uysal, Ü. E. (2012) "An Urban Social Movement Challenging Urban Regeneration: The Case of Sulukule, Istanbul," *Cities*, 29(1): 2–22.

Warren, M. E. (2008) "Democracy and the State," in J. S. Dryzek, B. Honig and A. Philipps (eds.), *The Oxford Handbook of Political Theory*, Oxford, UK: Oxford University Press: 381–399.

Yiftachel, O. and Huxley, M. (2000) "Debating Dominance and Relevance: Notes on the 'Communicative Turn' in Planning Theory," *International Journal of Urban and Regional Research*, 24(4): 907–913.

PART II
DYNAMICS OF CONTENTION AND COLLECTIVE MOBILIZATION IN PLANNING CONFLICTS

Introduction

Enrico Gualini

The contributions in Part II introduce a critical discussion of the conditions and forms under which conflict takes place in the framework of planning processes.

Through the exemplary cases presented, the authors highlight the need for a broader and more articulated understanding of planning conflicts than one resting solely on assuming their 'visibility' as overt and clearly defined contrasts between interest and positions; accordingly, they also highlight challenges in dealing with planning conflicts that go beyond assuming such aspects as defining features of conflicts. What these contributions highlight, rather, is the constitutive role of planning practices in defining the way conflicts are expressed and, accordingly, the selective and often ambiguous role planning practices play in shaping perceptions of what is at stake and in distributing resources for action.

Significantly, the contributions in this part point to the importance of understanding the absence, weakness or displacement of conflict not as phenomena external to planning, but as too often unexplored. Key to exploring this dimension is addressing 'conflict' as a moment of contention emerging in an intertemporal and co-evolutive dynamics of the mobilization of actors and of the formation of political subjectivities. As they define a field of practices and interactions, planning processes contribute to distributing opportunities and resources for a variety of actors to act upon the definition of policy issues and to appropriate them interpretively as objects of a claim and as matters of mobilization.

As the contributions in this part suggest, however, what remains too little explored is the uneven and selective influence exerted by planning on this—often, paradoxically, even when it allegedly addresses contentious issues through inclusive practices. From this perspective, the absence or marginality of conflict in the episodes presented is anything but the expression of a routine capacity of planning processes to lend voice and representation to competing social claims and to effectively settle them through negotiated agreements. Rather, it appears as an expression of an ambiguous capacity of hiding or disguising conflict by selectively (re)defining potential issues of contention and thus unevenly distributing resources and constraints for mobilization. While the construction of contentious policy issues is also addressed by several contributions in the following parts (particularly in Part III), the present chapters offer three distinctive interpretive perspectives centered on conditions and dynamics of mobilization.

Mössner and Del Romero Renau reflect on the cultural and institutional factors that influence the emergence and dynamics of collective mobilization and the capacity of actors to enact conflict through protest and contention. Their starting point is—both empirically and theoretically—the absence of protest in potentially contentious planning processes, and the importance of understanding non-protest or, as they put it, of exploring 'moments of non-protest.'

In emphasizing that explaining the absence of conflicts is as important as focusing on their presence, they point to the hidden or latent dimension of conflicts in urban policy and planning as a possible shortcoming of planning theory and, in particular, of the dominance of conflict resolution theories in thematizing planning conflicts. The perspective they adopt is that of radical political theories that see social conflicts not as moments of disturbance of the social order in need of 'resolution,' but as democratic moments essential to the political. Accordingly, understanding why conflict does not occur in certain situations amounts to addressing a paradox: that of 'planning without conflict' as a manifestation of a post-political trend in public policy.

The two case studies point to constraints to the emergence of social mobilization as a hegemonic result of growth-oriented politics and of the consensus orientation pursued by local urban elites. Against this background, the absence of protest or resistance highlights dominant consensus practices as a factor of exclusion, and poses democratic questions that have significant implications for research. For one, the authors take a critical stance towards conflict research focusing primarily on the relational interplay between protests, resistance and political consequences as an *explanans* of conflicts, as the empirical framework of such an approach neglects the reality of conflicts that do not find ways to emerge. For this, they propose a historically institutionalist-inspired interpretive framework, based on the interplay of a variety of factors such as, on the one hand, the path dependency of protest movements and the effects of their institutionalization on their capacity to act in an emergent situation, and, on the other hand, the role of an institutional framework based on consensus-building as an institutional conflict avoidance strategy and on related practices and discourses.

The influence of framework conditions on social mobilization is also at the center of the analysis by Pacchi and Pasqui, who address this in particular in relation to the institutional culture and practices embodied by recent developments in the form of urban plans. The core of their argument is an observation of the differentials of planning contexts—according to the different forms 'plans' or 'projects' may take in defining policy practices—with regard to the emergence and nature of conflict.

The case study of recent planning episodes in Milan offers a stage for exploring how different typologies of conflicts develop in relation to changing urban politics and policy frameworks. The main points they raise in this respect are: the differential capacity of projects/plans to become objects of explicit conflict; the different typologies of conflicts in relation to changing urban politics and policy frameworks; and the resulting 'space of possibilities' for conflicts and for their transformative potential.

If planning defines a 'space of possibilities' for conflicts to emerge and to be enacted, as moments of political subjectivation, democratic participation and potential social transformation, then a critical understanding is needed of the differential conditions and of the variable and uneven potential for conflict to emerge and to unfold democratization resources in different planning situations.

Again, this bears consequences for research as well as a potential for critique of the dimension of the political in planning practices. In line with the other contributions in Part II, Pacchi and Pasqui address the challenge of understanding the political nature of planning practices in times of radical decline and delegitimization of forms of political representation, and raise the question of how to conceive of conflict in times of post-political planning practices. The perspective they indicate is that of interpretive policy research focusing on specific relationships between actors, strategies, resources and tools in a particular field of structured planning practices. Directions for a repoliticization of planning practices, accordingly, rather than for a procedural focus on formal participation, may be drawn from understanding the differential potential of urban policies and plans for pluralist mobilization.

The observation of the inherent conflictual potential of planning processes, particularly as a marker of different social demands and rationalities as well as of the differentials in its expression, frames the contribution by Pizzo and Di Salvo, who also adopt an interpretive policy analysis approach to understanding an aspect they highlight as often neglected in considering planning practices: planning as a practice of disguising conflict. As they reject a simplified duality of considering planning either as source of or solution to conflicts, their contribution is critical with regard to the dominance of problem-solving attitudes and conflict resolution approaches in planning theory in conceptualizing planning conflicts.

Set within a broader urban research framework, addressing processes of neoliberalization and exploring their local specificities and variation in the case of Rome, this critique remarks on the centrality of this tradition in conceiving of conflict as a major factor for the divide between mainstream planning theory and critical urban research. Aiming at reconciling these traditions, the authors focus on an interpretation of conflict as an inherent dimension of planning practices, as a starting point for analyzing the hegemonic dimension involved in the way planning practices treat conflict.

As an interactive set of practices, planning co-defines the conditions under which conflicts can or cannot emerge: hence, in their words, the social responsibility of planning in determining the very conditions in which conflict emerges. Or, as they put it: planning becomes the chessboard, the strategic field on which conflict is played out. By analyzing the strategic-relational capacity of planning practices to predefine or predetermine conflicts, in the framework of the ambiguous and hybrid manifestations of neoliberal urban policy in Rome, Pizzo and Di Salvo unveil the tactical moves displayed in dealing with a contentious issue and their integrality to the strategies of development coalitions and policy-making elites.

The way the conflictual potential of urban development is dealt with in the Tor Marancia case reveals the ambiguity of an 'hybrid' neoliberal regime, in which 'innovative' forms of partnership appear as a cover-up of rather traditional forms of bargaining among selected actors, taking the form of 'disguised' negotiations rather than of an open and public 'collaborative' process. It reveals, moreover, the fundamental hypocrisy of such a form of negotiation as it is incorporated in planning practices that claim to represent a pursuit of public interests through public practices of negotiation.

The case delineates the picture of a defeat of planning, and in particular of the traditional masterplan, as a reference for debating public interests and for publicly negotiating trade-offs between public and private interests. While this appears to turn the plan into a merely rhetorical device, however, it also turns it—as the authors show—into a device for framing issues of contention and for manipulating their treatment. The implications are notable particularly in terms of the disempowerment of civil society; strategic scale-shifting and the trans-scalar implications of planning choices, for instance, exert a significant impact on the distribution of informational, symbolic and material resources for mobilization, significantly contributing to diffusing conflict.

3

What Makes a Protest (Not) Happen? The Fragmented Landscape of Post-Political Conflict Culture

Samuel Mössner and Luis del Romero Renau

Introduction

Geography, sociology, urban planning and other related social science disciplines have traditionally studied concrete conflicts in order to provide similarly definite and precise solutions for overcoming cleavages in society. Most of these studies focus on the emergence of conflicts in order to provide and discuss possible solutions aimed at overcoming the conflictual moment. Since the end of the 1970s, however, some scholars have claimed that explaining the absence of conflicts is as important as focusing on their presence (Newton 1978; Cox 1978). Such a comprehensive understanding of conflicts goes in line with a shift in the perspective on society. In contrast to the perspective of conflictual cleavages in society, another perspective evolved that, drawing on the work of German sociologist Ralf Dahrendorf, sees society rather as "a web of tensions and incompatible interests, which make conflict an ubiquitous part of the social order" (Newton 1978: 76) and, by doing so, distinguishes social reality from utopian ideas of society (Dahrendorf 1958).

More recently, this perspective re-emerges in the literature that broaches the issue of post-political and post-democratic tendencies in society and the urban in particular (Crouch 2004; Mouffe 2005; MacLeod 2011; Gill et al. 2012). These authors propose a perspective that denies the existence of a homogeneous society where conflicts are considered moments of disturbance. By doing so, they raise questions about the very moment of democracy that goes in line with conflicts and protests. Central to this perspective is Chantal Mouffe's work, in which she argues for an alternative perspective to the predominant belief in liberal democracy being the only legitimate governmental form (2000a). According to Mouffe, protests and conflicts particularly contribute to "a vibrant 'agonistic' public sphere" (Mouffe 2005: 3) that constitutes democratic life.

Frankfurt and Valencia have witnessed profound conflicts regarding the emergence of new urban regeneration projects that were contested by social movements for their impact on the capitalization and commodification of urban space. These criticisms were expressed in active and large protest movements pervading public space. Recent examples from both Germany and Spain demonstrate that protests seem to be rather well accepted as established ways of making conflicts visible and concrete. Protests, as such, are considered as a persistent element for stabilizing social order in both societies. However, despite the dramatic impact in the social and urban structure, in both case studies presented here surprisingly no protest emerged.

Newton (1978) and Cox (1978) claimed that there had been much work carried out explaining the emergence of conflicts in urban arenas. Most of this work was aimed at trying to understand whether urban conflicts occur. However, as both authors argue, it is not only the presence or absence of conflicts that is of interest. What is also of interest is understanding why in certain situations protests do or do not occur. Loudly expressed protest is an excellent medium for directing public attention to the conflict and, by doing so, placing the conflict at the center of democratic debate. Consequently, drawing on Mouffe (2000a), protests emerge as an essential factor for the democratization of society and the protest–conflict relationship appears crucial for understanding their influence on urban politics. Following Harvey Molotch's and John Logan's urban growth machine approach (Logan and Molotch 1987), we argue that the avoidance and suppression of protests in both cities is closely linked to the hegemony of urban elites grounded in a growth-oriented political consensus. As a central task, consensus secures the growth machine's objective of enhancing the "exchange value" of land regardless of "tangible detriments to the quality of life" for local populations (Purcell 2000: 86). This consensus excludes part of society, whose voices—borrowing a metaphor from Jacques Rancière (2001)—are only perceived as noise rather than articulated resistance. Consequently, this part of society remains excluded from participating in public-opinion-making. As protest and other forms of resistance represent a minimum possibility of participation in public life, it is the absence of protest that reveals political consensus to be a means of social exclusion. As such, non-protests are not considered as *simply* non-existing, but rather understood as particular forms of political action that are relevant in terms of local democracy.

In our chapter, we draw on this perspective provided by Mouffe and Rancière in investigating urban conflicts in Frankfurt and Valencia as critical moments for local democracy. While there is a broad strand of literature dealing with protests and other forms of resistance that make conflicts visible, concrete and observable, we are particularly keen on understanding those conflictual urban moments in which no significant protest (or any other form of resistance) occurs. It is the aim of our chapter to better understand such 'non-existences' of protests as relevant for conceptualizing urban conflicts from a post-political perspective. By doing so, we reject the oversimplified equation that conflicts only exist through the performance of protests and any other form of resistance. We further argue that the absence of protests does not primarily point to that fact that there are no conflicts in society but rather indicates a particular neoliberal order that suppresses critical voices from being heard. To make this case, we present two case studies of urban regeneration projects that had significant impact on urban form and social structure at the neighborhood level in Valencia and Frankfurt but witnessed no significant protest or resistance. By opposing yet not comparing these cases, we try to better understand the nexus between conflicts and protest in both cities and show that even though both Frankfurt and Valencia can look back on a long history of active protests, there is no 'automatism' of protesting and mechanisms of political exclusion do still exist.

This chapter is structured into three sections. In the first, we highlight the relationship between conflicts and protests and outline our conceptual approach to non-protests. The second deals with the case studies from Valencia and Frankfurt and the moments of non-protests that occurred in both cities. On the following pages, we analyze both case studies more deeply by providing more empirical details, and we finally point at the institutional setting that avoids protests and other forms of resistance in both cities.

On the Relationship Between Conflicts and Protests

Conflicts are usually defined as the observable expression of at least two opposing opinions or ideas that become evident by one or more concrete events or arguments (Bonacker 2009: 184–185) manifested in protests or other forms of resistance. This definition draws attention to the dissensus of at least two actors articulating their different interests in protest and by doing so making the conflict visible. Such a clash of interests or opinions occurs— according to established conflict literature—within a dynamic system of stimulus/response (or action/reaction) (Dunleavy 1977: 197), where a conflict functions as a stimulus for protests, which are responded to by political decisions, the change of a plan or a project, or in whatever form appears. Protest, conflicts and the political response are all interrelating parts of the same system. They occur in various forms and intensities, ranging from a civilized debate or discussion to violent confrontations. Large parts of the enormous repertoire of literature on conflict, which emerged in the last years in the interdisciplinary field of social sciences, deal with this trinity of conflicts—protests/resistance/political consequences—in order to develop appropriate models to manage or explain both causes of and potential solutions to conflicts (Joerin et al. 2006). By doing so, they underestimate the complex relationship between conflicts and protests as they take into account only those conflicts that are made observable by any form of protest. Many of the writings on urban and locational conflicts are based on an implicit 'desire for harmony.' This desire relates to a certain idea of a utopian society (Dahrendorf 1958) that unites all parts of society in a state of harmonic togetherness. Conflicts in such utopian societies are conceptualized by the consensus model (Newton 1978: 76–77). Here, society's cohesion is realized by "some kind of value consensus," whereas "conflict always implies some kind of dissensus and disagreement about values" (Dahrendorf 1958: 120).

Instead of treating conflicts as an anomaly of and threat to the actually existing social order, society must be seen as a web of tensions and incompatible interests, of which conflicts are a ubiquitous part (Newton 1978). Dahrendorf, who argues that conflicts should be seen rather as a necessary element to foster communication and cohesion between all the different social entities, also argues for this perspective. By doing so, however, he does not agree with approaching conflicts as the result of a deviant opinion that allegedly disequilibrates societal values. Social order, he insists, is realized through, but not threatened by, conflict. Following this perspective, protests are part of a political plurality and contribute to a vibrant democratic life. The crucial question is then neither why conflicts occur nor how they are resolved, but rather how society handles and deals with conflicts in the context of democracy. While the perspective of deliberative democracy focuses on consensus reached by participatory elements of democracy, our perspective results from different approaches, which contrast deliberative democracy with the idea of agonistic democracy (Mouffe 2000a, 2000b; Rancière 2001). Mouffe argues that conflicts create a "necessary condition for grasping the challenge to which democratic politics is confronted" (2005: 4). Conflicts in society express power constellations, hegemonies and antagonisms, which are sometimes hidden from the public debate. Accordingly, in our understanding, conflicts always exist and are part of our democratic systems. They can be expressed by many different forms of agitation, among which protests are considered an indicator for a vibrant democracy.

There is an emerging literature that is concerned with the decline of democracy as an egalitarian project (Crouch 2004) due to meta-consensual politics (Gill et al. 2012). This 'post-democracy' is described by people's disenchantment with politics by which democracy becomes reduced to elections. Rather than expressing contrasting opinions in the public realm, today most decisions are made behind closed doors away from the public, yet these decisions get accepted as kind of *natural laws*. This form of post-parliamentarianism (Crouch 2004) goes in line with new forms of "politainment" (Jörke 2005: 482) where making politics is transformed into an entertaining act.

Under post-democracy, political debates and decision-making have become quasi-privatized and removed from the public realm; it is politics outside of the political. There is a pacifying consensus in society over the principles and direction of policies to which protest and any form of political debate has been subordinated: "It is a politics reduced to the administration and management of processes whose parameters are defined by consensual socio-scientific knowledges" (Swyngedouw 2009: 602). Even though predefined by societal and economic constraints, this management process is open to everyone. By thus inviting resistant groups to participate and take responsibility for the outcome of these processes, antagonistic interests and perspectives are subordinated to the dogmatic search for societal consensus leading to the unification and standardization of society.

The exclusionary power of consensual politics, which suppresses any alternative form of political resistance, results from what Marchart (2010) calls the "political difference," i.e., the difference between *police* and *politics* (Rancière 2001). Following French philosopher Jacques Rancière, *police* is defined as specific procedures that constitute power and create or stabilize the consensus (Marchart 2010: 179) about what is visible and audible in society (Rancière 2010). The consensus that is usually reached by only a few persons denies that part of society that is not given a language to be heard. From this perspective, urban development as consensus-oriented police order is aimed at hierarchical orders and hegemonies (Chambers 2011: 306) that disallow different meanings, contrary opinions and societal dissensus.

Politics, by contrast, is about radical equality (Gill et al. 2012: 511) that results in the "demonstration of dissensus" (Rancière 2008: 33), of different political opinions, thoughts and ideologies that coexist within society. Dissensus is "not simply a conflict of interests, opinions, or values. It is a conflict over the common itself" (Rancière 2004: 6). Dissensus and equality are central arguments in Rancière's philosophy of the political that is aimed at criticizing the depoliticization of the urban. From the post-political perspective, the absence of protests is crucial for understanding the mechanisms of political exclusion. While the single reasons for not protesting are manifold and diverse for each group and individual, it is the absence of protest itself that speaks about the political situation in these cities.

Urban Conflicts in Valencia and Frankfurt

Valencia: The Formula 1 Circuit in the Poblats Marítims District

Since the 1970s, Valencia has experienced a profound shift in its economic structure. The containerization in freight transportation as well as the decline of the traditional manufacturing sector led to physical and social changes in the inner city. From the 1980s on, the city administration promoted landmark projects in order to foster tourism and the location of the newly emerging service sector in old industrial areas in the city. Flagship projects such as the construction of the 'city of arts and sciences' or the remodeling of the old Turia riverbed into an 'urban park' clearly reflect the new emerging political culture of 'festivalization' of urban policy (Häussermann and Siebel 1993). Although these projects were all located around the Poblats Marítims district, today this neighborhood is still considered one of the most deprived of the city. Social deprivation, high unemployment rates and a lack of social infrastructures were only few of the reasons for neighborhood associations to debate about the future and the political need for action in the district.

During the 1998–2008 real estate boom in Spain, Formula 1 tycoon Bernie Ecclestone visited Valencia in February 2006. Together with Ecclestone, the urban élite decided to bring the Formula 1 championship to Valencia. The construction of a circuit was in line with the marketing strategy of the urban politics at that time. Even though the project was expected to create ecological and infrastructural disadvantages for the local population—such as air pollution, traffic problems during the grand prix, privatization of public places and costs related to security issues during the event—the local growth machine expected to enhance significantly the amount of foreign investment in the city. At the beginning, the Formula 1 championship was expected to take place on the existing motorbike circuit in Cheste, which was built in 1999 and located nearly 30 km outside of Valencia. However on May 28, 2006 it was officially declared that the first grand prix would take place in June 2008, not on the motorbike circuit, but in the port district of Poblats Marítims, in accordance with Ecclestone's personal request (Badillo 2006).

Only a year after the decision to construct the circuit in Poblats Marítims, was a neighborhood association founded to fight against the realization of the project (Montesinos 2007). Under the name of Fórmula Verda (Green Formula), intellectuals and ecologists from existing neighborhood associations within the Poblats Marítims district called for more public participation and transparency during the implementation process of the project. They criticized particularly the lack of information about the exact amount of public funding for the project provided by the regional government, the privatization of public space and the transformation of the art deco ex-warehouses into garages and pit boxes during the race. In 2008 the association organized two protest events, in which, however, only a few hundred people participated. Regardless of its enormous impact on the urban space, the Formula 1 project provoked only few protests in society.

Frankfurt: The European Central Bank and the East End

As the executive board of the European Central Bank (ECB) announced in 2002, the headquarters of the ECB will move to a new building in the East End (Ostend) of Frankfurt in 2015. After a long and conflict-driven planning process starting in 1998, the European bankers have finally accepted the city's proposal, which preferred the former wholesale market hall as the best new location for the European financial institution. This building was inaugurated in 1928 as a wholesale market hall and symbol of the then progressive architectural movement *Neues Frankfurt*. The market hall is an immense brick building, officially listed for its historical and architectural singularity so that law prohibits larger structural modifications.

The winning architectural design of the new ECB headquarters includes two counter-rotating glass towers, which seem to unscrew out of the middle of the old wholesale market hall. In order to realize this architectural composition, Austrian architects Coop Himmelb(l)au connected two different buildings, the old market hall and the new glass towers, both representing different historical epochs, different urban modes of production and different political cultures. However, the design required the destruction of the middle part of the listed market hall building to which the glass towers are attached. The two buildings are physically connected, yet they remain ideologically detached. As a consequence of the relocation of the ECB to the East End, property speculation is leading to the displacement of former inhabitants, deeply transforming the built and social environment of the formerly working-class neighborhood.

Before the development of an international financial and service sector, Frankfurt witnessed a long Fordist tradition that had profoundly influenced its urban structure in the past. In particular, Frankfurt had been an important location for chemical, metal and paint production as well as the pharmaceutical industry that mostly emerged in the western and eastern periphery on the outskirts of the city. The first Global City formation started early in the 1960s (Keil and Ronneberger 2000) reconnecting to the path dependency of the financial sector and located in the inner-city upper-class neighborhood of the West End. In the very center of these transformations was a growth machine of mainly economic investors and local politicians. Since the beginning, the developments in the West End had encountered heavy resistance and protests by politically left-oriented, non-governmental groups. After the radical times of urban riots and housing struggles in the 1960s and the beginning of the 1970s (Noller and Ronneberger 1995), in the 1980s a conservative growth machine around Christian Democratic Union mayor Walter Wallmann (holding office from 1977 to 1986) and real estate speculator Ignatz Bubis came to power and brought the transformation of the West End to a new level. The housing struggles of the early 1970s failed to prevent the growth machine from achieving its objective of creating a built environment for establishing international financial institutions in Frankfurt, and so the city accomplished successfully the shift from Fordist to post-Fordist economic structures in the 1980s.

Only from the 1990s did political instruments such as the city's *Hochhausplan* (Skyscraper Development Plan) limit the further expansion of the financial sector. Since then, there have been 'two Frankfurts' independently coexisting due to a geographically unequal distribution of housing and labor markets as well as different life-chances, each developing its own materiality of the built environment and symbolic landmarks of specific modes of urban production:

- The western part is economically prosperous, creative, global and internationally connected with the most important information flows and offering the best individual life-chances. Expressions and marketing slogans such as 'Mainhattan' (referring to the River Main and a Manhattan-like skyline) or 'Frankfurt—City of the Euro' are symbolically related to that part of Frankfurt, which Jaschke (1997) described as the city of the suburban middle-class and the top of society.
- Besides the 'global west,' there was still a place in the East End for those citizens who have not benefited from booming service-sector-oriented economies, who are still suffering from the transformation towards post-Fordist employment structures and who are therefore excluded from the urban labor and housing markets. The old wholesale market hall, constructed by German architect Martin Elsaesser as an incisive symbol of the Fordist period, best represents this part of the city.

The relocation of the ECB headquarters to the East End symbolizes a second shift of the Global City formation that leads to unbalancing the economic, social and political duality. While in the 1970s there was enormous protest against the first formation, today, however, there are no voices heard expressing protest against either the partial demolition of the listed symbol of the *Neues Frankfurt*, or the property speculation that is leading to the displacement of the inhabitants of the East End. It seems as if the East End is out of sight of any critical perspectives on recent urban developments.

Moments of Non-Protest

Non-Protests Against Formula 1 in Valencia

In Valencia, the *movimientos vecinales* (neighborhood associations) used to play a crucial role in the resistance against Franco's dictatorship and attracted more people than the classical labor movement due to their cross-class character

(Pérez 2009). Born as a spontaneous response to the living conditions in Spanish cities forty years ago, they fought against a rather chaotic urban growth, which was and still is dominated by land speculation and profit-oriented real estate markets. During the 1980s the *movimientos vecinales* were the most important community actors. By the end of the decade, however, many of them had been institutionalized and partially assimilated by political parties (Cucó 2008). In the 1990s a new form of urban movement filled this gap, the *Salvem* ('Let's Save!') associations. At the local level they introduced new discourses such as environmental protection and sustainable development as well as life quality issues, and they claimed for a right to the city for all citizens and for social inclusion. However, each single *Salvem* association used to act in an independent way and only existed as long as the specific conflict it addressed. Some scholars call these associations the 'problem-associations,' referring to the fact that any association was founded for one specific problem (Cucó 2008: 187). Both movements failed in addressing the Formula 1 conflict. The *movimientos vecinales* were too reactive and institutionalized. For the *Salvem* movement, the Formula 1 project was positioned on a different scale. Effective protest would have required an internal reorganization in order to address the global actors. *Fórmula Verda*, the only association organizing two protests with moderate success, was rather acting according to the *Salvem* tradition and protested against the location of the project, but not against the project itself.

A second reason for the lack of protests is the time management of the project. The timescale between the public announcement of the decision to bring Formula 1 to the historic seashore district and the start of the construction was too short to organize efficient protests against the project, as the project plan was deliberately hidden from the public for months. In addition to the time factor, which inhibited an effective formation of protest, the city administration of Valencia tried to conceal and trivialize the project's impact during the planning process. The construction of the Formula 1 circuit would have required the formal approval of the Central and Regional Government and the Valencia Port Authority, and a revision of the land-use plan (*Plan General de Ordenación Urbana*) as well as the Valencia 2015 Strategic Master Plan. Additionally, all projects need to be evaluated according to the guidelines of the Environmental Impact Assessment (EIA) and to be subjected to a series of technical reports that assess their viability. In the Formula 1 case, these procedures were avoided by a legal loophole that allowed this project to be presented as a simple road system reform (Gaja 2009). Due to the legal declaration of the project as a 'temporary car exhibition,' the de facto complex urban development project was legally and formally approved without the EIA and other approvals (European Parliament 2009). In this case, the short timescale and trivialization led to the avoidance of the institutional assessment that could have brought to light the conflictual impacts of the project. This strategy must be understood within the notorious shift in city planning in Spain, from traditionally formalized, bureaucratized and top-down-oriented to a neoliberal urban policy spatially targeted and place-focused on projects such as the Valencia port, a model reproduced in many other European cities (Swyngedouw et al. 2002).

Furthermore, the city administration considered the Formula 1 championship a unique opportunity. The uniqueness of the event justified exceptional interventions by the public state. Accordingly, the city of Valencia decided to restrict the rights and the liberty of citizens during the race. Starting weeks before the event, the area was surveyed by 8,000 police officers for security reasons. The circuit, surrounding streets, avenues and parks were enclosed by a security fence, two meters high, and CCTV-monitored around the clock. Homeless people living in the neighborhood were evicted and the freedom of movement was simply suppressed. Residents were allowed to enter the area after an ID check by the police. A popular district of the inner city of Valencia was transformed into a monitored fortress. Protests in the area were simply prohibited and suppressed. Also, protests against the race were considered antipatriotic in character and an act against the urban and local society's interests. The *Fórmula Verda* protesters were accused of acting against "the general interest" and "against Valencia and the Valencians" by the mayor (Europa Press 2008). The project of the Formula 1 circuit was declared of 'general interest,' which is a legal act in Spain, and therefore the technical details and the costs of the project, substantially financed by the regional administration, still remain a mystery at the time of writing (Gaja 2009).

Non-Protests Against the ECB in Frankfurt

A key for explaining the lack of protest against the ECB in the East End is seen in the path dependency of protest movements in Frankfurt, particularly taking into account what happened the 1970s and 1980s in the West End, when a group of students and families squatted in a building in Eppsteiner Straße 47 in August 1970. It was their aim to protest against the speculations of the private real estate market and a shortage of affordable housing in the city. It was the first squatting of a building in the history of postwar Germany. Consequently, Frankfurt during the 1970s and 1980s witnessed numerous squatter movements (the so-called *Frankfurter Häuserkampf*), which mainly focused on the western part of the inner city—never on the East End. These protest movements were addressing two different political scales. Some protests were targeting the conservative political system of the whole German Federal Republic and were therefore rather detached from the objective of local residents to protect buildings from demolition or transformation into office spaces. Many of these protesters entered the national political arena afterwards and are now part of the regional and national political system. The Green Party, formed in 1980, ranked many of the Frankfurt West End protesters in its leading positions. Due to the political transformation at the national level, the local protest lost important actors and motivations. At the same time, the growth machine was following two strategies that turned out to be quite successful. The local politicians continued the tertiarization of the urban economy through a spatial reorganization, but this time the economization of the city was accompanied by the immense investment of approximately 11 percent of the city's budget into the urban cultural and art sector (Noller and Ronneberger 1995). Both strategies were accomplished through large support from private capital investments. The growth machine turned from a 'demolition machine' into a 'city promoter machine' and the successful linkage of economic and cultural objectives seemed to perfectly satisfy all critics.

In the meantime, the remaining protesters in the West End were stuck in local problems. Since the protest movements in the 1970s, much has changed in urban politics. The demand for housing has been satisfied by public investments in the housing sector and the construction of many new *Siedlungen*, even if affordable housing is still in decline. The transformation of the West End by constructing skyscrapers was limited by political instruments such as the Frankfurt *Hochhausplan* (Skyscraper Development Plan). New laws control even the transformation of residential flats into office space, which was one of the main reasons for squatting in apartment buildings. Finally in the 1990s, the situation in the West End was relative relaxed and the local neighborhood association concentrated on relatively banal problems such as the reduction of green spaces to provide car parking. Surprisingly hidden from the public awareness, a similar process of transformation started to occur in the East End. Up to the time of writing, however, social movements remain focused on the western part of the city, while the eastern part was rarely supported and defenseless, exposed to urban transformations.

Consensus-Building as Institutional Conflict Avoidance

At first glance, the case studies seem to contradict the historical perspective on social movements and urban resistance groups in both cities, who harken back to a long tradition of actively influencing and participating in urban politics and shaping local democracy. And indeed, still today, there is a vivid landscape of activism in both cities. In this chapter we argue, however, that these movements have neglected the Formula 1 circuit in Valencia or the relocation of the ECB in Frankfurt as they respond to a specific institutional setting that avoids protest and other forms of resistance and we highlight that there is a fragmented landscape in both cities of areas that are in the foreground for protest and other areas that are outside of the protest movement's range. There seems to be a societal consensus about both the institutional setting and the geographically uneven development in the cities. Our perspective is developed around what we call the 'institutional conflict avoidance strategy.' This idea directs attention to the institutional framework within which resistance may or may not occur and outlines a set of well-formed political strategies that have been rationally implemented in order to minimize public participation and any form of resistance.

In Valencia this set of strategies included sophisticated time management between the public announcement of the decision to bring Formula 1 to the historic seashore district and the start of construction. As a result, time to organize efficient protests against the project was too short, as the project plan was deliberately hidden from the public for months. In addition to the time factor, the city administration of Valencia tried to conceal and trivialize the project's impact during the planning process. This was realized by carefully providing limited information to the public. Another argument was the constraints of global competitiveness that enhanced acceptance for the project, as shortages in public financing were directly linked to the city's position within the global markets. The Formula 1 circuit was presented as a unique opportunity to enhance the financial situation of the city by investing in the city's global image. This argument, which is linked to the "festivalization of urban politics" (Häussermann and Siebel 1993), has been well known in Valencia for some time. Many large-scale urban development projects had been realized and promoted, such as the America's Cup 2007 and 2009, the MTV Winter Music Festival (2007–2011), the equestrian Global Champions Tour (2012) and the 500 Tennis Open (2011–2013). The impact of the Formula 1 circuit itself has furthermore been trivialized by avoiding an Environmental Impact Assessment and presenting different reports that only remark on the positive economic effects and omit the environmental consequences. The decision about the effects of the Formula 1 circuit has thus been reduced to what Swyngedouw calls the "administration and management of processes whose parameters are defined by consensual socio-scientific knowledges" (Swyngedouw 2009: 602). As a result, all reasons in favor of this postmodern amphitheater in Valencia were situated beyond the direct political responsibility of the urban government: global competitiveness, time constraints, unique opportunity and a positive scientific assessment.

Even though the construction of the European Central Bank in Frankfurt at first seems to be linked to a rather different set of policies than the Formula 1 circuit in Valencia, we can see some similar processes and mechanisms in the institutional context. First, the presence of the ECB in Frankfurt is accepted as a unique selling point to which Frankfurt marketing refers to on its webpage by stating that "as the seat of the European Central Bank, Frankfurt is the city of the Euro" (City of Frankfurt am Main 2013). Arguing against the movement of the European Central Bank to the East End would mean to call into question Frankfurt's position within the Global City ranking. Similar to the Formula 1 circuit, the discussion about the movement of the financial institution to another building has been discursively detached from the physical location. Since the beginning, the search for a new location for the ECB headquarters was politicized and reduced to the question: 'Is Frankfurt still able to offer an adequate place to the bank?' and any other arguments have been subverted. This became most evident during the trial when the bank became accused of destroying the listed building of the old wholesale market hall and the public heritage of the symbol of the *Neues Frankfurt* architectural movement that involved leading architects such as Ernst May, Walter Gropius, Bruno Taut and finally the architect of the wholesale market hall, Martin Elsaesser. There was a hegemonic consensus of finding a place for the bank and no alternative to this liberal-global hegemony seemed to be possible. The tertiarization of the city has become the governmental imperative of the urban organization avoiding any form of resistance against it. Last but not least, there was another strategy to enhance people's acceptance of the bank's decision to transform the listed building of the market hall. During summer 2008, there was an artistic illumination of the façade of the market hall during the *Luminale* exhibition. The illumination of the market hall represents what Hasse (2004: 415) refers to as the general "aestheticization of politics" by which the European city responds to its multiple crises, and so did Frankfurt. By paradoxically illuminating a building that later was partly demolished, people's attention has been focused on the project as a whole and another milestone of Frankfurt's 'Global City aesthetics' metaphorically illuminating the positive effects of the relocation of the ECB to the market hall that before had been outside of people's awareness.

The consensus to realize and implement both projects regardless of the negative and problematic impact on the neighborhoods around and the residents who live there is based on a set of rather rational political strategies that consists of five different elements. The first element refers to the planning procedure and the project management itself. While in Valencia time management aimed at short decision periods, in the case of the East End a rather long timescale was chosen in order to bring exceptional circumstances to normality. A second element refers to the participation of the public and the process to enhance people's acceptance. In both cases this was realized by 'festivalizing' the projects; in other projects around the world, participatory planning approaches can have the same effect. The third strategic element benefits from a fragmented urban landscape of protest movements, which are unevenly distributed across the city. While in some neighborhoods (the West

End in Frankfurt) awareness and resistance against neoliberal politics is still high, for historical reasons the East End is out of range. Fourth, both projects had socio-scientific and juridical certification, with the Formula 1 project presented as a street project in Valencia and the juridical trial in Frankfurt both underlining the 'rightness' of the projects from an allegedly neutral perspective. Finally, both projects created acceptance by drawing heavily on old-fashioned arguments—'trickle-down effects,' as argued in the context of financial constraints, resulted from the global competitiveness of both cities. Summing up, all elements refer to aspects that are beyond governmental responsibility regarding the implementation of the projects and that represent what Erik Swyngedouw refers to as "the making of a post-political and post-democratic condition, one that actually forecloses the possibilities of a real politics" (Swyngedouw 2007: 14).

Conclusions

The conflicts in Valencia and Frankfurt are both related to urban regeneration projects that have negative impacts for the local society. In both cases the urban projects have led to the displacement of inhabitants. Albeit both cities developed a vivid protest culture in the past, there were no protests against these transformations focusing on the single neighborhood and the local condition. In both cities the projects are the output of urban growth machines, strong coalitions of political and private actors focusing on the economization of the built environment.

We consider the analysis of non-protests as a desideratum in conflict research. Even though the analysis of non-protests implies methodological problems, we wish to open an academic debate on this issue by highlighting the relevance of institutionally avoided protests in the context of post-democracy. Furthermore, we would like to argue for a 'historical' perspective that takes into account the 1970s movements as key to understanding actually existing urban politics (see Mössner 2013).

This chapter does not provide any comparative study, but identifies some parallel moments of non-protest in both cities. Its aim is to underline the authors' conviction that it is important to take into account also those situations where no protest occurs. If we consider Touraine's famous statement, that the actors of protests promote social innovation in the city and contribute to the modernization process of societies (cited in Hamel 2005), and link it to Mouffe's and Rancière's approach about the importance of antagonisms in society, then the emergence of non-protests should be considered and analyzed more seriously by scholars of urban conflicts in order to better understand our local democracies.

References

Badillo, A. (2006) "La Fórmula Uno apuesta por un circuito urbano en Valencia para el Mundial 2008," *Las Provincias*, May 28, 2006, formerly available at: www.lasprovincias. es/alicante/pg060528/prensa/noticias/Deportes/200605/28/ALI-DEP-140.html (accessed September 10, 2011).

Bonacker, T. (2009) "Konflikttheorien," in G. Kneer and M. Schroer (eds.), *Handbuch Soziologische Theorien*, Wiesbaden, Germany: VS Verlag: 179–198.

Chambers, S. A. (2011) "Jacques Rancière and the Problem of Pure Politics," *European Journal of Political Theory*, 10(3): 303–326.

City of Frankfurt am Main (2013) Official webpage, available at: www.frankfurt.de (accessed November 1, 2013).

Cox, K. R. (1978) "Local Interests and Urban Political Processes in Market Societies," in K. R. Cox (ed.), *Urbanization and Conflict in Market Societies*, Chicago, IL: Maaroufa Press: 94–109.

Crouch, C. (2004) *Postdemocracy*, Cambridge, UK: Polity Press.

Cucó, J. (2008) *Antropología Urbana*, Barcelona, Spain: Ariel.

Dahrendorf, R. (1958) "Out of Utopia: Toward a Reorientation of Sociological Analysis," *American Journal of Sociology*, 64(2): 115–127.

Dunleavy, P. (1977) "Protest and Quiescence in Urban Politics: A Critique of Some Pluralist and Structuralist Myths," *International Journal of Urban and Regional Research*, 1(4): 193–218.

Europa Press (2008) "Rita Barberá lamenta que valencianos denuncien fuera de Valencia las posibilidades de progreso del circuito de F1," *Las Provincias*, November 6, available at: www.lasprovincias.es/valencia/20081106/local/valencia/rita-barbera-lamenta-valencianos-200811061422.html (accessed September 11, 2011).

European Parliament (2009) CM\797223ES *Communication to the Members from the European Parliament*, available at: www.europarl.europa.eu/meetdocs/2009_2014/ documents/peti/cm/797/797223/797223es.pdf (accessed September 10, 2011).

Gaja, F. (2009) "Grandes eventos, grandes proyectos: una apuesta de alto riesgo," paper presented at the seminar *Grandi Eventi: Casi internazionali a confronto per una riflessione sull'Expo Milano 2015*, Milan, Italy, April 1.

Gill, N., Johnstone, P. and Williams, A. (2012) "Towards a Geography of Tolerance: Post-Politics and Political Forms of Toleration," *Political Geography*, 31(8): 509–518.

Hamel, P. (2005) "Contemporary Cities and the Renewal of Local Democracy," in P. Booth and B. Jouve (eds.), *Metropolitan Democracies: Transformations of the State and Urban Policy in Canada, France and Great Britain*, Aldershot, UK: Ashgate: 31–46.

Hasse, J. (2004) "Die Stadt ins rechte Licht setzen: Stadtillumination—ein ästhetisches Dispositiv?" *Berichte zur deutschen Landeskunde*, 78(4): 413–439.

Häussermann, H. and Siebel, W. (1993) "Die Politik der Festivalisierung und die Festivalisierung der Politik," in H. Häussermann and W. Siebel (eds.), *Festivalisierung der Stadtpolitik: Stadtentwicklung durch große Projekte*, Opladen, Germany: VS Verlag (Leviathan Sonderheft, 13).

Jaschke, H.-G. (1997) *Öffentliche Sicherheit im Kulturkonflikt: Zur Entwicklung der städtischen Schutzpolizei in der multikulturellen Gesellschaft*, Frankfurt am Main, Germany: Campus Verlag.

Joerin, F., Pelletier, M., Trudelle, C. and Villeneuve, P. (2006) "Analyse spatiale des conflits urbains: enjeux et contextes dans la région de Québec," *Cahiers de Géographie de Québec*, 49(138): 319–342.

Jörke, D. (2005) "Auf dem Weg zur Postdemokratie," *Leviathan—Berliner Zeitschrift für Sozialwissenschaften*, 33(4): 482–491.

Keil, R. and Ronneberger, K. (2000) "The Globalization of Frankfurt am Main: Core, Periphery and Social Conflict," in N. Brenner and R. Keil (eds.), *The Global Cities Reader* (2006), London, UK: Routledge: 288–295.

Logan, J. and Molotch, H. (1987) *Urban Fortunes: The Political Economy of Place*, Berkeley, CA: University of California Press.

MacLeod, G. (2011) "Urban Politics Reconsidered: Growth Machine to Post-democratic City?" *Urban Studies*, 48(12): 2629–2660.

Marchart, O. (2010) *Die politische Differenz: Zum Denken des Politischen bei Nancy, Lefort, Badiou, Laclau und Agamben*, Berlin, Germany: Suhrkamp.

Montesinos, M. A. (2007) "Fórmula Verda considera incompatible el circuito y el delta verde de Nouvel," *Levante, El Mercantil Valenciano*, November 9, formerly available at: www.levante-emv.com/secciones/noticia.jsp?pRef=3715_16_367397__Valencia-Formula-Verda-considera-incompatible-circuito-delta-verde-Nouvel   (accessed September 10, 2011).

Mouffe, C. (2000a) *The Democratic Paradox*, London, UK: Verso.

Mouffe, C. (2000b) *Deliberative Democracy or Agonistic Pluralism*, Vienna, Austria: Institut für Höhere Studien (IHS), available at: www.ihs.ac.at/publications/pol/pw_72.pdf (accessed March 26, 2013).

Mouffe, C. (2005) *On the Political*, London, UK: Routledge.

Mössner, S. (2013) "Neoliberalisierung als Gesellschaftskrise: Kommentar zu Margit Mayers *Urbane soziale Bewegungen in der neoliberalisierenden Stadt*," *Suburban/zeitschrift für kritische Stadtforschung*, 1(1): 185–188.

Newton, K. (1978) "Conflict Avoidance and Conflict Suppression: The Case of Urban Politics in the United States," in K. R. Cox (ed.), *Urbanization and Conflict in Market Societies*, Chicago, IL: Maaroufa Press: 76–93.

Noller, P. and Ronneberger, K. (1995) *Die neue Dienstleistungsstadt: Berufsmilieus in Frankfurt am Main*, Frankfurt, Germany: Campus Verlag.

Pérez, A. (2009) *Movimiento vicinal, XXXV años de la Asociación de Vecinos de Benimaclet*, available at: http://avvbenimaclet.wordpress.com/archivo/movimiento-vecinal/ (accessed January 21, 2012).

Purcell, M. (2000) "The Decline of the Political Consensus for Urban Growth: Evidence from Los Angeles," *Urban Affairs Review*, 22(1): 85–100.

Rancière, J. (2001) "Ten Theses on Politics," *Theory & Event*, 5(3): 17–34.

Rancière, J. (2004) "Introducing Disagreement," *Angelaki*, 9(3): 3–9.

Rancière, J. (2008) *Zehn Thesen zur Politik*, Zurich, Switzerland: Diaphanes Verlag.

Rancière, J. (2010) "Gibt es eine politische Philosophie?" in J. Rancière and A. Badiou (eds.), *Politik der Wahrheit*, Vienna, Austria: Turia+Kant: 64–93.

Swyngedouw, E. (2007) "Impossible Sustainability and the Post-Political Condition," in R. Krueger and D. Gibbs (eds.), *The Sustainable Development Paradox: Urban Political Economy in the United States and Europe*, New York, NY: Guilford Press: 13–40.

Swyngedouw, E. (2009) "The Antinomies of the Postpolitical City: In Search of a Democratic Politics of Environmental Production," *International Journal of Urban and Regional Research*, 33(3): 601–620.

Swyngedouw, E., Moulaert, F. and Rodríguez, A. (2002) "Neoliberal Urbanization in Europe: Large-Scale Urban Development Projects and the New Urban Policy," *Antipode*, 3(3): 542–577.

4

Urban Planning Without Conflicts? Observations on the Nature of and Conditions for Urban Contestation in the Case of Milan

Carolina Pacchi and Gabriele Pasqui

The Research Question

Contemporary cities are increasingly characterized by highly fragmented decision-making processes, a complex and pluralist distribution of power and a crisis in the traditional forms of social and political representation; in such contexts, it is very difficult to find ways for a general public discussion about the spatial and economic strategies for city development. While in the past decades, in many European cities, issues concerning urban development and some distinctive urban themes have been the object of extensive mobilization, due to their highly conflictual nature, more recently there has been a sort of appeasement.

In the face of the significant urban transformations currently underway, and moving from an urban governance perspective, the question we want to raise is twofold:

- In this context of political and institutional fragmentation, pluralization and individualization of social problems, and absence of the traditional vehicles of social demand, is a public discussion about the spatial development of the city possible at all? Which are the (institutional, social, political) conditions that can produce this kind of discussion?
- What is the 'space' for general conflicts? Are there specific social and institutional conditions and tools that can enable the emergence of such conflicts, and what is the relationship between the 'technical' dimension and the dimension of social mobilization?

The chapter will use the case of Milan to critically discuss these issues. In particular we will analyze the differently contentious nature of urban projects and urban plans, their varying ability to become the object of explicit conflict, and we will argue that, in a highly fragmented and pluralist context, while urban redevelopment projects tend to be the object of locally rooted opposition, plans tend to offer a more structured framework/platform in which a more transversal urban voice can be raised. We will therefore argue that, under specific conditions, even such an ordinary and highly technical-bureaucratic tool as a land-use plan can become a platform for the emergence of conflict through opposition and mobilization.

Between 2007 and 2011 the Milan municipality promoted a new land-use plan for the city (*Piano di Governo del Territorio* [PGT]). During these years the right-wing municipal government faced a limited number of urban conflicts, and only a few of them were focused on planning strategies and decisions.

If we analyze Milan from the perspective of urban conflicts, we can recognize that the traditional political and social conflicts (against urban speculation, against gentrification or for new rights and new forms of citizenship) were limited and marginal. Even if Milan was characterized during those years by an array of urban transformations, following different types of plans and projects, the large majority of such transformations went apparently unnoticed: not the object of explicit public debate, apart from sporadic and advertisement-type articles in local media, and not the explicit object of conflict. In individual cases, local opposition to large urban transformation projects was organized by neighboring inhabitants, those most directly affected by the negative impacts of such projects. In general, we cannot say that this achieved the status of some forms of *voice*.

On the contrary, new kind of 'regressive' conflicts (against new urban populations, such as illegal immigrants or the Roma population, perceived as vehicles of crime and uncertainty) were at the center of media attention and influenced the urban agenda and the policies promoted by the public administration. Many other specific local themes explicitly became the object of conflict and public debate over the last few years, even if they did not significantly influence the political agenda: for instance, environmental issues (in particular air quality and traffic congestion); the quality of services and of local welfare; and the entitlement criteria adopted (in particular as far as school and nursery care are concerned).

The substantial absence of urban themes from the local debate was paradoxically overcome when the new master plan for the city was drafted between 2010 and 2011. A new phase began in May 2011, when a new left-wing political coalition won (for the first time in twenty years) the local elections, with a significant participation and mobilization on the part of citizens and associations. One of the first decisions taken by the new administration was to radically redefine the general plan strategies and rules, using as a basis the 4,000 written comments (*Osservazioni*) on the old version of the plan produced by citizens and associations.

The chapter tries to reflect upon the different typologies of conflicts occurring in urban contexts and their relationship with the radical change in urban politics and policy frameworks. Relying on the analysis of documents and on interviews with selected stakeholders, we will argue why, in a highly fragmented power context, the framework offered by the new plan has been able to raise contentious issues and to trigger a local *voice* explicitly focused on urban planning issues and their implicit distributional dimension. In conclusion, we propose a reflection on the theme of urban conflicts connected with planning debates and decisions, trying to use a conceptual framework based on the analysis of structural power relationships, but also on the role of political framing and urban agenda-making in the definition of the 'space of possibilities' for urban conflicts.

The chapter is organized in three sections, with some concluding remarks. In the first section the theoretical framework is introduced and discussed, impinging on both planning literature and sociological literature, from a wider perspective. The second section critically discusses the scarcely contentious nature of the main urban transformations in Milan in the last twenty years, underlying the connection between this absence of conflicts and the stability of the urban political agenda; and the third section critically retraces the story of the new urban plan, drafted between 2007 and 2010 and adopted in 2011, connecting each phase of the decision-making process with the voice it raised and the public debate it contributed to open up. Finally, the concluding remarks reflect upon the actual situation proposing some questions for further research.

Planning and Conflicts

Spatial Planning, Politics and Conflicts

Urban conflicts in contemporary cities tend to be fragmented along new lines and cleavages, compared to what happened during the period of early urbanization and industrialization, for a number of reasons. The emergence of general ideological conflicts about urban development models is becoming increasingly difficult due to the fragmentation of local societies, to the decoupling between political citizenship and the actual use of the city, and to the fact that very general images of the city are proposed starting from very local and specific issues. Moreover, the crisis in the traditional forms of representation of general interests (political parties, trade unions, cultural associations) has been exacerbated by the disjunction between political representation and territorial sovereignty, connected with new forms of deterritorialization of social and spatial practices. Still, spatial planning remains a domain strictly related to conflict or, more precisely, to a variety of conflicts.

In many recent important theoretical contributions Luigi Mazza has shown the connection between spatial planning and different typologies of social and political conflicts (Mazza 2002, 2009, 2010).

If we define spatial planning as a field of (social, technical, institutional) practices aimed at controlling and ordering territorial space, there are at least three main reasons explaining the intrinsically conflictual nature of planning activities.

First, the competition for space: "the uniqueness and irreproducibility of each portion of space, which are at the root of competition and sometimes conflicts over spatial control, means that any form of spatial plan and control works through the distinction between inclusion and exclusion" (Mazza 2009: 131). The conceptual pairing inclusion/exclusion can therefore explain many types of planning conflicts. The conflicts among different uses upon the same land—for example, the conflicts between public and private uses, or the conflict between residential and productive uses that was at the root of planning institutionalization in the Euclid–Ambler story in the US in the 1920s, but also the conflicts between old and new residents living in the same area—can be interpreted as consequences of processes of competition for space.

The second reason explaining the conflictual nature of planning is connected with the fact that planning is an activity that distributes economic and symbolic values and also citizenship rights. Access to public services, quality of built environment and public spaces, and control of the urban market are possible effects of planning decisions that affect the lives of individuals and social groups, generating inequalities and producing different citizenship statuses. So, there is always a connection between social and spatial control, because "planning manifests itself as an asymmetrical relationship of strengths between one party that has the power to decide (theoretically on behalf of the common interest) and parties or groups that defend particular interests" (Mazza 2009: 132).

It is very important to underline that this political dimension of planning practices is independent from the institutional, technical and social form assumed by planning activities (more or less based on authority, negotiation, participation …), and it is perfectly consistent with a pluralist interpretation of the governance of planning activities (Gualini 2011). Moreover, if planning has this contentious character because of the inclusion/exclusion principle and because of its political nature, there is also a third reason explaining the conflictual nature of spatial planning. Spatial planning is necessarily a local activity, involving portions of territory (an area, a community, a region …)

and planning decisions produce externalities that are not only local and that generate (environmental, aesthetic, social, economic) effects at a non-local level. Planning decisions, for this reason, are always associated with conflicts between local and non-local interests, which can be represented or not by institutional bodies.

Three Typologies of (Urban) Conflicts

If we consider the contentious dimension of spatial planning from a general theoretical and sociological perspective, we can identify different forms of (urban) conflicts connected with planning decisions. These different forms should be distinguished because their nature is very different and their logics are not always consistent.

A distinction proposed by Italian sociologist Alessandro Pizzorno (1993) can be very effective in identifying three typologies of conflicts. The first typology is that of *recognition conflicts*. In these conflicts a social group or actor promotes a conflict with the aim of imposing on other groups or on institutions the recognition of its identity. For Pizzorno identity, in this kind of conflict, is one of the possible outcomes, and is generated in conflicts themselves.

The second typology is that of *interest conflicts*. In this case the parts share the same values and the same systems of relations. The aim of interest conflicts is to produce clear benefits for the members of the conflicting groups that operate in a pluralist context.

The third is that of *ideological (or value) conflicts*. In these conflicts one party (or more) presumes to represent not a specific and particular interest, but a universalistic value or system of values. In these conflicts it is the same idea about 'how the world is (and then how it should be)' that is contentious.

If we consider urban conflicts connected with spatial planning, we can recognize all three of these typologies of conflicts.

Recognition conflicts take place when social groups (often local) want to be recognized through planning decisions that contribute to their identification. Often this kind of conflict is connected with the defense of 'local' (environmental, cultural, community) values, or with the claim for exclusive uses of a public space, against uses considered inconvenient.

Interest conflicts take place when scarce resources (and first land, and its possible uses) are distributed through planning decisions. Often this kind of conflict has an economic and financial dimension; for example, the competition among different uses of transformation areas is often a competition between developers and landowners, or between different promoters, or between financial operators and developers, and so on. If we think also of public administration, an economic actor producing resources through planning permissions, and the bargaining between institutional bodies and the private sector can be considered an interest conflict.

Ideological conflicts take place when beliefs and the very ontological frameworks in which they are grounded are objects of contention. In this kind of planning conflict there is no shared framework of reference between the parts; the framework itself is the object of conflict. Radical ecological conflicts, for example, can be considered ideological, because the parts want to produce (different) universal systems of values and meanings. Often in this kind of conflict scientific information and technical knowledge are at stake.

If we consider real urban conflicts connected with spatial planning, we see at work all three of these conflictual dimensions. Often it is not easy to clearly identify which kind of conflict predominates. Conflicts about identity and recognition are sometimes connected with value and beliefs conflicts; an interest dimension is hidden in universalistic and identity conflicts. Nevertheless, it is important to distinguish them, at least analytically, because the consequences of these different kinds of urban conflicts upon planning practices are different.

Urban Conflicts and Local Movements

When discussing local and urban conflicts, we need to identify the underlying forces; in each urban context, there will be different constellations of actors who mobilize and act contentiously.

As many observers have noted, the main cleavages of the Fordist era have been overcome in late modernity by the fragmentation that characterizes contemporary societies (Melucci 1982, 1996). This interpretive framework suggests shifting the attention from basic conflicts that divided society along main cleavages, like the one between capital and labor, to a multiplicity of conflicts, revealing the untreatable diversity of local societies and the emerging need to build shared identities.

Melucci's approach can be a good basis to read some relevant features of such conflicts in connection with emerging social movements, an analytical operation that enables us to bring the actors back to the scene. Social movements—and urban movements make no exception—are forms of collective action, which means that they are sets of social practices involving a number of individuals or groups, exhibiting similar morphological characteristics in contiguity of time and space, implying a field of social relationships and the capacity of the people involved to make sense of what they are doing.

Melucci observed that social movements in late modernity ('new social movements') are the expression of conflict, but at the same time imply solidarity and contribute to building shared identities, and tend to breach the limits of social systems. Similarly to the distinction operated by Pizzorno about types of conflicts, Melucci proposes the identification of different types of social movements: *claimant, political* and *antagonistic* movements.

In a *claimant movement* "the collective actor presses for a different distribution of resources within an organization and strives for a different functioning of the apparatus"; a *political movement* "campaigns to extend the criteria for participation in decision-making and fights against the bias in the political game that always privileges some interests above others"; and finally the *antagonistic movement* "consists of a collective conflictual action aimed at the production of a society's resources" (Melucci 1996: 35).

Moving from a claimant to a political and to an antagonistic movement, the symbolic content tends to increase, while the divisibility and negotiability of goals tends to decrease, and so does the reversibility of conflicts; in the end, such conflicts tend to become zero sum rather than positive sum games.

We can very clearly identify urban movements with these categories, excluding probably the one concerning the antagonistic movement. Every time there is an emerging request for the enlargement of public participation in a local decision, be it a plan or a policy, for instance, we recognize the existence of a political movement; while in connection with a typical interest conflict, in which the issue at stake is the allocation and division of costs and benefits, however defined, we identify a claimant movement.

Such categories can therefore be extremely useful to better interpret the emerging local voice in the Milan case, which we now analyze.

Milan: Transformation Without Conflicts?

Milan's Spatial Transformation in the Last Twenty Years

The theoretical analysis proposed above about urban conflicts, social mobilization and spatial planning can be used to describe Milan's spatial and social transformations in the last twenty years and the effects of this complex change on urban conflicts.

As in many other European cities, Milan underwent between the 1980s and the 1990s a radical social, economic, institutional and spatial metamorphosis. There were three main characteristics of this metamorphosis (OECD 2006; Balducci et al. 2011):

- the *changes in the urban economic base*, with a transition from a model based on manufacturing activities to a complex service-based economy, even if Milan was never a company town like Turin and also for this reason the economic transition was not comparable to that of other industrial cities;

- the *transformation of the social organization* and of demographic trends, with the growth of elderly population and immigrants, the reduction of the average number of households members, and the crisis of the traditional welfare state model (Ranci 2010);
- a *process of political and administrative fragmentation*, with the crisis of the party system and in particular of their local roots, the proliferation of administrative units and the growing complexity of decision-making processes in multilevel governance settings.

In twenty years (between the 1970s and the 1980s) the metamorphosis of Milan was completed, without serious social effects in terms of unemployment, economic crisis and shrinkage, and with a good performance by the Milanese society, economic actors and institutions in the management of this radical social transition.

In a spatial perspective, these economic, social and institutional processes have implied a complex territorial transformation. The central municipality of Milan has lost almost one-third of its population in the last thirty years (480,000 inhabitants) to reach a size today a little less than that of 1951. This population relocated, first, into the Province of Milan, until the beginning of the 1980s and afterwards into other bordering provinces that also grew due to their own capacity to attract. The reasons that led to this deconcentration were strong pressures on urban housing markets and the continued development of private transport that made it relatively easy to reach increasingly distant places.

The spatial consequences of these phenomena are well known: the dramatic growth of the volume and intensity of the flows that affect the Milan urban region, with an increasing importance of new urban populations that use the city either every day or temporarily without residing there; a significant urban expansion outside the central city; and a selective transformation of the metropolitan core.

This selective urban transformation during the last twenty years was characterized by two different dynamics (Balducci 2003). The first dynamic can be defined as diffused and incremental, and it is characterized by urban transformations affecting different parts of the city and spread throughout its territory, with fragmented and small changes in uses of buildings and small areas often connected with the social transformations of some neighborhoods (Diappi 2009).

The second dynamic is concentrated in some transformation areas, where large urban projects promoted by a limited number of private developers are transforming industrial, abandoned or under-used areas into new mixed-use (but often mainly residential and tertiary) urban centralities.

The analytical description of these two typologies of urban transformation is not possible in this chapter (Bolocan-Goldstein and Bonfantini 2007;

Bolocan-Goldstein and Pasqui 2011). It is enough to say that this cycle of urban transformation started in the 1990s, after a decade of substantial stability (Figure 4.1), and had a significant acceleration in the last ten years, with the implementation of the first important urban projects in semi-peripheral industrial areas (the most important being the re-use of Pirelli Bicocca area) and the take-off of a new group of relevant urban projects also in very central areas (the City Life project in the old area of Milan Fair, now relocated outside the central city in Rho-Pero, and the Porta Nuova project in the strongly connected and strategic Garibaldi Repubblica area, being probably the most important ones).

In the last few years these projects, promoted in the phase of real estate market explosion that started in 2001, have been affected by the severe crisis in the urban market. Some of the projects have been redefined (for example the Norman Foster project for Santa Giulia—Rogoredo or the different master plans for the Falck areas in Sesto San Giovanni); some operators are now undergoing a serious financial crisis and many ambitious projects have been completely abandoned (for example, a new international library in Porta Vittoria railway station area).

It is important to notice that these two typologies of urban transformation in the central city (incremental change affecting many different areas and parts of the city, and urban transformation projects promoted mainly by private actors) were promoted and implemented in the absence of a new planning framework.

The social, economic and territorial change in the 1980s and 1990s was in fact governed without a general plan, but using specific planning tools based on public–private agreements. In 2001, the Milan municipality approved a new 'strategic' document for planning policies, which was an interesting attempt to redefine the planning system and its rules and regulation forms (Comune di Milano 2001; Healey 2007), but only partially effective.

Milan has thus changed in the last twenty years without a clear strategic vision and also without a general planning framework. Nevertheless, the urban transformations it underwent were relevant, and some sectors of the city have changed or will change dramatically in the next years.

This change occurred in the absence of serious urban conflicts. The incremental but crucial changes that affected the consolidated city in general were accepted (sometimes well accepted, because they allowed the revitalization of specific parts of the city). The urban transformations generated by relevant urban projects often created a local opposition, but this opposition has not been able to produce radical and general urban conflicts.

Some of the large-scale urban projects (for example, the City Life project in the old Fair area) generated local opposition by the residents, whose urban quality standards were affected by the new transformations. However, this

Implemented, ongoing and planned transformations
Urban recovery and restoration plans
Transformation areas of general public interest
Municipality of Milan
Departments-districts

Figure 4.1 Urban transformations in Milan since the 1990s (source: Department of
Architecture and Urban Studies, Politecnico di Milano)

opposition was in almost all cases very local, without significant coordination
between the different local opposition groups, and the effectiveness was in
general limited. Some local associations created to oppose new urban projects
decided to use legal appeals to the courts, but without success.

In general, the opposition was limited, strongly connected with a very 'local'
perspective and unable to produce general effects at the political level. Moving
from Pizzorno's typology and Mazza's reflections, we can say that these limited
conflicts were in part connected with traditional opposition by previous residents

to new interventions, and in this sense they were interest conflicts; and in part had a problem with recognition by some social and professional groups and élites on the urban scene. In Melucci's terms, we would recognize the elements of a claimant movement, which mobilizes against a redistribution of resources (changes in real estate values, fear of a decreasing quality of existing services due to a population overload) and, less frequently, elements of a political movement, because in most cases the question of enlarging the opportunities for participation in the decision-making process has not been central. In general, we can see in most mobilization forms in this period the typical features of localism, short-sightedness and refusal to share public negative externalities usually associated with the NIMBY syndrome (Pacchi 2008).

In fact, during the period from 1992 to 2011, at the local elections, right-wing coalitions prevailed and the left-wing social and political coalition was always a minority.

Urban Conflicts, the Stability of the Urban Agenda and the Crisis of Political Representation

This limited role of radical urban conflicts in a phase of dramatic social and spatial changes can be interpreted using different explanations.

Here we propose the idea that one of the main reasons is political and cultural and it is connected with the stability of the urban agenda during the whole of this period and with the crisis of traditional forms of political representation in the urban arena.

If debate on urban development and on the critical issues present in the Milan public arena in the 2000s is analyzed, we can see that the main arguments and the dominating rhetoric appear very similar to those that emerged in Milan in the 1980s during the transition from a Fordist development model to an urban knowledge-based model.

Even after the break-up of the political system as a result of the 'Tangentopoli' corruption affair in 1992, the urban agenda was mainly dominated by the rhetoric of competitiveness, precisely along the lines of the debate started in the 1980s on the new role of cities in international competition and in globalization processes (Bagnasco and Le Galès 2000).

Even if radical and potentially contentious processes of social and spatial change characterized Milan in the last twenty years, the political and social elites (in the City of Milan, the Lombardy Region, the trade unions and employers' associations) found it difficult to interpret these processes and, as a consequence, to change the urban agenda.

An in-depth analysis of how public issues were constructed and defined in the Milan area performed a few years ago as part of a national research project

(Dente et al. 2005) shows that during the 1990s and again in the 2000s mainly old issues, inherited from previous years, were placed at the top of the urban agenda in Milan and the surrounding urban region.

The only, but very significant, exception was the issue of urban security, which has gradually become central in recent years, in relation, among other things, to the theme of managing large numbers of immigrants in Italy and in the Milan area in particular. The growing importance of the issue of security in Milan was also the main reason for the emergency of a limited but significant number of particularist and xenophobic conflicts; the opposition to the presence of Roma groups in different peripheral areas, for example, has been relevant since the mid-2000s, characterized by a high level of social mobilization and also by some episodes of serious conflict.

These 'regressive' conflicts were connected with problems of spatial planning as social control, and were influenced by the processes of individualization and the growing role of social insecurity connected with the crisis of the welfare state, especially for disadvantaged social groups.

In fact, if we compare the typology of social participation to 'regressive' urban conflicts (by residents against Roma or illegal immigrants) and to the limited conflicts opposing new transformation projects, we can observe that while the first kind of conflict was supported by lower-income and disadvantaged social groups living in peripheral areas, the conflict against urban development dynamics was usually conducted and led by high-skilled social élites (professionals, planners, architects) (Vitale 2007).

On the other side, the traditional vehicles of 'progressive' conflicts were affected in the same period by a deep crisis. Political parties, trade unions and business associations were not able to support a general discussion about different city visions and perspectives in the public sphere. This public sphere was more and more silent, and general issues were introduced only through particular questions and conflicts. The connection between specific local issues and a general vision of the future development of the city was very limited.

Even urban groups or populations that certainly represent quite general interests have not been fully able to raise new important issues about the idea of a future city and its development model on the urban scene. Two quite good examples are represented by urban cyclists on the one hand and by the vast population of commuters on the other. The growing cyclist population has been working on very specific and local issues (in particular linked to road safety for cyclists and on cycling lanes), and has not shown any ability to build a common mobilization framework with other groups working on urban environmental issues. On the other hand, the significant commuter population has not been able to raise questions of urban vision and political delegation, while the social problems connected with mobility in metropolitan areas have clear general consequences for city planning and policies.

The new urban populations, as cyclists and commuters, can be analyzed as aggregates of individuals defined by one or more simple common traits. An inhabitant's membership of a population group is usually not exclusive; it is momentary and partial. Each individual acts (and can be represented), as the occasion arises at different times of the day or week, according to their activities, as a commuter, motorist or cyclist, professional, art lover, etc. These actions involve a changing and plural relationship with the city and the region. Contrary to the kind of theoretical assumptions we need in order to analyze classes, movements, groups or organizations, it is possible to talk about populations without any significant assumption about their rational collective behavior (Martinotti 2005). Individuals belonging to urban populations share everyday practices, and sometimes their local actions can produce public effects. However, these effects are often unintentional, and these populations would not be able to express general visions about the city and its government (Pasqui 2008).

In conclusion, considering the period 1992–2010 we can say that the majority of the issues placed on the agenda and addressed with varying degrees of success seem to be characterized by a certain inability to 'frame' new issues and to deal with emerging challenges. The majority of the questions are path dependent, inherited from the 1980s, if not from previous decades. The consequences of this phenomenon of path dependency and the crisis of political representation are seen clearly in the inability to construct and address (let alone solve) emerging issues, and to connect specific opposition to new urban transformation in a wider urban conflict about strategies and visions.

Milan Master Plan: A Contentious Process?

From the Changing Regulatory Framework to the New Master Plan

The Milan master plan (PGT) has been defined according to the new regional regulatory framework, issued in 2005 (Regione Lombardia 2005). The main elements of this framework, which is quite innovative in the Italian planning context, are linked to the absence of any functional zoning, to very simplified density directions, to the centrality of public–private negotiations and to the diffused implementation of compensation and equalization mechanisms.

The elaboration of the new Milan plan started in 2007, with the aim of ending before the administrative term in spring 2011, also due to the final regional deadline of December 2012. The first elements of the plan to be published clearly showed that the Milan municipality had decided to fully attend to the regional prescriptions, and to interpret them in a way that significantly downplayed the strategic role of the public actor both in terms of selectivity and of assessment.

Contrary to the consensual climate that characterized the city for about twenty years, the elaboration of the new plan has always been under attentive public scrutiny, and has thus triggered almost immediate opposition. One early element of public debate has been linked to the dimensions of the city, and therefore the forecasts for real estate development. In November 2008, the cabinet member for urban planning, Carlo Masseroli, launched a proposal to bring back 700,000 inhabitants (subsequently reduced to 400,000) to the city, which now has a population of 1.3 million, after the sharp suburbanization trend of the previous decades. This proposal, not grounded in any technical evaluation or assessment, has been a first element of contentious debate, a debate during which technical experts, environmental NGOs and other local interests have started to make their voice heard.

In the subsequent two years, while the development of the plan was unfolding, this local voice became stronger and more organized. In particular, we can distinguish different phases: the development of this contentious voice up to the summer of 2010, when the plan was adopted by the city council, and the months immediately after the adoption, when citizens and local interests could prepare and send written comments to the published plan. Then, with the final version of the plan finally adopted by the city council in February 2011, a final phase started, which will continue until the change of political majority and the subsequent decisions of the new city government.

If, as we underlined in the preceding sections, in any urban planning activity there is an intrinsic conflictual or contentious dimension, we can also observe that this dimension becomes even stronger when the plan proposes significant innovations, in terms of form, method and contents, and this is certainly the case in this instance. The new structure of the plan, as defined by the regional regulatory framework, completely substitutes the traditional functional zoning with the division of the city into three or four different areas, defined on the basis of quite loose morphological and historical criteria (well-established urban fabric, heritage and similar quite open categories), and rural areas. Moreover, in the first version there was a standard building ratio applied to the whole municipal area, and no density threshold was defined. This meant that, due also to the equalization mechanism that we will describe in more depth, it would have been possible that parts of the city would be significantly densified without any technically defined limit.

The equalization mechanism, widely diffused in recent Italian plans, and the object of a very articulated scientific and technical debate (Micelli 2011), enables landowners and developers either to transfer building rights generated in a part of town in which it is not possible to build to other areas, or to acquire building rights in exchange of the original areas in which they were generated, which are acquired by the municipality in order to implement green spaces, parks or other public services. The combination of the standard and quite high building ratio with the equalization mechanism, in the absence of any strategic selection of areas for transformation on the public part, may have provoked, as many local voices underlined, unbalanced densifications, depending more on the contingent financial situation of developers than on long-term integrated assessments.

Finally, a point that became very visible in the local debate, helped by being easily understood by non-technical actors, is the fact that a standard building ratio, even if significantly lower than the general one, would be generated by the *Parco Sud* areas, a significant collection of rural areas situated in the southern part of the municipality and belonging to a vast regional agricultural park. Such building rights would not be implemented directly within the park, obviously, but they would be transferred to other parts of the city.

During most of 2009 and 2010, public opinion in the city was very much alert to the process of plan definition. No formal consultation or public participation activities having been planned and implemented by the city, the debate used the usual informal channels and networks (especially blogs and the institutional website of civil society, *Rete Civica Milanese*), echoed by the local editorial offices of one of the main Italian newspapers.

The City Responds

In July 2010 the city council finally adopted the plan. In the existing regulatory framework, after adoption there is a publication phase, during which the materials of the plan are available for citizens, landowners, developers and organized local interests to review, and after that phase there is a period in which it is possible to submit written comments on the plan itself. This, as we will see, has been a crucial phase of the decision-making process.

It is in this phase that four local organizations, expressions of different strands of organized local civil society (*Libertà e Giustizia*, *Legambiente*, *Arci* and *Acli*), decided to start up a very institutionalized consultation process, organized in a number of public presentations about the structure, innovations and basic technical and political choices of the plan, in each of the nine districts of the Milan municipality.

The objective of this phase is explicitly twofold. Since the municipality itself did not activate any form of consultation or participation, the first objective is to inform citizens and other local actors, and to let them get acquainted with the contents of the plan. Second, there is the explicit aim of helping local actors to define and submit written comments to the municipality, because this is the only way that would formally enable the city council to reopen a discussion on a number of contentious issues.

From this point of view, the participation and consultation exercise can be considered successful; more than 4,000 written comments were submitted in November 2010 by individual citizens, NGOs and community organizations, but also by private developers, landowners, their organizations and a range of technical bodies. Such written comments covered the whole range of urban topics, from the correction of analytical mistakes to the request for strategic changes in the building ratios and in other crucial planning and regulatory aspects; most of them concerned local aspects, but some had a cross-cutting and city-wide nature. In the face of this structured response on the part of the local community, the city council decided to aggregate the comments into eight large categories and to discuss them very quickly, also due to the very stringent deadlines for the approval of the plan before the interruption of political activity in view of the administrative elections; in the end only around 350 were accepted, and the plan was approved as such at the beginning of February 2011.

The New Plan

Maybe surprisingly, the master plan was not much used as a theme for debate during the electoral campaign for the administrative elections in 2011, also due to the wish expressed by the center-left candidate Giuliano Pisapia not to exacerbate the public debate. Nevertheless, the general awareness generated in the city in the previous months, and the conflictual approach to some crucial issues, worked under cover both in civil society and in the new left-wing political majority that resulted from the elections in May. In our opinion, this is one of the reasons behind the choice the new majority took in July to bring back the decision-making process and to re-examine the comments proposed by citizens and other actors in a more scrupulous way.

In the Milan case, a traditional participatory tool (the formal written comments to the plan) played a crucial role. Moreover, the new administration decided to review the plan (formally approved) starting from the 4,000 written comments received in 2010. These written comments were used as a device for correcting and changing some crucial aspects of the plan approved by the previous administration, thus internalizing a bottom-up approach in the new spatial planning strategies.

The changes between the two versions of the plan concern the densities and the possibility of proposing an overall spatial strategy, even within the very open basic framework of the regional law. The main change concerns the significant reduction of the overall building ratio, with the possibility of selectively densifying certain areas, provided that there is a public transit connection and that a certain amount of affordable housing is foreseen.

Moreover, an important change of a certain symbolic value is the impossibility for areas within the *Parco Sud* to generate any building rights. There is also a system of incentives linked to the energy performance of new buildings. The review mechanism, based on the comments on the previous plan, is clearly incremental; it impinges upon a significant local mobilization, but at the same time it responds to a variety of comments and points of view, so it is difficult to identify in it a radical revision of the main structure of the plan, and therefore a radically new vision of city development.

At the same time, it is possible to notice some first hints, some suggestions, that the structured voices that animated the public debate about future urban choices are ready to take an active part in the definition of the next steps in urban transformation. In 2012, a group of civil society organizations that actively took part in the consultation phase signed a strategic agreement with real estate operators and developers, a sort of memorandum of understanding setting priorities for the reframing of the plan itself, around some shared axes: the valorization of the *Parco Sud* as a real asset for the Milanese population; the improvement of public services through public–private partnerships; and the attention toward social housing and more generally toward the renewal of the housing stock, taking into account the energy-saving dimension, the public transportation issue and the opportunities offered by Expo 2015.

Concluding Remarks

The story of the approval and redefinition of the PGT seems to us interesting for at least three reasons that also open up new research questions.

First, there is a crucial relationship between the emergence of urban conflicts and the dynamics of the urban political agenda. In the Milan case, a huge spatial transformation occurred in twenty years without significant conflicts because in the same period the urban political agenda was stable and the actors (institutions and political parties, but also economic and social actors) were unable to redefine the problems and the critical issues for urban government and governance. The themes of spatial transformation assumed a new visibility in the public debate only when a more general cultural and political change infused Milanese society, and created the conditions for a radical political change and for a new political and administrative cycle, with the victory of the left-wing coalition in the 2011 municipal elections. Local actors have been able to find unity of action, and in doing so to show an understanding of a series of legitimation steps, as the representation of a plurality of existing worlds (political milieus, civil society, technical experts …).

Second, the typology of conflicts emerging through the opposition to the master plan were different from the limited and very local conflicts against specific large-scale development projects occurring in earlier years. The discussion about the general plan was conducted using general arguments, and trying to propose a different general vision for the urban development of the city. Nevertheless, the conflict was not ideological. The main actors involved were not the political parties, but civil society and its plural representatives. The arguments used were often based on technical expertise, and an important role was played by the public discussion promoted by experts and professionals. For these reasons it is possible to say that the public discussion about the new master plan for Milan represented both a return to a politicization of planning decisions and a radical shift from traditional ideological conflicts. In conditions of political change, the meeting of different actors became possible and enabled in turn the emergence of a new and different idea of city development. This can be seen as a reaction to the political and decision-making climate in the previous decades, in the first place to the systematic under-consideration of citizens and other stakeholders by the previous city government coalition, strictly connected to a closed network of powerful interests (especially in the real estate field), but significantly disconnected from the local community in its different articulations. Therefore, through the platform offered by the plan-making process, an opposition and mobilization of the idea of the city itself and its development model and not just of individual projects became possible.

Third, the fact that a very bureaucratic planning procedure, the formal written comments on the PGT, was one of the main planks of the conflicts framework seems to prove that the forms assumed by urban conflicts depend on the specific situation. If there are political and social conditions for the emergence of new public discussions and new conflicts, the actors will use the tools and the occasions that the circumstances offer them. This means also that we should probably put focus less on formal participation techniques, and more on the specific relationship between actors, strategies, resources and tools in a particular 'field' of structured practices. On the other hand, the conditions that led to the emergence of a local conflict about the future vision of the city, which found its way through the platform supplied by the new plan framework, have been so specific and contingent that they indeed proved to be necessary, but at the same time insufficient, to ensure a continuity of public mobilization and attention.

These final remarks open new research questions. How can we think of this new form of conflicts and planning politicization in the context of the radical crisis of the traditional forms of political representation and mediation? If these conflicts are different from traditional ideological conflicts, but cannot be reduced both to interest conflicts and to (self-)recognition conflicts, which categories should we use to describe and analyze these forms of conflictual social mobilization? What can the role of a general land-use plan be in the definition of a 'discussion platform' capable of creating the conditions for public discussions about spatial planning decisions that keep together a technical and a strategic dimension? The effectiveness of what happened in the Milan case, which was made possible by the specific context, leaves open the question about the continuity of this mobilization in the face of the existing social and political fragmentation.

References

Bagnasco, A. and Le Galès, P. (2000) *Cities in Contemporary Europe*, Cambridge, UK: Cambridge University Press.

Balducci, A. (2003) "Policies, Plans and Projects: Governing the City-Region of Milan," *DISP*, 152: 59–70.

Balducci, A., Fedeli, V. and Pasqui, G. (2011) *Strategic Planning for Contemporary Urban Regions*, London, UK: Ashgate.

Bolocan-Goldstein, M. and Bonfantini, B. (eds.) (2007) *Milano incompiuta: interpretazioni urbanistiche del mutamento*, Milan, Italy: Franco Angeli.

Bolocan-Goldstein, M. and Pasqui, G. (2011) "Oltre la crescita edilizia: una nuova agenda pubblica per Milano," in A. Arcidiacono and L. Pogliani (eds.), *Milano al futuro: riforma o crisi del governo urbano*, Milan, Italy: ed. e/o: 270–304.

Comune di Milano (2001) *Ricostruire la grande Milano: documento di inquadramento delle politiche urbanistiche*, Milan, Italy: Comune di Milano.

Dente, B., Bobbio, L. and Spada, A. (2005) "A Tale of Two Cities," *DISP*, 162: 41–52.

Diappi, L. (2009) *Rigenerazione urbana e ricambio sociale*, Milan, Italy: Franco Angeli.

Gualini, E. (2011) "Governance, Space and Politics: Exploring the Governmentality of Planning," in J. Hillier and P. Healey (eds.), *The Ashgate Research Companion to Planning Theory*, London, UK: Ashgate: 57–85.

Healey, P. (2007) *Urban Complexity and Spatial Strategies*, London, UK: Routledge.

Martinotti, G. (2005) "Social Morphology and Governance in the New Metropolis," in Y. Kazepov (ed.), *Cities of Europe: Changing Contexts, Local Arrangements, and the Challenge to Urban Cohesion*, Oxford, UK: Blackwell: 90–108.

Mazza, L. (2002) "Technical Knowledge and Planning Action," *Planning Theory*, 1(1): 11–26.

Mazza, L. (2009) "Plan and Constitution—Aristotle's Hippodamus: Towards an 'Ostensive' Definition of Spatial Planning," *Town Planning Review*, 80(2): 113–141.

Mazza, L. (2010) "Strategic Planning and Republicanism," *Spatium—International Review*, 22: 1–10.

Melucci, A. (1982) *L'invenzione del presente: movimenti, identità, bisogni individuali*, Bologna, Italy: Il Mulino.

Melucci, A. (1996) *Challenging Codes: Collective Action in the Information Age*, Cambridge, UK: Cambridge University Press.

Micelli, E. (2011) *La gestione dei piani urbanistici: perequazione, accordi, incentivi*, Venice, Italy: Marsilio.

OECD (2006) *Territorial Review: Milan*, Paris: OECD, available at: http://browse.oecdbookshop.org/oecd/pdfs/free/0406051e.pdf (accessed July 1, 2011).

Pacchi, C. (2008) "Cittadinanza a Milano: scelta democratica e trasformazione urbana," in AA.VV. *Per un'altra città: riflessioni e proposte sull'urbanistica milanese*, Santarcangelo di Romagna, Italy: Maggioli Editore.

Pasqui, G. (2008) *Città, popolazioni, politiche*, Milan, Italy: Jaca Book.

Pizzorno, A. (1993) "Come pensare il conflitto," in *Le radici della politica assoluta*, Milan, Italy: Feltrinelli: 43–81.

Ranci, C. (2010) *Città nella rete globale*, Milan, Italy: Bruno Mondadori.

Regione Lombardia (2005) *L.r. 11 marzo 2005, n. 12—Legge per il governo del territorio*, available at: http://smtp.consiglio.regione.lombardia.it/NormeLombardia/Accessibile/main.aspx?exp_coll=lr002005031100012&view=showdoc&iddoc=lr002005031100012&selnode=lr002005031100012 (accessed November 20, 2014).

Vitale, T. (ed.) (2007) *In nome di chi? Partecipazione e rappresentanza nelle mobilitazioni locali*, Milan, Italy: Franco Angeli.

5

A Muddled Landscape of Conflicts: What We Can Learn about Planning/Conflict Relationships from the Story of Tor Marancia, Rome, and Its Unexpected Shift

Barbara Pizzo and Giacomina Di Salvo

Introduction

There is a strong relationship between planning and conflict, as witnessed by the literature on planning theory. Within this literature, it is possible to distinguish very different issues, perspectives and approaches.

Conflicts have very different natures and origins, so that the actual chance for them to be treated or solved through planning depends on which definition of planning we assume.[1] Clearly, the stricter our conceptualization of planning and of its role in defining spaces as a way of intervening socially is (Mazza 1996, 1997, 2004), the weaker are its chances of directly solving profound socio-political conflicts (not to mention geo-political ones).

From an overview of the scholarly output on this issue, aside from the many different typologies of conflicts and the rather obvious observation of the coexistence of many different understandings and ways of practicing planning, an open question emerges. This is related to the form the planning–conflict relationship can assume in particular contexts, to the way in which the deliberative process can be designed and conducted and to the micro-level processes that can be hidden by, or within, macro-level governance configurations and/or power structures.

Our contribution aims at highlighting what we consider to be a fundamental ambiguity of this relationship, a point of view that deserves a wider and deeper reflection in planning theory, while becoming more developed, with its own specificities, in policy analysis. Policy analysis considers the inherent conflict potential of planning processes, particularly as the sign of different social demands and rationalities and consequently as a field of inquiry of public policy effectiveness and democratic legitimacy. Planning practices often leave these issues as implicit. In our research, we try to rejoin these two disciplinary approaches, making use of the range of both analytical and interpretive tools they provide.

Through an in-depth case-study analysis, we aim at overcoming here what we see as a sort of simplified duality determined by considering planning as the source or origin of conflict or, vice versa, as a tool for conflict resolution.

From the former perspective, there is a body of robust Marxist literature dedicated to the inherent conflictual potential of planning considered as a tool for the reproduction of capital related to land, as well as a tool for neoliberal practices of commodification of land and territory (Scott 1980; Dear and Scott 1981; Cenzatti 1987), and an even more influent sociological and geographical literature of the same stream that can be traced back to the work of Lefebvre (1968, 1972, 1974), Castells (1972, 1978, 1980, 1983), and Harvey (1973, 1985), though it entered the planning realm more as a suggestion than as a key issue for theory and practice.

From the latter perspective, most scholarly contributions and experiences are centered on a problem-solving approach, where planning is considered as a tool for conflict resolution (Susskind and Cruickshank 1987; Forester 1987, 1989, 2011; Kaufmann and Duncan 1989; Healey 1993; Hoch 1994; Innes 1995; see also the seminal work for conflict resolution scholarship of Schelling 1960). In particular, collaborative planning internalizes conflicts within the planning process, intended as the context where dialogue and interaction between all the involved parties is assured in order to find a shared solution (Habermas 1984; Sager 1994; Healey 1997; Rydin 2003; see also: Tewdwr-Jones and Allmendinger 1998; Allmendinger and Tewdwr-Jones 2002). The assumption is that planning acts 'in the face of power' (Forester 1989), that is, that it represents a positive force that can be used for disentangling contentious situations, and for defining a constructive context for overcoming or reducing distances between different interests, as well as for maximizing mutual gains (Susskind et al. 1999; Booher and Innes 2002). In our view, this dual interpretation is critical, particularly since it contributes to hiding the most intrinsic nature of planning as an interactive context of practices where the conditions of conflicts—as well as their course and outcomes—are (intentionally or even unintentionally) shaped.

In fact, despite conflicts often being described as the result of different and opposing views about the future of a place (e.g., development vs. protection or conservation) or of contrasting scales and rationales of policy intervention (e.g., 'local choices' vs. 'strategic necessities': Allmendinger and Tewdwr-Jones 1997), the actual responsibility of planning in determining the very conditions in which a conflict emerges or even explodes is in our view rather undervalued.

Since conflicts emerge any time stakeholders with different interests mobilize in order to obtain or to protect what they want (Kujala et al. 2012), and since planning has to do with competition over space (with the redistribution and reorganization of fundamental and limited goods such as space, or of resources related to space, being at stake), we can assume that conflicts are constitutive to planning, or, conversely, that planning is intrinsically contentious, and that planning procedures are key factors for conflicts (Mazza 2005).

By considering one of the most controversial cases of the recent history of planning in Rome-Tor Marancia—seemingly a 'clear' case of land-use conflict—we aim to make visible the intricacies and dynamics of conflicts over a whole planning process, showing quite clearly how planning itself can co-constitute the landscape of a conflict, and highlighting what in our view is still an open problem and a challenge for planning theory.

The case study site consists of a broad green area (220 ha) with a central and strategic position in the city of Rome. Its long story is rooted in the urban development provisions of the 1960s and 1970s, but it is only at the beginning of the latest planning process (early 1990s) that the actual implications of the former urban development provisions became clear. The area is situated at the border (and considered as a 'natural extension') of the *Parco dell'Appia Antica*, which since the 1950s, through the political action of an important group of intellectuals led by Antonio Cederna,[2] has been the object of a fierce civic battle for landscape protection. The land-use statute of about half of the area (114 ha) was that of a building site, deriving from precedent land-use regulations. Although ten years have elapsed (to the time of writing) since the planning controversy concerning Tor Marancia was legally solved, its territorial consequences at the urban and metropolitan scale are still largely unknown and in our view underestimated.

We will point out here three of the conventional understandings related to the planning–conflict relationship that our case study helps us to understand differently:

1. *Global–local relationships.* Related literature examines mostly cases where conflict is generated from supra-local decisions imposed on local communities. Citizens are mostly presented as reacting against supra-local decisions, while the local level is presented as that which represents bottom-up social expectations and demands. Our case study shows that the relationship is not always so neat, and that the 'scalar structuration' of a problem is crucial in that (Brenner 2001).
2. *Conflict and participation.* Related literature usually presents cases aimed at demonstrating how participative approaches—particularly if bottom-up and community-driven—play a fundamental role in conflict resolution,

also contributing to the empowerment of the communities involved, which are said to become increasingly aware of interdependencies between decisions, capable of linking different agendas and also more conscious about their own role in the deliberative process (Booher and Innes 2002). Our case study shows that this is not always the case, and that, particularly through a 'scalar shift' of the problem—as defined in critical interpretations of the 'politics of scales' (Brenner 2000; Swyngedouw 1997, 2000)—local communities may completely lose their control over choices, as well as their understanding of their implications, thus becoming, in actual fact, excluded from the planning process.

3. *Stakeholder relationships*. Related literature analyzes stakeholder relationships in conflict situations focusing on their ethical and strategic meaning and also on how different interests are justified in relation to the conflict (Kujala et al. 2012). Nevertheless, stakeholder relationships are described mostly as stable, in the sense that each actor is supposed to play a sort of fixed role throughout the process, while our case study shows the fluidity of relational dynamics, where different actors redefine themselves reciprocally and, while continuously redefining their interaction, they create different worlds, coming and going through them (Crosta 2003, 2010).

Framing the Case

Our contribution represents a first result of interdisciplinary research[3] the aim of which is an empirical analysis of neoliberal 'variegation' (Peck et al. 2009) in local contexts—that of Rome in our case—through looking at five dimensions of public action and decision-making: actors, representations, institutions, processes and outcomes. Urban planning is the field of public action we are involved in, and our reflection here derives mainly from intersecting an actor-oriented policy analysis (*who*) (Yanow 2000; Fischer and Gottweis 2012; Crosta 1998, 2006), with a critical assessment of planning tools and process (*how and why*) through their main outcomes (*what*) from a planning theory perspective. The issue of conflict emerges as a sign of the clashing of different interests and views, but also of conventional land-use regulation and new procedures, as well as the changing frame and orientation of the public action. Therefore we analyzed:

- the institutional, administrative, political, economic and cultural milieu;
- local policies and political deliberations, ongoing planning processes and planning frameworks in their changes through time (from the 1960s to the early 2010s);

- the actors involved: the interests each one of them brought; the dimension of the related interest (individual or private, collective, public); the spatial (territorial) roots of each interest; the capacity/attitude of each actor to revise and change its position according to changes over the course of time; the capacity/contribution of each actor in constructing and substantiating its own discourse and the role it played in structuring the decision process, and in determining choices;
- narratives and discourses constructed by different actors over the course of the action (through interviews and a full press review), for understanding how different interests are justified in relation to the conflict.

The definition of neoliberalism proposed by David Harvey is that

> a theory of political economic practices that proposes that human well-being can be best advanced by liberating individual entrepreneurial freedoms and skills within an institutional framework characterized by strong private property rights, free markets, and free trade. The role of the State is to create and preserve an institutional framework appropriate to such practices. (Harvey 2005: 2)

This means that the theoretical interpretation of neoliberalization follows the empirical analysis of facts and behaviors that, in the most common interpretation, are put into practice in order to answer the new needs of globalization—which, contrary to Jessop's valid observation, is assumed to be an *explanans* (Jessop 2003).[4] The need for neoliberal practices to be translated in particular places constitutes the reason for the renewed attention to context-specific conditions, going beyond bonds and restrictions.

In the case of Rome, if we unravel the particular socio-economic and socio-political conditions in the light of Harvey's discourse on neoliberalism, and more specifically on the role of the State in creating and preserving an 'appropriate' institutional framework for neoliberal practices, we cannot but agree that, without a clear and explicit reference to transnational capital and competitive processes at international level, the so-called neoliberal practices are (not too surprisingly) rather similar to the 'old' ones.

The socio-economic condition of Rome has always been closely related to its particular nature—that of a capital city, an all-important religious center and a main tourist destination. As to private enterprises, a decisive role has always been played by landowners (a few families, often formerly aristocratic ones linked to Catholic hierarchies) and by real estate and building companies—linked to or overlapping with landowners. The political and administrative life of the city was marked by cycles of different degrees of indulgence toward the pursuit of private interests through the exploitation of urban space, starting from land-use regulations used as tools for distributing privileges (and wealth) and obtaining political consent.[5] The soil has been considered a fundamental economic resource, the medium for exercising, distributing and strengthening hegemonic power. This interpretation does not fit *any* idea of a city and of its development or it fits *every* idea, instead. Here resides, in our view, the peculiar weakness of planning in Rome: on the one hand, its strength in terms of formal procedures, norms and prescriptions collides with its insubstantiality in terms of actual procedures, implementations and enforcement; on the other hand, market-driven development goals have been far more important than any consistent objective for the city as a whole, and short-term objectives have always been ahead of mid- or long-term objectives (let alone long-term strategies).

During the first decade of the 2000s, with Walter Veltroni as mayor, a main policy discourse emerged, the so-called *Modello Roma* ('Rome Model': Mattone 2004; for a critical point of view, see: AA.VV. 2007; Marcucci 2008). Its references are mainly to be found in newspapers, while scientific contributions are few, thus demonstrating that the "*Modello Roma* has significantly shaped the daily life of Roman people without having been seriously revised" (Violante and Annunziata 2011: 5). Its interpretation as the local translation of neoliberal practices in relation to transnational competition and globalization, as well as a hybrid context of neoliberal actors' constellations, has been put in question. By examining some of the main features of the *Modello Roma*, we will highlight points of continuity and discontinuity within conventional planning and policy approaches, in order to understand if and how we can talk about it as a sign of neoliberal variegation.

The main 'ingredients' of that model can be summarized as follows:

- A push toward the economy of culture, cultural tourism and leisure, through a strong support of cultural initiatives at all levels (from the international to the micro-local), a turn toward cultural policies and culture-led strategies that, far from being interpreted in the frame of the culture and knowledge turn of socio-economic policies at EU level, started to be recognized for their potential to play a decisive role in the growth of the city, and a driving force for its development and its positioning in the global market. What actually happened has been described as the 'spectacularization' of the city, and as a 'neo-Baroque' attitude that drew attention to the image of the city more than to the city itself (Maltese 2007). We also add that public attention was drawn mainly—if not exclusively—to the city center—the stage for representation—while much more relevant and actual territorial changes were happening in the suburbs. The gap between the quest for urban 'quality' between the city center and the suburbs is evident.

- A new (or renewed?) pact among politicians (starting with those involved in public administration) and entrepreneurs, especially those belonging to real estate and building companies, whose explicit meaning can be interpreted as twofold: to create a stronger link between public decisions and actions, addressed to the efficiency and to the credibility of the public administration; and to sustain public initiatives. As to this latter point, attention was mainly centered on the economic-financial support that some companies—usually entrepreneurial families—used to give to the public administration; in our view, however, their support in orienting public opinion was even more decisive. This they achieved particularly through their direct or indirect power within press agencies—which they sometime own—in order to create a positive context for action (it should be highlighted that this is a crucial point for framing the discourse on conflict in that period).
- The direct translation of public administration choices into spatial choices, through the redaction of the new Regulatory Plan, starting at the beginning of the 1990s, and formally ending in 2008 (just before the end of the second administrative cycle with Veltroni as mayor).

As to the last point, some further explanations should be provided, due to the close relationship between the case we are presenting and the planning process we have just referred to, and because of the role that our case played in it, as will emerge more clearly. Through the *Modello Roma*, public–private partnerships and negotiations have for the first time been extensively promoted and openly and convincingly sustained by the public administration as the only way to reach collective advantages related to urban transformations. This would have represented a major change in the political context, if it had brought to an end or to limited shadow negotiations and bargaining among economic and political elites, which have always been the gray side of the planning process. This is not what happened; decision-making became increasingly privately driven, while the competition between the State and the market, which is still used to clarify the contrast between the public and private character of interests expressed and pursued by the two actors, was perceived just as a window dressing that contributed to obscuring the nature of planning as a context of interaction.

A Brief History of Tor Marancia

Early in the 1990s, according to the Regulatory Plan of 1962, the land-use statute of the Tor Marancia estate was that of a building site, with impressive quantitative provisions: 4 million cubic meters for 40,000 new inhabitants.

In the 1990s, at the beginning of the planning process of the latest Regulatory Plan, two successive planning documents have been produced as *Varianti di Salvaguardia* ('Safeguard Variants'), with the explicit intention of protecting the fundamental ecological and historical elements of the urban landscape. These planning documents foresaw a reduction of the building provisions from 4 million to 2.4 million cubic meters, with a decrease in the territorial density of 40 percent. In 1995 an allotment project was presented to the city council. Meanwhile, the *Parco dell'Appia Antica* Committee[6] presented a plan for the enlargement of the park boundaries through the inclusion of Tor Marancia, according to its archeological and historical value, and in 1996 the Archeological Office asked the Ministry of Cultural and Environmental Heritage to impose a restriction for the protection of a large part of the site.

In 1997, the city council adopted the *Piano delle Certezze* ('Preliminary Plan of Certainties'); the land use for Tor Marancia was the same as in the Regulatory Plan of 1962, but with decreased provisions as in the *Varianti di Salvaguardia*. A few months later, the Lazio Region approved the inclusion of part of Tor Marancia (106 ha) within the boundaries of *Parco dell'Appia Antica*. In doing so, the land use of the estate changed in different zones: a regional park (106 ha) and a building site (114 ha).

In 1998, because of the application of a National Law on Landscape Protection (law 431/85), Tor Marancia was recognized as a restricted archeological site by the Ministry of Cultural and Environmental Heritage. This did not prohibit the building exploitation but submitted the project to assessment by the Archeological Office and by the regional administration.

In 1999, a new development project was presented, according to the directives of the city executive and the regional administration (1.9 million cubic meters for 14,000 new inhabitants). The implementation of the project was subjected also to the creation of public infrastructures and services for the realization of the park as a public space; moreover, the landowners had to transfer the other part of their property (114 ha) to the public. The final version of the project was presented to the press.[7] Real estate investors provided an Environmental Impact Assessment of the project, as requested by the regional administration.

While landowners took legal action against the restriction imposed in 1998, members of the public, sustained by important cultural associations, NGOs and by three political parties,[8] constituted a committee against *any* building development in the Tor Marancia estate (*Comitato per il no all'edificazione a Tor Marancia*). Their 'zero option' position was sustained also by 140 members of the national parliament, and the committee drew up a petition that collected 5,000 signatures, asking the city council to put the cancellation of the whole exploitation project to the vote. The project was confirmed, instead, even if by a margin of just one vote.

This represented one of the most intense phases of the debate at the civil society and political level, and it was through this debate that contradictions and controversies emerged more clearly. The first ambiguous sign was that one of the most powerful real estate investors, who sustained the mayor and was also the owner of the most widely read of local newspapers,[9] started a press campaign against the development project of Tor Marancia precisely the day after the vote at the city council. At the same time the regional president of World Wide Fund for Nature, who was fighting against the development provisions of the new Regulatory Plan (while the Green Party was within the city council majority), asked for 'at least' the cancellation of the project for Tor Marancia.

It became increasingly clear that this project played a decisive role within the whole urban planning process, becoming a major consideration in the policy the city executive was conducting.

In 2001, the Archeological Office of Rome together with the Ministry of Cultural and Environmental Heritage declared that there was no development compatible with the Tor Marancia estate. Thus in 2002, the regional administration included the whole site within the borders of the *Parco dell'Appia Antica*, notwithstanding that the ownership of the land was still private. It is important to note that this act required no refund or compensation; it was not necessary to acquire the land (however, most of the whole park is still private at the time of writing).

In 2002, during a public debate in the district of Tor Marancia, the town councilor in charge of planning declared that, after lengthy negotiation, landowners and real estate investors had 'agreed to renounce' their building rights, while the municipality would give them in turn 'compensation.' [10] The city executive decided to reward the landowners, presenting this as the only possible choice, while from a juridical point of view it was not compulsory.

In 2003, through an Act of the City Council, the compensation program started; building rights were transferred from Tor Marancia to 15 development areas in the suburbs. They were implemented through *Accordi di Programma* ('Program Agreement'), a simplified administrative procedure that relies on 'one-by-one' agreements. Through this procedure, begun in 2006, landowners were 'compensated' for their lost building rights and for having agreed to shift them, and 'refunded' for the public acquisition of their property (Figure 5.1).

The actual meaning and effects of compensation for the city emerged only when the first compensation agreement has been signed:[11] an enormous increase in construction at each of the 15 sites, which turned into 4.1 million cubic meters—even more than the former planning provisions of 1962.

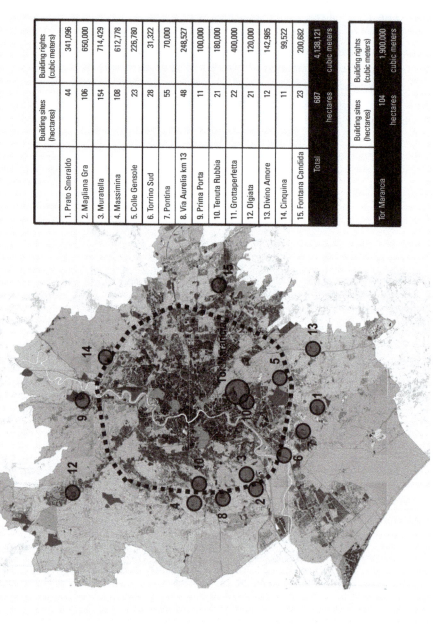

	Building sites (hectares)	Building rights (cubic meters)
1. Prato Smeraldo	44	341,096
2. Magliana Gra	106	650,000
3. Muratella	154	714,429
4. Massimina	108	612,778
5. Colle Gensole	23	226,780
6. Torrino Sud	28	31,322
7. Pontina	55	70,000
8. Via Aurelia km 13	48	248,527
9. Prima Porta	11	100,000
10. Tenuta Rubbia	21	180,000
11. Grottaperfetta	22	400,000
12. Olgiata	21	120,000
13. Divino Amore	12	142,985
14. Cinquina	11	99,522
15. Fontana Candida	23	200,682
Total	687 hectares	4,138,121 cubic meters

	Building sites (hectares)	Building rights (cubic meters)
Tor Marancia	104 hectares	1,900,000 cubic meters

Figure 5.1 Outcomes of the compensation program for Tor Marancia: transfer of building rights (source: authors)

Although the Regulatory Plan was almost ready, most of the 'landing zones' of these compensations were recognized in rural, even protected areas—parts of the well-known *Campagna Romana* (and not, as initially declared, in already urbanized ones).

Table 5.1 Chronology of planning procedures leading to the compensation program for Tor Marancia

Tor Marancia as a Development Area

Year	Planning Tools	Building Rights
PRG 1962–1965		
1962	Implementation project of PRG ("piano attuativo")	4,000,000 m³ 40,000 inhabitants
1971	"piano attuativo"	As 1962 (confirmed)
1987	"piano attuativo"	As 1962 (confirmed)
Varianti de Salvaguardia		
1991	"piano attuativo"	−20% (3,200,000 m³)
1996	"piano attuativo"	−40% (2,400,000 m³) (+106 ha for green public area)
1997	"piano attuativo" (+ EIA)[1]	−50% (1,900,000 m³) (+106 ha for green public area)
1999	"piano attuativo" (+ EIA)	As 1997 (confirmed)

Tor Marancia as a Park—the Transfer of Building Rights in the Compensation Areas

Year	Public Acts	Building Rights
2001	Declaration of Archeological Office of Rome and Ministry of Cultural and Environmental Heritage: incompatibility of any real estate development in Tor Marancia	Cancellation of building rights on the site of Tor Marancia
2002	Decision of the city executive to reward with 'compensation' the landowners who renounced their building rights in Tor Marancia	Transfer of building rights to other sites ('landing zones')
2003	Deliberation of the city council on the 'compensation agreement' that defined: • dimension (scale of new building rights) • location (15 'landing zones' in the suburb) of transferred building rights from Tor Marancia	Enormous increase in construction at each of the 15 sites, which turned into 4,100,000 m³—even more than the former planning provision of 1962
2006	First compensation agreement—Grottaperfetta	Increase in building rights in the 'landing zone' due to compensation—from 180,000 m³ to 400,000 m³

Note:
[1] EIA = Environmental Impact Assessment
(source: authors)

Discursive Change of Meanings/Interests: Planning as the Creation and Perpetuation of an Urban Conflict Matrix

The case we presented was intertwined with the planning process, showing conflicting interests over the city and its development: a conflict between exploitation and conservation, rooted in the land-use and property rights regime.

The origin of the controversy resides in:

- the over-scaling of the Regulatory Plan of 1962—Its expectation of a population of six million inhabitants has been contradicted by the actual growth of the city but its development provisions remained;
- the inconsistency of the environmental and landscape protection goals expressed by the preliminary documents of the new Regulatory Plan with the still valid provision of the old one; and
- the high environmental and historical value of Tor Marancia, as well as its huge economic potential as a building site.

The solution through compensation followed a lengthy conflict that set in opposition public institutions at all levels, landowners and real estate investors, NGOs, associations and the public, together with all of the political parties. First of all, the nature of the conflict has been questioned. It is of some interest to note that during that period, the word 'conflict' was rarely used in newspapers, in public debates or in the political discourse.[12] It was the course of events that attracted our attention. Astonishingly, a quite unexpected unanimous consent followed the final decision about the future of the site. Where was the trickery? Starting from the advantages and disadvantages at stake and actually produced, the role of actors and their interaction has been examined, as well as the role of planning through the procedures it used, and the particular form the planning–conflict relationship assumed.

Actors were distributed in a sort of double-track setting. On one side, we found those who played a single role throughout the process. Among them, together with environmental and landscape associations, were representatives of political parties in the minority on the city council; they sustained the 'zero option' coalition, refusing negotiation and wishing to use the conflict to achieve political consensus among the citizenry. On the other side, there were those who demonstrated interest in negotiating and proved adept at changing their position according to a changing context. The main public actor (the mayor and executive) played an ambiguous role: formally a *super partes* one, expressing a strong will to find a solution without conflict, while actually assuming a partisan position with the most powerful coalition, that of landowners and real estate investors. Between these two groups there was no real interplay and, as had happened with the conflict, also negotiations

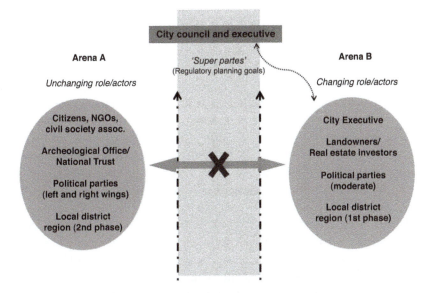

Figure 5.2 Actors and their double-track setting (source: authors)

(including those for compensation) were withheld from the public debate. In this way, the meaning of planning as a co-evolutive context of interaction that defines the conditions in which conflicts can (or cannot) emerge and develop was concealed.

In sum, planning and the new Regulatory Plan strongly contributed to structuring the public discourse about the city, and power relationships between the mayor, the city council and the other actors involved at various levels in decision processes about city development. In the following, we pinpoint three main points of content, the relevance of which should be validated throughout the planning process, which are:

1. the urban plan as a sign of the political and administrative turn toward transparency and open democracy;
2. the urban plan as a guarantee of the consistency of planning proposals; and
3. the urban plan as a work-in-progress which demonstrates the efficiency of public action.

In more detail, point by point:

1. At the beginning of the planning process especially, there was a precise intention to show how the debate about the city was more open and transparent than ever before. While previous urban plans had been presented as technical products, public participation was in this case highly

emphasized. The political message was that the new plan was important for the city and for all citizens, and that it was in everyone's interests.[13] The pre-electoral policy (which produced forms of 'pacts' among actors) was expressed also (and largely) through a preliminary plan, or planning scheme, which tended to hide the contradictions (and potential conflicts) between public and private objectives. The ambiguity of the mayor's policy consisted in seemingly sustaining public-driven policies and planning while systematically practicing forms of market-driven negotiations on single development choices. A fundamental question remains; namely who are the actors who actually co-produce choices and their implementation, or who are the actors whose initiative the public sustains, and why?[14]

2. Many difficult or contested choices have been accepted within the frame of a master plan that—in the mind of the planning staff—has both 'structural' and 'strategic' contents. The first preliminary plan (*Piano delle Certezze*) defined the main elements of urban quality to be pursued, but its principles were later contradicted or even negated. The master plan was presented as a precondition, and as a guarantee of the consistency of planning proposals, but its implementation through single development projects negotiated with real estate developers focused on single areas, often in open contradiction with the declared general goals. The two main strategies, intended to increase public services and transportation and to preserve and improve environmental quality and the landscape—presented as the 'iron therapy' and the 'green wheel'—tended to hide millions of cubic meters of new buildings that would have been realized through various forms of public–private negotiations in order to get private financing for public spaces and public goals, while a general look at what the plan has actually produced until now shows the enormous gap between private and public advantages.

3. Given the direct link between public action and the length of the political administrative cycle, the problem of planning temporalities (a too-long and expensive process that often follows urban changes rather than guiding them) acquires a very important role,[15] since urban planning can contribute to demonstrating the efficiency of public action within the political mandate of the mayor. In Rome, where the last Regulatory Plan was 40 years old, the problem has been 'solved' through starting the implementation of the new Plan during its redaction. This has been realized through some tools (practices), interpreted as a planning 'style' that has been called 'planning by doing.'[16] Notwithstanding the choices already taken, and the partial implementation of the Plan during its redaction, it had to be 'adopted' and then 'approved' by the city council.

The case of Tor Marancia triggered off such an intricate and muddled landscape of interests, solutions (with very different contents and meanings) and potential conflicts that the political setting at the city council became progressively unclear and uncertain, so much so that the professionals involved in the planning and the mayor himself more than once feared not being able to bring the Plan to its final approval. The risk was in not reaching the majority during the vote for the adoption of the Plan, which was a priority in the political agenda of the mayor. Rather than being the instrument for demonstrating the mayor's policy efficiency, it risked demonstrating its failure. In this sense, we can say that the case of Tor Marancia is a paradigmatic example of the setback that the public can suffer; the mayor, who defended private rights on Tor Marancia, started to fear losing the support of part of his own political coalition—linked to environmental associations that were fighting to preserve Tor Marancia—during the approval of the Regulatory Plan. Compensation was chosen as a way to overcome this impasse without disappointing any actors involved. However, in so doing, some of the fundamental planning objectives—starting from land consumption control—have been definitely contradicted.

Planning appeared to be the chessboard on which the game has been conducted. In our opinion, the conflicts were not between different ideas concerning the development of the city and its future, but between a conception of the city as an objective (a mid- to long-term objective to be reached progressively) and a conception of the city as a tool for reaching aspatial economic goals while exercising hegemonic power on and through space. This critical perspective assumes a more general meaning within the discourse on the logic of global markets and the very mechanisms of globalization, and imposes a need to rethink the State–market dichotomy.

Actors set themselves in a sort of 'unbalanced' form of mutual adjustment (Lindblom 1965). From an actor-oriented policy analysis perspective, it seems to us that the question of the unsettled position of the different actors is clear enough in this case, together with their different capacity of being involved with, or even managing, the conflict. From analyzing actors' interactions, it emerges that those able to adapt themselves and to change their position more often drive the conflict, and are stronger than those whose interests are linked to a particular place. The mechanism of compensation increased further the power of real estate investors by abstracting the building rights from their former location.

Concluding Remarks

Planning theory mostly builds on an understanding of planning as (1) an institutional instrument of power, and of the attribution/distribution of power—so to say, as a cause or origin of conflict; and (2) a tool for conflict resolution, aimed at achieving public or collective goals in a context of ruling private interests and market-driven imperatives. This dual interpretation of planning is in our view limited and rather problematic, since it tends to hide its functioning as a co-evolutive, interactive context of practices where the very conditions of conflicts are—intentionally or even unintentionally— shaped, and the different dimensions of decision-making—actors, representations, institutions—are continuously redefined. Planning, and particularly the urban plan, rather than being either the cause of conflict or the tool for its resolution, becomes its chessboard, the field on which the game is played and where its rules are defined.

Looking beyond the common bipolar interpretation of planning as the source or the resolution of conflicts, the planning episode of a broad green area with a strategic position in the city of Rome that we have analyzed demonstrates how planning defines the conditions in which conflicts can, or cannot, emerge, and the way they develop. The role of the public, and the planning procedures it implements, are key factors for the rise and the progress of a controversy. The ambiguous role the public actors played in this case, preaching planning as a public-driven initiative pursuing public-interest objectives, as opposed to market-oriented ones, while systematically practicing shadow negotiation, prevented planning from being clearly recognized as functioning as a context of interaction and of co-evolution of context–actors relationships. This had decisive implications for the different positions of the actors involved, in terms of: different levels of awareness of the ongoing process as a context of negotiation and interaction; different capacities and attitudes to changing position according to changes within the planning context; and different levels of knowledge amounting to different levels of power among actors. In our view, these points are relevant both empirically and theoretically. In fact, the case also revealed the need for an advanced interpretation of actors' relationships, more attentive to consideration of how their different attitudes to changing position according to changes within the context are dependent on their power, but also on the ideological content of their position, which can determine different understandings of (and different attitudes in revising) the problem, its frame and its implications.

Instead of contributing to its empowerment, conflict can lead a local community to lose control of options and to be excluded from the decision-making process, by ignoring interdependencies among choices and their implications, particularly through a scalar shift of the problem. Moreover, as the politics of scale argument (Brenner 2000; Swyngedouw 1997, 2000) helps us to understand, the question of trans-scalar implications of a planning choice become particularly critical, since a scalar shift could lead to a 'scalar trap.'

It was not a shared victory that led to the unexpected unanimous consent that followed the resolution about Tor Marancia, when its status changed from a building site to a park. Landowners and real estate investors have been the only winners, and no other outcome would have been expected, given the planning preconditions, context and procedures, which became increasingly evident over the course of the action and through its results. In fact, the landscape and environmental associations lost. They say they won, because they achieved the goal of having Tor Marancia included within the *Parco dell'Appia Antica*. However, the very principles that guided their fight have been negated, and the results have been much worse than could have been expected. In fact (even if unintentionally on their part), the case of Tor Marancia contributed to determining an impressive waste of land and a reckless exploitation of the soil, so that the *Campagna Romana* has been deeply jeopardized. However, the mayor and executive were defeated; they also lost the elections that followed this story, and (according to a widely shared opinion at political and civil society level) they lost first and foremost because of the failure of their urban policy and of their choices regarding the city, expressed by urban planning. Surely the city has been the main loser, considering both its spatial and societal dimension. We can say that the problem was not 'solved,' but just moved—from a highly conflictual context, to a very broad context (many areas far away in the suburbs), where the space to exercise citizenship is more fragmented and frail, so that no immediate opposition nor conflict conditions were to be expected. Moreover, it can be said that positions that had a strong ideological content proved weaker than those characterized by well-defined but non-site-specific 'un-spatial' interests, as required by the present forms of the market. Unlike the former, who expressed a specific interest for a place, real estate interests could have been moved almost anywhere, as the public administration itself helped to do, through the mechanism of compensation; and this outcome, which the case clarifies, can be ascribed to the neoliberal variegation interpretation. Furthermore, the mechanism that has been used, relying on new planning procedures (compensations through *Accordi di Programma* in particular) while perpetuating the same elitist dynamics of power that have always been a dark side of planning, fits perfectly into the discourse of neoliberalization and its logics. Such a 'hybrid' context still represents in our view an open problem, requiring further investigation.

Notes

1. By 'planning' in the present reflection, we imply a complex of spatial public policies and planning tools (from zoning to urban design) addressed to govern and to regulate spatial transformation processes. This activity is conceived in Italy, for instance, as part of the State's goals and functions and as public-driven.

2. Antonio Cederna (1921–1996), archeologist, journalist and political activist, co-founder of Italia Nostra, spent his life studying, disseminating and fighting for the protection of Italian cultural and environmental heritage. The committee against the development of the Tor Marancia estate was named 'Comitato Cederna' in his honor.

3. "I percorsi della neoliberalizzazione a Roma: una prospettiva di analisi 'interpretive'" ("Pathways of Neoliberalism in Rome: An Interpretive Analysis"), with E. D'Albergo and G. Moini, Department of Social Sciences, La Sapienza Università di Roma.

4. In Jessop's view, globalization has to be presented more as an *explanandum* than as an *explanans*.

5. The most important and complete work on the history of Rome from this critical perspective is still that of Italo Insolera, *Roma Moderna*, whose first edition, dated 1962, has been continuously reprinted and recently updated.

6. The technical-scientific committee presented the results of different expert studies: Sovrintendenza Archeologica di Roma (Archeological Office/National Trust)—which was directed by Adriano La Regina; CNR (National Research Institute); Dipartimento di Geologia (Geological Department—University of RomaTre); and Pontificia Commissione di Archeologia Sacra (Pontifical Commission of Sacred Archeology).

7. The name of the project changed to *Parco Numisia*, cunningly alluding to its environmental value (it is intended as a park), and to its historical and archeological value (it makes reference to an ancient Roman family, the Numisi).

8. The Green Party, plus the left and the right wings within the city council.

9. Gaetano Caltagirone. The newspaper is *Il Messaggero*.

10. Compensation is a tool that allows the 'transfer' of development (building) provisions involving protected or high-value sites (from an ecological or landscape point of view) to other sites. The former landowners would be refunded for their lost ownership and building rights, and also rewarded for agreeing to move, through an increase of building rights rather than in monetary terms. This tool represents an alternative solution to that of expropriation for public utility, which consists of a cash payment to the owner of the cost of his land. The estimated cost for the expropriation of the Tor Marancia estate was €35 billion. Moreover, the restriction related to the declaration of public utility (preliminary to the expropriation) is time-limited (to five years), and owners can appeal to the court rejecting the restriction. This represents a further difficulty for public administrations, which consider time as one of the main problems planning has to face. It must be also said that case laws recognize the private right more often than the public one.

11. The first agreement was for the 'landing zone' of Grottaperfetta, the only one that remains near Tor Marancia. In quantitative terms, the increase is more than double, from $180,000\,m^3$ to $400,000\,m^3$. This building site is now at the core of a new public protest.

12. Instead, the word 'battle' has often been used (the battle for landscape and environmental protection), as well as 'problem' and 'question' (intending what the mayor and the city council had to face and to solve).

13. The plan was presented by the moderate left-wing administration as its most (or one of its most) significant political act. For about 15 years (this was the duration of the planning process), almost every day something related to its elaboration occupied newspaper pages, public debates, TV shows and radio talk shows, so that it seemed as if planning was at the core of public action, and as if planning choices, which were of public interest, were collectively and transparently taken. The website of the City of Rome was functioning perfectly and regularly updated so that, to the general public, it

seemed that one could find there whatever was needed in order to be fully informed. Public arenas were generally weakly conflictual and this was particularly true up to the definition of the master plan with its strategic choices, while conflicts emerged when strategies came up against land-use regime, regulations and ownerships. However, as we already said, the word 'conflicts' did not appear anyway. Most of the potential conflicts had been prevented and avoided, confining decision-making to élites of politicians, professionals and investors.

14. This question is well expressed by Claus Offe, when, talking about governance, he poses the question: "With whom does the 'cooperative State' cooperate and which role does the veto-power of the partners in negotiations play in the 'informal' choice of the partners themselves?" (Offe 2008: 72, our translation).

15. There is an increasing distance, and an increasing conflict, between the different temporalities of the State and the market. The economy of time imposed by the present phase of capitalism determines a growing temporal pressure in policy-making and implementation, with a turn to 'fast-policy', "which privileges those who can operate within compressed time scales, narrows the range of participants in the policy process, and limits the scope for deliberation, consultation, and negotiation"; fast-policy is "antagonistic [...] to the routines and cycles of democratic politics." Moreover, "this can significantly affect the choice of policies, the initial targets of policy, the sites where policy is implemented, and the criteria adopted to demonstrate success. It also affects whether any lessons learnt are relevant to other targets, sites, or criteria; and it discourages proper evaluation of a policy impact over different spatio-temporal horizons, including delayed and/or unintended consequences and feedback effects" (Jessop 2003: 17). One may now wonder whether there is still a chance for planning to act: surely, the changes imposed by the new temporalities of globalized neoliberalization cannot but deeply influence it (Pizzo 2010: 6).

16. Giuseppe Campos Venuti, talking about the *Piano delle Certezze* (Preliminary Plan of Certainties), said that 'planning by doing' was the pragmatic answer to the paralyses of public action, aiming to restart and to increase public interventions. He said also, talking about the Plan in 1995, that it would be not a drawing, but a 'machine' (see the special issue of *Urbanistica* dedicated to the Regulatory Plan of Rome: *Urbanistica* 2001). Giuseppe Campos Venuti was chosen as chief director of the planning staff by Francesco Rutelli. Walter Veltroni described him as the 'father' of the Regulatory Plan. He later decided to withdraw his name from it due to decisions taken during the mandate of the same Veltroni, inconsistent with his own.

References

AA.VV. (2007) *Modello Roma: l'ambigua modernità*, Rome, Italy: Odradek.

Allmendinger, P. and Tewdwr-Jones, M. (1997) "Post-Thatcherite Urban Planning and Politics: A Major Change?" *International Journal of Urban and Regional Research*, 22(1): 100–116.

Allmendinger, P. and Tewdwr-Jones, M. (2002) "The Communicative Turn in Urban Planning: Unravelling Paradigmatic, Imperialistic and Moralistic Dimensions," *Space and Polity*, 6(1): 5–24.

Booher, D. E. and Innes, J. E. (2002) "Network Power in Collaborative Planning," *Journal of Planning Education and Research*, 21(3): 221–236.

Brenner, N. (2000) "The Urban Question as a Scale Question: Reflections on Henri Lefebvre, Urban Theory and the Politics of Scale," *International Journal of Urban and Regional Research*, 24(2): 361–378.

Brenner, N. (2001) "The Limits to Scale? Methodological Reflections on Scalar Structuration," *Progress in Human Geography*, 25(4): 591–614.

Castells, M. (1972) *La question urbaine*, Paris, France: François Maspero.

Castells, M. (1978) *City, Class and Power*, Basingstoke, UK: Macmillan.

Castells, M. (1980) *The Economic Crisis and American Society*, Princeton, NJ: Princeton University Press.

Castells, M. (1983) *The City and the Grassroots: A Cross-Cultural Theory of Urban Social Movements*, Berkeley, CA: University of California Press.

Cenzatti, M. (1987) "Marxism and Planning Theory," in J. Friedmann (ed.), *Planning in the Public Domain: From Knowledge to Action*, Princeton, NJ: Princeton University Press: 437–447.

Crosta, P. L. (1998) *Politiche: quale conoscenza per l'azione territoriale*, Milan, Italy: Franco Angeli.

Crosta, P. L. (2003) "Pubblici locali: l'interattività del piano rivisitata," *Urbanistica*, 119: 20–23.

Crosta, P. L. (2006) "Interazioni: pratiche, politiche e produzione di pubblico: un percorso attraversola letteratura con attenzione al conflitto," *Critica della razionalità urbanistica*, 19: 27–52.

Crosta, P. L. (2010) *Pratiche: Il territorio "è l'uso che se ne fa,"* Milan, Italy: Franco Angeli.

Dear, M. and Scott, A. J. (eds.) (1981) *Urbanization and Urban Planning in Capitalist Society*, London, UK: Methuen.

Fischer, F. and Gottweis, H. (eds.) (2012) *The Argumentative Turn Revisited: Public Policy as Communicative Practice*, Durham, NC: Duke University Press.

Forester, J. (1987) "Planning in the Face of Conflict: Negotiation and Mediation Strategies in Local Land Use Regulation," *Journal of the American Planning Association*, 53(3): 303–314.

Forester, J. (1989) *Planning in the Face of Power*, Berkeley, CA: University of California Press.

Forester, J. (2011) "Learning from Practice in the Face of Conflict and Integrating Technical Expertise with Participatory Planning: Critical Commentaries on the Practice of Planner-Architect Laurence Sherman," *Planning Theory and Practice*, 12(2): 287–310.

Habermas, J. (1984) *The Theory of Communicative Action: Reason and the Rationalization of Society*, Vol. 1, Boston, MA: Beacon Press.

Harvey, D. (1973) *Social Justice and the City*, Baltimore, MD: Johns Hopkins University Press [revised edition, 2009, Athens, GA: The University of Georgia Press].

Harvey, D. (1985) *The Urbanization of Capital: Studies in the History and Theory of Capitalist Urbanization*, Baltimore, MD: Johns Hopkins University Press.

Harvey, D. (2005) *A Brief History of Neoliberalism*, Oxford, UK: Oxford University Press.

Healey, P. (1993) "Planning Through Debate: The Communicative Turn in Planning Theory," in F. Fischer and J. Forester (eds.), *The Argumentative Turn in Policy Analysis and Planning*, Durham, NC: Duke University Press: 233–253.

Healey, P. (1997) *Collaborative Planning: Shaping Places in Fragmented Societies*, Basingstoke, UK: Macmillan.

Hoch, C. (1994) *What Planners Do: Power, Politics and Persuasion*, Chicago, IL: Planners.

Innes, J. E. (1995) "Planning Theory's Emerging Paradigm: Communicative Action and Interactive Practice," *Journal of Planning Education and Research*, 14(3): 183–189.

Insolera, I. (1962) *Roma Moderna*, Turin, Italy: Einaudi [revised and extended edition, 2011, Turin, Italy: Einaudi].

Jessop, B. (2003) *Globalization: It's About Time Too!* Vienna, Austria: Institute for Advanced Studies, available at: www.ihs.ac.at/publications/pol/pw_85.pdf (accessed September 25, 2014).

Kaufmann, S. and Duncan, G. T. (1989) *Third Party Intervention in Managing Conflict: An Interdisciplinary Approach*, New York, NY: Praeger.

Kujala, J., Heikkinen, A. and Lehtimäki, H. (2012) "Understanding the Nature of Stakeholder Relationships: An Empirical Examination of a Conflict Situation," *Journal of Business Ethics*, 109(1): 53–65.

Lefebvre, H. (1968) *Le droit à la ville*, Paris, France: Anthropos.

Lefebvre, H. (1972) *La pensée marxiste et la ville*, Paris-Tournai, France: Casterman.

Lefebvre, H. (1974) *La production de l'espace*, Paris, France: Anthropos.

Lindblom, C. E. (1965) *The Intelligence of Democracy: Decision Making Through Mutual Adjustment*, New York, NY: The Free Press.

Maltese, C. (2007) *I padroni delle città*, Milan, Italy: Feltrinelli.

Marcucci, B. (2008) *Modello Roma, il grande bluff*, Catanzaro, Italy: Rubbettino.

Mattone, A. (2004) "Veltroni: ecco il Modello Roma," *La Repubblica*, January 13.

Mazza, L. (1996) "Funzioni e sistemi di regolazione degli usi del suolo," *Urbanistica*, 106: 104–108.

Mazza, L. (1997) *Le trasformazioni del piano*, Milan, Italy: Franco Angeli.

Mazza, L. (2004) "Piani ordinativi e piani strategici," in *Piano, progetti, strategie*, Milan, Italy: Franco Angeli: 18–28.

Mazza, L. (2005) *Dispense di Urbanistica*, Milan, Italy: Politecnico di Milano [revised edition in L. Gaeta, U. Janin Rivolin and L. Mazza (eds.) (2013), *Governo del territorio e pianificazione spaziale*, Turin, Italy: Cittàstudi].

Offe, C. (2008) "Governance: Empty Signifier oder sozialwissenschaftliches Forschungsprogramm?" in G. F. Schuppert and M. Zürn (eds.), *Governance in einer sich wandelnden Welt*, Wiesbaden, Germany: VS Verlag für Sozialwissenschaften: 61–76.

Peck, J., Theodore, N. and Brenner, N. (2009) "Neoliberal Urbanism: Models, Moments, Mutations," *SAIS Review*, 29(1): 49–66.

Pizzo, B. (2010) "Space, Time and Planning," paper delivered at the 24th AESOP Annual Conference (Track 1: Planning Theory and Methods), Helsinki, July 7–10.

Rydin, Y. (2003) *Conflict, Consensus and Rationality in Environmental Planning: An Institutional Discourse Approach*, Oxford, UK: Oxford University Press.

Sager, T. (1994) *Communicative Planning Theory*, Aldershot, UK: Avebury.

Schelling, T. C. (1960) *The Strategy of Conflict*, Cambridge, MA: Harvard University Press.

Scott, A. J. (1980) *The Urban Land Nexus and the State*, London, UK: Pion.

Susskind, L. and Cruickshank, J. (1987) *Breaking the Impasse: Consensual Approaches to Resolving Public Disputes*, New York, NY: Basic Books.

Susskind, L., McKearnan, S. and Thomas-Larmer, J. (1999) *The Consensus Building Handbook: A Comprehensive Guide to Reaching Agreement*, Thousand Oaks, CA: Sage.

Swyngedouw, E. (1997) "Neither Global nor Local: Glocalization and the Politics of Scale," in K. Cox (ed.), *Spaces of Globalization: Reasserting the Power of the Local*, New York, NY: Guilford Press: 137–166.

Swyngedouw, E. (2000) "Authoritarian Governance, Power and the Politics of Rescaling," *Environment and Planning D: Society and Space*, 18(1): 63–76.

Tewdwr-Jones, M. and Allmendinger, P. (1998) "Deconstructing Communicative Rationality: A Critique of Habermasian Collaborative Planning," *Environment and Planning A*, 30(11): 1975–1989.

Urbanistica (2001) *Il nuovo piano di Roma* (special issue): *Urbanistica*, 116.

Violante, A. and Annunziata, S. (2011) "Rome-Model: Rise and Fall of an Hybrid Neoliberal Paradigm in Southern Europe," paper delivered at RC21 Conference 'The Struggle to Belong: Dealing with Diversity in 21st Century Urban Settings,' Amsterdam, July 7–9.

Yanow, D. (2000) *Conducting Interpretive Policy Analysis*, Thousand Oaks, CA: Sage.

PART III
KNOWLEDGE, POWER AND HEGEMONY: EXPLORING THE GOVERNMENTALITY OF PLANNING CONFLICTS

Introduction

Enrico Gualini

The issue of the relationship between planning and power is anything but new and has constituted a major thread of planning theory debates for decades. It is, in many respects, an undecidable issue—or, in other terms, an issue that can only be seen as openly dialectical—in a realm of practices, like planning, that conceives of itself and of its progressive nature as a distinctive combination of critical and normative attitudes, of acting critically and performing normatively. It is, however, a defining one, in particular, as concerns the attitude of planning—and planning theory—toward urban policy conflicts.

The contributions presented in this part, as they explore planning episodes and contexts that highlight their conflictual and political dimension, take issue with the ambiguity often still inherent in an understanding of planning as a set of practices being played out 'in the face of' power and politics. Their aim is rather to explore the constitutively political dimension of planning practices. By this, they also highlight dimensions of power in planning practice that defy progressive attempts at their reduction within a deliberative 'design rationality.'

Planning is involved in the practices of production of the material and symbolic-cognitive conditions for agency that define urban citizenship, and thus is constitutively implicated in the exercise of power. Moving from this assumption, Leffers takes a critical stance toward consensus-based deliberative approaches to local politics and planning and toward the post-political drifting of a depoliticized consensus-oriented populism. Against this background, practices of conflict resolution appear as part of local 'de-radicalization' strategies and as the disciplining counterpart to the instrumentality of planning in sustaining capital accumulation strategies.

Leffers discusses these issues against the background of governmentality debates, adopting a combined Gramscian-Foucauldian analytics of power and hegemony, which highlights the similarity between a Gramscian understanding of hegemonic power and a Foucauldian conceptualization of power as the relational ability to exercise the 'conduct of conduct.' His reading accordingly highlights the ideological dimension of planning concepts and paradigms, and the role of planning as part of the "myriad strategies and technologies of government" (Chapter 6 this volume: 123) that define citizenship in relation to space.

Urban citizenship is hence the terrain of hegemonic struggles, of which planning practices and discourses are a major expression. Leffers, however, also reminds us of the need to look at these struggles dialectically. As hegemonic and counter-hegemonic practices are played out in the public domain, they continuously push the boundaries of urban citizenship. Thus, the nature of citizenship and of the urban public are defined through conflicts and their negotiation.

In this context, Leffers stresses the productive nature of conflict in the context of freedom and democratic engagement. Therefore, struggles for urban citizenship have a critical role to play in both the production and the resolution of conflict, and in turning it into a democratic resource. In his view, such struggles are played out exemplarily against the background of contradictions and tensions arising around planning, around its concepts and paradigms and their application, as their social effects highlight the dimension of power and hegemonic practices that sustain it. What is required, then, is neither a planning doctrine aimed at a routine application of deliberative and negotiating practices, nor a planning critique advocating their wholesale rejection: rather, what is required is a critical inquiry into the capacity of related practices to produce counter-hegemonic effects and to contribute to expanding the boundaries of citizenship instead of realizing effects merely instrumental to hegemony power.

Questioning relationships between planning and politics is also the starting point of Allegra and Rokem's contribution as they ask whether there can be a 'planning answer' to "systemic turbulence and entrenched political polarization" (Chapter 7 this volume: 153). In their aim to contribute to advancing our understanding of the relationship between planning, conflicts and power, they take stock of the dualism between Habermasian normative ideals of deliberative rationality and public space on the one hand, and agonistic conceptions of politics inspired by the work of the likes of Foucault and Mouffe, on the other hand. Rejoining critique of the neglect of context in deliberative approaches and practices, they direct attention to the social, political and institutional environment and to the *Realrationalität*—that is, to the contingent, non-ideal and non-normative rationality—that informs any specific planning process. Against this background, they address a theoretically oriented analysis of the conduct of planners practicing 'amidst the storm'—that is, in situations in which politics, conflict and power relations are constitutive of the planners' identity and agency rationale.

Allegra and Rokem adopt the Israeli–Palestinian conflict as an 'extreme' case for exploring these issues. The core of their contribution is an inquiry into the way the political dimension of planning is reflected in the self-perception and self-assessment of planners' roles and conduct. They explore how different cultural understandings of governing planning and policy frameworks are affected by different contextual factors that shape planners' perceptions of the planning process and of its political nature and how this, in turn, contributes to determining their agency and its outcomes. In this, differences in forms of identification are played out largely beyond normative disciplinary ideals, as a result of divergent perceptions of possibilities and constraints due to structural inequalities and the partisan nature of the planning system.

Through an analysis of the specific intersection of arguments, storylines and narratives mobilized by planners in different positions and roles—such as, in their reconstruction, 'mainstream' and 'activist' planners—the authors show how the politicization of planning issues becomes constitutive of their identity and strategies of conduct. The result of their analysis questions the usefulness of conceiving of planning and politics as distinct realms and, in particular, of unreflectively reproducing an exogenic understanding of politics' influence on planning, resulting in the assumption that "what planners really need is to 'learn to deal with politics' to develop the progressive potential that is inherent to their profession." Their suggestion is rather to direct attention to planners' agency as part and parcel of politics as a practice of puzzling and empowering, and to "focus instead on the difficult and painful reconstruction of the actual dynamics of social and political phenomena" they experience in their practice (Chapter 7 this volume: 157).

Gribat and Huxley also emphasize the role of discourses—and not only of material framework conditions—in defining the 'political' in planning. The core of their contribution is an analysis of how policy and planning paradigms, concepts and discourses perform, and with which effects, on the constitution of spatial planning issues—such as, in their case study, 'shrinkage'—as a policy problem.

Reference is made to the notion of 'problematization' as the constitution of a policy problem—i.e., the way a policy issue is discursively identified and defined as a problem. The way Gribat and Huxley treat 'problematizations' directs attention to the discursive construction of policies. While this is a classic issue of policy analysis—in particular in connection to the analysis of agenda-setting and 'policy-framing'—and similarly addressed to other interpretive approaches, such as frame analysis and narrative analysis, it is revisited here from a Foucauldian governmentality perspective. Their analysis questions the governmentality effects of policy practices related to certain problematizations, and the way they performatively affect forms of agency, rather than simply assuming them as the environment of agency. In addition, it distinctively refrains from the 'normative leap' that typically characterizes interpretive approaches as they become part of mediated deliberative practices. Rather, problematizations are seen as being defined and played out on a terrain of hegemonic struggles.

Discursive policy and planning constructs define, as the authors call it, a causal 'spatial rationality' that links spaces and subjectivities leading to functionalized problem–solution combinations. They are thus expression of a governmental rationality that is distinctively grounded in factors of cultural hegemony. Accordingly, the authors' concern is for change as a result of counter-hegemonic forms of contestation. Their seeds are identified in local socio-cultural practices and in their potential to break open the contradictions of planning problematizations. On the one hand, they discuss the potential for "thinking and acting differently" (Chapter 8 this volume: 162) that may be present even with a certain problematization, as the solution it envisions may produce unexpected or deviant effects and open up cracks within its alleged self-contained coherence. On the other hand, they highlight the importance of alternative socio-cultural practices in the 'framing' of contestations that may result in the emergence of such contradictions and, eventually, in the rise of new problematizations. Their case study shows how local culturally driven contestation may highlight the contradictions inherent in certain problematizations as they bring about the materiality of lives and the related emotional and experiential dimension of locally rooted everyday practices.

The case of Stuttgart 21, finally, is presented here as paradigmatic for the ambiguity of relationships between politics and planning in the face of conflicts. This ambiguity is explored here with reference to a peculiar moment in the contentious development of this case: the moment policy-making and planning adopt ex post a deliberative rationality as a way out of the contradictions and conflicts that are inherent to open political contention. As an epochal case, one that has significantly shaken public moods and questioned beliefs in the democratic nature of public policy in Germany, the conflict around Stuttgart 21 presents a remarkable complexity. The chapter focuses on a specific and limited aspect of this contentious planning episode—one that is, admittedly, hard to separate from the whole process, but the peculiar nature of which makes it amenable to a specific critical analysis: the conduct of a mediated negotiation process, as an attempt to 'solve' the conflict, after political contention and public outrage had reached an unexpected degree of escalation. Against a background of high and diffuse expectations for the prospects of democratization attached to it by the public, and under unprecedented public scrutiny, the experiment in mediated negotiation conducted in Stuttgart in 2010 highlights the contradictions inherent in attempts to turn an ingrained social conflict into a democratization event, and the manipulatory potential attached to this. These critical observations also realize a virtual transition to the chapters in Part IV, which present reflections for a renewal in the design and conduct of deliberative practices in planning conflicts.

6

Conflict in the Face of Planning?
Power, Knowledge and Hegemony
in Planning Practice

Donald Leffers

Introduction

Conflict in urban planning and development can be understood and theorized in many ways. Here I attempt to do so using Foucauldian theories (or 'analytics') of power and Gramscian notions of hegemony as "subtle forms of rule" (Ekers and Loftus 2008: 698). A central question in this regard is: in what way is planning implicated in the myriad strategies and technologies of government that shape how urban citizens relate to urban spaces, both discursively and materially, especially in the context of use or exchange value? I also draw on Isin's (2002) notion of 'being political' as well as various other works on the post-political (e.g., Swyngedouw 2009; Allmendinger and Haughton 2012). I use these bodies of work to interrogate how the urban public—often through conflict—exercises its citizenship, and to analyze how the negotiation with urban planning can be characterized. Here questions revolve around how and when acts are merely 'aesthetic' and serve the status quo, and when they are, more meaningfully, political acts of citizenship. This framework can and may be perceived as a direct challenge to consensus-based approaches to public participation in planning, suggesting that consensus often means little more than a depoliticized form of populism (Swyngedouw 2009). However, I find it more useful to use these literatures dialectically as a way to bring the dangers of consensus-based approaches to the fore while at the same time recognizing some of the possibilities contained within them.

Drawing on case study research conducted in Ottawa, Canada, I suggest that conflict in planning can have a specific purpose, and can be analyzed in ways that lead to productive insights for critical planning theory and practice. These insights have direct implications for analyzing what has been, is and should be the purpose of planning, and how conflict can be understood in the context of freedom and democratic engagement. Using the principle of urban intensification—a particular form of urban containment—in Ottawa as a subject of analysis, I suggest that planning, although often purported to be outside the realm of power (Forester 1982) and 'between' government and the public (Boyer 1983), is in many ways a powerful system that contributes to knowledge production around what constitutes sustainable and socially just urbanism. In this context, planning has a critical role to play in both the production and resolution of conflict. Yet exactly how conflict should be understood and dealt with is not immediately clear. Although planning has often been framed as a tool to enable and promote the smooth functioning of capital (e.g., Harvey 1978; Boyer 1983; Gunder 2010), planners also have a role to play in producing a just city, one that moves beyond capitalist space into one that emphasizes social and environmental justice and democracy.

This chapter is divided into three main sections. The first outlines case study research conducted in a 1920s-era neighborhood in Ottawa, Canada, that analyzed urban intensification policies and practices. The second draws on Gramsci and Foucault to discuss how knowledge and specific practices in planning are produced through the exercise of power. The third section discusses what it means for urban citizens to 'be political' and how this notion relates to planning.

Urban Intensification in Ottawa, Canada

Like many North American cities concerned with urban sprawl, the City of Ottawa has enacted policies intended to manage growth, often through the language of sustainability. The connection between sustainable urbanism and built form, often through discourses of smart growth and urban intensification, has been the subject of much research (e.g., Williams et al. 1996; Tregoning et al. 2002; Filion 2003; Wheeler 2003; Bunce 2004; Neuman 2005; Krueger and Gibbs 2008). In Canadian cities such as Ottawa and Toronto, the concept of urban intensification is well known and widely used in planning (Campsie 1995; Winfield 2003; Searle and Filion 2011). Urban intensification can mean a variety of things, including an increase in building density within a given area (often termed 'densification'), an increase in population within a given area, and/or an increase in economic activity in a given area (Campsie 1995; Bunce 2004). Despite often being portrayed as a progressive form of growth management and a move toward urban sustainability, intensification in practice often fuels local contestation, and in Ottawa has at times been deployed more for economic than environmental purposes (Leffers and Ballamingie 2013). Recent policies and practices rationalized through urban intensification have generated a number of tensions in Ottawa, and empirical research has suggested that most local resistance to intensification projects stems from a perceived failure in execution. However, other tensions revolve around, among other things, loss of certain types of urban space and conflicting constructions of nature. These tensions will be discussed in turn.

Failure in Execution

For many community residents interviewed as part of the case study, intensification as a policy represented highly progressive and sustainable urbanism; it was its execution that was generally framed as flawed and inappropriate, usually gauged in terms of existing neighborhood 'character' or compared with ideal principles of sustainability on which zoning and infill guidelines are based (see Leffers forthcoming for more details on the case study). A particularly illustrative example of this 'flawed' execution of intensification is the replacement of a small house with a large semi-detached building that was built to the maximum allowable buildable area of the lot. Oppositions to this development were based on its overwhelming size, its lack of 'fit' with the neighborhood and the replacement of a modest and affordable home with two large luxury homes valued at over $1 million each (compared with the average resale house price in the city of Ottawa of $367,279: City of Ottawa 2012). This development required no zoning changes as it conformed to new zoning intended to promote, among other things, increased residential density (City of Ottawa 2008). Residential zoning bylaws privilege technical specifications, such as dwelling densities and heights, and setbacks from streets and lot lines (ibid.). Despite the publicized commitment to decreased ecological footprint and increased green space in the context of urban sustainability and intensification (City of Ottawa 2007c), as well as 'community' and 'neighborhood character' (City of Ottawa 2007b), it is zoning bylaws that establish the parameters for development in practice. In this local context, broad notions of urban sustainability, smart growth, community and neighborhood character are part of the planning discourse, but in everyday planning practice these complex concepts are much reduced (Leffers 2015).

Loss of 'Space'

The second tension around the intensification discourse has to do with loss of particular types of space, often cited as being important for sustainability but also chronically undermined by urban intensification, in part because they do not fall under the purview of a capitalist market system, at least not in obvious ways. These range from so-called natural or green spaces, to things like civic and community spaces that provide various 'services' for urban residents. In the case study, conflict due to the 'inappropriate' use of or loss of space characterized each contested development. These included the redevelopment of a mainstreet commercial space, which purportedly both under-utilized and over-utilized space, albeit in different ways. This redevelopment involved the construction of a large-format commercial building on a remediated brownfield site.[1] Some community residents claimed that this redevelopment did not include *enough* development since it was built 'slab on grade' instead of on top of a below-grade parking structure, and that much of the space remained as surface parking. The building was also limited to two stories in a space zoned for four. Many other local residents and nearby small business owners, on the other hand, contested the scale and format of the building, suggesting that as a 'big box' retail building, this development undermined the small business context of a so-called 'traditional mainstreet.'[2] Conflict also arose due to the perception by some of inadequate parking provision, a perception that contradicts somewhat the assertion that traditional mainstreets should not include large amounts of parking, since the neighborhood is intended to be 'walkable' (City of Ottawa 2006). Others defended the development, stressing its status as a brownfield redevelopment that would result in a more effective use of the land than the gas station and parking lot formerly located there. This narrative characterizes space in terms of the degree to which it is developed, which is reminiscent of the smart growth discourse, especially in the context of reusing existing land resources, and providing for more business space in walkable neighborhoods. According to the smart growth narrative, 'nature' or 'environment' take on meaning based on a localized efficient use of resources (including less reliance on the personal automobile), but also based on more global processes, such as climate change and peak oil (Reeds 2010). Thus local initiatives, such as urban intensification, are given coherence through their connections with global sustainability, with the understanding that local actions and commitments influence environmental processes at a variety of scales (Robinson 2009).

Whose Nature?

A further tension around intensification has to do with how nature is construed within intensification policies and planning practice, and what other natures are overlooked as a result. Most of the conflicts mentioned so far have a central issue in common and highlight a key tension: that of the 'built' versus the 'natural' environment. In this context, the relationship between what counts as urban versus what is natural depends for the most part on whether it is considered part of the central urban area (the target for intensification) and thus not 'natural' space but 'undeveloped' space. In Ottawa, intensification policies suggest a core periphery model and perceive more central areas as spaces that *should* be developed more densely—they *should* be more built-up than spaces further from the center. The environmental narrative of urban intensification is thus quite disjoined from one that connects environmentalism with such imagined natures as urban forests, green spaces and urban parks. In the intensification discourse in Ottawa, these are not considered natural spaces but spaces of potential development and increased building density. That said, parks and green spaces do exist in central urban areas in Ottawa, although they often also fulfill utility functions (utility corridors, municipal parks, storm water runoff collectors etc.) rather than exist on their own accord.

Tensions between the built environment and nature have important implications, not only for sustainability, but also for incrementally increasing densities and continued granting of development permits seem to invite. Although planners and policy makers often downplay the value of ecosystem services or the non-market value of so-called 'urban natures,' pushback by residents living in the sites of these developments seems to highlight those very things as important. Furthermore, local biophysical consequences of development (e.g., storm water runoff problems and increased reliance on infrastructure; the urban heat island effect; pollution) are all downplayed in the compact city model of sustainability but ultimately emerge to reveal their contradictions (Melia et al. 2011).

Challenging the Coherence of Urban Intensification

However urban intensification is defined and assessed, it is not as coherent as municipal policies suggest it is. It does not simply refer to processes that are inherently more sustainable—processes that automatically lead to sustainable cities through rezoning and density targeting. Intensification is certainly not immune to misuse and cooptation. This is the very point that Bunce (2004: 188) makes when she asserts that intensification can be used to mask "straight-ahead plan[s] for economic revitalization," in effect using the discourse of sustainability to legitimate an underlying growth agenda. So what is the role of the planner when policies such as urban intensification lead to conflict, especially at local spaces of urban (re)development? How can power, knowledge and rationality be conceptualized from the perspective of planning practice within processes of capitalist urbanization?

Planning Power/Knowledge

One of the central arguments of this chapter is that planning is not outside of power but is actively implicated in its exercise and produces a particular form of knowledge. In Ottawa, intensification is usually linked to sustainability, specifically by drawing on the smart growth narrative to argue that urban form can contribute both to increased use of resources and increased sense of community (City of Ottawa 2007b). Smart growth and urban intensification are planning concepts that have become widespread in Ottawa and the rest of Canada. Yet the inherent virtues of intensification are far from self-evident. Intensification is a discourse—a particular form of knowledge that is legitimated by particular claims to truth. Production of this knowledge is not innocent but has a particular context and history within which it operates.

The Ideology of Intensification

In some ways therefore, intensification, as a relatively unquestioned proxy for urban sustainability, relies on ideological foundations that particular planning practices are inherently and universally beneficial to the common good, that any negative effects are outweighed by the positives and that those who cannot understand this simply need to be educated by experts. Gunder (2006) discusses the discursive production and dissemination of expert knowledge, suggesting that planning officials in Melbourne, Australia, used the structure and authority of the municipal planning department to 'educate' and change the behavior of the community. Gunder elaborates:

> some planners take the position that the ends justify the means and that they should have the right bestowed on them in the name of sustainability to impose their vision and the necessary behavioral changes to achieve such an outcome. (Gunder 2006: 217)

Similar to Melbourne's city planners, one Ottawa city councilor has been particularly aggressive and outspoken about the need for urban intensification, even in the face of direct opposition within his own council ward. A local newspaper reporter quotes this councilor in an explanation of how communities must be educated to understand intensification:

> the challenge to municipal leaders who want to succeed in changing the face of the city is to show people why intensification is good ... communities will work against change if they don't see the point ... we will have to lead them through an intensification phase. (Rupert 2008)

The councilor constructs community members not as intelligent and capable people who have their own needs and desires within the community, but as uninformed subjects who must be educated and led in the appropriate direction by an authoritative expert.

'Scientizing' Planning Principles

The reliance on scientific, expert knowledge legitimates discourses by giving them authority and rules in which to operate, and dismisses competing discourses as uninformed and incapable of accessing the truth. Current governance and planning in Ottawa rely on expert claims put forward and normalized by planners and politicians; reaction to these discursive norms has come from communities that are disproportionately affected by planning initiatives that these communities perceive to be harmful to themselves and to the environment. A recent contested infill project in Ottawa illustrates this tension well. During a community meeting about this project, a city planner expressed what he thought an appropriate infill would be. Neighboring residents challenged the position of the city planner, speaking of the long-term and neighborhood-altering effects and loss of green space such an infill would produce. The planner countered with arguments that as a planner, he was more capable of determining the effects and appropriateness of a particular infill development on a neighborhood than were its residents. Similarly, Finlay (2010) posits that one role of planners is to educate the public and city councilors, and to convince them of the merits of 'good planning practices,' such as urban intensification.

Toward Hegemony?

Although this is clearly not the only role of the planner, the notion of 'educating' the public suggests that opposition to the expert position, activism against 'good planning practice' or deviance from planning discipline are conditions that must be controlled and overcome. Educating the public suggests that the public do not realize what is good for them but those in élite positions of leadership can fulfill the role of providing a certain knowledge to render subjects docile and compliant. Gramsci's conceptualization of hegemony can perhaps provide a starting point for understanding how ideas are produced, and especially how dominant ideas become accepted and consented to. The rendering dominant of certain ideas can then be juxtaposed with the purported goals of conflict resolution to gain a deeper understanding of what might be the more subtle and disturbing intent of diminishing conflict in the name of order and stability.

Gramsci (1999: 145) distinguishes between social hegemony, "which the dominant group exercises through society," and direct authoritarian domination or juridical power. Social hegemony comprises two main components: consent of the population and legally enforced coercive power (ibid.). In other words, an élite group maintains domination through the 'consent of the masses,' only using coercive acts when necessary. Some components of coercion can likely be described in terms of repression, but clearly Gramsci's notion of power within social hegemony cannot be reduced to repression. Yet repression seems to be important within the coercive juridical power than serves to prohibit. In some ways, Foucault's theorization of power rejects what appears to be this negative aspect of power within Gramsci's social hegemony, although in other ways Foucault does indeed accept prohibition or repression as one possible way to exercise power if it induces subjects to act—if it can be described in terms of 'conduct of conduct.' For Foucault, repression is a difficult notion to reject conceptually, precisely because it often seems to be so evidently at work. Nevertheless he cautions that power should not be reduced to repression. As Foucault explains,

> [repression] does indeed appear to correspond so well with a whole range of phenomena that belong among the effects of power [...] [however], [i]n defining the effects of power as repression, one adopts a purely juridical conception of such power, one identifies power with a law that says no [...] [but] it also traverses and produces things, it induces pleasure, forms of knowledge, produces discourse. It needs to be considered as a productive network that runs through the whole social body. (Foucault 1994b: 119–120)

In this context, repression can indeed be implicated in the exercise of power, but repression itself is not power. Rather, power flows through the effects of that repression: the conduct that repression 'freely' produces in subjects given a range of possible choices. For Foucault, however, power is exercised not so much as repression but as 'government,' "the way in which the conduct of individuals or of groups might be directed [...] to govern in this sense is to structure the possible field of action of others" (Foucault 1994a: 341). Power as a matter of government in this sense does not preclude the possibility of violence or repression, but it certainly would not seek or use domination or violence as a matter of course. Domination and violence are only powerful if they induce subjects to act.

This differs somewhat from what some theorists, often following Gramsci, conceptualize as power or hegemony. For example, Ekers and Loftus (2008) cite theorists who differentiate 'realist' views of power (attributed to historical materialists, such as Gramsci) and more 'relational' (i.e., Foucauldian) views of power. In this context, power is held and deployed by élites who literally possess the physical and authoritative capability to control a resource, such as water, and thus the ability of people to access it. Although in this example it appears that power is something that can be held and wielded, this is not necessarily Gramscian. For Gramsci, hegemony refers to 'consent of the masses,' in every aspect of daily life, including social (e.g., division of labor) and political forces (Gramsci 1999: 145, 404–405; Ekers 2009). If control of water is an active contributing part of this consent, then power here is operating more in terms of 'conduct of conduct' than direct authoritarian control. Power is exercised in the show of ability to control a resource, and less so in the control of the resource itself. Thus in some ways, social hegemony might be understood to conflict with the Foucauldian conceptualization if it is understood primarily as domination, coercion and repression of a ruling class over its subject masses. However, in other ways, social hegemony can also be framed as productive in that it directs action—if it is actively involved in the 'conduct of conduct.'

Theorizing Power

Whether by consent, coercion or 'government' (in the Foucauldian sense), power is something that is exercised; it produces action in addition to, or separate from, forced and direct domination. It is this point I wish to highlight as crucial vis-à-vis conflict and the desire for its resolution in planning practice. An additional caution about using the concept of hegemony is that Gramsci referred to the social domination of almost all aspects of daily life: the internalization and permeation of beliefs, values, morals—in short, ideology—into the everyday such that this way of knowing becomes common sense. Or as Loftus (2009: 326) succinctly phrases it, hegemony involves "the ways in which power is both consolidated and contested within the taken-for-granted aspects of everyday life." On the one hand, therefore, it is unlikely that land-use planning principles rely on ideas permeating through all aspects of everyday life. On the other hand, however, as Harvey (1978), Dear and Scott (1981), Boyer (1983) and many others suggest, planning exists primarily to enable capitalist urbanization, or is at least a contradictory and hybrid activity, dedicated to utopian and humanistic ideals while transforming opposition in order to uphold the status quo of market logics (Knox 2008)—in essence, an extension of state power that serves to consolidate the dominant class position (Jessop 2008). One might then begin to recognize in certain fundamental principles (e.g., the fetishization of growth, the 'creative' city discourse, nature as resource, etc.) a permeation of worldviews, ideologies, 'philosophies' and so on with these discourses to which planning is closely connected.

As such, these fundamental principles also demand adherence to a normalized status quo, and it is here that we can recognize in conflict resolution a diminution of the 'radical element' in order to draw it into the mainstream: a desire to resolve conflict not by meaningful engagement with activists or 'deviants' or anyone else who disagrees, but by 'educating' them as to what appropriate urbanism (including built form) should be. Indeed Kipfer, drawing specifically on Lefebvre and his conceptualization of 'everyday life' (drawing as well on Gramsci), suggests that planners (as well as architects, developers and even academics) can act as "key agents in making the production of space hegemonic" (Kipfer 2008: 201). They do so particularly by the very practical, material, technical and 'everyday' practices that both integrate urban citizens into urban processes and 'demobilize' them at the same time (ibid.): 'integrated' through utopian promises realized through such things as idealized built form; and 'demobilized,' since these utopias are captured within normalized processes of capitalism that stimulate little resistance, in effect depoliticizing planning and development processes (Allmendinger and Haughton 2012). In the process, capitalist urbanization remains 'common sense' and unquestioned, as do those utopian notions, such as urban intensification, that claim to reconcile capitalist growth and environmental protection.

Using the example of urban intensification, conflict resolution in the context of a hegemonic (neo)liberal governmentality would not likely include or even permit a critical appraisal of intensification itself, and surely not of capitalism. Conflict resolution here would focus on convincing opponents of its merits and perhaps shifting attention to things like design details or building heights in order to make the entire notion more palatable, or at least slightly less intolerable to detractors. The ultimate goal of this neoliberal governmentality is conflict resolution, and consensus is the desired and least costly (financially and politically) means to resolve conflict (Isin and Siemiatycki 1999).

Is Conflict Constitutive of Democracy?

One can often find the notion of freedom from conflict implicit in liberal democracy, and particularly in communicative planning principles, where actors are expected to reach consensus using 'rational' dialogue and debate (Flyvbjerg and Richardson 2002). Democracy can also be framed in terms of acts of citizenship and rights (Grant 1994). Yet when it comes to planning and policy, as Grant notes, these aspects of democracy are often difficult to discern in practice, and democratic engagement seems to lead to conflict more often than consensus. Flyvbjerg and Richardson (2002), drawing on Foucault, adopt a different approach to democracy, arguing that conflict (rather than consensus) is a key component; it is conflict itself that opens up the possibility for debate, dialogue and a glimpse of freedom from domination. If social hegemony implies consent or coerced compliance to the dominant group—if this is what conflict resolution means and if this is what planning is about—then the ultimate challenge to planning and policy might be democracy itself (and vice versa).

Indeed, it often seems as if the purported need to avoid complexity and conflict—the large time and effort required to resolve issues, 'hostile' public reaction, increased political pressure to appease diverse interests, in short the messiness of democracy—seems to be a key motivation for the mobilization of élite groups and the 'need' for authoritative bodies to keep the development ball rolling to ensure that the growth machine progresses. Seen in this light, liberalism and planning in the (neo)liberal, capitalist city is very undemocratic indeed. What are the implications, therefore, for democratic urban citizenship, and how can planning contribute to democracy rather than domination?

Is Public Consultation Being 'Properly' Political?

In many ways, the city can be described as one of the key sites for active citizen engagement. As Sassen (1996), Isin (2007) and others assert, the city is one of the localized places where citizenship happens. One of the purported connections between urban citizenship and the governing of the city is through public involvement in planning. Yet a growing concern surrounds the way in which the planning arena is 'properly political' (Swyngedouw 2009), especially when neoliberal ideologies within planning emphasize economic competitiveness and markets rather than direct concern for the public good or the environment (Fainstein 1991). Perhaps public consultation is simply a "technology of government" (Rose 1999: 52), a carefully staged and choreo-graphed performance of democracy—what Rancière (2004; see also Nash 1996), Swyngedouw (2007, 2009), Allmendinger and Haughton (2012) and others call a post-political or post-democratic condition—designed to lead to specific desired endpoints, while minimizing the potential for undesirable alternatives. Furthermore, as Grant (1994) notes, public participation tends to favor those with connections, expertise or resources:

> Well financed interests can participate effectively and see that decision makers address their concerns […] citizens without resources often grow cynical and frustrated in the face of their inability to influence outcomes. Participation is a luxury for citizens in modern industrial societies. It requires skill (e.g., in public speaking), resources (e.g., for child care), money (e.g., for legal advice), and time. Can we legitimately speak of democratic participation when so few citizens can take advantage of the opportunities provided? (Grant 1994: 205–206)

Valverde (2012) makes a similar point, arguing that the segment of the population that is given a voice in planning disputes rarely includes those who most need to be heard.

Claims by dominant groups to represent the city are always problematic and contested, but they are also normalized and institutionalized using political technologies and economic rationalization that serve to create images of unity. Isin and Siemiatycki (1999) suggest that planning, particularly land-use planning, favors corporate developer interests at the expense of the needs of urban residents, while at the same time it tries to maintain the status quo—an image of unity—so as not to disrupt the majority of tax-paying voters. Conceptualizing the city as a 'unified order' is, according to Isin (2002: 281), "a solidaristic and agonistic strategy that enable[s] dominant segments of dominant groups to constitute themselves as virtuous, righteous, and moral agents, justified in inculcating their vision of the city in other groups." As this vision becomes more and more normalized and the dominant ideology reframed as common sense, one can recognize a move toward social hegemony as conceptualized by Gramsci. In this context, Grant (1994: 5) sees planning as a normalizing tactic: a "cultural apparatus for dealing with conflict and social control." Since politics, as Magnusson (2011) states, is a source of conflict, disorder, complexity and uncertainty, planning as an exercise in resolution of these factors works to produce a consensual condition geared toward subverting politics.

In many ways, current urban planning in Ottawa creates unity by removing the public from the process or by regulating public participation. Although public participation pervades planning, including planning in Ottawa, Grant argues that the very institutionalization of public participation has made citizen involvement much less radical and less meaningful, in essence a post-political condition: "by institutionalizing public meetings and citizen committees, governments incorporated or dissipated potentially disruptive forces. Planners and politicians acknowledge the need to allow citizens a role in community decision making, but citizens often find their role frustratingly ineffective" (Grant 1994: 13). This frustration is fueled at least somewhat by the highly regulated channels through which the public are 'permitted' to have their voices heard (see, for example City of Ottawa 2010, which outlines the highly regulated procedures around public participation).

According to Gunder (2010), planning is centered on an ideology that defines the use of urban space within the dominant order of neoliberalism, depoliticizing resistance in the process through its incorporation within formalized procedures. Resistance here includes the desire to participate in planning, since public participation usually only occurs when citizens feel compelled to contest particular planning decisions. Gunder (2010) here draws to some extent on Gramscian notions of hegemony that theorize how values and beliefs become dominant in society, conceptualized as "serving the preservation of the existing order" (Gunder 2010: 300). As already discussed above, similar to this framework of 'neoliberal ideologies' as a dominant order,

I found discursive constructions of urban intensification to be deeply entrenched in Ottawa in political policies, in planning 'best practices' and in the values of individual residents. Thus, public consultations around intensification projects did not begin with criticisms of or opposition to intensification. Intensification was already firmly entrenched within the dominant discourse as a way to create sustainable urbanism and reduce sprawl; public consultations were centered on how to carry out intensification most appropriately, not whether to carry it out. Thus, even though specific intensification initiatives were being contested, many residents nevertheless claimed to support intensification in principle, and deemed as logical and rational the notion that the city should strive for a particular built form. According to Rose (2001: 156), based on the work of Foucault, "part of the power of a specific discursive formation may rest precisely on the multiplicity of different arguments that can be produced in its terms." The 'expert' knowledge of planners and policy makers is surely an important factor in legitimizing this particular discourse, rendering it dominant and stable.

According to Purcell (2009: 141), "neoliberalization has had a corrosive impact on cities and urban life, and democratic movements are a particularly promising way we might resist it." If this is the case, then democratic movements must question and resist the very 'doctrines' of neoliberalism, including those that promise a brighter future through a more competitive economy. According to Rankin (2009: 221) such neoliberal futures are epitomized by 'green capitalism' that promises sustainability without disrupting the flow of corporate capital, as well as "'creative city' ideologies that constitute the latest version of supply-side inducements to global capital." These are ecomodernist futures that rely on the market and scientific management to solve the problem of environmental degradation for future generations (Hajer 1995), but that are really "fantas[ies] of socioecological cohesion" (Cook and Swyngedouw 2012) where social and environmental costs are recast as win-win opportunities for society, markets and the environment (Escobar 1996; Harvey 1996). What might an alternative future look like?

Toward a More Political Urban Planning: Some Conclusions

A number of authors propose theoretical avenues to shift planning practice away from modernist technologies of governance, toward a more democratic and socially just ethics of planning and governance. According to Holston (1999), urban planning for the most part excludes 'the social,' resorting to governance strategies that privilege aesthetics and consumption. A focus on consumption is also manifested by the primary concern of the state with its budget rather than the welfare of its citizens (Isin and Wood 1999). Other planning theorists have made recent contributions to the literature around public participation in planning, albeit from very different theoretical positions. Examples of such literature include: updated versions of communicative planning (e.g., Hillier 1998; Healey 2007, 2012); a 'three-dimensional view' of planning that focuses on the power and ideologies of participatory stakeholders (Aitken 2010); and Ananya Roy's (2008) 'postliberal' ethics of planning. As this is not the place for an in-depth critique of the various approaches to theorizing public participation in planning, I will conclude this chapter with some thoughts about the role of conflict in planning.

Planning need not always be resistant to conflict, as something that necessarily needs to be 'resolved.' Neither does power need to be conceptualized simply as domination—as 'power over.' It is here that Foucault can provide a politics of hope and possibility, despite the association of Foucault with the 'dark side' of planning theory. It is also within the space of counter-hegemonic discourse that Isin (2002) suggests one can be political not by aesthetic and superficial engagement but by meaningful questioning of dominant narratives around who is included and who is excluded from the possibility of urban citizenship. In this context, Foucauldian theories of planning are 'dark' only if one relies upon arguments that meaningful engagement can only occur 'outside of power.' Reframing power as "an interplay of enabling capabilities and constraining powers" (Rabinow and Rose 2003: 12) opens up power to something beyond authoritative domination. However, it also suggests increased engagement, less certainty about who exercises power and how it is manifested, and perhaps more conflict as subjects resist domination through activism, dialogue, everyday practices and even active political engagement.

The Ottawa planner mentioned above, who expressed indignation at having his credentials questioned, in other ways shows himself to be a very progressive planner who communicates often with residents and spends a great deal of time participating in community meetings. In this way, power is operating in a different way than when he makes claims to a certain superior expertise and (apolitical) scientific rationality, all geared to minimizing opposition within a liberal 'democracy.' Community meetings and public consultations can be quite conflictual (and political) settings. Yet participating in this type of scenario, if done in a meaningful way that actually responds to resident concerns, no matter how much they conflict with established norms and dominant ideologies, is one way of negotiating conflict. It is not dismissing conflict—it is not 'educating' the public or coercing them into something that conflicts with their values, morals, beliefs, knowledge and so on. Or at least it does not have to be. This planner also responds quite diligently to inquiries from urban residents, writes extensively in online blogs and magazines, and seems genuinely engaged with the concerns of a wide variety of social actors. Of course, this may simply be part of a politics geared toward 'consent of the masses.' But not necessarily. This type of planning practice also likely falls outside the purview of 'rational planning,' especially when debates do not reach a happy consensus but drag on and on through conflict-ridden processes of community meetings and public consultations. People may even hold grudges and plans may die on the table. Yet one could argue that this messy engagement with the urban populus is much more in keeping with freedom and democracy than carefully calculated procedures and public consultations and perhaps in this lies the hope for a more just planning practice.

Notes

1. The City of Ottawa defines brownfields as "abandoned, vacant, or underutilized commercial and industrial properties where past actions have resulted in actual or perceived environmental contamination and/or derelict or deteriorated buildings" (City of Ottawa 2007a: 3).
2. According to the City of Ottawa (2006), a mainstreet is 'traditional' if the community through which it runs was developed primarily prior to 1945. These streets tend to have small-scale mixed-use buildings set close to the street, resulting in "a lively mix of uses and a pedestrian-friendly environment" (ibid.: 1).

References

Aitken, M. (2010) "A Three-Dimensional View of Public Participation in Scottish Land-Use Planning: Empowerment or Social Control?" *Planning Theory*, 9(3): 248–264.

Allmendinger, P. and Haughton, G. (2012) "Post-Political Spatial Planning in England: A Crisis of Consensus?" *Transactions of the Institute of British Geographers*, 37(1): 89–103.

Boyer, C. M. (1983) *Dreaming the Rational City: The Myth of American City Planning*, Cambridge, MA: MIT Press.

Bunce, S. (2004) "The Emergence of 'Smart Growth' Intensification in Toronto: Environment and Economy in the New Official Plan," *Local Environment*, 9(2): 177–191.

Campsie, P. (1995) *The Social Consequences of Planning Talk: A Case Study in Urban Intensification*, Toronto, Canada: University of Toronto Centre for Urban and Community Studies.

City of Ottawa (2006) *Urban Design Guidelines for Development along Traditional Mainstreets*, Ottawa, Canada: City of Ottawa Planning and Growth Management Department.

City of Ottawa (2007a) *Brownfield Redevelopment Community Improvement Plan*, Ottawa, Canada: City of Ottawa, available at: www.ottawa.ca/residents/planning/brownfields/images/cip_2007_en.pdf (accessed May 30, 2012).

City of Ottawa (2007b) *City of Ottawa Official Plan: Consolidation (Vol. 1)*, Ottawa, Canada: City of Ottawa.

City of Ottawa (2007c) *Getting Greener: On the Path of Sustainability*, Ottawa, Canada: City of Ottawa.

City of Ottawa (2008) *Zoning By-Law 2008-250 Consolidation*, Ottawa, Canada: City of Ottawa.

City of Ottawa (2010) "Public Consultations," available at: www.ottawa.ca/residents/public_consult/index_en.html (accessed December 1, 2010).

City of Ottawa (2012) *2011 Annual Development Report*, Ottawa, Canada: City of Ottawa, Planning and Growth Management Research and Forecasting Unit.

Cook, I. and Swyngedouw, E. (2012) "Cities, Social Cohesion and the Environment: Towards a Future Research Agenda," *Urban Studies*, 49(9): 1959–1979.

Dear, M. and Scott, A. J. (eds.) (1981) *Urbanization and Urban Planning in Capitalist Society*, London, UK: Methuen.

Ekers, M. (2009) "The Political Ecology of Hegemony in Depression-Era British Columbia, Canada: Masculinities, Work and the Production of the Forestscape," *Geoforum*, 40(3): 303–315.

Ekers, M. and Loftus, A. (2008) "The Power of Water: Developing Dialogues Between Foucault and Gramsci," *Environment and Planning D*, 26(4): 698–718.

Escobar, A. (1996) "Constructing Nature: Elements for a Poststructural Political Ecology," in R. Peet and M. Watts (eds.), *Liberation Ecologies: Environment, Development, Social Movements*, London, UK: Routledge: 46–68.

Fainstein, S. S. (1991) "Promoting Economic Development: Urban Planning in the United States and Great Britain," *Journal of the American Planning Association*, 57(1): 22–33.

Filion, P. (2003) "Towards Smart Growth? The Difficult Implementation of Alternatives to Urban Dispersion," *Canadian Journal of Urban Research*, 12(1): 48–70.

Finlay, B. (2010) *The Planning and Growth Management Department: Where Do We Fit In? Planning Primer Session I*, April 10, Ottawa, Canada: City of Ottawa Planning and Growth Management Department.

Flyvbjerg, B. and Richardson, T. (2002) "Planning and Foucault: In Search of the Dark Side of Planning Theory," in P. Allmendinger and M. Tewdwr-Jones (eds.), *Planning Futures: New Directions for Planning Theory*, London, UK: Routledge: 44–62.

Forester, J. (1982) "Planning in the Face of Power," *Journal of the American Planning Association*, 48(1): 67–80.

Foucault, M. (1994a) "The Subject and Power," in J. D. Faubion (ed.), *Power*, New York, NY: The New Press: 326–348.

Foucault, M. (1994b) "Truth and Power," in J. D. Faubion (ed.), *Power*, New York, NY: The New Press: 111–133.

Gramsci, A. (1999) *Selections from the Prison Notebooks* [e-book], London, UK: ElecBook, available at: www.elecbook.com (accessed September 6, 2011).

Grant, J. (1994) *The Drama of Democracy: Contention and Dispute in Community Planning*, Toronto, Canada: University of Toronto Press.

Gunder, M. (2006) "Sustainability: Planning's Saving Grace or Road to Perdition?" *Journal of Planning Education and Research*, 26(2): 208–221.

Gunder, M. (2010) "Planning as the Ideology of (Neoliberal) Space," *Planning Theory*, 9(4): 298–314.

Hajer, M. A. (1995) *The Politics of Environmental Discourse: Ecological Modernization and the Policy Process*, Oxford, UK: Clarendon Press.

Harvey, D. (1978) "On Planning the Ideology of Planning," in R. Burchell and G. Sternlieb (eds.), *Planning Theory in the 1980s*, New Brunswick, NJ: Center for Urban Policy Research: 213–233.

Harvey, D. (1996) *Justice, Nature and the Geography of Difference*, Oxford, UK: Blackwell.

Healey, P. (2007) *Urban Complexity and Spatial Strategies: Towards a Relational Planning for Our Times*, London, UK: Routledge.

Healey, P. (2012) "Communicative Planning: Practices, Concepts and Rhetorics," in B. Sanyal, L. Vale and C. Rosan (eds.), *Planning Ideas that Matter: Livability, Territoriality, Governance, and Reflective Practice*, Cambridge, MA: MIT Press: 333–358.

Hillier J. (1998) "Beyond Confused Noise: Ideas Towards Communicative Procedural Justice,' *Journal of Planning Education and Research*, 18(1): 14–24.

Holston, J. (1999) "Spaces of Insurgent Citizenship," in J. Holston (ed.), *Cities and Citizenship*, Durham, NC: Duke University Press: 155–173.

Isin, E. (2002) *Being Political: Genealogies of Citizenship*, Minneapolis, MN: University of Minnesota Press.

Isin, E. (2007) "City.State: Critique of Scalar Thought," *Citizenship Studies*, 11(2): 211–228.

Isin, E. and Siemiatycki, M. (1999) *Fate and Faith: Claiming Urban Citizenship in Immigrant Toronto*, CERIS, Working Paper Number 8.

Isin, E. and Wood, P. (1999) *Citizenship and Identity*, London, UK: Sage.

Jessop, R. (2008) *State Power: A Strategic-Relational Approach*, Cambridge, UK: Polity.

Kipfer, S. (2008) "How Lefebvre Urbanized Gramsci," in K. Goonewardena, S. Kipfer, R. Milgrom and C. Schmid (eds.), *Space, Difference, Everyday Life: Reading Henri Lefebvre*, London, UK: Routledge: 193–211.

Knox, P. (2008) *Metroburbia, USA*, New Brunswick, NJ: Rutgers University Press.

Krueger, R. and Gibbs, D. (2008) " 'Third Wave' Sustainability? Smart Growth and Regional Development in the USA," *Regional Studies*, 42(9): 1263–1274.

Leffers, D. (2015) "Urban Sustainability as a 'Boundary Object': Interrogating Discourses of Urban Intensification in Ottawa, Canada," in C. Isenhour, G. McDonogh and M. Checker (eds.), *Sustainability as Myth and Practice in the Global City*, Cambridge, UK: Cambridge University Press.

Leffers, D. and Ballamingie, P. (2013) "Governmentality, Environmental Subjectivity, and Urban Intensification," *Local Environment*, 18(2): 134–151.

Loftus, A. (2009) "Intervening in the Environment of the Everyday," *Geoforum*, 40(3): 326–334.

Magnusson, W. (2011) *Politics of Urbanism: Seeing Like a City*, London, UK: Routledge.

Melia, S., Parkhurst, G. and Barton, H. (2011) "The Paradox of Intensification," *Transport Policy*, 18(1): 46–52.

Nash, K. (1996) "Post-Democracy, Politics and Philosophy: An Interview with Jacques Rancière," *Angelaki*, 1(3): 171–178.

Neuman, M. (2005) "The Compact City Fallacy," *Journal of Planning Education and Research*, 25(1): 11–26.

Purcell, M. (2009) "Resisting Neoliberalization: Communicative Planning or Counter-Hegemonic Movements?" *Planning Theory*, 8(2): 140–165.

Rabinow, P. and Rose, N. (eds.) (2003) *The Essential Foucault: Selections from Essential Works of Foucault, 1954–1984*, New York, NY: The New Press.

Rancière, J. (2004) "Introducing Disagreement 1," *Angelaki*, 9(3): 3–9.

Rankin, K. (2009) "Critical Development Studies and the Praxis of Planning," *City*, 13(2/3): 219–229.

Reeds, J. (2010) *Smart Growth: From Sprawl to Sustainability*, White River, VT: Chelsea Green.

Robinson, P. (2009) "Urban Sustainability in Canada: The Global–Local Connection," in C. Gore and P. Stott (eds.), *Environmental Challenges and Opportunities: Local–Global Perspectives on Canadian Issues*, Toronto, Canada: EMP: 159–181.

Rose, G. (2001) *Visual Methodologies*, London, UK: Sage.

Rose, N. (1999) *Powers of Freedom: Reframing Political Thought*, Cambridge, UK: Cambridge University Press.

Roy, A. (2008) "Post-Liberalism: On the Ethico-Politics of Planning," *Planning Theory*, 7(1): 92–102.

Rupert, J. (2008) "City, Neighbourhood at Odds Over Apartment: Intensification on Trial in Fight Over Tower on Industrial," *The Ottawa Citizen*, available at: www.peterhume. ca/OttCit-340Industrial.pdf (accessed April 30, 2010).

Sassen, S. (1996) "Whose City Is It? Globalization and the Formation of New Claims," *Public Culture*, 8(2): 205–223.

Searle, G. and Filion, P. (2011) "Planning Context and Urban Intensification Outcomes: Sydney Versus Toronto," *Urban Studies*, 48(7): 1419–1438.

Swyngedouw, E. (2007) "Impossible 'Sustainability' and the Post-Political Condition," in R. Krueger and D. Gibbs (eds.), *The Sustainable Development Paradox: Urban Political Economy in the United States and Europe*, New York, NY: Guilford Press: 13–40.

Swyngedouw, E. (2009) "The Antinomies of the Postpolitical City: In Search of a Democratic Politics of Environmental Production," *International Journal of Urban and Regional Research*, 33(3): 601–620.

Tregoning, H., Agyeman, J. and Shenot, C. (2002) "Sprawl, Smart Growth, and Sustainability," *Local Environment*, 7(4): 341–347.

Valverde, M. (2012) *Everyday Law on the Street: City Governance in an Age of Diversity*, Chicago, IL: University of Chicago Press.

Wheeler, S. (2003) "The Evolution of Urban Form in Portland and Toronto: Implications for Sustainability Planning," *Local Environment*, 8(3): 317–336.

Williams, K., Burton, E. and Jenks, M. (1996) "Achieving the Compact City Through Intensification: An Acceptable Option?" in M. Jenks, E. Burton and K. Williams (eds.), *The Compact City: A Sustainable Urban Form?* London, UK: E&FN Spon: 83–96.

Winfield, M. (2003) *Smart Growth in Ontario: The Promise vs. Provincial Performance*, Drayton Valley, Canada: Pembina Institute.

7

Planners Amid the Storm: Planning and Politics in the Contested Metropolitan Area of Jerusalem

Marco Allegra and Jonathan Rokem

Introduction

This chapter delves into the contentious nature of the planning process in the metropolitan area of Jerusalem by examining the role played by planners; it investigates the complex and nuanced relation between planners and conflict by observing how contextual factors shape the planning process and determine its outcomes, and how planning is embedded in the surrounding society.

As far as the relation between planning and politics is concerned, Jerusalem represents a rather exceptional case study because of the partisan urban policies developed by Israel after the reunification of the city in 1967. Still, we maintain that the observation of such an exceptional case study can be useful in advancing our understanding of the relation between planning, conflicts and power.

Our work is based on the examination of a variety of primary and secondary sources, including a number of in-depth interviews with Israeli planners conducted in 2010. The use of these sources—along with our academic and professional background—allows us to present a firsthand account of planners' self-perceptions, discourses and practices in the Jerusalem region.

Planning in the Face of Power

Since the pathbreaking contribution by John Forester (1982, 1989), the relation between planning and politics has been one of the major themes of inquiry and discussion among planning theorists. The background of this chapter is therefore the ongoing debate on planning theory and practice, and its relation to issues of power, conflict and collective identities. As far as the theoretical foundations of planning are concerned, this debate can be imagined as contained between two opposed philosophical outlooks represented by Jurgen Habermas's ideal of deliberative rationality and public space (1979, 1983, 1987, 1990) and the more power-oriented, agonistic conceptions of politics inspired by the work of Michel Foucault (1979) and Chantal Mouffe (1993, 1999, 2000, 2005).

Drawing on Habermas's work, a large and diverse stream of literature—commonly referred to as 'communicative' or 'collaborative' planning—has been developed (Forester 1989, 1999; Innes 1995; Healey 1992, 1996, 1997). This 'communicative turn' in planning theory emphasized the role of debate among the stakeholders as an appropriate practice of deliberation, as well as its potential in reducing conflict among them through appropriate discursive practices. The success of the communicative turn in reframing planning theory and practices prompted a wave of criticism from scholars who deemed that communicative theorists placed too much emphasis on inclusive arenas of deliberation and communicative practices. Communicative theorists, the critique goes, devote little attention to the social and political context where deliberation—and ultimately planning—takes place (Yiftachel 1998, 1999; Yiftachel and Huxley 2000; Flyvbjerg and Richardson 2002).

It is not our intention to elaborate "a pragmatic and progressive planning role for all those planning in the face of power" (Forester 1982: 67), or to provide a 'test' of communicative theories by using the case of Jerusalem—for a similar effort in the deeply polarized context of Northern Ireland, see Brand and Gaffikin (2007). Indeed, in few other cities in the world would the partisan asymmetry of planning—as well as the absence of either 'soft' or 'hard institutions' (Healey 1997) to promote 'conversation between groups' and a fair representation of all stakeholders in the public arena—be more evident than in post-1967 Jerusalem. As Sandercock (2000: 29) notes, "a political space had to be created for this approach [communicative planning] through political action" before actually implementing the good planning practices described by communicative theorists. Still, the debate provides us with a valid theoretical starting point and with methodological suggestions. In turn, we maintain that the observation of such politicized, contentious urban development processes can advance our understanding of the role of planning in different kinds of conflict situations by exploring its embeddedness in the surrounding social, political and institutional environment (Yiftachel 1998) and its *Realrationalität* (Flyvbjerg 1996)—the contingent, non-ideal and non-normative rationality informing any specific planning process.

In this respect, we argue that Jerusalem represents at the same time what Bent Flyvbjerg (2006) defines as an *extreme* and a *critical* case. It is an extreme case—a case that makes a point in "an especially dramatic way" (Flyvbjerg 2006: 229)—with respect to fundamental issues at the center of the debate on communicative planning (e.g., the dynamics of the inclusion/exclusion of stakeholders, the retreat into professional space in the face of power and the ambiguous nature of the notion of 'good planning practices,' etc.). More subtly, Jerusalem represents a critical case as it has a "strategic importance in relation to the general problem" (ibid.), namely the issue of planners' agency; in other words, observing planners' autonomous agency in Jerusalem—where, as the rhetoric goes, 'everything is politics,' and planning policy is dictated by political imperatives—implicitly strengthens the argument for understanding the relation between planning and politics in a non-linear, non-hierarchical fashion.

This chapter delves therefore into issues such as: the planners' assessments of the interplay between planning and politics; their perceptions of their own professional roles in the polarized environment of Jerusalem; and the interaction of professional and political arguments in shaping the planning process. In doing so, we aim to explore the role of planners in conflict situations, and their delicate role in framing the perspectives of coexistence in the city. Our goal is therefore twofold: on the one hand, we aim to go beyond the definition of ethical, professional and normative ideals of 'good' planning practices; on the other hand, we aim to escape the reductionist image of planners as one-dimensional agents of unprofessional or altogether unethical political interests—a recurrent theme in politically polarized environments such as Jerusalem.

Planners Amid the Storm

It has been suggested that cities in general are undergoing "a radical restructuring in geographical distribution of human activity and in the political-economic dynamics of uneven geographical development" (Harvey 2001: 346). As a result, the diversity of cities and their residents' different identities have become a central topic of concern for planning policy and practice, and for urban theory in general (Fincher and Jacobs 1998: 1; Fincher and Iveson 2008: 2). In any planning process there is an interaction of professional and political arguments shaping the planning outcome and the delicate role of planners in framing the perspectives of coexistence in the city. In few cities is the planning–politics nexus more evident than in Jerusalem, to the point that a vast number of contributions portray the city as a case where one of the cardinal functions of planning—the mediation between the State and competing societal interest—is severely undermined by the structural exclusion of the Palestinian community from the planning process itself, and more broadly from decision-making arenas. The unavoidable starting point of our exploration of planners in Jerusalem is the realization of the deep, entrenched politicization of planning in the city, as well as the partisan nature of the latter; paraphrasing Carl von Clausewitz, Anthony Coon said that, if "[w]ar has been described as politics carried out by other means[,] in the West Bank [including conquered East Jerusalem] planning is war carried out by other means" (Coon 1992: 210).

At the same time, Jerusalem represents a case of "planning in turbulence" (Morley and Shachar 1986: 3), where the professionals involved in planning have to cope with radical, and to a certain extent unpredictable, changes, with problems that are well beyond the field of intervention of planning itself—however broadly we define it—and with a diffused social perception of crisis, anxiety and imminent disaster. While these conditions determine a situation where the lack of a 'planning doctrine' is manifest, "what is evident, however, is a strong sense of purpose [...] behind developments in East Jerusalem," namely, "[t]he widely, if not unanimously shared political goal [of] the permanent unification of Jerusalem under Israeli rule" (Faludi 1997: 98). In the immediate aftermath of the Six-Day War, crucial decisions regarding land use, housing and infrastructure were taken directly by the highest ranking policy makers of the Israeli government. Those decisions "aimed [...] at minimizing uncertainty":

> This strategy called for the creation of facts that would constrain possibilities, limit options, or even close certain options for the city in the future. To be specific, the option that had to be closed was the redivision of the city, and closing it was not only conceived as an action taken against external bodies but also by the government itself. (Schweid 1986: 112)

This outlook determined some fundamental planning choices—such as the choice of a 'dispersed' model of urban development over a 'compact' city (Schweid 1986; Faludi 1997)—and resulted in a marked gap between communities in terms of housing, services provisions and infrastructure investment. In this sense, "the Israeli 'place' is a product of a contested socio-historical process, characterized by motivation for controlling national space and framing it in a total manner. Such a decisive approach generates counter-products which are also spatially expressed" (Yacobi 2004: 7).

Indeed, in this chapter we try instead to delve into the complex and nuanced relation between planners and conflict by observing how different contextual factors shape planners' perceptions of the planning process and determine its outcomes. In order to do so, we interviewed both planners working in administrative offices and bodies—such as the Ministry of Housing and the Civil Administration, the military agency administering the West Bank, but also the Jerusalem Institute for Israeli Studies (JIIS), the independent research center that publishes for example the authoritative *Statistical Yearbook* of the city—and planners working in NGOs—such as Bimkom, Peace Now, BTselem,

Ir Amim and others—explicitly committed to the achievement of a just Israeli–Palestinian peace, democracy and human rights.

We refer to these two categories as 'mainstream' and 'activist' planners. This distinction is, in the first place, a pragmatic starting point to refer to the different professional affiliation of the respondents, and the different institutional roles they have in the planning process. More generally, "norms of the governing culture are usually embedded in institutional frameworks of planning and policy expressing the values of the ethnically prevailing majority" (Sandercock 2000: 15), or as Maarten Hajer put it, in 'story-lines,' which he defines as

> exclusionary systems because they only authorize certain people to participate in them [...]. [S]tory-lines are narratives on social reality through which elements from many different domains are combined providing actors with a set of symbolic references that suggest a common understanding. (Hajer 1997: 49)

In this respect, the distinction also points to different narratives about planning developed by the two groups. In Jerusalem, 'mainstream' planners tend to represent the official Israeli planning discourse, or 'story-line,' about planning in the city and to regard their activity as determined by adherence to a set of (neutral) professional practices. On the other hand, the activity of 'activist' planners can be conceptualized through the model expressed by the notion of 'insurgent planning' (Sandercock 1998), to the extent that 'activists' not only tend to challenge the conventional wisdom of 'mainstream' planners about Israeli planning in Jerusalem and operate outside the formal institutions of the planning system, but also emphasize the socio-political and ultimately controversial nature of planning practices themselves.

It is important to stress, however, that even in the polarized environment of Jerusalem multiple overlaps exist between these two categories. 'Mainstream' planners become 'activists' and stern critics of policies they themselves have contributed to implementing; 'activist' planners work in West Jerusalem with the same municipal officers whose policies in East Jerusalem they criticize. Different degrees of endorsement and criticism toward Israeli official policies— as well as political positions in general—are voiced by individuals and organizations.

Planners in the Face of Power

How do planners see the interplay between planning and politics with respect to major urban development issues in the metropolitan area? As John Forester notes, "[i]f planners ignore those in power, they assure their own powerlessness" (Forester 1982: 67). To begin with, the community of planners in Jerusalem is deeply aware of power issues and the politicization of planning; still, this consciousness seems to have provided little relief or guidance to planners themselves.

As a whole, the planners working in the Israeli administration—whom we call 'mainstream' planners—are almost unanimous in regretting the absence of what Faludi calls a 'planning doctrine.' As a senior municipal planner remarks, the political choice to opt for a dispersed urban model was "imposed on the planners to handle," and

[i]f it was left to the planners, they probably would not decide to [put] in the south Gilo [a Jewish settlement included in the municipal boundaries] somewhere ... But to grow gradually, step by step toward that ... The major decisions are political decisions and the planners have to cope with it. (I. Kimhi, interview)

In the same vein, a senior city planner of the Jewish settlement of Ma'ale Adummim comments:

I think that Jerusalem lacks a lot in planning: it does not have a general view. After 1967, the Ministry of Housing and the government tried to achieve certain political goals in Jerusalem […]. I don't think that there was a really [much thought] about […] how this town will function, if it's good to put these neighborhoods as an addition to the small and very weak city of Jerusalem. (G. Brandeis, interview)

The deteriorated situation of housing in Jerusalem is another of the recurrent concerns of 'mainstream' planners. On the one hand, as a planner in the JIIS observes, noting the "conflict between urban goals and government goals:"

every time a developer wants to develop something in the city center […] they would tell him to develop residences there [for the Jewish population]. Why? Because they want to keep the demographic balance. Residences, residences, residences ... and then the city center is not functioning, or it's much less functional than it used to be because every time they develop residences instead of services, arts, museums, employment, as it should be. (A. Shapira, interview)

On the other hand, many 'mainstream' planners point out the interference of international political pressures in restricting access to the housing reserves available (for the growth of Jewish population) in the settlements located in the West Bank:

> [t]here's a growing demand for housing in Jerusalem, it can't all be met in West Jerusalem, some of it has to be met in the neighborhoods around Jerusalem [...]. And the non-building of Ma'ale Adummim [and] Beitar [two Jewish settlements built after 1967 in the periphery of the city, whose expansion plans had been frozen by the Israeli government], because of the political issues, has basically brought about the fact that the youngsters of Jerusalem have nowhere to go. (B. Weil, interview)

Most 'mainstream' planners tend to interpret these political obstacles on the road to good, rational planning in terms of a burden imposed by the conflict as a whole on the metropolitan area. 'Politics' is therefore often depicted as hostile to the creation of a positive atmosphere for planning discussion. As a senior planner in the Ministry of Housing notes in explaining the shelving of the 1994 Metropolitan Plan, "[i]t's hard to implement an idea when you have bombs in the buses" (Z. Efrati, interview); others point out that the development of a professionally balanced scheme created conflicts with the political process by setting preconditions to the negotiations (R. Khamaisi, interview; a similar view about the 1994 Metropolitan plan is put forward by Adam Mazor, see Bollens 2000: 153–154). Similarly, the chaotic residential sprawl in Jerusalem is interpreted as the result of the competition for land resources, and not of Israeli policies. When asked about the effect of the Israeli policy of 'facts on the ground' and the encroachment of Jewish settlements into Palestinian areas, a former city planner and senior researcher at the JIIS replies:

> fact on the ground was done both by Israelis and Palestinians. There is a tremendous amount of construction by the Palestinians—although they are shouting that we are not allowing them, and so on, so forth ... But if I compare the situation on the ground, from air photographs and so on, I can see the difference ... There is a tremendous housing development by the Palestinians, they are growing twice as quickly as the Israelis. (I. Kimhi, interview)

The divergence between politics and planning, however, does not account for the whole narrative of planning in Jerusalem. This is obviously true for those planners who hold a more critical view of Israeli-established policies—whom we call 'activist' planners for their widespread engagement in the activity of progressive, pro-peace NGOs such as Bimkom, Ir Amim, BTselem, etc. 'Activist' planners, indeed, share the sentiment of frustration in confronting the urban reality of Jerusalem, but they reject indefinite notions of 'politics' and 'conflict' as obstacles to planning, pointing instead to structural inequalities generated by the partisan nature of Israeli policies.

In explaining the distortions of urban development, they point to the demographic imperatives behind Israel's policy, the late and poor planning in Palestinian neighborhoods, the collusion between government officials and the Jewish settlers, the political use of national parks and green areas to limit Palestinian growth and, in the end, the substantial consensus among the different branches of local and national government about the fundamental goals and principles of urban policy (A. Cohen-Lifshitz, E. Cohen-Bar, interviews; see also Kaminker 1997).

From this point of view, the impossibility of planning for the entire metropolitan area depends on the overall coherence between planning and politics. The partisan nature of the system would shape the dynamics of inclusion and exclusion in the planning process and determine the intrinsic ambiguities between political-demographic and functional definitions of the region. As a Palestinian-Israeli planner who participated to the drafting of the 1994 Metropolitan Plan notes:

> I do not think that the term 'metropolitan'—according to how it's known in the Western countries, which is the notion of metropolitan [integration] from the functional point of view—[…] actually fits the situation here in Jerusalem … We have a dual system, one for the Palestinians and the second for the Israelis, OK? […] The functional actually follows, or is limited [by], the political agenda. (R. Khamaisi, interview)

Their frustration is therefore derived from the perception of conducting an uphill battle against public authorities and planning institutions, and of their own relative isolation in the political arena, as well as in public opinion. Our respondents are unanimous in stressing the huge costs of their activities of 'counter-planning'—monitoring the sensitive areas of urban development, preparing alternative planning schemes, submitting objections to planning authorities and filing petitions to courts—against the very small results they achieve. They describe a trade-off between the importance and political sensitivity of the debated issue and their chance of success:

> [t]he planners in the offices, they say, "This is politics, don't talk to us here in this committee about politics; we are talking about planning." (E. Cohen-Bar, interview)

> I am not very optimistic about [going to courts] either […]. For example, in the petition against E-1 in 1998, it was rejected on the ground that is a general petition that deals with issues that are primarily political in nature.

Now, you can argue this almost on everything in the West Bank, so that's why we actually avoid as much as possible, anything that can hit on a political argumentation, but still, if they want they can always say it. (N. Shalev, interview)

Planners in the Mirror

Given the widespread realization of the politicization of planning issues, how do planners make sense of their own professional role? How do they reconcile their activities with the existence of partisan policy goals and power asymmetries? These questions directly address not only the role of planners as professionals, but also their personal political and ideological worldviews; they force us to take into account the subtle ways in which living in an extremely polarized context influences this worldview, as well as the role of lies and self-deception (Flyvbjerg 1996).

As David Morley and Arie Shachar point out, a common answer to these environmental pressures is for planners to

> base their proposals on a discourse that avoids viewing them from a particular ideological perspective. This approach becomes a strategy to create legitimation for the objective methodology of planning as a way to hold in check the strongly held and conflicting positions among planners and their clients regarding critical issues. (Morley and Shachar 1986: 145)

Indeed, many of the 'mainstream' planners seem to adopt this strategy. The separation is in the first place a personal, "psychological separation of an administrative 'me' from a political 'them'" (Bollens 2000: 109). Our interviews contain several passages in which the planner stresses his non-political role. As one respondent puts it, "I am not a politician [...]. The attitude of this office is very professional; we are not into political issues" (B. Weil, interview). Though never requested to do so, the planners interviewed often declare their political preferences—usually in a convoluted manner: "I am not known as very right-wing, on the contrary" (I. Kimhi, interview)—only to immediately distance themselves from any political stance by recalling their professional attitude. Planners and politicians would belong to two separate types: in an interview, a senior member of the Ma'ale Adummim planning team in the 1970s argues that he could have an open and fair dialogue with any planner irrespectively of his ethnic background, while openly blaming politicians of both communities for the continuation of the conflict (T. Leitersdorf, interview). The separation between the roles of planning and politics also implies what we could call a differentiation in time; planners begin their work after politicians finish theirs. Planners do not make decisions and act within a context whose boundaries are determined by politicians; their role is to make sure that political deliberation is translated on the ground in a professional way.

The second barrier is a methodological one. The planners as professionals would look at urban problems through a different set of lenses and instruments to the ones used by politicians, and act following a different code. Israel Kimhi stresses the need to "postpone issues of sovereignty; […] let's talk over the next five–ten years on a practical level—how we can live together" (Bollens 2000: 107). More broadly, the advantage of long-term planning would therefore be "to get rid of the organizational distortions" (Adam Mazor on the 1994 Metropolitan Plan, ibid.: 148) linked to present political uncertainties; the use of functional definitions would bypass issues of sovereignty. Specific professional techniques—such as the 'potential model' (I. Kimhi, B. Weil, Z. Efrati, interviews)—could even have an inherent value in terms of conflict management and resolution.

Those barriers ultimately provide the planners with the feeling that a 'safe space' of planning ultimately exists, where they can exercise their professional expertise. In this space they can maintain their non-ideological posture and deal with contentious issues as purely urban issues. An interview with a planner in the JIIS is worth quoting at length:

> I am speaking about the basic urban level of services, employment, transportation. […]. I think that the basis for a joint life does not have to include any political restructuring […] [and] whatever be the political structure, those urban problems can be solved and solving them would be the beginning of a joint urban […] life, even if it would be under Jewish control […]. In my opinion […] there are a lot of problems and well, of course, political change of frameworks would do … may advance things greatly—maybe it won't—but it may advance things greatly, but I think that things can advance even without any change of political framework. I know that the facts in the last forty years are against what I am saying, but I think that [recently] there is an advancement. (A. Shapira, interview)

From time to time, however, a more porous relation between planning and politics emerges in the activity of planners. Despite their constant reminding of the frustrating subordination of planning to politics, many senior 'mainstream' planners can refer to "glorious times" where "planning and political considerations went hand in hand" (Thomas Leitersdorf on the planning of Ma'ale Adummim, quoted in Tamir-Tawil 2003: 155–156). Israel Kimhi recalls the early times after Jerusalem's reunification as the most fortunate situation for a planner—that you are needed. We were needed by the politicians—what road to open, what to knock down, where is the sewage, what to do. They simply came to us—we had all the information. We were prepared for this act of reunification. It was a glorious time. (Bollens 2000: 109)

In a more self-reflective vein, another member of the Ma'ale Adummim planning team during the 1970s elaborates on the (politically motivated) decision to 'build eastwards':

If we do not regard the political aspect of it, I think it was a normal step [...] giving Jerusalem more time to deal with building in the city [...], as within the city you have to [proceed very slowly and carefully] [...]; if there would [have been] no political pressure, and still you would say: "No, we are not going to let the market dictate it, but we are going to plan it," [...] where would you recommend to build a new city? It would be [eastwards]. (E. Barzacchi, interview)

This coherence does not have a simple instrumental value for the planners; sometimes it harmonizes with the planners' feelings and values. David Best defines his experience of planning the neighborhood of East Talpiot as an effort to do something new in terms of planning practice (in relation to design, organizational elements, even communicative planning practices). At the same time, he states:

I was convinced it was right. It was beyond the border, but only just, and it was a project that should go ahead, for the defense of a united Jerusalem. From a geo-political point of view I thought it was right. I also thought that it was right from a social point of view, creating a strongly built edge to Jerusalem on the southeast desert landscape. (quoted in Forester et al. 2001: 60)

The analysis of the 'glorious times' of planning in Jerusalem raises an important issue. Despite the recurrent argument of the subordination of planning to politics, the issue of planners' agency surfaces from time to time. As David Best notes, the interaction between a planner and his client is one of reciprocal exchange and manipulation:

generally, my major aim is to try to get people to believe that they have arrived at conclusions which they feel are right [...]. I don't work with people who say, "Look, you do as I say; you have no say in the matter." (quoted in Forester et al. 2001: 61, 63)

Best's description of his struggle over the location of the residential neighborhood of East Talpiot is a telling episode of how planners can be able to form coalitions, anticipate political opposition, make an opportunistic use of a variety of planning and political arguments, and jump the hierarchy in order to achieve their goals (ibid.). Who was manipulating whom in that 'glorious time'? Thomas Leitersdorf, chief architect in the Ma'ale Adummim planning team, offers us an insightful picture of Israeli decision-making by describing the way the final location of the settlement was chosen:

> When we put the alternatives to the Ministerial Committee for Settlement, headed at the time by Ariel Sharon, the only questions asked were: "Which of the alternative locations has better control over the main routes?" And "Which town has a better chance to grow quickly and offer qualities that would make it competitive with Jerusalem?" I replied that according to these criteria the ideal location would be location A [the present site of Ma'ale Adummim] [...]. At that moment Sharon rose and declared, without consulting the Committee, that "the State of Israel decides on location A." (quoted in Tamir-Tawil 2003: 153–154)

In the case of Ma'ale Adummim, the planners wanted to change the location of the settlement *before* the meeting of the Committee, wishing to do so for architectural and planning reasons: climate, morphology of the terrain, proximity to employment centers, accessibility to infrastructures and to be able "to see the light of Jerusalem from Ma'ale Adummim" (E. Barzacchi, interview; also T. Leitersdorf, interview, and Tamir-Tawil 2003: 153). If we dig below the surface of Leitersdorf's quote—apparently a crystal-clear case of top-down, politico-strategic decision-making—we get the sense of how the planners managed to steer the process because they strategically interpreted the planning–politics bundle inherent to decision-making.

For 'activist' planners, the barriers between political and planning considerations are much more porous. On the one hand, they hardly bother to claim any professional neutrality, and are far more outspoken about the political role of planners in Jerusalem. NGOs such as Bimkom, BTselem, Ir Amim and Peace Now define their missions in terms of commitment to human rights and democracy, and their involvement in planning issues is a direct consequence of the politics–planning nexus in Jerusalem. On the other hand, their judgment of the role of Israeli planners in shaping post-reunification Jerusalem is straightforwardly negative. Meron Benvenisti, formerly deputy mayor of Jerusalem and senior planner of the municipality, sums up this attitude, harshly rejecting any claim of neutrality from the 'mainstream' planner community:

Planners want to get jobs. They are part of the political systems, of the power relationship ... The fact that they find excuses is something else. I don't trust them at all. [...] There are very few planners who refuse to plan in the occupied territories, most of them hide behind that excuse, "We are trying to be [neutral]." The fact that you do that plan is political ... otherwise you should refuse. If you don't refuse, you become part of the process. (M. Benvenisti, interview)

Indeed, the history of planning in Jerusalem presents well-known cases of 'conversions'—and especially among the older generation of city planners. Meron Benvenisti, Sara Kaminker and Elinoar Barzacchi, to name but three, have gone from holding key positions in the municipal planning offices to a stern opposition to Israeli policies in the city after completely breaking their ties with the Israeli administration.

In our interviews with 'activist' planners—as well as in the documents published by the NGOs in which they work—the shift between political and planning considerations is much more straightforward; for them the emphasis on the legal ground of their objections and the need for good planning practices is directly anchored to a political commitment toward more equitable relations between communities. Planning is therefore perceived as a political tool to act on the behalf of a disadvantaged community; its inherent political value is testified to by the emphasis on the goal of "[empowering] the [Palestinian] residents themselves with the skills and knowledge that will enable them to continue to actively participate and protect their rights in matters of planning" (Bimkom 2006: 2); the same outlook is reflected in the activity of Ir Amim's joint Israeli–Palestinian urban planning working group, aiming at enhancing community participation in planning for Palestinians by creating a Palestinian planning administration and a separate master plan for East Jerusalem (The Peace and Democracy Forum/Ir Amim 2009: 4–5). As an architect working for Bimkom notes, this is a justification of their action well beyond the achievement of tangible results in planning terms; citing a case of house demolition, she declares "[w]e don't believe that our petition [...] will stop demolitions, but we want to raise awareness" (E. Cohen-Bar, interview).

Discussion

Jerusalem represents a particularly dramatic example—an 'extreme case,' as Flyvbjerg (2006) would put it—of the nexus between politics and planning. The question implicitly raised by this chapter—is there a 'planning answer' to systemic turbulence and entrenched political polarization?—should therefore be considered in the light of an understanding of planning as a social practice embedded in the contradictions of the society as a whole.

From this point of view, probably in few places other than Jerusalem, it is more obvious that planning issues are more broadly issues of power and democracy, and that planners face not only narrow technical issues, but political and systemic problems. In this respect, there can be no narrow 'planning answer' to political problems; Robert Dahl's (1989) caveat about the inability of procedural democracy itself to deliver substantive democracy also applies to those technical tools of social engineering and decision-making procedures that make up the planning system. Before discussing planning in terms of technicalities and 'good planning practices'—a central theme in the debate on communicative planning—we should therefore consider the criteria for the inclusion of stakeholders, the drawing-up of the agenda to be discussed, and the basic rules of decision-making—in other words, the social, political and economic context in which planning takes place.

Jerusalem offers multiple examples of how crucial planning questions cannot be resolved through the narrow reference to 'good' or 'professional' planning practices. If we look, for example, at any single moment of the planning process, the case for the advantages of a narrowly professional approach can be made by stressing the latter's potential for minimizing conflicts within the boundaries of a given situation; still, the long-term adoption of such a strategy of depoliticization of urban issues is likely to accommodate the status quo and perpetuate conflicts (see for example Forester 1982; Bollens 2000: 23–27). The acknowledgment of the contextual nature of planning is also crucial to evaluate the scale and location of planning interventions. To what extent can single projects or local episodes of 'good planning'—let us say preserving green areas in West Jerusalem through the development of a participatory process with the local (Jewish) community—be separated from their systemic consequences (the increased pressure to accommodate Jewish housing needs by building in the eastern part of the city)?[1] More generally, to what extent is it realistic to focus on what has been done—and neglect what *has not* been done? By referring to specific 'good planning practices,' we risk missing the fact that the most important factor affecting the Palestinian community in Jerusalem has not been the active curtailment of population growth—which took place anyhow—through restrictive planning or demolition orders, but instead the outright absence of planning for Palestinian neighborhoods.

The acknowledgment of the social nature of planning practices is crucial, not only for evaluating planning practices per se or the functioning of the planning system as a whole. Situating the experience of planners helps us in making sense of their subjectivity; the social context is the background against which they frame urban issues, look to their professional role and make significant personal and career choices.

Two recurrent themes emerge, for example, in our interviews, both among 'activist' and 'mainstream' planners. On the one hand, there is the reference to a set of 'good practices' rooted in the methodology of their profession—the need to collect direct, firsthand knowledge of the urban issues and landscape, to adopt sophisticated technical tools and to consider the stakeholders' needs and voices—also signaling the discursive and professional shift from the once widely held rationalistic conceptions of planning as a problem-solving, cost–benefit technique toward a more process-oriented, participative ideal of planning. On the other hand, there is the planners' frustration in the face of uncertainty, political impasse and polarized attitudes of the stakeholders, and the subordination of the planning issues to political imperatives.

Both the reference to good planning practices and the feeling of frustration, however, assume different meanings for 'mainstream' and 'activist' planners. For the majority of 'mainstream' planners, good practices represent the first and foremost requirements of the profession and are a way to minimize conflicts on the way to urban development; conflicts originate because 'politics get in the way' of good planning. For 'activist' planners, 'good planning' is instead framed in terms of a revolutionary or insurgent action—and a colossal and often unfruitful effort, hence their frustration—against the status quo. The inclusion of all stakeholders in the planning process, for example, is at the same time good professional practice and a radical claim for the political inclusion of the Palestinian community—a call for a dramatic reorientation of past Israeli policies.

Last but not least, the embeddedness of planners in the socio-political environment—of which they are a product themselves—allows us to investigate planners' agency. Planners do face political issues beyond the narrow realm of planning; yet, on the other hand, they are also political actors in the decision-making process. Indeed, planners can adopt a wide range of strategies in order to steer the planning process, from the strategic use of their professional expertise to lobbying and political activism, from opportunistic tactics to the deception of clients and public opinion.

In Jerusalem, the narrower, professional frame adopted by 'mainstream' planners needs therefore to be problematized. First, the 'retreat' to the neutrality of the profession represents a strategy in dealing with political issues, and therefore, implicitly, a political action. Moreover, in the face of the complex overlap between planning and politics in Jerusalem, the statement 'I don't deal with political issues'—expressed by individual planners, planning offices and commissions or by the court system—is inherently ambiguous and allows ample room to maneuver. Second, planners' personal experiences and worldviews are never immune from the political culture and climate. In our interviews, the rhetoric about the planners' ability to 'keep a balance' does not hide the recurrent emergence of political arguments, inclinations and passions as factors in their professional choices and therefore in the planning process. Third—as anecdotes such as those recounted by David Best, Thomas Leitersdorf and Israel Kimhi, among others, reveal—planners do have agency in steering the planning process by using both the tools of their profession and more 'political' personal and institutional devices.

The case of 'activist' planners provides us with yet another example of socially situated agency. As Amit Ron and Galit Cohen-Blankshtain observe about the Kaminker project—a deliberative planning initiative conducted by Bimkom in the Palestinian neighborhood of Issawiya—"[h]ad we chosen to measure Bimkom's planning process against any ideal model of deliberative planning, we would have to deem it a failure" (Ron and Cohen-Blankshtain 2011: 646), citing the limitations inherent in the process itself and the impossibility of passing the plan through hostile planning commissions. Still, as the authors put it, deliberation can be understood "as a form of political representation that competes with other forms of representation" (ibid.: 637). In this case, planners' agency goes well beyond the narrow boundaries of the planning system and of professional practice.

The issue of planners' agency reveals the value of Jerusalem as a 'critical case' in the relation between politics and planning. What we mean is that observing planners' autonomous agency in Jerusalem—where, as the rhetoric goes, 'everything is political' and planning policy is dictated by political imperatives—implicitly strengthens the argument for understanding the relation between planning and politics in a non-linear, non-hierarchical fashion.

Without considering carefully the interplay of planning and politics, one would support a misleading and somehow dangerous notion of the separability between the two realms of politics and planning—or between politics and any other technical knowledge involved in decision-making or policy imple-mentation. Following that thread risks ending up with the idea that a precise hierarchy exists between the two—be it the subordination of the latter to the former or vice versa—and that what planners really need is to 'learn to deal with politics' to develop the progressive potential that is inherent to their profession (this is the outlook emerging from the contributions by John Forester 1982, 1984; see also Forester et al. 2001).

In the case of Jerusalem, this illusion tends to be translated into the artificial dichotomy between all-powerful politicians making use of powerless planners—either in the role of victims or in that of disciplined soldiers of the politicians themselves. Still, we suspect that, should we focus our analysis exclusively on politicians, we could very easily report the same perception of the intractability of the problems—uncertainty, frustration and impotence. The interviews could be repeated again, with very similar results, for every category of actor: Israeli grassroots activists, Palestinian businessmen, Jerusalem notables, etc. Should we then conclude—in what can be either a very deep insight on the nature of life or, more likely, a poor and superficial understanding of social phenomena—that nobody is steering urban development in any measure?

This is obviously not the case in Jerusalem, where partisan planning has decisively contributed to shaping urban development over almost half a century. Nevertheless, our feeling is that, rather than looking for a 'plan' or a neatly defined set of instrumental and hierarchical relations, we should delve instead into the complexity of Israeli decision-making—a bundle of institutional and individual networks, ideology and expertise, strengths and pathologies developing against the background of the polarized environment of municipal and national politics. We should allow for the relaxation of the predetermined assumptions of roles, patterns of behavior and reciprocal interactions of the actors involved, and focus instead on the difficult and painful reconstruction of the actual dynamics of social and political phenomena.

Appendix: List of Interviewees

Elinoar Barzacchi (Former City Engineer, Municipality of Jerusalem; Co-Director, Steering Committee—Jerusalem Metropolitan Plan and Development Plan; Planner, Ma'ale Adummim Planning Team).
Meron Benvenisti (Former Deputy Mayor and City Council Member, Jerusalem Municipality).
Gadi Brandeis (City Planner, Municipality of Ma'ale Adummim).
Efrat Cohen-Bar (Architect, Community Planning Department—Bimkom).
Alon Cohen-Lifshitz (Architect, Community Planning Department—Bimkom).
Zvia Efrati (Head, Program Department—Ministry of Housing).
Rassem Khamaisi (Planner, IPCC; Planner, Jerusalem Metropolitan Plan and Development Plan Planning Team).
Israel Kimhi (Senior Researcher, Jerusalem Institute for Israeli Studies; Former City Planner, Municipality of Jerusalem).
Thomas Leitersdorf (Chief Architect, Ma'ale Adummim Planning Team).
Nir Shalev (Researcher, Community Planning Department—Bimkom).
Asaf Shapira (Researcher, Jerusalem Institute for Israeli Studies).
Benjamin Weil (Head, Jerusalem District Office—Ministry of Housing).

Note

1. It is interesting to note that the largest mobilization by Israeli citizens against a single development project in Jerusalem (with a total of 16,000 planning objections presented to the planning commission) was organized against the so-called 'Safdie Plan' (Outline Plan 37/1, foreseeing the construction of about 20,000 housing units over an area of 26.6 km^2 of open space to the west of Jerusalem), mostly by environmentalist organizations; since 2006, the protest so far has been successful in sinking the plan. Without mentioning the Safdie Plan specifically, many respondents

pointed to the exhaustion of housing reserves in West Jerusalem as a factor in strengthening the need of such development in the eastern part of the city—for example in the E-1 area.

References

Bimkom (2006) *The Kaminker Project in the East Jerusalem Neighborhood of Issawiya: Report of the First Two Years of Activity*, available at: http://eng.bimkom.org/_Uploads/6IssawiyaReport.pdf (accessed March 3, 2013).

Bollens, S. A. (2000) *On Narrow Ground: Urban Policy and Conflict in Jerusalem and Belfast*, Albany, NY: State University of New York Press.

Brand, R. and Gaffikin, F. (2007) "Collaborative Planning in an Uncollaborative World," *Planning Theory*, 6(3): 282–313.

Coon, A. (1992) *Town Planning Under Military Occupation*, Aldershot, UK: Dartmouth Press.

Dahl, R. A. (1989) *Democracy and Its Critics*, New Haven, CT: Yale University Press.

Faludi, A. (1997) "A Planning Doctrine for Jerusalem?" *International Planning Studies*, 2(1): 83–102.

Fincher, R. and Iveson, K. (2008) *Planning and Diversity in the City: Redistribution, Recognition and Encounter*, Basingstoke, UK: Palgrave Macmillan.

Fincher, R. and Jacobs, J. M. (eds.) (1998) *Cities of Difference*, New York, NY: Guilford Press.

Flyvbjerg, B. (1996) "The Dark Side of Planning: Rationality and 'Realrationalitat'," in S. J. Mandelbaum, L. Mazza and R. W. Burchell (eds.), *Explorations in Planning Theory*, New Brunswick, NJ: Center for Urban Policy Research Press: 383–394.

Flyvbjerg, B. (2006) "Five Misunderstandings about Case-Study Research," *Qualitative Inquiry*, 12(2): 219–245.

Flyvbjerg, B. and Richardson, T. (2002) "Planning and Foucault: In Search of the Dark Side of Planning Theory," in P. Allmendinger and M. Tewdwr-Jones (eds.), *Planning Futures: New Directions for Planning Theory*, London, UK: Routledge: 44–62.

Forester, J. (1982) "Planning in the Face of Power," *Journal of the American Planning Association*, 48(1): 67–80.

Forester, J. (1984) "Bounded Rationality and the Politics of Muddling Through," *Public Administration Review*, 444: 23–31.

Forester, J. (1989) *Planning in the Face of Power*, Berkeley, CA: University of California Press.

Forester, J. (1999) *The Deliberative Practitioner: Encouraging Participatory Planning Processes*, Cambridge, MA: MIT Press.

Forester, J., Fischler, R. and Shmueli, D. (eds.) (2001) *Israeli Planners and Designers: Profiles of Community Builders*, Albany, NY: SUNY Press.

Foucault, M. (1979) *Discipline and Punish: The Birth of the Prison*, New York, NY: Vintage.

Habermas, J. (1979) *Communication and the Evolution of Society*, London, UK: Heinemann.

Habermas, J. (1983) *The Theory of Communicative Action, Vol. 1: Reason and the Rationalization of Society*, Cambridge, MA: MIT Press.

Habermas, J. (1987) *The Philosophical Discourse of Modernity*, Cambridge, MA: MIT Press.

Habermas, J. (1990) *Moral Consciousness and Communicative Action*, Cambridge, MA: MIT Press.

Hajer, A. M. (1997) *The Politics of Environmental Discourse: Ecological Modernization and the Policy Process*, Oxford, UK: Clarendon Press.

Harvey, D. (2001) *Spaces of Capital: Towards a Critical Geography*, London, UK: Routledge.

Healey, P. (1992) "A Planner's Day: Knowledge and Action in Communicative Practice," *Journal of the American Planning Association*, 58(1): 9–20.

Healey, P. (1996) "The Communicative Turn in Planning Theory and Its Implication for Spatial Strategy Formation," *Environment and Planning B: Planning and Design*, 23(2): 217–234.

Healey, P. (1997) *Collaborative Planning: Shaping Places in Fragmented Societies*, Basingstoke, UK: Palgrave Macmillan.

Innes, J. (1995) "Planning Theory's Emerging Paradigm: Communicative Action and Interactive Practice," *Journal of Planning Education and Research*, 14(3): 183–190.

Kaminker, S. (1997) "For Arabs Only: Building Restrictions in East Jerusalem," *Journal of Palestine Studies*, 26(4): 5–16.

Morley, D. and Shachar, A. (eds.) (1986) *Planning in Turbulence*, Jerusalem, Israel: Magnes Press.

Mouffe, C. (1993) *The Return of the Political*, London, UK: Verso.

Mouffe, C. (1999) "Deliberative Democracy or Agonistic Pluralism," *Social Research*, 66(3): 745–758.

Mouffe, C. (2000) *The Democratic Paradox*, London, UK: Verso.

Mouffe, C. (2005) *On the Political*, London, UK: Routledge.

The Peace and Democracy Forum/Ir Amim (2009) *Toward Resolving the Planning Disparity in Jerusalem*, available at: www.pdf-palestine.org/The%20Urban%20Planning%20Dispute%20-JPF.pdf (accessed March 3, 2013).

Ron, A. and Cohen-Blankshtain, G. (2011) "The Representative Claim of Deliberative Planning: The Case of Isawiyah in East Jerusalem," *Environment and Planning D: Society and Space*, 29(4): 633–648.

Sandercock, L. (ed.) (1998) *Making the Invisible Visible: A Multicultural Planning History*, Berkeley, CA: University of California Press.

Sandercock, L. (2000) "When Strangers Become Neighbours: Managing Cities of Difference," *Planning Theory & Practice*, 1(1): 13–30.

Schweid, Y. (1986) "The Planning of Jerusalem Before and After 1967: Attitudes Toward Uncertainty," in D. Morley and A. Shachar (eds.), *Planning in Turbulence*, Jerusalem, Israel: Magnes Press: 107–113.

Tamir-Tawil, E. (2003) "To Start a City from Scratch: An Interview with Architect Thomas M. Leitersdorf," in R. Segal and E. Weizman (eds.), *A Civilian Occupation: The Politics of Israeli Architecture*, London, UK: Babel and Verso Press: 151–162.

Yacobi, H. (2004) "Whose Order, Whose Planning?" in H. Yacobi (ed.), *Constructing a Sense of Place: Architecture and the Zionist Discourse*, Aldershot, UK: Ashgate: 3–13.

Yiftachel, O. (1998) "Planning and Social Control: Exploring the Dark Side," *Journal of Planning Literature*, 12(2): 395–406.

Yiftachel, O. (1999) "Planning Theory at a Crossroads: The Third Oxford Conference," *Journal of Planning Education and Research*, 18(3): 267–271.

Yiftachel, O. and Huxley, M. (2000) "New Paradigm or Old Myopia? Unsettling the Communicative Turn in Planning Theory," *Journal of Planning Education and Research*, 19(4): 333–342.

8

Problem Spaces, Problem Subjects: Contesting Policies in a Shrinking City

Nina Gribat and Margo Huxley

Introduction: Contention Over the Problem of Urban Shrinkage

[Problematization is] what has made possible the transformation of the difficulties and obstacles of a practice into a general problem for which one proposes diverse practical solutions. [...] [I]n connection with [these obstacles] it develops the conditions in which possible responses can be given; it defines the elements that will constitute what the different solutions attempt to respond to. (Foucault 1996: 421–422)

It's only the *Neustadt* [new town] that people move away from. [Whereas] even if people left the *Altstadt* [old town], there would be others to take their places, because—very simply—that's an urban environment and you just want to live there. (Interview: planner, December 4, 2007)

[The policy makers] fool themselves if they believe that the problem of shrinkage is only a problem of the *Neustadt*. It's completely wrong. It's a problem of the whole city. (Interview: architect-activist, December 12, 2007)

Across North America, Europe and elsewhere, 'urban shrinkage' has been identified as a problem for policy makers in cities where former large-scale industrial production has shut down or moved 'off-shore' and urban population numbers have rapidly declined. This is nowhere more evident than in Hoyerswerda, a town on the eastern borders of Germany, which exhibits one of the fastest rates of population loss in the country (O'Brien 2004; Glock and Häußermann 2004: 922). Since the early 2000s, *Bund* (federal), *Land* (state) and local urban policies in Germany have attempted to deal with the causes and effects of shrinkage, principally through programs for the demolition of 'excess' housing and infrastructure and the regeneration of the traditional urban cores.

In the analysis that follows, we examine the ways in which urban shrinkage has been identified as a problem, and the forms this took in post-unification Germany, in particular, in the town of Hoyerswerda. We explore the policies that were put in place to deal with the problem of shrinkage in Hoyerswerda to show how certain areas of the city were attributed with characteristics equated with a negative past while others were held to exemplify the good future. These characteristics were not just matters of population numbers or spatial and built-form deficiencies, but were seen as attributes of the inhabitants. That is, a causal rationality can be identified that links spaces and subjectivities. These attributions of causes and correlates of the problem of shrinkage produce forms of policy solutions in terms of the demolition of 'excess German Democratic Republic (GDR) housing' and the revaluation of the urbanity of the 'European' old town, and the worth or otherwise of certain sections of the population (Gribat 2010).

In highlighting these aspects of shrinkage policy, we argue that a governmentality perspective helps both to productively question the taken-for-granted ideas underlying policies and to assess the positions taken in contesting them. In particular, we argue that examining shrinkage as a form of 'problematization'—a crystallization of difficulties encountered by urban policy into an identifiable problem that then shapes possible solutions—can provide valuable insights into both the policies of shrinkage and the responses to them. The solutions implicit in the constitution of the problem incite contestations that challenge the judgments of spaces and subjects. The forms of contestation enacted in Hoyerswerda question the particular evaluations of different parts of the city and their role in shaping future trajectories, and assert the equal worth of different spaces and their inhabitants in the present. Nevertheless, while the contestations are posed within the terms of the same governmental rationalities that frame the problem as one of shrinkage, in the process of contestation through a variety of cultural projects, practices have emerged that can be seen to push beyond the framework set by the problematization of shrinkage.

We conclude by suggesting a need for further research exploring the critical potentials of Foucauldian understandings of government and problematization, and the possibilities for productive practices of critique they imply.

The Problematization of Shrinkage

In his study of Leipzig, Bernt (2009b: 83) concludes that housing markets— "not discourses and planning paradigms"—are what is fundamental to the success of urban renaissance in eastern Germany. We do not dispute the importance of understanding housing markets, and their implication in wider economic processes. However, we argue that understanding how discourses and planning paradigms shape urban problems and their solutions are not peripheral issues, but have profound material and social implications.

The governmentality approach we adopt in this chapter, focusing on policies as problematizations, serves to unpick the idea of urban shrinkage and to interrogate policy discourses that attempt to act on the problem. Our approach draws on a case study of Hoyerswerda, a shrinking city in eastern Germany, to show how embedded assumptions about spaces, urban subjects and the city's future frame the problem and set limits on the acceptability of possible solutions. However, even though reactions to, and contestations of, the policies are enfolded in the form of the problematization, they also contain potentials for thinking and acting differently beyond the boundaries set by shrinkage.

A starting point for examining shrinkage policy as problematization is the way in which certain urban problems came to be identified under the heading of 'shrinking cities.' As Beauregard (2009; see also Lampen and Owzar 2008) demonstrates in his analysis of 180 years of urban population change in the US, urban areas do not follow a unidirectional upward trend in population over time, but fluctuate according to economic, technological and demographic circumstances. So while there have been periods of concern about the decline of certain cities (Beauregard 1993), this has not necessarily been labelled with an overarching term such as 'shrinking cities' (although terms like 'rust belt' and 'sun belt' attempted to capture the geographical restructuring of the US economy in the 1970s and 1980s). Similarly, Cunningham-Sabot and Fol (2009: 25) point out that in France and Great Britain, "when surrounded by growth areas, pockets of decline pass unnoticed." This being the case, it can be asked: what is at stake in thinking about, and acting on, these problems in terms of shrinkage (rather than, e.g., 'decline,' 'rust belt' or as the result of 'fluctuations in economic cycles'?). How are solutions formulated and responses shaped by the form of a problematization? What possibilities might be opened up by thinking differently about the 'problem'? (Gribat 2010: 11–17).

In asking these questions, we draw on studies that 'decenter' familiar and taken-for-granted assumptions such as 'the Economy' (e.g., Gibson-Graham 1996, 2006). Such decentering enables questions to be posed about the very conception of the Economic itself:

> Where does this idea of a[n economic] system come from and what are its power effects? What function does it serve in making the real thinkable and amenable to intervention? Who can speak in its name, and what claims to authority can they make? (Walters 1999: 321)

Similarly, by examining the assumptions underpinning the policies and practices of 'urban regeneration,' for instance, it is possible see how they are variously put to work according to the way in which the problem to be solved by 'regeneration' has been posed (Cochrane 2007: 3–4). That is, urban policy does not intervene in natural or given spaces, but is an important factor in constituting spaces as spaces of intervention, as spaces and environments made governable (Dikeç 2007). The focus of interest lies in asking questions about how such policy concepts and discourses are put into use, what work they do, what reactions they provoke and with what consequences.

Questions such as these are enabled by a perspective developed from Foucault's (2007, 2008) notion of 'governmentality' and the conceptions of problematization and governmental rationalities that accompany it. The outlines of the idea of governmentality are generally familiar (see Burchell et al. 1991; O'Malley et al. 1997; Dean 1999; Rose 1999; Rose et al. 2006; Huxley 2008; Walters 2012). Government, understood as governmentality—and in particular, liberal governmentality—indicates a field that includes the state, political government and governance, but these are seen as particular instances of the more extensive occurrence of

> any more or less calculated and rational activity, undertaken by a multiplicity of authorities and agencies, employing a variety of techniques and forms of knowledge, that seeks to shape conduct by working through our desires, aspirations, interests and beliefs, for definite but shifting ends and with a diverse set of relatively unpredictable consequences, effects and outcomes. (Dean 1999: 11)

Studies of governmentality show how processes of government have identifiable rationalities and techniques that, importantly for the critical examination of urban policies, rest on suppositions of causal connections between qualities of spaces and characteristics of individuals and populations (Foucault 1984; Elden 2001; Huxley 2006). In this way, a governmentality approach can probe

> how different kinds of spaces are constituted as objects and aims of government; how they figure in programs and practices of government; and how material spaces and built forms are deployed as techniques of rule by multiple institutions of reform and control, which may or may not be linked to the state. (Huxley 2008: 1649)

That is, governmentality seeks to foster, manage and guide productive relations in an "individual-population-environment" complex (Burchell 1991: 142). In addition to this set of causal 'spatial rationalities' (Huxley 2008) envisaging reciprocal relations between subjects, groups and spaces, governmentality has a utopian aspect that seeks to produce better configurations of these relationships in the future. "Every theory or programme of government presupposes an end of this kind—a type of person, community, organisation, society or even world which is to be achieved" (Dean 1999: 33). Identifying problematizations, therefore, also involves seeing how the way in which the problem is specified frames the ends to which the solutions are directed in the future (Dean 1999: 27–39).

However, far from being 'merely discourses,' the presuppositions and aims of government and the way in which problematic conditions or subjects are identified have material effects on what comes to be acted on in any given situation. 'Problematization' indicates how certain issues are constituted as objects of governmental concern in response to conditions that are seen to require remediation. Examining problematizations involves asking

> how and why certain things (behaviour, phenomena, processes) became a problem [...] while other similar forms were completely neglected at a given historical moment. [...] [I]t was precisely some real existent in the world which was the target of social regulation at a given moment. (Foucault 2001: 171)

The identification of a problem also already presupposes that there are answers or solutions. However, a particular answer is not necessarily the inevitable or only logical solution, and how it comes to appear as 'natural' or 'normal' and unquestioned, or as a frame within which conflict and contestation take place, can also be critically examined. In this process, other answers become possible (Gribat 2010: 83–86).

In relation to shrinking cities, the reality of the phenomena that led to the problematization of shrinkage—the loss of population and jobs—is not denied (there is a 'reality' beyond discourse). Shrinkage encapsulated these phenomena as a problem that appeared in places where such a process had previously not even been imaginable. However, once named as shrinkage and particular causes assumed or constituted and other possibilities ignored, the problem could be provided with a solution or solutions according to the specific situation; or rather, particular kinds of solutions became feasible, and entered into a contested, contestable field of discourse. Thus different aspects of the problem of shrinkage were given as causes: population loss and ageing; economic decline and unemployment; abandoned physical environments and underused infrastructure; the economic viability of the housing market and the cultural devaluing of GDR built form and history. Each was a distinctive but interrelated problem. The identification of these problems played a part in the constitution of solutions such as the demolition of excess housing and infrastructures, the regeneration of city centers and other measures that were considered to contribute to overcoming the problem of shrinkage. Solutions, thus, involve envisaging particular futures, which follow from the form of the problematization.

It is important to note here that an analysis of the spatial rationalities of shrinkage does not assume that discourses and practices automatically achieve the effects they seek. Not only do programs for the government of space and subjects intersect with, modify or contradict myriads of other programs seeking different ends, but in regimes of liberal government, subjects are constituted and governed as free and autonomous individuals, and effects and outcomes are indeterminate, unstable and open to contestation. This approach differs from studies of 'resistance,' participation or direct democracy in not seeking to identify the seeds of revolution or the possibility of (mediated) participatory democracy in every instance of protest. Nevertheless, the idea of analyzing more closely the different problematizations and solutions holds the possibility of examining, in any given situation, "how not to be governed like that, by that, [or] in the name of those principles" (Foucault 1997: 28; Cadman 2010; see also: Chatterjee 2004).

With these perspectives in mind, we briefly examine the constitution of the problem of shrinkage in Germany and Hoyerswerda. We then turn to examining the way in which policies constitute problem spaces and problem residents in Hoyerswerda and show how the civic and cultural projects undertaken in reaction to the policies are forms of contestation that question these valuations.

Shrinkage as a Policy Problem in Germany[1]

The notion of shrinking cities applied to whole urban areas only became a widespread term in Germany in the late 1990s and early 2000s, when population loss in east German cities was brought into the federal urban policy agenda in the context of the financial difficulties of east German housing associations (Gribat 2010; see also report by Pfeiffer et al. 2000). Before this, it had been considered taboo to acknowledge the possibility of decline. Since then, especially in relation to post-socialist towns and cities in Europe, a growing number of English- and German-language studies have called attention to the phenomena of dramatic population loss and economic decline (Kil 2004; Wiechmann 2008; Bernt 2009a, 2009b; Pallagst et al. 2009; Gribat 2010: 2–5).

Many cities in Germany have attempted to overcome shrinkage by promoting policies to support transformation into forms of cosmopolitan historic European city centers. In Leipzig, for example (Bernt 2009b; see also

Bontje 2004), visions of culture-led revitalization as a 'showcase European City,' patterns of property ownership and misplaced support for owner-occupation have produced a "hotchpotch in which renovated buildings and ruins, nicely developed pocket parks and garbage dumps, community gardens and dog runs all stand cheek by jowl" (Bernt 2009b: 81). Similarly, in Dresden (Wiechmann 2008), policy dreams of a compact 'European City' with managed demolition of excess housing stock and a stable population were challenged by an unexpected growth in population, the result of which has seen a patchwork of new suburban housing constructed next to areas of decline.

There are studies of local residents' reactions to these policies or the protests or conflicts that may be engendered (Kabisch et al. 2004: 141–158; Weiske et al. 2005). These tend to focus on the familiar themes of participation, communication and how differences can be negotiated. That is, they focus on the mediation and negotiation of conflict rather than the assumptions and discourses that frame the contestation itself.

Here, we focus on the experience of shrinkage in Hoyerswerda in order to bring to light some of the assumptions underlying the policies—notions of shrinkage as the opposite of growth (physical or economic); the need to replace one kind of urbanization (industrial) with another (European urbanity)—and to show how policies seek the recreation of spaces and subjects as solutions to these constitutions of the problem. The official responses to the shrinkage of Hoyerswerda took forms that reacted to the specific situation, its history and particular visualizations of its future. The policies so constituted then called forth particular forms of contestations and protests framed in these terms.

The Problem of Shrinkage in Hoyerswerda

Until the mid-1950s, Hoyerswerda was a small rural town with around 7,000 inhabitants, all of whom lived in what is today known as the city's *Altstadt*—in and around the original medieval center. At this time, the *Altstadt* was, in fact, equal to Hoyerswerda altogether (see Figure 8.1, year 1950). This changed when the GDR government decided to extend the city in order to house the workers of the new GDR Energy Center in *Schwarze Pumpe*, under construction near the open-cut brown-coal mines in the areas surrounding Hoyerswerda. The *Neustadt* extension to Hoyerswerda was of great importance for the whole GDR, and in 1955 an urban design competition was held for what was to be the 'Second Socialist Model City' to be constructed on a site opposite the *Altstadt* across the River Elster.

Within ten years, most of the planned new districts of the *Neustadt* were complete (Figure 8.1, year 1965) and the extension of the city had already

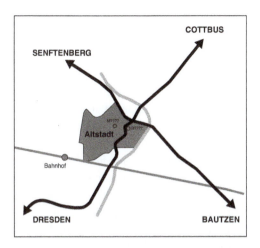

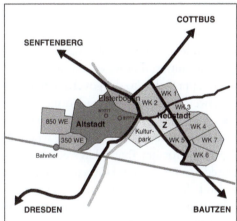

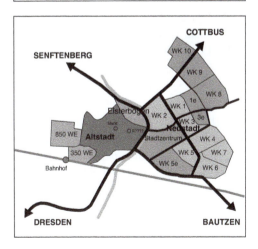

Figure 8.1 Urban development in Hoyerswerda: 1950, 1965, 1990 (source: Gröbe 2008)

exceeded the original plans. The population of Hoyerswerda continued to grow due to the demand for workers in the Energy Center; additional housing complexes were still being constructed in 1989, when the Berlin Wall came down (Figure 8.1, year 1990). By this date, the majority of the population lived in the *Neustadt* with only 10 percent of Hoyerswerda's now 70,000 inhabitants living in the increasingly derelict, 'outdated' and 'pre-socialist' *Altstadt*.

No one predicted the dramatic changes that lay ahead in terms of population loss in Hoyerswerda. However, with Germany's reunification, the GDR Energy Center was closed down and its workers made redundant. There were no other large industries in the area; residents were forced to look for jobs elsewhere and Hoyerswerda started to lose population: from 67,881 inhabitants in 1989 (data: Staatliche Zentralverwaltung für Statistik) to 50,203 in 2000 and 37,379 in 2010 (data: Statistisches Landesamt des Freistaates Sachsen). In the first ten years after reunification, around 17,000 people left (or died) and in the subsequent ten years around 13,000. In total, Hoyerswerda has lost around 45 percent of its population in 20 years. It is in this context that policies identifying the problem of and possible solutions to shrinkage in Hoyerswerda emerged, which provoked the contestation that we examine below.

Two slightly different approaches to the government of urban shrinkage can be identified in Hoyerswerda. First, an early identification of urban shrinkage as a problem can be seen in 1999, in Hoyerswerda's *Urban Development Concept 2030* (UDC) (Stadt Hoyerswerda 1999) at a time when there was no wider regional or federal policy program that addressed this issue. Second, urban shrinkage was addressed as a problem in Hoyerswerda in 2003 and 2008, in the context of the federal *Stadtumbau* (urban redevelopment) policy. Two *Stadtumbau* policy documents have so far been produced in Hoyerswerda in response to the policy parameters set by the federal government: the *Integrated Urban Development Concept 2003* (InSEK I)[2] (Stadt Hoyerswerda 2003); and the second set of *Stadtumbau* policy documents *Integrated Urban Development Concept 2008* (InSEK II) (Stadt Hoyerswerda 2008a, 2008b, 2008c, 2008d, 2008e). Although there are some differences between the earlier, locally produced document and the federally influenced *Stadtumbau* policies, in this analysis we mainly focus on the second set of documents, which express the different valuations of the spaces and subjects of the city most clearly.

Both federally influenced InSEKs were based on reducing the physical size of the city following the principle of 'deconstruction'—that is, demolishing housing starting from the peripheries. In line with federal requirements, demolition sites were to remain free from new construction activities and could only be transformed through landscaping. Depending on the location of the demolition sites and available finances, forms of landscaping on the vacant sites ranged between reforestation (peripheral sites; relatively cheap to produce and maintain) and parks (central sites; relatively expensive to produce and maintain).

In the next section, we analyze how different urban areas of the city, and the subjects associated with them, were related to different possible futures in the urban policy discourse. We then show how these issues were contested by urban professionals and activists. The emergence of protest coincided with the initial problematization of urban shrinkage in Hoyerswerda's urban policy and has not diminished since. This conflict has divided those engaging in debates on the future of the city into two camps. On one side are the policy makers, the city administration, the service providers and the housing associations; and on the other are a group of architects, engineers and social workers, all more or less involved in cultural initiatives. However, rather than assuming that conflict emerged because groups employed radically different rationalities—as suggested by Watson (2003) in relation to South Africa, for instance—it can be argued that contestation of the policies took place within the presumptions at the base of discourses of shrinkage, and were attempts to engage with and influence the government of shrinkage.

Problematic Environments and Subjects: Neustadt *vs.* Altstadt *as Policy Problem*

The problematization of different parts of Hoyerswerda's urban structure (exemplified in the opening quotations of the chapter) is based on a general assessment of the current population loss being a 'foreseeable' consequence of the city's role in GDR history.

> Hoyerswerda [pulled in] … people from the whole Republic … lured with apartments, with good money, with good services. Many people moved there, then the economy broke down, and people moved away … This aspect [of shrinkage] was foreseeable. (Interview: Saxon Ministry for Economy Technology and Transportation, March 18, 2008)

In contrast to places that did not develop as rapidly in the GDR and that are, therefore, seen to have grown 'naturally,' Hoyerswerda's *Neustadt*—with its 'artificial' urban development based on planned in-migration of workers from the whole country—is now cast as an obvious case of decline. In this context, urban shrinkage is identified as a correction that will lead to a healthier (more natural) size for the city: "[Hoyerswerda] has developed artificially … it has developed enormously through brown-coal mining in GDR times … And now it shrinks to, perhaps, a healthy size …" (Interview: Regional Administrative Authority, March 13, 2008). The way in which cities grew in the GDR economy is considered unsustainable and unnatural (no matter that economic policies in 'the West' were also based on industrializing formerly peripheral areas). The issue of historical continuity in terms of economic structures and in relation to urban and regional economic tradition is central for this assessment; GDR history is seen as a diversion from an otherwise undisturbed and naturally progressing (Western) capitalist urban and economic history (Gribat 2012).

The spaces of the *Neustadt* are now seen to represent a 'bad' era, evident in the form and design of the standardized and prefabricated residential building types commonly known as *Plattenbau* (no matter that such modernist architecture was also produced and subsequently reviled in the 'West'). In InSEK I, for instance, the 'City Wall'—a long eleven-story *Plattenbau* building in the center of the *Neustadt*—is characterized as "emanat[ing] a negative urban design atmosphere because the monotony of the façade is paired with the intensity of its built mass, which put a strain on general human sensations" (Stadt Hoyerswerda 2003: 107).

In contrast, the *Altstadt* is seen to embody a desirable continuity between a European past and a contemporary valuation of diversity and cosmopolitan urbanity: "In the central *Altstadt*-area the building development exhibits a structure of a small town with European imprint [...] The existing settlement-structure possesses a healthy mix of uses of the areas housing, work and leisure" (Stadt Hoyerswerda 2008a: 13).

> It's only the *Neustadt* that people move away from. [Whereas] even if people left the *Altstadt*, there would be others to take their places, because—very simply—that's an urban environment and you just want to live there. (Interview: planner, December 4, 2007)

Here, the spaces of the city are problematized and differentiated in terms of their relation to GDR history and the built form. Population loss is seen to result from the fact that *Plattenbau* (or indeed the whole *Neustadt*) are socialist relics and out of keeping with contemporary theories of urbanity. However, the spatial rationalities underpinning the valuations also attribute to these environments causal effects on the characteristics of the inhabitants. The problematization of space correlates with a distinction between the characteristics of the residents of the *Altstadt* and the *Neustadt* in which the *Neustadt* embodies all that is wrong with Hoyerswerda.

> high-rise building is always a social trouble-spot. There you can find what is typical of the *Neustadt* of Hoyerswerda ... You can see what's going on there in these flats: the TV is on all day long, there are beer bottles—that's how it is. And the worst thing is, these are the [people] who have kids. Yes, and these kids are subjected to this lifestyle. (Interview: planner, December 4, 2007)

In addition to associating building types with certain unwanted residents, similar connections are drawn between the context of the *Neustadt's* influx of population in the boom years and the current population loss. In particular, the movement of people in the GDR planned economy is seen to have produced a lack of commitment to the city on the part of working-migrants from other areas. People who came to the *Neustadt* from elsewhere are now perceived to lack loyalty and attachment to Hoyerswerda, even though they may have been there for thirty years before the closure of the Energy Center and subsequent loss of jobs:

> In the [*Neustadt*] the population is particularly young and has not lived there for a long time yet. The resulting low psychological attachment to the city may be of advantage for the individual who is looking for potential employment [elsewhere, but] for the city it is of considerable disadvantage that the population is less involved in the city and moves away more readily than is the case in grown cities. (Stadt Hoyerswerda 1999: 76)

The longer people have resided in a place, the more they are seen to be involved in it and the higher their 'psychological attachment' to the city. From this perspective, the traditional built form of the *Altstadt* represents, and indeed fosters in its residents, desirable qualities of continuity of residence and loyalty to the city.

InSEK II emphasizes that the different parts of the city and their populations cannot be expected to 'work together' in the near future:

> It is accepted that the bipolarity of the city will continue to exist in the future [...] We are aware that the different parts [of the city] with their different inhabitants and user-mentalities cannot be immediately united in a renewed city structure in the near future. A joint 'functioning' of the city cannot be automatically realized simply by combining the parts of the city, because of the differences in the built environment and in the mentalities of the residents. (Stadt Hoyerswerda 2008a: 10)

Thus, these assumptions—governmental rationalities—imagine a fragmented and divided city that cannot easily be reunited physically or socially. They point to policy solutions of demolition, or at least reduction of the extent, of *Plattenbau* housing, in order to remove problematic spaces that are emblematic of a problematized history and that harbor problematized subjects. These assumptions then also contain within them solutions that envisage a particular kind of future—a future in which these disparities have been dissolved in a desirable urban form that fosters and reflects appropriate qualities in its residents.

The Altstadt as the Future

The 'naturally grown' 'European City'—the Altstadt—based on a compact urban form; short distances between housing, work and leisure; and mixture of uses and types of buildings, is idealized in relation to the planned GDR residential city—the Neustadt (Stadt Hoyerswerda 2003: 3, 45, 58). The Altstadt, thus, serves as an object or aim for governing urban shrinkage and creating a future in Hoyerswerda:

> The ideal of the traditional bourgeois/civic city of European imprint should be achieved as closely as possible. [In] Neustadt the degree of necessary changes is considerably different from [those in] the Altstadt [...] With the development of urban diversity the big disadvantage of the monotony of Plattenbau areas will be corrected. (Stadt Hoyerswerda 2003: 45–46)

Thus, the federally instigated Stadtumbau policy can be seen as a process of rescuing the physical form of the city from decay. In his election campaign in 2006 the new mayor, Skora, is reputed to have used the analogy of an apple: to keep the core of an apple you have to cut off the moldy bits on the outside (Interview: Christian Democrat Union Party, December 4, 2007). That is, in order to keep the core of the city (its historical Altstadt center), the decaying areas at the peripheries have to be got rid of. Furthermore, in demolishing the peripheries, the city can keep the center free from the rot—the 'moldiness' of the Neustadt peripheries is prevented from infecting the core.

The (largely taken-for-granted) positive end of the whole Stadtumbau process—preserving the desirable parts of the city—justifies the means of demolition of the rest. The Neustadt is considered to be beyond help because its construction, built form, expansion and residents were the products of the planned economy of the GDR. The Neustadt thus represents the rejected socialist past and the Altstadt promises a different, European future. Demolitions appear as a well-founded and coordinated process directed toward a positive end:

> Urban planners understand demolitions as a chance to remove the gravest shortcomings of the urban design of Hoyerswerda-Neustadt such as too high density, diffuse urban form and lack of centrality. For the whole city, Stadtumbau bears a chance to change the adverse relationship between Alt- and Neustadt [...] and to arrive at a sustainable urban structure. (Stadt Hoyerswerda 2003: 42)

Thus, in the urban policy discourse the future of Hoyerswerda is seen to belong to, and to be created by, the pre-GDR urban structures and people. However, these solutions to the problems thrown up by the identification of shrinkage were not automatically accepted. In the next section, we examine some of the forms of contestation emerging in reaction to policy discourses on shrinkage.

Contestations: Same Problems, Different Solutions

Urban shrinkage policies in Hoyerswerda were first publicly challenged in 2001 when a group of architects, urban planners and theorists from Saxony chose Hoyerswerda as the subject of one of their annual field trips. After the visit, a few residents formed a citizens' initiative, *SubVersionen*, with the aim of rescuing a particular building from demolition and of improving public participation in the *Stadtumbau* processes. Subsequently, cultural and artistic projects were organized by a local architect-activist and the socio-cultural center *KuFa* ('Culture Factory') to raise issues about the future of the city.

These initiatives were forms of policy critique. For instance, *SubVersionen* sought to show that the *Stadtumbau* practices of demolition in Hoyerswerda were not properly coordinated, and that they would contribute to the city's problems rather than ameliorate them:

> [Un-coordinated demolitions] have destroyed the heart of [*Neustadt*]. Is it still worth maintaining the city [around it]? It's clear, [the urban policy idea is] we 'build-back' and return to nature, that's fine. But for people who are to be moved who would potentially stay, there are no alternative [apartments] on offer for them. There is nothing left in the core area of [*Neustadt*], that's the problem … They all see that [the center of *Neustadt*] is desert, that there is nothing left. (Interview, *SubVersionen*, March 12, 2008)

Similarly, the project *Superumbau* ('Super Regeneration') in 2003, had two aims: to fuel a wider debate about urban shrinkage in Germany and to change the negative image of Hoyerswerda.[3] Two *Plattenbau* housing blocks, scheduled for demolition, were used as a location for a six-week festival. Artists were invited to work with the residents of the city and staged an exhibition of their works in one of the empty buildings, while the other was being demolished.

The *Superumbau* project received good press, both nationally and internationally. However, locally in Hoyerswerda, the event was seen as negative and counterproductive to the aims of *Stadtumbau*. Commenting on the negative reactions of the policy makers, one of the organizers of the project said: "Those on the inside [of the policy process] believed: 'Now [the organizer] pokes her finger into the wound and even says it loudly'" (Interview: architect-activist, December 12, 2007). The problem of shrinkage was not to be debated openly, and indeed, among the residents views were divided, because aspects of the *Superumbau* projects challenged local sensibilities. Some of the artists from elsewhere were seen to deal with the urban environment of the *Neustadt* too freely—almost disrespectfully—for example, by baking a *Plattenbau* cake, which was to be consumed during the exhibition. In later projects, fewer artists from elsewhere were involved and work with the local population was put center stage.

However, as well as directly engaging with the technical terms of the policies—*Superumbau*, for instance, is a play on the word *Stadtumbau*—these contestations of solutions to shrinkage challenged the policies' negative constitution of the spaces and environments of the *Neustadt* and the negative evaluations of the residents; by instituting different practices in the present, they opened up possibilities for creating different futures for the whole city.

In this work by residents, artists and activists, different perceptions of the city's problems from those emphasized in the urban policy discourse came to the fore. The *Neustadt* was not considered the sole source of Hoyerswerda's problems. Instead, the construction of the *Neustadt* and the influx of so many people during the boom years were seen as having raised Hoyerswerda from insignificance and as having introduced a more urban spirit to the city. The guiding vision of *Stadtumbau* policy—to achieve a 'European City'—was considered as far too unspecific and too much focused on the difference in urban form between the *Neustadt* and the *Altstadt*. Instead, the solution should envisage the city as an integral whole: "[The policy makers] fool themselves if they believe that the problem of shrinkage is only a problem of the *Neustadt*. It's completely wrong. It's a problem of the whole city" (Interview: architect-activist, December 12, 2007).

Several of the cultural projects focused on reversing the association of the *Neustadt* with a lack of commitment or loyalty on the part of its residents. In one of the projects—*Die dritte Stadt* ('The Third City'), which was held on the occasion of the fiftieth anniversary of the *Neustadt* conception—residents of all ages were asked to work with their memories and their visions of the city in different formats: several theater pieces, a musical, a photo project, a future workshop and an exhibition. Another project, *Hier bin ich geborn* ('I Was Born Here') focused on the children who were born in Hoyerswerda, highlighting that the young generation is as connected and committed to the city as residents from what is considered in the policies as the original desirable *Altstadt*. In a similar fashion, a pensioner's theater group, most members of which used to live or still live in the *Neustadt*, call themselves *Die Herzogen* ('Those Who Moved Here').

These alternative formulations drew attention to the subjects of shrinkage and sought ways of dealing with emotions of loss and needs to express farewell (to buildings and people alike)—experiences that are not addressed, or even acknowledged, in current policy practices of *Stadtumbau*. The strong attachment of many people to the *Neustadt* was recognized in the cultural projects, in contrast to the supposed lack of attachment problematized in official discourses. The projects celebrated the *Neustadt* and its residents—past and present—and their experiences and memories, as integral and important aspects of the whole city.

These cultural and artistic contestations also challenged the versions of Hoyerswerda's future envisaged in the policies. Rather than a merely passive and backward-looking stance in relation to shrinkage, a further aim of the *Superumbau* project was to put Hoyerswerda in an important position in the then relatively new urban shrinkage discourse. As an instigator of the project put it: "I wanted to make clear that this city has the damn obligation to act as a pioneer [a model] again with this new issue of shrinkage after its history [as the Second Socialist Model City of the GDR]" (Interview: architect-activist, December 12, 2007). As the site of the innovative Second Socialist Model City, Hoyerswerda is seen to have taken a positive pioneering role in the GDR. Now, current urban shrinkage is positioned as a new challenge rather than a negative problem, in response to which the city could take a new pioneering role—rather than reverting to the pre-GDR times of the *Altstadt*.

Equally importantly, these projects explored possibilities for experimentation offered by shrinkage, focusing on everyday experiences in contrast to the policies' emphasis on an undefined future. The general perspective was not only of celebrating the past, or working toward a better future, but also finding ways of relating to urban transformation in the present. The different initiatives started as direct responses to the problematization of shrinkage in the urban policy discourse. However, over the following years, while the transformation of the city was still an important point of reference (e.g., The 'Third City' project), other activities and events that brought people together in different circumstances, such as dance pieces (e.g., *Eine Stadt tanzt I und II*, 'A City Dances I and II'), gained importance, producing a sense of collective endeavor.

Over the course of the different projects, the criticism of the practices of *Stadtumbau* shifted to the aim of improving the current quality of life and of encouraging residents' active involvement:

> To be in contact with people ... has ... created a different form of culture ... what we really continually play with is this new cityscape and [we] don't just say: "Critique, critique ...!" ... It is also important to say: "We want to live here, and that's got to do with culture so we have to create our [own] culture. And if many things don't work here any longer, then I will create them in a different manner." People don't meet at the Italian [restaurant], because it doesn't exist any longer. [But] they put on a play or deal with an issue or just have fun, that's part of it. I do have to have an idea about life. We try to test new ways of living or to occupy ourselves in a different manner and that I find quite exciting. (Interview: architect-activist, July 9, 2009)

In providing opportunities for people to get involved in debates, otherwise held behind closed doors or limited to urban policy documents, these urban socio-cultural projects constitute solutions in relation to shrinkage that are defined in different ways from urban policy. The impacts of shrinkage and the effects of Stadtumbau policy on people's lives are recognized and the contribution of the Neustadt and its inhabitants to making Hoyerswerda a city are emphasized. The loss of services because of shrinkage (like the Italian restaurant mentioned above) can encourage experimentation in how to live one's life. Cultural projects can thus be seen to push the question of how to deal with the day-to-day material present in a context in which most policies attempt to imagine a better, but unspecific, future.

These cultural initiatives contest the forms of solutions that policies present to the problem of shrinkage. They seek to reverse the valuations of different spaces, environments and inhabitants of the city by engaging in criticisms and practices that re-present negative characteristics as positive qualities. In this way, the projects work within the frames set by the problematization of urban shrinkage underlying the policies. Nevertheless, in encouraging residents' involvement in projects and in suggesting the need to engage with emotions, memories and the experiences of day-to-day living, possibilities for creating different kinds of futures may be enabled.

Conclusion

In viewing policies as problematizations and examining assumptions under-pinning governmental rationalities of the solutions, it "is a question of a movement of critical analysis in which one tries to see how the different solutions to a problem have been constructed; but also how these different solutions result from a specific form of problematisation" (Foucault 1996: 421–422).

In this chapter, we have tried to indicate the productive critical focus made possible by seeing urban shrinkage policies as forms of problematization. From such a perspective, shrinkage is not a self-evident given, but the condensation of a variety of phenomena into a manageable, governable problem to which solutions can be proposed. This form of analysis itself has the potential to subvert the seeming solidity of governmental rationalities and point to the fragility of their underpinnings. It can do this, first of all, by critique of particular problematizations, and second, by paying attention to the local, specific acts of contestation to particular programs of government.

Critiques of problematizations attempt to

grasp how and why that-which-is might no longer be that-which-is [...] to describe that-which-is by making it appear as something that might not be, or that might not be as it is. […] [T]he things that seem most evident to us […] reside on a base of human practice and human history, and since these things have been made, they can be unmade, as long as we know how it was that they were made. (Foucault 1988: 36–37)

In examining shrinkage as a problem that constitutes certain solutions, we hope to have shown how the idea of shrinkage is itself problematic and need not necessarily take the form assumed in policies. Once this self-evidence is questioned, other ways of thinking and acting in relation to the phenomena gathered under this heading can be conceived. However, these will be specific to each instance of the problematization and need to be studied in relation to the local times and places where phenomena have been identified as shrinkage.

We have examined the specific forms of problematization and contestation in Hoyerswerda. Here, the problem is posed in terms of the negative qualities of the GDR *Neustadt*, its role as the source of population loss, its place in the structure of the city, its built form and the 'disloyal' characteristics of its inhabitants. The solutions that follow from this form of problematization lead to positive valuations of the qualities of the pre-GDR *Altstadt*—its centrality and historical continuity, its European urbanity, the supposed commitment of its inhabitants to the future of Hoyerswerda—and in the policies' visualization of a future for the city, the *Altstadt* forms a utopian horizon as a model and a goal.

However, these problematizations of the city are at odds with the 'messy realities' and experiences of present-day life in Hoyerswerda, and their solutions do not automatically produce the consequences that they seek. Shrinkage policies are contested by cultural projects involving artists, academics and residents opposing the fragmentation of the city into 'good' and 'bad' areas, and reversing the negative valuations of the inhabitants of the *Neustadt*.

The contestations are thus framed by the form of the problematizations and solutions inherent in the policies. Attention to the emotional, social and cultural responses to demolition and the revaluing of the lives and contributions of residents of the *Neustadt* does not necessarily fundamentally question the assumptions of wider urban shrinkage discourses about, for instance, the constitution of 'the Economic,' or the need to manage shrinkage such as better coordinated demolition. Rather, the cultural projects are oppositional actions located in very specific contexts of time, place and discourses; they do not necessarily aim to instigate, or even unconsciously herald, wider radical social change.

Nevertheless, in directing attention to the material lives of the residents and the potentialities for living differently in the changed conditions of the city—testing 'new ways of living' or 'occupying ourselves in a different manner'—the cultural projects and the interactions between residents, artists, architects and activists do open up spaces for questions and practices that push beyond the envelope set by the policies. Such everyday practices in the here-and-now have the potential to sow the seeds of different futures.

Notes

1. The empirical material that is used in the following sections was taken from Nina Gribat's doctoral thesis (Gribat 2010). Interviews were held between 2007 and 2009.
2. InSEK—*Integriertes Stadtentwicklungskonzept* (*Integrated Urban Development Concept*). Cities that applied for funding in the *Stadtumbau* framework were required to produce InSEKs.
3. As well as being known as the fastest-shrinking city in Germany, Hoyerswerda also had a reputation as the 'Neo-Nazi City' following xenophobic attacks on asylum seekers' and foreign workers' homes in 1991.

References

Beauregard, R. A. (1993) *Voices of Decline: The Postwar Fate of US Cities*, Oxford, UK: Blackwell.

Beauregard, R. A. (2009) "Urban Population Loss in Historical Perspective: U.S. 1820–2000," *Environment and Planning A*, 41(3): 514–528.

Bernt, M. (2009a) "Partnerships for Demolition: The Governance of Urban Renewal in East Germany's Shrinking Cities," *International Journal of Urban and Regional Research*, 33(3): 745–769.

Bernt, M. (2009b) 'Renaissance Through Demolition in Leipzig," in K. Shaw and L. Porter (eds.), *Whose Urban Renaissance? An International Comparison of Urban Regeneration Strategies*, London, UK: Routledge: 75–83.

Bontje, M. (2004) "Facing the Challenges of Shrinking Cities in East Germany: The Case of Leipzig," *GeoJournal*, 61(1): 13–21.

Burchell, G. (1991) "Civil Society and 'the System of Natural Liberty'," in G. Burchell, C. Gordon and P. Miller (eds.), *The Foucault Effect: Studies in Governmentality*, Chicago, IL: University of Chicago Press: 119–150.

Burchell, G., Gordon, C. and Miller, P. (eds.) (1991) *The Foucault Effect: Studies in Governmentality*, Chicago, IL: University of Chicago Press.

Cadman, L. (2010) "How (Not) To Be Governed: Foucault, Critique, and the Political," *Environment and Planning D: Society and Space*, 28(3): 539–556.

Chatterjee, P. (2004) *The Politics of the Governed: Reflections on Popular Politics in Most of the World*, New York, NY: Columbia University Press.

Cochrane, A. (2007) *Understanding Urban Policy: A Critical Approach*, Oxford, UK: Blackwell.

Cunningham-Sabot, E. and Fol, S. (2009) "Shrinking Cities in France and Great Britain: A Silent Process?" in K. Pallagst, J. Aber, I. Audirac, E. Cunningham-Sabot, S. Fol, C. Martinez-Fernandez, S. Moraes, H. Mulligan, J. Vargas-Hernandez, T. Wiechmann and T. Wu (eds.) (2009), *The Future of Shrinking Cities— Problems, Patterns and Strategies of Urban Transformation in a Global Context*, Berkeley, CA: Center for Global Metropolitan Studies, Institute of Urban and Regional Development, and the Shrinking Cities International Research Network, Monograph Series: 17–28.

Dean, M. (1999) *Governmentality: Power and Rule in Modern Society*, London, UK: Sage.

Dikeç, M. (2007) *Badlands of the Republic: Space, Politics and Urban Policy*, Oxford, UK: Blackwell.

Elden, S. (2001) *Mapping the Present: Heidegger, Foucault and the Project of a Spatial History*, London, UK: Continuum.

Foucault, M. (1984) "Space, Knowledge, and Power: Interview with Foucault" in P. Rabinow (ed.) *The Foucault Reader*, London, UK: Penguin Books: 239–256.

Foucault, M. (1988) *Politics, Philosophy, Culture: Interviews and Other Writings 1977–1984*, New York, NY: Routledge.

Foucault, M. (1996) *Foucault Live: Interviews 1961–84*, New York, NY: Semiotext(e).

Foucault, M. (1997) *The Politics of Truth*, Los Angeles, CA: Semiotext(e).

Foucault, M. (2001) *Fearless Speech*, New York, NY: Semiotext(e).

Foucault, M. (2007) *Security, Territory, Population: Lectures at the College de France 1978–1979*, Basingstoke, UK: Palgrave Macmillan.

Foucault, M. (2008) *The Birth of Biopolitics: Lectures at the College de France 1978–1979*, Basingstoke, UK: Palgrave Macmillan.

Gibson-Graham, J. K. (1996) *The End of Capitalism (As We Knew It): A Feminist Critique of Political Economy*, Cambridge, UK: Blackwell.

Gibson-Graham, J. K. (2006) *A Postcapitalist Politics*, London, UK: University of Minnesota Press.

Glock, B. and Häußermann, H. (2004) "New Trends in Urban Development and Public Policy in Eastern Germany: Dealing with the Vacant Housing Problem at the Local Level," *International Journal of Urban and Regional Research*, 28(4): 919–929.

Gribat, N. (2010) "Governing the Future of a Shrinking City: Hoyerswerda, East Germany," doctoral thesis, Sheffield, UK: Sheffield Hallam University.

Gribat, N. (2012) "Conflicting Economic and Cultural Subjectivities: Governing the Future of a Small and Shrinking City," in A. Lorentzen and B. van Heur (eds.), *Cultural Political Economy of Small Cities*, London, UK: Routledge: 179–193.

Gröbe, T. (2008) "Ein kleiner Ausschnitt aus der Stadtplanung in Hoyerswerda" (presentation), symposium Literatur und Lebensraum Stadt 'Grüße an Franziska Linkerhand,' June 18–20, Hoyerswerda, Germany.

Huxley, M. (2006) "Spatial Rationalities: Order, Environment, Evolution and Government," *Social and Cultural Geography*, 7(5): 771–787.

Huxley, M. (2008) "Space and Government: Governmentality and Geography," *Geography Compass*, 2(5): 1635–1658.

Kabisch, S., Bernt, M. and Peter, A. (2004) *Stadtumbau unter Schrumpfungsbedingungen: Eine sozialwissenschaftliche Fallstudie*, Wiesbaden, Germany: VS Verlag für Sozialwissenschaften.

Kil, W. (2004) *Luxus der Leere: Vom schwierigen Rückzug aus der Wachstumswelt, Eine Streitschrift*, Wuppertal, Germany: Müller + Busmann KG.

Lampen, A. and Owzar, A. (eds.) (2008) *Schrumpfende Städte: Ein Phänomen zwischen Antike und Moderne*, Cologne, Germany: Böhlau Verlag.

O'Brien, K. (2004) "Last Out, Please Turn Off the Lights," *The New York Times*, May 28, New York.

O'Malley, P., Weir, L. and Shearing, C. (1997) "Governmentality, Criticism, Politics," *Economy and Society*, 26(4): 501–517.

Pallagst, K., Aber, J., Audirac, I., Cunningham-Sabot, E., Fol, S., Martinez-Fernandez, C., Moraes, S., Mulligan, H., Vargas-Hernandez, J., Wiechmann, T. and Wu, T. (2009) *The Future of Shrinking Cities: Problems, Patterns and Strategies of Urban Transformation in a*

Global Context, Berkeley, CA: Institute of Urban and Regional Development, University of California.

Pfeiffer, U., Simons, H. and Porsch, L. (2000) *Wohnungswirtschaftlicher Strukturwandel in den neuen Bundesländern: Bericht der Kommission*, Berlin, Germany: empirica, on behalf of BMVBW.

Rose, N. (1999) *Powers of Freedom: Reframing Political Thought*, Cambridge, UK: Cambridge University Press.

Rose, N., O'Malley, P. and Valverde, M. (2006) "Governmentality," *Annual Review of Law and Social Sciences*, 2: 83–104.

Stadt Hoyerswerda (1999) *Stadt Hoyerswerda: Städtebauliches Leitbild 2030*, Hoyerswerda.

Stadt Hoyerswerda (2003) *Integriertes Stadtentwicklungskonzept (INSEK) der Stadt Hoyerswerda: Entwicklungskonzept Wohnen*, Hoyerswerda, Germany.

Stadt Hoyerswerda (2008a) *Integriertes Stadtentwicklungskonzept (INSEK) für die Stadt Hoyerswerda, Fortschreibung 2008: Allgemeine Angaben/Gesamtstädtische Situation*, Hoyerswerda, Germany.

Stadt Hoyerswerda (2008b) *Integriertes Stadtentwicklungskonzept (INSEK) für die Stadt Hoyerswerda, Fortschreibung 2008: Fachkonzept Demografische Entwicklung*, Hoyerswerda, Germany.

Stadt Hoyerswerda (2008c) *Integriertes Stadtentwicklungskonzept (INSEK) für die Stadt Hoyerswerda, Fortschreibung 2008: Fachkonzept Städtebau*, Hoyerswerda, Germany.

Stadt Hoyerswerda (2008d) *Integriertes Stadtentwicklungskonzept (INSEK) für die Stadt Hoyerswerda, Fortschreibung 2008: Fachkonzept Wohnen*, Hoyerswerda, Germany.

Stadt Hoyerswerda (2008e) *Integriertes Stadtentwicklungskonzept (INSEK) für die Stadt Hoyerswerda, Fortschreibung 2008: Kernaussagen und ihre Auswirkungen auf die anderen Fachkonzepte*, Hoyerswerda, Germany.

Walters, W. (1999) "Decentering the Economy," *Economy and Society*, 28(2): 312–323.

Walters, W. (2012) *Governmentality: Critical Encounters*, London, UK: Routledge.

Watson, V. (2003) "Conflicting Rationalities: Implications for Planning Theory and Ethics," *Planning Theory and Practice*, 4(4): 395–407.

Weiske, C., Kabisch, S. and Hannemann, C. (eds.) (2005) *Kommunikative Steuerung des Stadtumbaus: Interessensgegensätze, Koalitionen und Entscheidungsstrukturen in schrumpfenden Städten*, Wiesbaden, Germany: VS Verlag für Sozialwissenschaften.

Wiechmann, T. (2008) "Errors Expected: Aligning Urban Strategy with Demographic Uncertainty in Shrinking Cities," *International Planning Studies*, 13(4): 431–446.

9

Mediating Stuttgart 21: The Struggle for Reconstructing Local Democracy Between Agonistic and Deliberative Practices

Enrico Gualini

Introduction

Stuttgart 21 is a project at the center of a complex and ongoing social and political conflict, with an escalating point at the turn of the last decade. As such, it has acquired a paradigmatic position in public debate as well as in various strands of social research. Its most striking aspects, uncommon in public policy processes in Germany, are the intensity, diffusion and pluralist nature of antagonism around the project, and the cross-sectional and intergenerational features of social mobilization, prompting scholarly attention for the 'new' sociological features of urban protest and citizen mobilization. Above all, however, Stuttgart 21 (henceforth: S21) has triggered a major public debate on issues of the apparent legitimacy deficit of public decision-making, on its incapacity to enable a truly agonistic politics and on the need for a 'renewal' of local democracy.

This chapter does not present an overall assessment of this complex case. It is rather a critical exploration of one specific aspect, which notably stands out in its public perception: that S21 has become both a marker of a democratic legitimacy crisis of local politics and a watershed experiment in overcoming it through a practice of mediated negotiation.[1] While there has been a clear perception of exceptionality and emergency around the *Schlichtung* (as this mediation was called) among the German public, this experiment has in fact been generally associated by several participants, observers and opinion makers alike with an almost redeeming potential for democratization. This chapter is an attempt at defining some criteria for a critical assessment of these expectations.

Public Policy Mediation as a Discursive Situation

Policy analysis has a significant tradition of understanding agonism and conflict as constructive and constitutive elements of social relations, as sources of their strength and ability to innovate and transform (e.g., Lindblom 1965; Hirschman 1994). This line of reasoning has exerted a significant influence on planning theory. In particular, mediated forms of negotiation and dispute resolution—as they have developed out of the practical engagement with alternative approaches to solving conflicts since the late 1970s—have played a central role in reasoning about deliberative practices capable of dealing constructively with the conflictual potential of public policy and planning. Mediated negotiation is understood as an interactive process in which the achievement of agreement and joint decision-making is premised upon interest- (rather than position-)based argumentation and on the readiness of participants to enter processes of a cognitive displacement and realignment within an iteratively and communicatively connoted situation. A key dimension of the mediation process is identified in the ability of the mediator to actively create and sustain conditions for a structured form of argumentation. Most of the literature has accordingly tended to concentrate on the key role of mediators in defining such conditions, in dealing as 'institutional entrepreneurs' in fostering the constitution of an interactive and communicative situation, in shaping the very conditions for an alternative to conflict to take place.

There is significant convergence in the literature, underlining the virtues and even the ethical sensitivity that mediators must put to work in the situations in which they operate (e.g., Fisher and Ury 1981; Raiffa 1982; Sullivan 1984; Susskind and Cruickshank 1987; Fisher and Brown 1988; Kelman 1996; Raiffa et al. 2002). In the first place, mediators play a key role in 'assessing' a conflict situation and the prospects of success of mediated negotiation. This implies facing situated, specific, applied problems about which planners-mediators need to learn in order to do their work. In so doing, they need to pursue a process of "full, open, truthful exchange" (Raiffa et al. 2002: 86) and to become the gatekeepers of conditions of 'fairness,' 'efficiency,' 'stability' and 'wisdom' (Susskind and Cruikshank 1987), actively dealing with deceit and manipulation in the treatment of 'information' and with the strategic misrepresentation of situations, with the way knowledge around an issue is argumentatively constructed and intersubjectively shared. They face challenges of trust, respect and representation. Their repertoire of skills and abilities includes therefore the capacity to feel and promote 'empathy' and to direct participants toward developing an attitude of sharing one another's perspective and viewpoint (Fisher and Ury 1981; Kelman 1996). In sum, mediators are required to perform context and background sensitivity, to exert practical judgments and to enhance cognitive and relational emotional attitudes to learning.

In this view, as summarized by e.g., Forester and Laws (2009), mediators working with conflicting parties conduct practical research as they "help the parties explore the issues in dispute, they foster a creative process of exploring and proposing new options for joint action, they empower parties to create their own agreements, and more." They engage in a situated, practical analysis with significant ethical dimensions to it, as the way the knowledge is brought into a mediated process "might influence emerging relationships among these actors and contribute to, or detract from, their subsequent flourishing and development." In sum: "mediators' work helps disputing parties to do better" (Forester and Laws 2009: 179–180). The ultimate mediators' goal is thus seen as that of "extending the learning they initiate to the parties involved," while openly and transparently "dealing with differences" inscribed in a situation (ibid.: 180, 182)

There is no doubt that lessons drawn from practical engagements and with experienced-based theorizing on mediated forms of dispute and conflict resolution have significantly influenced the 'argumentative turn' in planning theory, promoting extensive theoretical programs that aim to translate their original remedial, ex post attitude toward conflict into a direction for redefining planning as a deliberative practice capable of anticipating conflict and constructively incorporating structured agonism (e.g., Christensen 1985; Healey 1997; Innes and Booher 2010). Nevertheless, the diffusion and influence of theories of mediated negotiation is undeniably to a large extent tied to the definition and diffusion of model-like approaches to defined conflict situations. In planning practices, this not only implies very often a prevalence of a form of remedial instrumentality, but also a certain degree of stereotyping in the understanding and representation of conflict situations. The subjectivist emphasis on the role of mediators in defining the conditions for this process is a case in point. In principle, mediated negotiation is understood as a strategic-relational game in which mutual partisan adjustment among positions ideally takes the form of a learning process that affects the definition of interests through a situationally redefined understanding of interests and preferences. The key of the matter, however, is usually identified in the skills the mediator subjectively brings into the process in order to foster such a learning process—along, maybe, with providing for some external institutional conditions.

The apparent paradox is a reduction of attention to the situational features of the process that are attached to the behavior of the participants—e.g., the performance of their subjective skills and, above all, those of the mediator— and a widespread neglect of determinants of the situation that 'frame' their behavior. It is, in other words, as if the obsession with the situational skills required from the participants in a mediation process would exert a 'black-boxing' effect with regard to an understanding of the way the mediation process itself is defined as a situation.

We can illustrate this point leaning on Laws and Forester (2006). Moving from Rein and Schön's work on policy controversies and on the role of the framing of policy issues (Rein and Schön 1993; Schön and Rein 1994), Laws and Forester (2006) discuss situations in which the nature of scientific 'facts' is at the core of the controversy. Their analysis moves from the observation of two ideal-typical situations: one in which technical-scientific knowledge and the facts it advances are undisputed, and where the matter of controversy is their contingent and situational interpretation in relation to the policy issue at hand; and one in which technical-scientific knowledge and the 'facts' are themselves disputed, as insufficient, inadequate or false. The latter defines a situation of 'uncertainty' in the socio-political sense defined by Christensen (1985), as absence or temporary impossibility of consensus, and as a situation in which strategic behavior in twisting the matter of controversy defies rational communication. Laws and Forester (2006) suggest that overcoming an escalation of the controversy into overt conflict can be realized through procedures of 'joint fact-finding' around practical problems, enabled through mediating practice. In analogy to the contradictions of Rein and Schön's 'normative leap' in addressing a 'design rationality' for reframing controversies, however, this appears to be premised upon the possibility of the existence of a subject capable of realizing a mediation by virtue of abstracting from epistemological controversies and by enabling the establishment of a pragmatic ground for collective understanding. To a certain extent, then, the professional mediator must be a subject floating over the controversy, immune to it, and set free of the contradictions that define the knowledge put at play in the situation.

The case presented here contradicts such assumptions, not due to lack of professional distance and expertise in the mediation effort, but rather due to two interrelated aspects: first, that a distinction between the two situations is, at best, an abstraction, since even situational interpretation makes the meaning of facts; and, second, that the mediator is part of the experience represented by the controversy, entangled—with others—in its epistemological contradictions.

Discursive Situations as Strategic-Relational Constructs

This is not to deny a notion of 'situatedness' as a dynamic, co-evolutive, and potentially transformative feature of social agency (cf. Lave and Wenger 1991). This notion implies that a 'situation' is not only a 'context' for social agency (in the sense, for example, of a conditionally dependent relational arena or setting or of a particular cultural or cognitive frame), but what is constituted (in terms e.g., of relations or knowledge) through interactive practices within that context. Moreover, what constitutes a social situation must be understood as a co-evolutive interplay of these dimensions. Thus, 'situatedness' is to be intended as a strategic-relational game, as a game in which the strategic intentionality of subjects is confronted with the "tendency for specific structures and structural configurations to reinforce selectively specific forms of action, tactics, or strategies and to discourage others" (Jessop 2001: 1224). In that, the relational environment may exert forms of "structurally inscribed strategic selectivity" that influence the capacity of the actors to (endogenously) reconstitute a situation as it (exogenously) defined. This capacity "depends both on the changing selectivities of given institutions and on their own changing opportunities to engage in strategic action" within a certain relational setting (ibid.: 1226). Strategic actors face "structurally inscribed strategic selectivity that rewards actions that are compatible with the recursive reproduction of the structure(s) in question" (ibid.: 1225).

In this chapter, attention is directed to the way in which a process of mediated negotiation is constituted as a discursive situation, intended as a strategic-relational construct. A deliberative practice—like the mediated negotiation process—is understood here as an instance of how socially produced meanings are discursively defined in a specific situation. As such, it is a set of interactive and communicative practices by which a dynamics of discourse production unfolds. As discourse is made of practices, and is part and parcel of the development of practices, in which knowledge sources and resources are constructed and put at play in an interactive and communicative way, understanding a discursive situation requires an understanding of these practices and the conditions under which they take place.

Mediated negotiation represents a discursive situation or 'event' (Fairclough 1992) defined by the way in which knowledge-based arguments are framed by both the discursive practices of their selection and combination and the social practices of their conduct.

A mediation exercise, characterized as a defining moment in a controversy, is embedded in a discursive situation—and, in fact, it embodies and reproduces it at the same time as it is purportedly called to enlighten it for the sake of transforming it. The latter would be conceivable only in the presence of a third party epistemologically and existentially above the controversy. Any discussion of mediating practices that underlines the learning experience involved can avoid this aporia only at the price of neglecting the dimension of hegemony and antagonism in the political process.

Constituents of a Discursive Situation

If we take this perspective on a mediation process, we can detect several mechanisms at play in defining a discursive situation.

First of all, the exercise of mediation in a conflict situation is predicated upon a selective process of boundary-setting. Practices of boundary-setting or 'boundary-work' can be understood as the activity of "defining a practice in contrast with other practices, to protect it from unwanted participants and interference, while trying to ascribe proper ways of behavior for participants and non-participants (demarcation)," and "defin[ing] proper ways for interaction between these practices and mak[ing] such an interaction possible and conceivable (co-ordination)" (Halffman 2003: 70, in Metze 2006: 78).

Highlighting what is consensually deemed possible and fencing off what cannot be consensually dealt with is a precondition for a process of mediated negotiation to be initiated at all. Thus, as they constitute the possibility for a mediated resolution to a dispute or a conflict, practices of boundary-setting may enable as well as constrain certain options, and enable as well as constrain innovations; they literally co-define the 'range of possibilities' of a situation. Hence, while there may be potential for creativity and learning in a mediation process, these are at the same time 'bounded' to the selectivity of the discursive situation being constituted.

One obvious possible expression of boundary-setting is agenda-setting, the definition of an agreed-upon agenda that, in itself, constitutes a requisite condition for the mediation process to become possible. Agenda-setting in this respect expresses a form of strategic selectivity as it selectively frames the issue at stake—i.e., what is 'negotiable'—not only in substantive, but also in symbolic-cognitive terms. As such, there is also an—often implicit or 'hidden'—boundary-setting effect attached to the way the agenda of a mediation process selects the forms and styles of arguments and the kind of knowledge that is appropriate and required for the mediation to be possible.

As highlighted in science and technology studies (cf. Callon et al. 1986; Latour 1987; Gieryn 1995), knowledge as a justification of a policy can be constructed as a natural given, as 'objective'; accordingly, the 'truths' a certain knowledge construct conveys in turn exert a performative role in legitimizing the actors and institutions whose values and interests inform that knowledge frame or conform with it. Knowledge as a construct acts therefore as a key factor for building alliances that may secure a dominant or hegemonic position in a controversy.

As these values and interests are contested, becoming an issue of controversy, however, the knowledge mobilized is at stake. Knowledge as a construct becomes the center of the controversy precisely as it is a key matter of contestation (Latour 1987). This obviously 'challenges' knowledge constructs and may unleash a significant 'deconstructive' potential. For instance, in the context of a knowledge controversy, a confrontation of knowledge constructs that takes the form of arguments about 'facts' can become a powerful factor for deconstruction of the opponent's knowledge-base; it can reveal how 'facticity' is a function of symbolic-cognitive frames and of their narrative enactment into storylines and, as such, it bears an important reframing potential. As it becomes the center of a controversy, however, it also binds the actors to certain argumentative rules. This is particularly apparent when—as in a mediated negotiation context—this is premised on the acceptance of rules defined through boundary-setting.

As a discursive situation is being constituted, it obviously develops as a process and, as such, is amenable to internal evolution; on the other hand, while no deterministic mechanisms can be assumed to define its trajectory, measures of boundary-setting that define a situation exogenously may exert a reinforcing effect as they are reflected in the adaptive behavior of participants, which enacts and, to a certain extent, endogenously enforces its selectivity.

This may establish a significant tension between the aim of change and innovation, on the one hand, and the pressure to adapt, on the other hand. In the field of sociological institutionalism, the tendency has been, for instance, explored toward the development of forms of isomorphism, as a result of the strategic-relational constraints of the pursuit of strategic orientations by actors or organizations. Accordingly, isomorphic behavior is an adaptive mechanism for ensuring legitimation which is linked to conditions of uncertainty and ambiguity pervasive in organizational-institutional fields (cf. March and Olsen 1976, 1989; Weick 1979; DiMaggio and Powell 1983); this uncertainty is related to aspects of a strategic order (e.g., knowing about one's own knowledge as a condition for defining one's own strategies and preferences) as well as to aspects of a relational order (e.g., knowing about the other's knowledge as a condition for repositioning and reorienting one's own preferences and strategies with regard to it).

The extent to which actors or organizations can affect factors of a strategic and relational order in a situation—making them, for instance, capable of acting as 'institutional entrepreneurs'—introduces a significant differential in the direction of adaptation they will address, or even in their potential to break out of adaptive behavior. However, this differential is not only dependent on exogenous factors, but is also endogenously defined by the behaviors of actors or organizations as they interpret the situation as a framework for developing a strategic-relationally 'appropriate' behavior. By this, they co-constitute the situation through their specific adaptive behavior. The interplay of factors for adaptation hence bears a significant reproductive potential, which affects prospects and modes of change. The dynamics described may even lead at times to forms of discursive institutionalization as a local, situated effect: to forms of 'local institutionalization' of aspects or features of discourse (Gualini 2001, 2004; Schmidt 2010) that contribute to reinforcing a discursive situation in terms of isomorphic adaptation.

Finally, the mediator is him/herself entangled in the strategic-relational game which defines mediation as a discursive situation. Far from being primarily—let alone exclusively—a reflective 'enabler,' the mediator is, in the first place, an agent of practices of boundary-setting; and, far from being 'unpolitical,' the mediator is a political subject, entering the scene upon condition of enacting a certain discursive framing of the situation. By co-defining conditions for mediation, the mediator acts as an agent of boundary-setting—and this is the very condition for legitimation of his/her role. By defining the agenda and conduct of the process, the mediator contributes to the strategically selective definition of a discursive situation. This does not necessarily mean that these practices are the expression of a subjective intentionality. The mediator is, among the participants in a mediation process, the first to be caught in a 'double-bind' that influences the way the situation is constituted.

Mediated Negotiation as a Discursive Situation: A Critical Analysis of *Schlichtung Stuttgart 21*

Our case certainly lends itself to being analyzed as a 'drama' of mediating public disputes, in the tradition and exemplarily represented by e.g., Forester (1999, 2009). However, it also lends itself to some other observations.

In the following section, attention is directed to the way the *Schlichtung* was constituted as a discursive situation. The hypothesis is that the nature of a discursive situation thus defined results from the co-constitutive interplay between (exogenous) forms of strategic selectivity inscribed in the situation and the influence these exert on the (endogenous) strategic-relational behavior of actors. The analysis will look at the following dimensions:

1. The way boundaries are set within which a mediated negotiation process is conceivable; this involves setting a series of politically and institutionally determined conditions of possibility, which involve e.g., exerting selectivity on issues, predefining agendas, sorting out participants/representatives, discriminating among argumentative styles …;
2. A specific effect of such boundary-setting: drawing a line between what is deemed to be political or non-political—involving assumptions about which knowledge and arguments are legitimized to come to bear in the process;
3. The way this influences how knowledge controversies are played out in terms of the strategic-relational development of participants' positions and

arguments, implying e.g., the emergence of disputes over cognitive frames or narrative storylines inscribed in the knowledge brought to bear;
4. The effects these conditions have on the scope for frame-reflection and reframing of participants' positions and arguments.

Making Mediation Possible: Setting Boundaries for Schlichtung Stuttgart 21

When the parties representing this most remarkable of recent public controversies in Germany gathered in Stuttgart town hall on October 22, 2010—the starting date of *Schlichtung Stuttgart 21*—this was just a chapter in a long story.[2] Yet—as stated by a protester during the symbolic occupation of the railway station's hall in spring 2010—the story had just about started to enter a new phase.[3] A key aspect of this new phase—after the escalation of fall 2010, with the violent police repression of civic protests, which had largely shocked German public opinion—was the mediated negotiation process conducted between October and November 2010 in Stuttgart, known as the *Schlichtung*.[4]

The proposal for Dr. Heiner Geißler[5] to be appointed as the mediator in the S21 controversy was first advanced in early October by the leader of the Green Party on Stuttgart city council, Werner Wölfle. After several failed attempts in September, attitudes toward accepting a mediation process had significantly changed in the aftermath of the events of September 30 ('Black Thursday'—see note 1). Formally proposed on October 6 by the president of the Land Baden-Württemberg, Mappus, Geißler was accepted by all parties in the Land parliament as a *Schlichter* in the controversy around S21 and the new Wendlingen–Ulm railway line—previous agreement by the head of the Green Party group, Wolfgang Kretschmann, having been a precondition. The *Aktionsbündnis* (the association of civic initiatives against S21) followed suit, and on October 15 the involved parties agreed on the modalities of conduct of a mediated negotiation process, upon condition of the suspension of both public protests and construction works. Thus, on October 22, the *Schlichtung Stuttgart 21* could start (9, 36).[6]

According to Geißler, at the outset it was not clear to participants[7] what kind of outcome the process would have—for instance, whether it would have to put forward a clear resolution mediated through a 'decision' (*Votum*) by the mediator (9, 36). However, the process itself was obviously premised upon mutual recognition of the fact that the results would not be legally binding, but rather—in Geißler's words—a significant "psychological and political effect" (ibid.). As a matter of fact, Geißler made clear in several declarations, in advance of assuming the position of *Schlichter*, that he would not see his role as one of questioning the project's legal and formal political legitimation. By this, Geißler referred to two crucial but contradictory conditions for the mediation to take place: on the one hand, that all the parties—including the mighty Deutsche Bahn—agreed to accept its outcomes; on the other hand, that formal decisions—and in particular contracts signed with Deutsche Bahn—would not be directly reverted by them. By this, Geißler ambiguously stated a fait accompli argument as a precondition for the whole process. The question then was: what might these outcomes be?

Despite pains taken on all sides—first and foremost by Geißler himself—in order to play down any direct transformative effects of the *Schlichtung*, it became obvious by fall 2010 that the public mood around S21 placed extremely high public expectations on the *Schlichtung*. In particular, given the highly contentious features taken by the conflict, the breakthrough represented by the parties agreeing to face each other argumentatively was seen with some skepticism, and a resolutory word from the mediator himself—the so-called *Schlichterspruch* (the '*Schlichter*'s statement')—was expected with almost messianic fervor. This aspect bears a peculiar interest in itself. While public opinion—most notably, media opinion-makers—was far from agreed on the conflict and its prospects of resolution, the exceptional nature of the situation led most observers to take the role of the *Schlichter* in sorting out the issue for granted, almost as a matter of last resort. Expectation for the final *Schlichterspruch* shaped this highly publicized and mediatized event.[8]

One could argue here that, first, this is nothing other than what we would expect from a textbook mediator as the active broker and public testimonial of a negotiated consensus reached among conflicting parties, and, second, what could have possibly been 'messianic' in this expectation obviously was in the eye of the beholder. To play down this aspect, however, means to neglect a significant feature of the discursive situation of *Schlichtung S21*—one which the mediator Geißler embodied in person: the ambiguous and mutually reinforcing connection between the real political conditions for mediation and the aim of realizing mediation around a de-politicized 'facticity.'

The Schlichtung as 'Fact-Checking': De-Politicizing Within a Politicized Framework

From the beginning—and as the very condition for its conduct—Geißler's aim was 'fact-finding,' as a way for achieving pacification (*Befriedung*) of the controversy. He explicitly connected this with an aim of 'objectivating' (*Versachlichung*) debate, which he intended as a form of sound 'realism.' Introducing the mediation process by reminding of its antecedents, Geißler declared:

Opponents and supporters of this project alike shared the opinion that an attempt should be made, with the help of a mediator [*Schlichter*], to contribute to a pacification and objectivation of confrontation. I declared myself available for assuming the role of mediator, after I had been asked by both sides to take on this task. I want to say from the outset, however: we cannot invent a new station in the framework of this mediation. (Geißler: 1, 1)[9]

This approach was reflected in the agenda of the *Schlichtung*. Session 1 was to deal with the strategic meaning and the technical transportation performance of the Stuttgart railway node in relation to the S21 project and the new Wendlingen–Ulm railway line.[10] Then a discussion of the Wendlingen–Ulm line itself was on the agenda, followed by a discussion of the alternative concept called K21 brought forward by the opponents of S21, and a critical comparison of the two. A further issue would be a discussion of cost–benefit forecasts, followed by issues of geology, security and the construction process. Ecology and urban development issues would close the agenda of the mediation process before the reaching of a mediated consensus was expected.[11]

Fact-finding or 'fact-checking' (*Faktencheck*) was to become a recurrent argument, particularly in the first sessions, and—time and again in connection to the 'pacification issue'—a key moderating device in the course of the process. However, this was more than a mere rhetorical trope by the mediator-moderator; reference to 'fact-checking,' and understanding the process as, above all, a 'mediation about facts' (intended as objective and testable under scientific disciplinary criteria: this being the meaning of the recurrent expressions "*Sach- und Fachschlichtung*," or also "*Faktenschlichtung*," cf. Geißler: 1, 2 and 5, 2) was shared by the participants. Some examples: Palmer (opponent), declaring that he will express his key statements "in the form of a 'does-it-apply-that'-question …" (1, 114–115); Kefer (supporter), stating that: "The view of all those involved was: pacification is necessary. Hence this substantive mediation [*Fachschlichtung*] was initiated under the motto: facts on the table" (9, 5); and Geißler, repeatedly using expressions like: "Exchanging facts face to face—I say it once again: at eye level" (2, 10), and "*Faktencheck*" (2, 32). What was meant and implied by all this, however, soon becomes a matter of struggle: in fact, a knowledge controversy.

That 'fact-checking' would imply fighting out a controversy over knowledge was quite obvious to the participants, it was part, as can be assumed, of their strategic awareness. There were significant underpinnings for this—including the remarkable level of preparation and of expertise brought into play on all sides. The role played by 'arguments about facts' and by the knowledge that was conveyed through them must be seen in strategic-relational terms; that is, it unfolded within the constitution of an interactive situation that involved mutual adjustment and experiential learning.

One significant example was the behavior of the mediator himself.[12] While the *Schlichtung* developed—as programmed—as a sequence of increasingly lengthy expert reports and counter-reports, Geißler was first and foremost dealing with establishing a mutually acceptable argumentation style. In this, however, he faced a series of emerging issues.

From the outset, two issues stood out as problematic: first, 'facticity' is dependent on a framework of assumptions—or 'premises'—requiring scrutiny themselves, whether in their tacit nature or in their truthfulness; second, 'facticity-checking' as such depends on the relational framing of arguments.

The issue of 'premises,' for instance, appeared in the very first counter-intervention of opponents (Palmer: 1, 20) and became recurrent on both sides throughout the *Schlichtung*. Some examples:

> Our counter-statement is: You have managed to define framework conditions—we have presented a catalog of them we would like to work out in writing—in such a way as to let it appear as if the station would perform better. (Palmer, opponent: 1, 71)

> I believe, the heart of the matter is, all that is available up to date to our advisors and experts—I am referring to a respectful and honorable way of dealing with each as previously mentioned, Mr. Kefer—the assumptions and inferences that have been drawn from them, and what is said to underscore them, are not plausible. That is why we are struggling with each other. (Dahlbender, opponent: 1, 88)

While these aspects became stakes in the knowledge controversy, Geißler took pains to keep technical jargon at bay, to separate issues and argumentative levels by sorting out the agreed-upon agenda, and, especially, to try to reach partial agreement on 'factual' statements that could bring the discussion further—only to increasingly realize that precisely these aspects are strategically at stake.[13]

Geißler, for instance, tried time and again to draw consensual conclusions. Examples of this—at times contradictory—attitude are his attempts at postponing a controversial issue by first trying to clarify "what the issue is" (1, 82) and his attempts to put a full-stop behind disputes about 'facts':

> It is worthless to debate further about the premises, which have underscored the simulatory analyses that have been made. This way we come to no end. We need to assume for now that you have done this all well and correctly according to scientific standards. What you just said, you also said based on scientific good conscience. But, by holding expertise against each other, we cannot get ahead. (Geißler: 2, 76–77)

Similarly, in a later session, he attempted to at least secure consensus on the fact that an aspect of the project will bring improvements "given certain conditions," in order to shift the issue—however, meeting harsh disagreement by the opponents (3, 110). Geißler regularly failed to settle the matter of controversies: hence his attempts to move on to other issues as a way out of the dilemma—at times showing overt uncertainty, at times almost losing his temper. A significant example:

> I have been trying for about half an hour to make clear that we are really dealing here with the transportation performance of the terminal station and of the transit station. The people who have been listening to us over the last one-and-a-half hours must be completely confused. (Geißler: 2, 88).

Meanwhile, however, his style expressed an increasing realization of the contradictions of 'facticity'; for instance, arguments meant to be 'factual' may require arguments that are 'counter-factual' in order to become amenable to intersubjective scrutiny. By this, despite resistance and the initial insistence on exchanging facts, a shift occurred progressively in his conduct of mediation. Requests for comparable counter-views, for instance, became more resolute. An example is a moment in Session 3 (114) in which, despite a comparison of the alternative projects S21 and K21 not being on the agenda yet, Geißler intervened strongly calling the opponent for a comparable alternative—which was not available in detail—in order to discuss the data brought by the project supporters; again in Session 3, he intervened in a similar vein:

> It would be helpful, Mr. Rockenbauch, if the Bündnis could possibly give a thought to what an alternative could look like. I am saying it once again in your own interest: it would interest people out there, if the Bündnis would not only say 'no.' (Geißler: 3, 145)

Far from being trivial, the issue of whether a comparison was admissible or desirable as a foundation for expert arguments had already caused heated discussions in Session 2 (133–134), when comparison between S21 and K21 had repeatedly popped up despite being scheduled for a later session.

Behind the mantra of 'fact-checking'—and beyond its outward rhetorical function—a quite different situation developed: a situation in which mere 'political information'—if ever 'fact-checking' had been intended as such—could only reveal its limits. Beyond the mere managing of 'factual' information, it became apparent in the development of the argumentative process—and in the mediator's learning how to conduct it—that the participants were strategically realigning to deal with a situation in which knowledge was in dispute. Nevertheless, appeals to facticity and objectivity remained upheld—and were mobilized on all sides—throughout the *Schlichtung*. This aspect needs to be observed in order to understand the way this knowledge controversy took form.

The Schlichtung as Knowledge Controversy: Confronting Conflicting Storylines/Frames

As it developed, a series of recognizable features of the mediation process became apparent. It turned out to be, first of all, a dispute about knowledge-bases and the 'premises' behind statements; this involved conflicts over issues such as the availability and update of databases and documents, as well as disputes on the representation of technical aspects and of the context for factual statements, for instance planning procedures.

A significant example of the former aspect is a quarrel that arose on the correct technical representation of situations, for instance in the graphics used in expert presentations (Session 3, beginning), on which Geißler concluded: "Now you can see, scientific controversies need not be dry, they can be even quite lively. (Laughter and cheers from the supporters)" (3, 44). Another example is when, in connection to a detailed discussion of geotechnics and water management issues, opponents questioned whether the right conclusions were drawn from statements contained in expert reports and *Planfeststellungsverfahren*; this would lead to a key shift in arguments by the opponents based on addressing the precautionary principle (Session 4, 102).

The latter aspect became a matter of heated controversy, for instance, in Session 5, when the presentation of formal planning procedures as producing 'facts' (a systematic argument of supporters), while in reality in progress and not fully concluded, was detected with reference to the issue being discussed and was harshly condemned by opponents.

Time and again, such disputes turned into questions of truthfulness and trustworthiness. Allegations of potential manipulation recurrently concerned the way 'facts' are dealt with and how they may conceal either premises or interpretations that may lead to untrue conclusions. Here is an example of this aspect, from one of the project's opponents:

> It becomes evident again that the project is based on premises that, in transportation and economic terms, are unfortunately false. You are leading us into a cul-de-sac. You are leading us into a fallacy. (Palmer, opponent: 2, 142)

This led to accusations of willful deception, for instance in the form of allegations concerning recourse to deceptive rhetorical devices. Here is an example from an exchange between proponents, opponents and the mediator-moderator:

WITTKE (SUPPORTER): One moment, may I answer the questions one after another?

PALMER (OPPONENT): If you could answer them with yes or no?

GEISSLER: Yes, go ahead, please answer them. Your turn will be next, Mr. Palmer.

WITTKE (SUPPORTER): I would like to answer the questions one after another ...

GEISSLER: That's absolutely right.

WITTKE (SUPPORTER): ... because it is a common tactic, to ask ten questions at once in order to confuse the speaker. At the end, the first question is already forgotten. I do not like to be treated like that. (6, 49)

Occasionally, even overt accusations of lacking trustworthiness were raised—despite self-restraint being repeatedly required from the participants by Geißler. An interesting example is how the following quarrel developed over time (in connection to a dispute over cost calculations, in which a counter-expert maintained that expected costs systematically exceeded planning cost calculations presented by Deutsche Bahn):

ROCKENBAUCH (OPPONENT, INTERRUPTING GEISSLER): [...] the question rather is: if he now draws from his hat live in front of us all these figures, that is hardly to be proved! He does not keep to what we have agreed to: facts on the table! This, what he is sketching in front of us, this cannot be checked in time ... [interruption] ... even if it appears plausible! Mr. Kefer is so smart, he manages to present things as if they were plausible, consistent— only, the premises we cannot check! That is the key point! (8, 4) [...]

VIEREGG (OPPONENT): Formally correct, but the figures aren't right.

GEISSLER: The premises are different, according to you?

VIEREGG (OPPONENT): The input figures are wrong.

GEISSLER: The input figures. All right then, expose your own calculations now. (8, 11) [...]

[The dispute becomes increasingly heated: open allegations of untruthfulness]

ROCKENBAUCH (OPPONENT, OBJECTING TO KEFER, SUPPORTER): Keep to the truth!

GEISSLER: I have to expressly object to this. You have no reason at all to say this. This would in fact mean the opposite, that he is lying. Do you say this in earnest?

ROCKENBAUCH (OPPONENT): He needs to stick to it!

GEISSLER: He needs to stick to the truth? Well, all right. Hence you are assuming he has said the truth so far. (8, 13–14).

On the other hand, unveiling contradictions was recurrently countered by upholding technical and expert knowledge and its merits, only to be repeatedly followed by Geißler's calls for considering communication with a broader non-expert audience:

> Mr. Geißler, I would like to point to the fact that we have undertaken an attempt to talk about facts. It was always clear to us that we would enter details which are not always very easy [...] A certain amount of expertise [*Fachlichkeit*] will not be avoidable in a fact-mediation [*in einer Fach- und Sachschlichtung, in einer Faktenschlichtung*], rather we will need to allow this. (Gönner, supporter: 1, 92–93)

And again the same speaker from the supporters, contrasting 'factual' with 'political' arguments: "Otherwise I think, it is about time to end this debate, which is quite political, since we are not getting ahead" (Gönner: 8, 31).

On a different level of analysis, different storylines were seen emerging from this controversy over knowledge: different 'causal stories,' whereby reference to a different knowledge-base within different relational causality frames was enacted.

One of the most notable examples concerns different conceptions of planning progressively outlined in the debate: one that is framed by some sort of 'expert realism' that understands the rationality of the planning process as leaning on the context-dependent systemic legitimation provided by legal-administrative procedures, and one that is systematically inclined to transcend this systemic context in order to highlight the substantive conceptual contradictions of the planning process.

This conflict between storylines, which consistently affected the way the planning process was represented, focused on the opposition between German practices of transportation and infrastructure planning and the longed-for alternative, symbolically represented by the Swiss system of integrated railway timetable planning. This turned out to be a most apparent source of incommensurability among positions. The German approach was readily accused by opponents of the project of being counter-intuitive and counter-effective (e.g., Conradi: 1, 90; Palmer: 1, 108), involving realizing infrastructure projects before adequate performance evaluations, and ultimately contributing to S21 being a "*Jahrhundertprojekt* of the last century" (a recurrent theme: e.g., Palmer: 1, 108; Wölfle: 6, 21). This view (and the counter-example of Swiss integrated timetable planning) was countered by project supporters by basically upholding the inherent procedural rationality of German planning procedures as an uncontestable fact.

A striking example is this exchange between two speakers of respectively supporters and opponents in which, at an early stage, the controversy on understandings of planning already arises:

Mr. Palmer and Mr. Conradi, I feel this discussion, as we are conducting it at the moment, is quite unfair. I am willing to say why I feel this way. In my presentation I said from the outset, we have in Germany a certain system and certain processes, which we adopt, when large projects are planned. I ask you to accept these processes, because planning processes [*Raumordnungs-, Planfeststellungverfahren und sonstige Verfahren*] are mandated by law and lead to certain reactions in the planning. [...] I object to the fact that you time and again bring arguments like that, if at a certain point of the system a conflict is found, then the whole system has to be put in question. I reject this. This cannot be done. (Kefer, supporter: 1, 111–112)

Your argument was: we do it this way. This is how we do it in Germany. If you wish to have it differently, you need to move to Switzerland. (Palmer, opponent, replying to Kefer: 1, 114)

An interesting side-effect of this is that, when substantive critique is brought against aspects of the project, replies by the supporters recurrently imply a defensive hint at the open, in-progress character of the planning procedure, allegedly allowing margins for further definition (e.g., Palmer, opponent and reply Starke, supporter: 1, 108).

Another significant conflict among storylines emerged around different causal relationships established between issues—one key example being the relationship between restructuring the station and building the new Wendlingen–Ulm line as a justification of S21 as a whole. It is interesting to note that, while there were apparent differences in interpretive frames even among the opponents of the new railway line (e.g., between arguments of economic-ecologic balance, cost–benefit ratio, or priority: 3, 101–110), it was ultimately the difference in storyline pursued in representing the project that was important in defining the knowledge controversy. Two examples from the arguments of the opponents:

S21 is almost worthless transportation-wise without the new line. Without it, you would almost only have it for urban development purposes. The other way round, however, does not apply. This is in itself an important thing to be acknowledged. The new railway line can have a value on its own. We maintain, not as it is today, but definitely it does not need to have Stuttgart 21. That is how it is. The economist would say, it is a coupling, but only one way around. (Holzey, opponent: 3, 28).

Against Stuttgart 21 there are great concerns and protests. We have never been among those who have posited a connection between Stuttgart 21 and the new line. We never did it, but you did it. [...] This is why we should not primarily actually deal with the new railway line in isolation—that is a whole different debate—but you should rather take the step and finally say: Stuttgart 21 needs the new line, otherwise it leads to nothing. That is why I would like to conclude again by saying: this is the decisive debate. It is up to you to separate the issues and to make it possible for us to conduct separate debates. (Kretschmann, opponent: 3, 165–166).

Another significant example is the discussion—enlightening, as it revealed the potential for manipulation of policy concepts, but relatively marginal in the overall process—on the concept of the European *Magistrale* Paris–Budapest (Session 3, starting at 38): a lengthy, at times hilarious, and extremely interesting excursus on the political rhetoric in which the project was embedded, with a significant potential for deconstruction which, however, soon faded out from the discussion. Yet another example—focusing on differences in understandings of priorities—could be the 'Porsche vs. Golf' controversy (starting in Session 3, 116 and recursively emerging in following sessions) concerning the relative priority and cost–benefit ratios of intensity/speed in point-to-point connections over extension/reliability in network performance.

While more analysis of these aspects would be required, the question is now what influence they had on the process as a whole.

The Schlichtung as 'Dialogue of the Deaf': Contesting Technical Expertise with Technical Expertise

As the *Schlichtung* progressed and developed as a knowledge controversy— under scrutiny of the media and the public—one aspect becomes strikingly clear: the fact that 'factual arguments' based on technical expertise remained substantially unchallenged as the focus of the mediation process. While this was obviously a significant political premise for the exercise to take place, as the careful boundary-setting of its agenda showed, this feature was co-constituted by the nature of the arguments brought to bear. In other words, it appears as if none of the contrasting frames underpinning the participants' arguments was actually subverting the overarching frame defining the *Schlichtung* as a technical-expert dialogue. More importantly, it appears that the participants' conduct and their arguments co-constituted the *Schlichtung* as a peculiar discursive situation in which, despite differences in positions, a basically empiricist understanding of knowledge and expertise was shared and reproduced as conditional for exchange and communication. The dominance of what—in the terms of Habermas (1984)—we could define as rational-technical knowledge remained unchallenged and was actually reproduced even while the knowledge controversy came to a climax. It was, in other words, as if the conduct of the knowledge controversy would stick to a practical order of technical or situational justification that did not address an argumentative connection with more reflective, value-sensitive and moral order of reasoning that has been so important as a motivation for the protest (Fischer 1980; Fischer and Forester 1987). First, rational-technical knowledge and expertise and their related objectivity bias were consistently claimed on both sides as a legitimation for their own arguments; and, second, that rational-technical knowledge and expertise ultimately conferred a mutual legitimation on the participants, as it constituted within the mediation setting the very condition for structured argumentation. Accordingly, the *Schlichtung* developed consistently—and almost unchallenged—as a game of expertise and counter-expertise, and rational-technical knowledge dominated over the controversy, so far as to prevail over the capacity of working out contradictions among frames and of possibly addressing their reframing.

A striking aspect in this sense was the dominance of extensive and intensive, increasingly lengthy and detailed technical discussions. We already mentioned the importance, for instance, of a discussion on timetables: a discussion that started very early in Session 2 and dominated most of it, until (2, 100) it was postponed as the latest documentation appeared not to be available ... only to come back at length in Session 8 as a key matter in the comparison between S21 and K21 (8, 47–177). A similar importance was placed on discussions on regional transportation networks and traffic data (dominating most of Session 3) and on geology issues (Session 6).

It is trivial to note that, as substantive technical matters, the aspects involved in these discussions were important in arguments about the performance and feasibility of S21, and hence also in the knowledge controversy. The point, however, is that, despite potentials for insisting on conflicting frames or storylines, arguments and counter-arguments rather converged on an attitude that realized an isomorphic argumentative rationality in questioning expert knowledge by expert knowledge.

The discussion on timetables is a case in point. In line with the agenda, the discussion on timetable plans was part of the aim of assessing the performance of S21; hence, the timetable issue was discussed at great length, mainly as an issue of whether it was technically feasible or not—even while an alternative view of what a timetable might be at all loomed behind it (e.g., Wölfle: 2, 90). While it is apparent that the way in which an isomorphic argumentation is pursued with an apparent 'falsificationist' or de-constructivist intent—as in this case—may provide a significant foundation for counter-arguments and for alternative proposals, it is also apparent that it expresses the dominance of a defined discursive frame that is predicated on this isomorphism.

A significant effect of these isomorphic arguments was the difficulty of exiting a discursive frame of expertise vs. counter-expertise. This became apparent precisely when this frame was openly questioned: for instance, as questioning the 'evidence' of the opponents was countered by requirements for 'counter-evidence' from the supporters—requirements that the opponents systematically refused to accept (e.g., Palmer: 2, 91), reminding the actors of the asymmetry of competences and responsibilities between the parties, and of the planning authorities' own responsibility to include alternative counter-arguments in their planning procedures—only to turn to arguments defined precisely by an isomorphic frame of counter-arguments in presenting their alternatives (most notably, K21 as an alternative to S21: Session 8).

These aspects underlined the constraints defined by the discursive situation, for both sides, to exiting an empiricist frame of argument; on the other hand, they underlined the way the development of arguments reinforced this isomorphism, co-constituting the features of the discursive situation.

Some key features of the development of arguments during the *Schlichtung* exemplify this aspect. One of these is the centrality gained by cost–benefit arguments, as applied to the various performance criteria for assessing the project; while developing initially within the frame of 'fact-finding' and 'fact-checking,' as an apparent issue of sharing information and establishing a common knowledge-base, cost–benefit arguments soon became markers of what was at stake in the process, while also constraining the discussion within a strictly technical domain of argumentation. This had effects, for instance, when the cost–benefit argument, at a certain point in the process, established itself even in the awareness of the participants as a key argument of the opponents—exerting a dominance in their arguments that progressively marginalized other significant frames:

> We have no agreement here, because we have just got the cost–benefit issue from Mr. Kretschmann as the central point. The line as such is not contested, but what the thing costs and what benefits it delivers. That is the real issue. (Geißler: 3, 144)

A similar observation can be made about a key shift in arguments introduced by the opponents in Session 6 (in light of highly technical discussions on the expected geological impact of construction) when, as part of a controversy over the interpretation of evidential data, risk-related arguments were introduced, leading to the introduction of an argumentative frame based on precautionary principles: the whole discussion turning out to adopt the same argumentative repertoire of cost–benefit analysis adopted in previous performance discussions.

Conclusions

No doubt, the *Schlichtung* has been an exceptionally important and necessary event in recent German politics and society: first of all, for the public awareness it has raised about mechanisms of policy-making and planning usually shielded from broad public insight and scrutiny. The *Schlichtung*, as a peculiar response to the social mobilization that had prompted it in the first place, has made it possible to articulate demands for new legitimating sources of public policy-making and to channel them into potential directions of reform. In this respect—even if no progressive outcome can, at the time of writing, be taken for granted—its critical deconstruction of public policy practices and its long-term effects should not be underestimated.

There is also little doubt, however, that the *Schlichtung* did not provide the resolution for any of the conflicts around S21. Too many and too momentous contradictions loom behind this experiment, as the conditions at the outset made clear, and as events following the spring 2011 state elections and the constitution of a new government coalition in Baden-Württemberg confirmed.[14] As a consequence, despite its political-cultural significance, the *Schlichtung* has paradoxically turned out to be a minor episode in terms of concrete outcomes. This is not the least of the contradictions worthy of exploration, in the framework of more general critical engagement with the S21 case.

When expectations for democratization are emphasized in connection to a deliberation event, having a closer look at what is at play is warranted. This chapter has done this by looking at a specific, limited but crucial aspect: understanding the way mediated negotiation is constituted as a discursive situation. A key reason why the *Schlichtung* could hardly resolve the S21 conflict is the set of constraints to reframing the issue inscribed in the mediated negotiation process as it was constituted as a discursive situation.

The point being made here is that this aspect is largely neglected in pragmatic, application-oriented theories of mediated negotiation that exert a mainstream influence in planning theory and practice. Conversely, this neglect bears significant limitations on our understanding of the nature of conflict situations and on our assessment of the potential outcomes of mediated negotiation practices.

There is no denying the meaning of deliberation and mediation practices for democratization. We need, however, to look at them as part of hegemonic practices (Laclau and Mouffe 1985; Mouffe 2013). The way in which these practices are played out is key for defining conditions under which mediated negotiation can become part of the (re)framing or, conversely, a factor for reproducing a certain framing. In order for this to contribute to turning antagonism into a truly democratic practice of agonistic pluralism—to use

Mouffe's terms (2000)—a critical analysis of the nature of the discursive situation in which democratization hopes are raised is required.

Notes

1. A caveat: defining the *Schlichtung* as 'mediated negotiation' is not unproblematic, and would require a discussion not only of mediated negotiation itself, but also of some ambiguous features of the *Schlichtung* specific to the Stuttgart experience. In this chapter, I propose 'mediated negotiation' as an apt definition, provided it is not understood too dogmatically and as distinct from 'deliberation.'

2. Here a brief chronology and some basic data on the project:

   First concepts date back to 1988, when experts' proposals for an underground railway station became the foundation for exploratory planning by the government of Land Baden-Württemberg, leading in September 1992 to a first intergovernmental agreement on a solution combining a new station with a specific railway development option. In 1994, Stuttgart 21 was officially presented as a partnership project of the German federal government, the Land Baden-Württemberg, the City of Stuttgart and Deutsche Bahn AG, involving a new underground station on the location of the extant railway grounds, to be dismissed for urban redevelopment purposes, and an improved railway connection to Stuttgart airport. Following feasibility studies, in November 1995 the institutional partners signed a framework agreement defining mutual responsibilities in the development and financing of the project. In February 1997, according to the timing foreseen by the legal planning procedure—the *Raumordnungsverfahren*—a first phase of formal public insight and consultation was opened: over 13,000 entries, mostly referring to environmental impacts and local nuisances, made manifest the potential for conflict attached to the project. Nevertheless, in November 1997 the project surmounted the hurdle of environmental impact assessment and the operational planning phase began. Financing—in particular on the federal side in charge for railway infrastructure—however, turned out to be a major issue in the ensuing years, leading to delay of the official release of the project until March 2001, when a covenant between the Bund and Deutsche Bahn AG was finally signed. While the city started purchasing land from DB in the areas targeted for redevelopment, a controversy over the listed station hall building by architect Paul Bonatz (completed 1927) arose in 2005, leading to a compromise decision that safeguarded the main hall but sacrificed the northern wing to the plan's provisions. Pending lawsuits were decided in favor of the project by the Land lawcourts in 2006, but this only led to public opposition getting stronger in the ensuing years: 2007 marked a significant escalation in the public protest and led to mobilization for a local referendum on the project that—despite the backing of about 67,000 signatures—was dismissed by the Stuttgart government in December. With a further financial covenant signed by the project partners in April 2009, the realization phase officially started. However, success for the Greens in June 2009 local elections and the start of regular so-called 'Monday demonstrations' at the central station in November marked the start of a new public mobilization phase, which was further fueled by developments unveiling contradictions in the financial prospects of the project. In February 2010, construction works at the station began, countered by mass demonstrations with up to 60,000 participants taking part throughout the year. Meanwhile, politics at the federal, state and city level became fully involved with the issue, with the Greens as the party-political wing of opposition against the project, the Social Democrats in Stuttgart finally accepting the idea of a referendum, the federal and Land government coalitions overtly supporting the project and rejecting any claim for political or legal revision, and citizens' protests extending to the occupation of public spaces in central Stuttgart. As a consequence of this pattern of politicization, and in view of state elections to be held in early 2011, any attempt at mediation conducted during September 2010 failed. This phase dramatically culminated in the events of 'black Thursday' when, on September 30, 2010, ruthless police attacks on protesters left about a hundred citizens hurt and two seriously injured.

3. "Jetzt geht es erst recht los" ("Now things really get started," statement by an anonymous protester interviewed on February 2, 2010, as broadcast by DeutschlandRadio Kultur: personal recollection).

4. Henceforth, S21 stands for Stuttgart 21 as—according to context—either to the development project (similarly to the alternative project K21, standing for Kopfbahnhof 21) or to the controversy as a whole. I will refer to the mediated negotiation process—as customary in Germany—as the *Schlichtung*.

5. Heiner Geißler (born 1930) is a key but eccentric figure of the German Christian Democratic party (CDU), which he also led as secretary-general between 1977 and 1989. As a jurist and former justice in the state administrative court of the Land Baden-Württemberg, he started his career as a CDU politician in Baden-Württemberg (1962–1965 head of office of the Ministry of Labor and Social Policy), the Land this party ruled for several decades until state elections in 2011. His career in public office developed since the 1960s with a focus on social policy (1967–1977 Minister of Social Policy, Youth, Health and Sports of the Land Rheinland-Pfalz, 1982–1985 Minister of Youth, Family and Health of the federal government) introducing significant reforms. A long-term MP in the German *Bundestag*, in later years Geißler has developed a remarkable attitude for transparency and unorthodox positions, culminating in his over-critical anti-globalist and internationalist positions and his joining of Attac in 2007. Geißler also has a significant experience with private contracting disputes, having served recurrently since the late 1990s as a mediator in nationwide wage contract negotiations—one of which, significantly, involved Deutsche Bahn AG (in 2007).

6. The numbers (number of the session followed by page number) refer to the stenographic protocols of the *Schlichtung* (see note 11), available at: www.schlichtung-s21.de/dokumente.html, accessed: May 2011 and May 2014. This chapter is mainly based on text analysis of the stenographic protocols, backed by extensive review of media coverage and public debates. Video recordings of the sessions have been partially consulted but not explicitly used as a source.

7. The *Schlichtung* developed along nine day-long sessions held in Stuttgart town hall between October 22 and November 30, 2010 (for more details, see below, note 11). Participation was flexible but subject to the rule that seven representatives would represent each side at the table at each individual session. Each side could also involve a non-predefined number of experts. It was agreed that only the formal representatives would be included in the sessions program and allowed to intervene as speakers; formal representatives were entitled to pass on the right to intervene to their own experts, according to need. As Geißler put it: "All will run through the seven protagonists—I will call them thus—and it will be they who decide which expert is to talk" (Geißler: 2, 34). The name of experts participating are not listed in the protocols of the *Schlichtung* but named when intervening; here they are quoted as in the protocols. A

complete listing of participants in each session can be found on the website: www.schlichtung-s21.de (accessed October 2014).

To give a sense of the table's composition, here are the formal representatives participating in the concluding session of November 30:

Representatives of the opponents of S21:

- Hannes Rockenbauch, member of Stuttgart city council and of the civic association SÖS Stuttgart Ökologisch Sozial;
- Winfried Kretschmann, MP in the Land Parliament and head of the Green Party group therein;
- Werner Wölfle, MP in the Land Parliament and head of the Green Party group in Stuttgart city council;
- Brigitte Dahlbender, head of the civic association BUND in Land Baden-Württemberg;
- Peter Conradi, architect in Stuttgart and former MP of the Social Democratic Party in the German Bundestag;
- Gangolf Stocker, initiator of the civic initiative Leben in Stuttgart—kein Stuttgart 21;
- Klaus Arnoldi of the civic association Verkehrsclub Deutschland.

Representatives of the supporters of S21:

- Johannes Bräuchle, a protestant pastor, of the civic association Bündnis der Befürworter—Wir sind Stuttgart 21;
- Thomas Bopp, MP in the Land Parliament and Head of the Stuttgart regional government (Verband Region Stuttgart);
- Tanja Gönner, Minister of the Environment, Nature Protection and Transportation of the Land Baden-Württemberg;
- Stefan Mappus, MP in the Land Parliament and Minister President of the Land Baden-Württemberg;
- Rüdiger Grube, CEO of Deutsche Bahn AG;
- Volker Kefer, managing director of Deutsche Bahn AG;
- Wolfgang Schuster, Mayor of the City of Stuttgart.

8. One important feature of exceptionality in the S21 case resides in the wave of public attention it raised and in its coverage throughout the media. In particular, the sessions of the *Schlichtung* were entirely broadcast live as well as live-streamed over its website by the national public information TV channel Phoenix, and partially by regional channels like Südwestrundfunk and Flügel TV. According to a communication by Geißler himself (2, 9–10), during the first session on October 22, the live broadcast had a share of 6.8 percent on Südwestrundfunk in Baden-Württemberg and of 2.9 percent on Phoenix on a national basis, with 370,000 hits registered via the website.

9. All translations from German are mine.

10. A key issue concerning the relation between S21 and the Wendlingen–Ulm railway line was not only an assessment of their specific performance and functionality but also of their mutual implications, the opponents being open—and rather divided—with regard to the merits of the new railway line but contending that these did not imply a project like S21, while the reverse was true; in this respect, contesting the Wendlingen–Ulm line had a rather equivocal function in the opponents' arguments, serving both as a proof of faulty planning as a whole and as a proof of the arbitrariness of linkages to the need of a new transit station.

11. Despite minor shifts, in part resulting from interim checks and the need to agree on redefinitions of the agenda, this basic structure was consistently upheld by the mediator. For the sake of comparison, the headings of the protocols referring to the issues discussed read as follows (simplified):

- Session 1, October 22, 2010: 'Strategic meaning and transportation performance of the node Stuttgart 21';
- Session 2, October 29, 2010: 'Performance of the railway node Stuttgart 21';
- Session 3, November 4, 2010: 'New railway line Ulm–Wendlingen (general concept, passenger traffic national–international, goods traffic/K21');
- Session 4, November 12, 2010: 'Terminal Station Kopfbahnhof 21';
- Session 5, November 19, 2010: 'Ecology and urban development';
- Session 6, November 20, 2010: 'Geology, security and construction process';
- Session 7, November 26, 2010: 'Costs–benefit calculation';
- Session 8, November 27, 2010: 'Performance and management concept S21/K21, effects on regional and local transportation, open questions, construction process';
- Session 9, November 30, 2010: 'Closing session, closing pledges, recommendations by the *Schlichter*' (the so-called *Schlichterspruch*).

12. One could argue that, despite emphasis on learning processes by participants, there is a significant underrating of the learning experienced by mediators themselves in the literature.

13. That such a realization is also part of this learning process is exemplified by a moment in Session 5 (108), when Geißler declared himself almost shocked by some of the discrepancies highlighted by the exposure of 'facts.'

14. The results presented to the public on November 30, 2010 had a most important provision: the parties agreed to make the realization of S21 dependent upon the result of a 'stress-test' assessing its performance. Albeit agreed upon as 'binding,' this decision was contradictory in two ways. First, it was basically technical and—despite aims of 'objectivity'—it was hardly neutral, as it was framed as a test of the S21 project—not of alternative solutions or of different framings of the issue. Second, all possible exit strategies following a negative stress-test were dependent on extant contractual agreements among the institutional partners. This actually amounted to Deutsche Bahn being able to blackmail both the Land Baden-Württemberg and the City of Stuttgart. Moreover, as it turned out, granting independence and transparency in conducting the stress-test proved impossible under such conditions, lending Deutsche Bahn a position of undue vantage. Significantly, after a contested presentation of its results on July 29, 2011 (SMA+Partner AG 2011)—allegedly confirming Deutsche Bahn's technical expectations and thus upholding the project—its validity was broadly dismissed by representatives of the *Aktionsbündnis*. Attempts by the mediator, Heiner Geißler, to bring into play a new 'integrative' solution based on K21 (SMA+Partner AG and Geißler 2011) were in turn readily dismissed by S21 supporters, as they had already been assessed in the *Planfeststellungsverfahren*.

References

Callon, M., Law, J. and Rip, A. (eds.) (1986) *Mapping the Dynamics of Science and Technology*, Basingstoke, UK: Macmillan.

Christensen, K. S. (1985) "Coping with Uncertainty in Planning," *Journal of the American Planning Association*, 51(1): 63–73.

DiMaggio, P. J. and Powell, W. W. (1983) "The Iron Cage Revisited: Institutional Isomorphism and Collective Rationality in Organizational Fields," *American Sociological Review*, 48(2): 147–60; now in W. W. Powell and P. J. DiMaggio (eds.) (1991), *The New Institutionalism in Organizational Analysis*, Chicago, IL: University of Chicago Press: 63–82.

Fairclough, N. (1992) *Discourse and Social Change*, Cambridge, UK: Polity Press.

Fischer, F. (1980) *Politics, Values and Public Policy*, Boulder, CO: Westview Press.

Fischer, F. and Forester, J. (1987) *Confronting Values in Policy Analysis*, Newbury Park, CA: Sage.

Fisher, R. and Brown, S. (1988) *Getting Together: Building a Relationship that Gets to Yes*, Boston, MA: Houghton Mifflin.

Fisher, R. and Ury, W. L. (1981), *Getting to Yes: Negotiating Agreement without Giving In*, New York, NY: Penguin.

Forester, J. (1999) *The Deliberative Practitioner*, Cambridge, MA: MIT Press.

Forester, J. (2009) *Dealing with Differences: Dramas of Mediating Public Disputes*, Oxford, UK: Oxford University Press.

Forester, J. and Laws, D. (2009) "Toward a Naturalistic Research Ethic: Or How Mediators Must Act Well to Learn, If They Are to Practice Effectively," in F. Lo Piccolo and H. Thomas (eds.), *Ethics and Planning Research*, Aldershot, UK: Ashgate: 179–189.

Gieryn, T. (1995) "Boundaries of Science," in S. Jasanoff, G. E. Markle, J. C. Petersen and T. Pinch (eds.), *Handbook of Science and Technology Studies*, Thousand Oaks, CA: Sage: 393–443.

Gualini, E. (2001) *Planning and the Intelligence of Institutions: Interactive Planning Approaches Between Institutional Design and Institution-Building*, Aldershot, UK: Ashgate.

Gualini, E. (2004) *Multi-Level Governance and Institutional Change: The Europeanization of Regional Policy in Italy*, Aldershot, UK: Ashgate.

Habermas, J. (1984) *The Theory of Communicative Action*, Boston, MA: Beacon Press.

Halffman, W. (2003) *Boundaries of Regulatory Science*, Boechout, Belgium: Albatros.

Healey, P. (1997) *Collaborative Planning: Shaping Places in Fragmented Societies*, Basingstoke, UK: Macmillan.

Hirschman, A. O. (1994) "Social Conflicts as Pillars of Democratic Market Society," *Political Theory*, 22(2): 203–218.

Innes, J. E. and Booher, D. E. (2010) *Planning with Complexity*, London, UK: Routledge.

Jessop, B. (2001) "Institutional Re(turns) and the Strategic-Relational Approach," *Environment and Planning A*, 33(7): 1213–1235.

Kelman, H. C. (1996) "Negotiation as Interactive Problem-Solving," *International Negotiation*, 1(1): 99–123.

Laclau, E. and Mouffe, C. (1985) *Hegemony and Socialist Strategy: Towards a Radical Democratic Politics*, London, UK: Verso.

Latour, B. (1987) *Science in Action*, Cambridge, MA: Harvard University Press.

Lave, J. and Wenger, E. (1991) *Situated Learning*, Cambridge, UK: Cambridge University Press.

Laws, D. and Forester, J. (2006) "Learning in Practice: Public Policy Mediation," *Critical Policy Analysis*, 1(4): 342–371.

Lindblom, C. E. (1965) *The Intelligence of Democracy*, New York, NY: The Free Press.

March, J. G. and Olsen, J. P. (1976) *Ambiguity and Choice in Organizations*, Bergen, Norway: Bergen Universitetsforlaget.

March, J. G. and Olsen, J. P. (1989) *Rediscovering Institutions: The Organizational Basis of Politics*, New York, NY: The Free Press.

Metze, T. (2006) "Keep Out of the Bijlmerpark: Boundary Work in Experimental Policy Discourse and Practice," in M. van den Brink and T. Metze (eds.), *Words Matter in Policy and Planning*, Utrecht, Netherlands: NGS: 77–89.

Mouffe, C. (2000) *The Democratic Paradox*, London, UK: Verso.

Mouffe, C. (2013) *Agonistics: Thinking the World Politically*, London, UK: Verso.

Raiffa, H. (1982) *The Art and Science of Negotiation*, Cambridge, MA: Harvard University Press.

Raiffa, H., Richardson, J. and Metcalfe, D. (2002) *Negotiation Analysis: The Science and Art of Collaborative Decision Making*, Cambridge, MA: Harvard University Press.

Rein, M. and Schön, D. A. (1993) "Reframing Policy Discourse," in F. Fischer and J. Forester (eds.), *The Argumentative Turn in Policy Analysis and Planning*, Durham, NC: Duke University Press: 145–166.

Schmidt, V. E. (2010) "Taking Ideas and Discourse Seriously: Explaining Change Through Discursive Institutionalism as the Fourth 'New Institutionalism'," *European Political Science Review*, 2(1): 1–25.

Schön, D. and Rein, M. (1994) *Frame Reflection: Toward the Resolution of Intractable Policy Controversies*, New York, NY: Basic Books.

SMA+Partner AG (eds.) (2011) *Audit zur Betriebsqualitätsüberprüfung Stuttgart 21. Schlussbericht*, Zurich: author.

SMA+Partner AG and Geißler, H. (2011) *Frieden in Stuttgart: Eine Kompromisslösung zur Befriedung der Auseinandersetzung um Stuttgart 21*, Zurich: author.

Sullivan, T. (1984) *Resolving Development Disputes Through Negotiation*, New York, NY: Plenum Press.

Susskind, L. and Cruickshank, J. (1987) *Breaking the Impasse: Consensual Approaches to Resolving Public Disputes*, New York, NY: Basic Books.

Weick, K. E. (1979) *The Social Psychology of Organizing*, second edition, New York, NY: Addison-Wesley.

PART IV
INTERPRETIVE POLICY ANALYSIS AND DELIBERATIVE APPROACHES TO PLANNING CONFLICTS

Introduction

Enrico Gualini

The contributions in this concluding section of the volume are representative of contemporary attempts at rethinking critically and renewing deliberative approaches to the treatment of planning conflicts. Each chapter takes a different perspective and derives in part from different theoretical premises, but all share, in the first place, a belief in the need for critical scrutiny of established normative models of deliberative practice—in face of their frequently disappointing application and results—and, in the second place, an interest in the renewal of their theoretical underpinnings, with a focus on recent developments in interpretive policy analysis.

The chapters establish a virtual dialogue across themselves, and in particular among pairs developing complementary arguments from distinctive perspectives. Pucci and Allain discuss the combination of deliberative and negotiating practices in the light of new theoretical contributions as well as against the background of recent public approaches. Durnová and Verloo combine an attention to the role of emotions in the policy process with an interest in understanding the discursive and narrative construction of policy controversies and conflicts. The combination of interpretive proposals advanced by these chapters defines new significant avenues for planning theory and practice in dealing with conflicts.

The starting point of Allain's arguments is her observation of the separation between deliberative approaches and conflict resolution approaches in practice. There is significant acknowledgment in planning theory of the fact that negotiations over meanings, roles, positions and interests among actors are ongoing in planning situations. This is in line with directions of interpretive policy analysis that understand negotiations over the meaning of a situation as being a constitutive component of social interactions. Accordingly, planning theory inspired by interpretive policy analysis identifies a key task for the design of a deliberative planning process precisely in allowing these negotiations to develop in transparent and integrative ways. In contrast to this, however, Allain stresses the prevailing distinction between understandings of deliberation, on the one hand, and of negotiation, on the other hand, in related literature and practice; in her opinion, this has in the long run developed into a gap in understanding the dynamics of conflict—a gap that derives from assumptions about deliberative democracy, and their application within deliberative planning approaches, that have neglected the role of negotiation. She accordingly pleads for the development of an interpretive framework for grasping conflict dynamics within contexts of deliberation by focusing on the practice of negotiation as a key interpretive moment.

For Allain, negotiation can be seen as an interpretive tool of conflict transformation in deliberative situations, helping to address the traditional distortions in deliberative settings due to asymmetries in the positions and in the conducts of the participants. In fact, her aim is similar to the one pursued by Pucci in searching for a medium for negotiation within the constraints and challenges facing public deliberation in real-world contexts. For both Allain and Pucci the context of research is represented by attempts at new approaches in the framework of a rearticulation of institutional deliberation arenas and practices in France and Italy.

Pucci thematizes the challenges of deliberation under conditions—as typical, i.e., in the case of large infrastructure projects—where the general public does not have real opportunities to influence decision-making processes. Deliberation efforts are then hampered by a double asymmetry of decision-making, which relates to the mismatch between scales of decision-making and implied conceptions of the public—with locally concentrated costs and burdens and distributed benefits, in the face of dominant utilitarian assumptions on collective interests and the 'public good'—and to an unbalanced role in decision-making between public institutions and local communities. The result is all too often a mode of planning dominated by a logic of technical verification and by a functionalist understanding of planning issues that assumes collective interests to be served by state-centered decision-making procedures a priori of local evaluation and independently of articulations of scale. The consequences are the difficulty of conducting effective participatory efforts and the frustration resulting from practices that do not reach beyond mere consultation. In Pucci's analysis, negotiated compromises emphasize these asymmetries as, under such conditions, they tend to result in highly selective and partial or uneven compensations, highlighting even more exclusionary effects.

Under these conditions, prone to the prevalence of vested interests and to promoting polarization and conflict escalation, consensus on policy issues appears as an impossible and even hampering ideal. The search for viable alternatives is opened by reference to the concept of 'boundary objects' as a device for addressing a combined deliberative and negotiating practice targeted at reaching practicable policy improvements. The assumption is that identifying 'boundary objects' as the matter of deliberation may open up a 'neutral' space, delineated to include a diversity of viewpoints around the reasons and problems—and not the solution—represented by the policy. As such, a 'boundary object' is a device for sharing an issue, even if from different, even conflicting, perspectives; it may become a device for cooperation beyond consensus-building, for a dialogue in an agonistic space.

Regarding the space of agonism and contention as a space full of emotions is starting point for Durnová's analysis of planning conflicts. Tying into a growing body of research on the role of emotions developing in interpretive policy analysis, Durnová maintains that "emotions are neither the side-effects nor the faults of planning processes" (Chapter 12 this volume: 268), but are rather a constitutive component of their contested political nature. Emotions shape actors' narratives and define their grouping and conduct. As such, they are key to understanding the features of planning controversies and their escalation into overt conflict—in particular when escalating emotions are tied to processes of escalation of opposing, conflicting discourses.

The co-constitutive and co-evolutive relationship between emotions and discourses is the core of Durnová's analysis. She argues for the need to develop an understanding of emotions and of the role they play in defining policy discourses. For this purpose, she advances the notion of 'emotional experiences of discourses' as a key for understanding discourse formation in policy interactions. According to this notion, emotions are inherent to the formation of discourses, and yet also have the potential to transform them. Emotions organize and, so to speak, steer the development of discourses, rather than just 'charging' them: thus, "they have a governing role" in policy processes (Chapter 12 this volume: 253), as they co-define the conditions for actors' identification, the features of opposition and antagonism, and the possible conditions for mediation. This opens up new perspectives for interpreting and acting upon the ambivalence of knowledge(s) at play and at stake in policy conflicts as well as upon the ambiguities of actors' relationships in the policy process.

Verloo characteristically defines emotions as "the story behind the words" (Chapter 13 this volume: 273). Her contribution is a further development in a narrative policy analysis approach connected to emotions. The central tenet is that emotions affect our ability to 'understand' others' stories—and thus deeply affect our modes of interaction. From her perspective, failure to account for emotions is often the origin of failures of deliberative processes to effectively address conflict—even resulting in deeper ingrained feelings of marginality, in "unintended processes of exclusion" (Chapter 13 this volume: 275), and possibly in new stages of escalation.

Verloo is particularly interested in developing a pragmatics of dealing with narratives in the planning process as a means of overcoming prevailing power relations, through "an approach to narrative practice that seeks to engage and acknowledge each distinct storyline in the process of conflict" (Chapter 13 this volume: 287). By this, she further develops a tradition of planning theory that views storytelling as a planning approach or method *for* planning by connecting it with one that views storytelling as a way to start the process of conflict resolution. Her approach also critically engages with others—and in particular Roe's meta-narratives approach—that share similar assumptions, but fail to include the power dynamics involved in the development and mutual relationship of narratives and storylines in the process. As an alternative to the construction of meta-narrative as an additive, mediated and selective outcome of planner's intervention, she advocates a process of 'narrative braiding,' as the expression of the ability of the planner-mediator to render narratives shared by a plurality of actors in their development and mutual relationship.

Narratives are political, also according to Verloo, and their analysis is a contribution to dealing with the political nature of conflicts. In fact, "stories are means to make sense of conflict, but [...] these understandings also shape our ability to act in the process of dealing with conflict" (Chapter 13 this volume: 282); thus dealing with conflict often relies on repertoires of actions that render some stories dominant—as 'master plots'—and others marginal— as 'counter plots'—resulting in effects of hegemony and domination. "Planning conflicts take place exactly at that intersection of dominant and counter plots"; thus, according to Verloo, "[t]he challenge of narrative practice is not to be responsive to or summarize different stories, but instead braid them through the storytelling of decision-making" (Chapter 13 this volume: 284).

Finally, in her Afterword, Patsy Healey takes a longer view in discussing the contributions in this volume. She offers us her reflections on planning as a cause of and response to conflict, putting at the center of attention again a concern for practice, for progressive planners' responsibility and for practicable avenues of engagement.

10

Negotiation as an Interpretive Tool of Conflict Transformation in Deliberative Situations: Learning from the French 'Public Debate' on the Extension of the Highway La Francilienne

Sophie Allain

Introduction

Since the 1970s, many plans have been confronted with urban conflicts and have reached deadlocks. Planners have then come to rethink their practices, seeking to get the public more involved in decision-making. More specifically, new practices of planning giving more room for deliberation have been employed in many countries. Deliberation is indeed expected to allow dialogue between planners and the public, to further mutual understanding and then to improve the quality of the decision and strengthen its legitimacy, avoiding conflicts or their escalation.

Because deliberative practices imply an idealistic context in which opinions are shaped through respectful dialogue, they do not pay attention to the way deliberation may help to handle those conflicts in practice, either in their emergence or in their development. As Susskind (2006: 5) stresses, "deliberative democracy and public dispute resolution have been developing separately for some time. Now it is time for them to begin learning from each other." In June 2005, under the auspices of the MIT-Harvard Public Disputes Program at Harvard Law School, a two-day conference brought together leading dispute resolution professionals and political theorists in the field of deliberative democracy to share ideas and experiences (Susskind 2006, 2009). The aim here is to pursue this path. More specifically, as theories devoted to deliberation in political science or in planning do not really conceptualize conflicts and then do not offer the possibility of understanding their dynamics, the aim of the chapter is to propose an interpretive framework likely to grasp the conflict dynamics in a context of deliberation. This framework relies on the concept of negotiation. After explaining how negotiation may be an interesting deciphering tool to grasp the conflict dynamics in a context of deliberation, I will present a case study (Allain 2007): the French public debate on the extension of the highway La Francilienne in a very urbanized area of the western part of Paris, which took place in 2006. This public debate was organized in the framework of a specific procedure created in 1995 and extended in 2002, which aims to organize public debates on plans of general interest under the control of an independent commission, the National Commission for Public Debate. While many plans are subject to controversies, this specific public debate took place in the context of a very severe local conflict, and particularly brings to the fore how deliberation may help us to understand conflicts and deal with them.

Negotiation as a Deciphering Tool to Grasp the Conflict Dynamics in a Context of Deliberation

While conflict is not a new question as such in planning theory, the development of practices giving more room to deliberation requires new insights into the analysis of conflict dynamics in a context of deliberation. An examination of deliberative theories either in political science or in planning, however, reveals the incomplete dimension of conflict, which is only considered from a discursive viewpoint. Conflict has been recognized as a natural feature of any deliberative and decisional situation concerning public affairs and as undermining genuine and constructive dialogue by scholars of the conflict resolution field. This calls for bringing together both fields. Along these lines, I shall suggest that negotiation may be an interpretive tool to decipher conflict dynamics in a context of deliberation.

The Incomplete Dimension of Conflict in Deliberative Theories

Generally speaking, deliberative theories do not handle the issue of conflict as such or remain superficial. As Aragaki (2009) stresses, in the field of political science, theoreticians of democratic deliberation tend to view conflict as 'disagreement' about different 'philosophies of life' (Cohen 1998) or 'moral arguments' (Gutmann and Thompson 1996). The appropriate response to the 'controversies' that arise is a process of 'rational argumentation,' through which participants try to accommodate the moral convictions of their opponents to the greatest extent possible, without compromising their own moral convictions, in a spirit of mutual respect. Success at resolving such conflicts hinges on the ability of each party to convince the other parties by means of 'reasonable' arguments, within the building of a common good process.

In the field of planning, the 'communicative' or 'argumentative' turn (Forester 1989; Fischer and Forester 1993b; Innes 1995; Healey 1997; Innes and Booher 2010), which has developed as a "challenge to systematized reason" (Healey 1993: 235) dominating professional practices, insists on the value of discourse. Along these lines, politics is "a discursive struggle" (Fischer and Forester 1993a: 1–2) between different definitions of social problems and political solutions, and deliberative settings represent one type of political arena in which discursive struggles take place. Planning as "a communicative enterprise" (Healey 1993: 240) is "a process for collectively, and interactively, addressing and working out how to act with respect to shared concerns about how far to go and how to 'manage' [...] change." Theoreticians of communicative planning then try to develop collaborative practices (Healey 1997; Innes 2003; Innes and Booher 2010), considered as a new mode of governance. While they recognize that conflicts are "a routine part of our experience" (Healey 1997: 31) and "ever present throughout" a collaborative process (Innes 2004: 14), and while several scholars build upon conflict resolution approaches (Innes 2003, 2004; Forester 2009; Innes and Booher 2010), they do not analyze the conflicts and their dynamics per se. This is partly because, in their work, the very idea of conflict is, first, associated with pluralism, namely "the recognition of a diversity of ways of living everyday life and of valuing local environmental qualities" (Healey 1997: 32). Along these lines, it is a matter of planning in 'fragmented societies' (Healey 1997) and dealing with 'complexity' (Innes and Booher 2010) in order to handle 'wicked problems.' However, it is also because attention remains at the level of discourses, and is therefore placed on the issue of "resolving conflicts of frame" (Rein and Schön 1993: 145), 'dealing with value differences' (Forester 2009), or improving the 'quality of dialogue' (Innes 2003; Innes and Booher 2010).

While several scholars have criticized deliberative democracy and communicative planning approaches sharply (Flyvbjerg 1998; Huxley 2000; Huxley and Yiftachel 2000; Lauria 2000; Yiftachel et al. 2002), they have not highlighted clearly the incomplete dimension of conflict in those theories. Actually, they have rather contested the effectiveness of deliberative practices because of unbalanced power relations and questioned the feasibility of consensus-building. In the field of planning, Healey (2003) and Innes (2004) have clarified several misunderstandings and brought several answers to the critics, and today there is rather a call for a 'post-collaborative era' (Brownill and Parker 2010), which does not reject communicative planning, but suggests analyzing the actual dynamics unfolding at the micro-level more thoroughly and understanding how participation refigures local governance.

Along these lines, how to take conflict better into account in the analysis of deliberative processes appears a key question. Several scholars have therefore undertaken to bring deliberative and conflict resolution theories together (Mansbridge 2006; Aragaki 2009; Menkel-Meadow 2011). These scholars not only emphasize that conflict dynamics always interfere with dialogue; following scholars in conflict resolution, they also highlight that while conflict may have positive functions (Simmel 1955; Coser 1956), ranging from clarifying problems to integration, it may also have destructive effects (Deutsch 1973). As Aragaki (2009) summarizes, conflict actually affects our experience of ourselves and others, which distorts the very process of giving reasons and listening to the other parties' arguments. Conflict then tends to harden positions and to polarize discussions, each party being convinced that it is right and the other wrong. Conflict inhibits empathy and the ability to listen carefully to each other. If one party listens to the other parties' discourses, it is more often to identify errors and weaknesses, or seek evidence that supports its interests while ignoring evidence that does not. What is a good argument to one side is seen by the other as further proof that the speaker is wrong or seeks to deceive. An explanation or an appeal to moral considerations may be considered an attack. Therefore, while deliberative theories consider conflict only at a conceptual and intellectual level as a struggle of arguments, conflict resolution scholars emphasize the relational dimension of conflict.

These reflections suggest that new insights are required to understand conflict dynamics in a context of deliberation; it is necessary to analyze not only the exchange of arguments and how they contribute to clarify the problem through a process of inquiry, but also how the relationships between the participants progress and how both dimensions interact to transform the conflict, in the direction either of more cooperation or more competition. It means that arguments have to be considered not only as elements of reasoning regarding the specific project under debate but also as expressions of human beings integrated in complex networks of relationships and then pursuing several objectives or submitted to a variety of influences. Deliberative situations have then to be seen as temporary discursive arenas opened to a larger public and political sphere. I shall argue that negotiation may be used as an interpretive tool of conflict transformation in deliberative situations. However, I shall first explain how the concepts of conflict, deliberation and negotiation may be linked.

Linking the Concepts of Conflict, Deliberation and Negotiation

At first glance, linking the concepts of conflict, deliberation and negotiation appears very challenging. This especially concerns the links between deliberation and negotiation, as many scholars have defined deliberation and negotiation in contrast (Urfalino 2005). As we have seen previously, in deliberative theories, deliberation representations tend to be grounded in the 'conversation' (Remer 2000; Urfalino 2005) or 'discussion' paradigm (Lavelle 2007). Such a concept has developed under the influence of Jürgen Habermas (1984), who has distinguished between 'communicative action' and 'strategic action.' The first refers to the interaction between at least two people, who seek to reach a mutual understanding regarding an action through rational argumentation, in order to consensually coordinate their own actions. The notion of 'strategic action' is an extension of the 'teleological action,' which refers to an actor choosing the means that he or she considers the most efficient to reach a predefined aim. In the strategic model, the actor takes the behavior of at least one other actor into account in his or her calculus. In 'communicative action,' actors are disinterested and only prompted by the pursuit of the common good, and then seek to cooperate, while, in 'strategic action,' actors only defend their own interests and can only compete. 'Communicative action' and 'strategic action' then seem opposite conceptions of social interaction. While Habermas has stressed that both are "two equally fundamental elements of social interaction" and aspired to accommodate them, he has not realized this aspiration, which remains a goal to be reached (quoted in Johnson 1991: 181).

I suggest that negotiation can articulate both conceptions, on condition that the notion of 'strategic action' is not restricted to the idea of selfish actors unable to cooperate, and that 'communicative action' does not rely on the model of disinterested rational argumentation. 'Communicative action' and 'strategic action' are indeed not so irreconcilable as they appear at first glance (Allain 2009). First, while 'communicative action' relies on the idea of disinterested rational argumentation, Remer (2000) has suggested that deliberative situations are better described by the 'oratory model,' where it is a matter of persuading the others, and then winning them over. Furthermore, interaction among disinterested actors is an unrealistic situation in policy-making, because the actors who commit themselves in such processes are stakeholders. Therefore, communication among interacting actors may have strategic dimensions. Conversely, 'strategic action' does not imply selfish actors, unable to take the common good into account. It only suggests that in situations of interdependency, where actors cannot decide alone on the course of their action, they have to take the opinions, expectations or wills of the others into account, as the game theory and the definition of negotiation proposed by Thomas Schelling (1981 [1960]) put it; indeed, in this scholar's view, negotiation refers to a situation where each actor perfectly knows that his or her own acts are observed and may be anticipated by his or her adversary, which he or she has to include in his or her analysis. Furthermore, policy-making relies on multilateral negotiations, which cannot be restricted to pure situations of bargaining, where each position is well-known from the beginning and which only implies trade-offs among players in an exchange considered as a transaction. Indeed, Zartman (1994) has shown that the variety of issues and interests involved in multilateral negotiations leads to a more open dynamic of interactions, because the game is not clearly structured by positions giving rise to stable coalitons and oppositions, and because there is room for innovation. Besides, in situations where people have to go on living together (such as in a city), and then have to maintain good relationships, they cannot behave as if they were purely adversarial and are so prone to cooperate at least at a minimal level. Finally, Mansbridge (2006: 110) has stressed that "although negotiations often produce compromises, which by their nature leave both sides to some degree unsatisfied, they can also produce 'integrated' solutions." She borrows this idea of integration from Mary Parker Follett (1942), an idea that has since been used by Walton and McKersie (1965) and renamed 'win-win' solutions (Fisher and Ury 1981). Mansbridge (2006) adds that integrated solutions achieved through behavior of cooperation produce a common good.

Communicative and strategic action may then be articulated as soon as we admit that the actors interacting in policy-making are stakeholders, who defend their own interests but are also able to cooperate, and that the interactive process gives them matter for thought and then for evolution of their viewpoints, expectations or demands.

The links between conflict and negotiation are easier to establish. Indeed, many scholars have stressed that the border between conflict and negotiation is not clear. Dupont (1994) has emphasized that negotiation is a social activity that has to be distinguished from both 'pure conflict' and 'pure problem-solving.' In a pure conflict, each party only seeks to win against the others and may use any means it considers as appropriate to achieve its own aims, including coercion, strength, trickery, rigging and so on. In contrast, in a negotiation, parties look for a mutually satisfying agreement. However, Schelling (1981 [1960]) has stressed that most situations of conflict are also situations of negotiation, because the possibility for one party to achieve its aims often broadly depends on the choices and decisions made by the others. Negotiation may then be explicit, but it may also be tacit. Such a representation highlights that, in a conflict, the parties always have a common interest to seek a solution likely to settle this unsatisfying situation without jeopardizing each other, interests too much. Actually, as soon as a notion of interdependency is recognized in a conflict, there is a continuum between conflict and negotiation. Along these lines, conflict can be described as a kind of 'distributive' negotiation defined by Walton and McKersie (1965) as a pure situation of bargaining where the objectives of at least two parties referring to an area of common concern are assumed to be in conflict and where what one party may gain is a loss to the other. Such a definition is close to the description proposed by

Deutsch (1973: 10), who stresses that "a conflict exists whenever *incompatible* activities occur." It is also close to that of Rubin et al. (1994: 5), for whom "conflict means perceived divergence of interest, or a belief that the parties' current aspirations cannot be achieved simultaneously."

Let us now look at how negotiation may be used as an interpretive tool of conflict transformation in deliberative situations.

Negotiation as an Interpretive Tool of Conflict Transformation in Deliberative Situations

The introduction of any deliberative situation in the public and political sphere always opens an area of uncertainty. Planners know it and often dread facing this moment of public testing. Deliberative situations then present a transformative potential, and negotiation may help to grasp this potential. More specifically, negotiation can be used as an interpretive tool of conflict transformation in deliberative situations.

Deliberative situations are often considered by planners as plan-related negotiations de facto (Forester 1989). Whatever the nature of the issues debated, planners have often already reflected upon them, made some choices and dismissed some options. Therefore, they behave more like stakeholders defending a position (or a range of positions) than practitioners widely open to exchanges with the public in order to define a common strategy. Deliberative situations are for them an opportunity to make their plan acceptable by identifying the adjustments likely to satisfy the malcontents, and then being able to coming to an agreement after the debate.

However, considering deliberative situations as sequences of plan negotiations restricts the possibility of understanding the transformative potential of conflicts. In planning, conflicts are actually much more complex than the picture of NIMBY ('Not In My Backyard') underlying the conception of a plan negotiation suggests. According to the NIMBY theory (Wolsink 1994), any opposition to facility-siting is purely based on local residents' self-interest, namely avoiding having the facilities situated in their own backyard, but the public interest of the project is not questioned. Elliott (1988) has, however, advanced the idea that conflicts in planning often present four overlapping dimensions related to the effects of the new facility on the local environment and the risks associated with it; the nature of the facility; the decisional procedures; and the underlying political principles. Along these lines, examining the transformational potential of deliberative situations implies referring to a wider negotiation of governance, moving beyond the narrow area of the plan to consider a field of territorial problems likely to be handled by different options.

A deliberative situation can then be considered as a specific interactive sequence in such a negotiation of governance, which presents the following features. It is a mediated discursive arena in which a variety of stakeholders confront each other by negotiating the progress of governance. It is mediated, because as soon as deliberative situations give every participant the opportunity to express his or her viewpoint, they can actually be considered as devices of mediation equalizing each party's strength or at least reducing unbalanced power.

The aim of the analysis is to understand how the negotiation of governance progresses within this mediated discursive arena when it starts with a conflict. What does the deliberative situation reveal about this negotiation of governance? Who are the stakeholders? Were all of them already identified? How does each one frame the project in terms of resulting benefits or problems? What does their framing reveal about their underlying interests beyond the positions that they defend? How does it help to understand the conflict and governance situation that has to be improved? Do collective governance stakes emerge? How do the justification processes make it possible to transform the initial positions by discovering new problems or, on the contrary, new solutions? Does the deliberation enable a turn toward a more cooperative negotiation of governance? What are the new possibilities created by the deliberative situation (new options, new kinds of interactions among the participants and so on)? On the contrary, what impedes the progression of the negotiation? Is it possible to come to a cognitive agreement about the governance situation that has to be improved, the reasons for the conflict, or the ways to go on and move forward?

The progression of the negotiation is analyzed from a mediative standpoint in the deliberative situation. This can be the virtual position of an external observer or the actual position of a practitioner in charge of the organization of the debates (whether both positions are clearly different in terms of action, they are indeed not in terms of the understanding of the situation, as soon as the same mediative standpoint is assumed). The analysis relies on a study of the concrete interactions among the participants, especially the planner and the public. By concrete interactions, I mean not only the arguments exchanged but also how the participants behave on the debate stage and around. It is a matter of identifying advances, turning points or formation of deadlocks. The outcomes of the interactions are seen as the product of the participants' strategies and the concrete conditions of deliberation created during the whole process. Empirical data stem from the inquiries conducted by practitioners in charge of the organization of the debates, the arguments exchanged during the debates (mostly oral discourses, which are recorded, but also any kind of written texts publicly available) and the observation of the participants' behavior and concrete conditions of deliberation.

Understanding Conflict Dynamics in the French 'Public Debate': The Case of the Extension of the Highway La Francilienne

The French 'public debate' on the extension of the highway La Francilienne, which took place in 2006 in a very urbanized area of the western part of Paris, started in the context of a very severe local conflict, particularly brings to the fore what deliberation can bring to urban conflicts. I shall begin by presenting the features of the French public debate procedure and the history of this conflict before turning to the analysis of the public debate on this project.

The French 'Public Debate' Procedure

The 'public debate' procedure (*débat public*) was created in France in 1995 by the so-called Barnier Law and extended in 2002 by the Local Democracy Law (*Loi de Démocratie de Proximité*) in order to organize public debates on plans of general interest under the control of an independent commission, the National Commission for Public Debate. This procedure was introduced after the severe conflicts over the High-Speed Méditerranée Train project, which was to link two large cities, Lyon and Marseille, in one hour (De Carlo 2006). The decision-making process, which unfolded between 1989 and 1994, has given rise to major institutional innovations in the framework of the Bianco Memo, the Barnier Law and the Local Democracy Law.

First, on December 15, 1992, the French Minister of Transportation Jean-Louis Bianco sent a memo to departmental and regional prefects, in which he called for "a transparent and democratic debate on the design and implementation of large facilities planned by the State."[1] Such a debate would revolve around a series of meetings giving a broad spectrum of stakeholders the opportunity to discuss project proposals. This orientation was strengthened in the framework of the Law on the Reinforcement of Environmental Protection (February 2, 1995) initiated by the Minister of the Environment Michel Barnier. This law broadened the spectrum of projects to which the procedure would apply. It also extended the scope of the debate by allowing the discussion of project objectives and main features early in the decision-making process. It also created the National Commission for Public Debate (CNDP) in charge of the organization of the debates. For each project, the CNDP would appoint a special commission of three to seven members, which is autonomous for organizing the debate between the planner and the public. The debate on a project could not last more than four months unless the special commission decided to ask for a complementary expert's assessment. The commission had to give an account of the debate without playing an arbitrator role and the planner had to take the debate into account. The Local Democracy Law (February 27, 2002) strengthened the CNDP by transforming it in an independent body, broadening further the spectrum of projects likely to be subject to a public debate, and introduced the possibility of questioning the very opportunity of realizing the project.

The Long-Standing Conflict over the Extension of the Highway La Francilienne

The project of the extension of the highway La Francilienne in order to link the two cities Méry-sur-Oise and Orgeval over a distance of 22 km in the western part of Paris is very old. A first project was indeed included in the first Master Plan (*Schéma Directeur*) of the Parisian area in 1965. Studies were made for a toll highway from 1988 to 1991 and an association was created to defend the residents, the COPRA184. After having consulted local people and because of the mobilization against this project, the Transportation Ministry gave up this option in 1993. A new project was included in the Master Plan of the Ile-de-France Region in 1994. A Bianco debate was organized from 1994 to 1997, which aimed to compare two groups of routes, one in the northwestern part of Cergy-Pontoise and the other one in the more urbanized southeastern part. The Transportation Ministry made a decision concerning this project on January 27, 1997, and chose one from the southeastern group of routes, along the right bank of the River Seine through the Chanteloup area. Because of the strong local opposition to this choice, new studies were made in 1998 to analyze the feasibility of another route in the northeastern group. Those studies showed that such a route was technically feasible but did not meet the objectives of the project. Later, in 2003, State experts recommended the solution on the right bank of the River Seine again, but stressed that it was necessary to add environmental measures. Because of the intractable conflict on this project and the impossibility of finding a satisfying solution, the Transportation Ministry finally called for a public debate on this project in September 2004.

This briefly summarized history of the project shows that it has been subject to a strong social mobilization since the beginning and that a severe conflict has developed between the people potentially affected by the project and the planner, namely the Transportation Ministry. It is especially the route along the right bank of the River Seine that has been rejected by local people. COPRA184 appears as the main local association of opponents and malcontents.

Analysis of the Conflict Dynamics During the Public Debate

The public debate on the extension of the highway La Francilienne unfolded from March to July 2006. Fives routes, or lines, were to be debated: one in the northwestern part of Cergy-Pontoise (called the pink line) and the four others in the more urbanized southeastern part (known as the red, green, blue and black lines). The special commission in charge of the organization of the debate was composed of five members—of which I was one—and mainly worked from November 2005 to July 2006. Before the beginning of the debate, it had indeed to help the planner to prepare the document presenting the project, which would be submitted to the public. It also had to choose a strategy of deliberation in order to organize the first meeting and at least define the approximate number of meetings, their location and their orientation (of general interest or thematic). The special commission then met several parties before the launch of the debate to begin to understand the conflict. Because this first understanding framed the strategy of deliberation, and then influenced the concrete conditions of deliberation and the dynamics of conflict, I shall begin by presenting it before examining how and to what extent the public debate has transformed the conflict.

The Initial Understanding of the Conflict by the Special Commission

The first inquiries made by the special commission made it aware of the severity of the conflict. Mayors and other elected officials, as well as representatives of COPRA184, indeed, emphasized the bitter clashes that had happened in the past and the hostile relationships they had with the planner. They especially complained about the rigidity of the planner and the absence of dialogue. They had an ambiguous feeling about the public debate; on the one hand, they eagerly wished to show their hostility to the planner, but on the other hand, they did expect the emergence of a solution after such a long-standing conflict. They all recognized that there was a severe transportation problem in the area, resulting in ever-increasing traffic congestion, and that something had to be done. However, because of their resentment toward the planner, they were not inclined to accept a dialogue with the planner from the first meeting, and rejected the idea of a public round-table beginning to clarify the controversies about the project, as the special commission had suggested. While the parties met the special commission did not seem to have clear ideas about what should be done in the area, most of them stressed that more attention had to be paid to the negative effects of the project, especially the high level of health risks caused by noise and air pollution in such urbanized area. The very idea of building a new highway, however, did not seem to be rejected.

These discussions convinced the special commission to organize the public debate in order to be really able to listen to local people and show them its will to do so, and to extend the scope of the debate enough to clarify all the issues, especially those concerning health risks. Let us now examine how the conflict progressed during the public debate.

The Difficult Establishment of a Deliberative Regime

Aware of the picture of rigidity offered by the planner, the special commission first helped him to prepare a more communicative document of presentation of the project. It especially prompted him to show in this document that he had heard the claims previously expressed by local people and taken them into account. It then concretely suggested that he present the history of the project, and show that the new project submitted to the debate had been improved by the previous exchanges. The special commission also encouraged the planner to give information concerning the negative effects of the project, especially the health risks. Though there was not much time to work on the document again, the planner agreed to make some changes.

The first meeting, which took place in the main city of the area, Cergy-Pontoise, attracted more than 2,000 people, and was, as expected, highly conflictual. COPRA184 had organized strong demonstrations of opposition to the project in the room, making an indescribable noise—which reached the level of 104 decibels, namely the noise made by a plane at takeoff—and hardly let anyone who was suspected of being close to the planner speak. The prefect himself was then interrupted. It was the same for the president of the special commission, partly because the neutral role of this body was still not understood and partly because the experience of the president (previously at the head of the national electricity company and then the national train company) gave him the appearance of a planner. The representative of the Transportation Ministry could not really present the project and the five routes submitted to the debate. Each institutional representative who mounted the platform just expressed positions for or against one route, or general ideas, but did not really argue. After such a difficult meeting, the special commission then faced a serious challenge to conduct the second meeting. If it were impossible to start with deliberation, then the public debate could not take place and should be cancelled. This second meeting was to be held in a small city, Andrésy, concerned by the red line proposed by the planner. This line was very similar to the route along the right bank of the River Seine, which had already been chosen in the past and was strongly rejected by COPRA184. Demonstrations of strong opposition were then still expected. At the same time, the special commission had decided to accept holding the second meeting in this city, as its mayor had asked, precisely because the city was concerned by this red line, and because choosing this place for the first local meeting could show the real will of an open debate. This second meeting began in an atmosphere as tumultuous as the first one, even if there were not so many people because of the local focus of this meeting. The special commission then decided to hand over to the former president of COPRA184, letting him express all the resentment built up for years against the planner. Such a public expression of the past difficulties was actually necessary to start the debate on pacified foundations. The planner understood this point himself and spontaneously offered his apologies to the local population. Another choice was to put the planner in the position of answering questions from the public, rather than developing a presentation of the project, and to let local stakeholders explain what problems arose from the red line for the city. After this second meeting, the next ones could then happen in a pacified atmosphere, at least when the mayor expressed a position in line with the public, namely when he claimed that he rejected a route through his city. Even if it was not the case, the meetings could be held, though in a much tenser atmosphere.

The special commission had initially planned 13 local meetings, thereby covering almost all the cities concerned by a route in the area, then four thematic meetings. The importance given to local meetings and their position at the beginning of the debate aimed to show the local population the will of the special commission to listen carefully to it and to be able to clarify the impacts of the project for each city and understanding the variety of interests involved. Six other local meetings were added to cover all the cities concerned by a route in the southeastern part of the area, the most urbanized part of the territory. The preparation of the local meetings with the mayor and his team helped the special commission to adjust those meetings to specific problems and expectations and to develop an atmosphere of trust, or at least reduce distrust.

Despite the severity of the initial conflict, it was then possible to establish a deliberative regime, by paying close and permanent attention to local expectations and reactions and by organizing the debate in line with this priority objective. Let us now examine how the negotiation of governance has progressed.

Toward an Uncertain Negotiation of Governance

The local meetings offered the possibility of clarifying the impacts of the project on the area and questioning several assumptions made by the planner. For instance, while the planner had not identified negative effects of the project on the environment around Herblay, the local population put forward the proximal existence of old quarries, which belonged to their common heritage and should not be destroyed. Another example concerns the highly contested crossing of the highway above a charming little island of the River Seine (Ile des Migneaux), by the means of a bridge. Some participants suggested that another option could be examined, namely going under the Seine. Others argued that it was not possible, because of the presence of withdrawal points used for water consumption in the vicinity and the necessity of protecting groundwater. Others still stressed that several of them would not be used any more in the future, and therefore there was some leeway in this field. Step-by-step, then, new possibilities and new constraints for the project emerged.

A new route called the white line was even proposed by the mayor of Andrésy and presented as 'a line of possible consensus,' as it seemed to impact less people than the other routes, while still remaining in the southeastern part of the area, considered the most appropriate location to meet the objectives of the project. Generally speaking, the will to come to an agreement on a route was clearly expressed during the public debate, even if it was not in the remit of the special commission. The beginning of a dialogue between the mayor of Saint-Ouen l'Aumône in favor of the project and the former president of COPRA184 at the public meeting held in the mayor's city led the president of the special commission to propose an ambiguous 'fifth thematic meeting' on the topic of: 'Is it possible to imagine a solution?' The media clearly understood the intention, as the headlines of the local newspapers showed after this meeting; "Francilienne: The Debate at a Turning-Point" ran in the newspaper Le Parisien. While the white line could have been a line of consensus, the public meeting added by the special commission at the end of the process, just before the final meeting, did not offer the chance of making any progress in this direction. This is partly because this proposition was not well received by different local stakeholders, some of them emphasizing that the mayor of Andrésy could easily speak of a line of consensus that would not go through his city, and others stressing that this route also presented problems. This is also because the local stakeholders had not had enough time to really study this new option.

Furthermore, while the inquiries conducted before the debate could indicate that there was no real opposition to the principle of building a new highway in the area, the public meetings revealed much more contrasting positions. Several people questioned the very need for the project, calling for more attention to the problems of public transport and stressing the heavy cost of a highway and the competition for funding between the different means of transportation. Other people argued that it was necessary to decrease our reliance on cars, because of peak oil, which would happen in the near future, and the urgency of taking climate change into account. Elected officials of the

Ile-de-France Region especially emphasized that to debate the extension of the Francilienne highway had no meaning at this period, while the Master Plan, which would define the future orientation of the Region concerning transportation, was still being debated, especially when the State expected that the Region would contribute to the financing of the project. The existence of the project was above all questioned because of the high level of health risks that would ensue. While the thematic meetings aimed at debating and clarifying all these questions, they hardly fulfilled their role. It was indeed difficult to change the mode of deliberation after the local meetings. Whereas the thematic meetings would have required a new type of investigation calling for confrontation between experts questioned by the public, the process followed the logic of the local meetings. It was especially difficult to debate about the usefulness of a new highway, which would have required a territorial framing going beyond the scope of this specific public debate or real foresight, and a complex crossing between different issues. The debate about the health risks also revealed two divergent conceptions; for some people, the health risks were only constraints that had to be reduced by added measures, while for some other people, the risks were so severe and the possible solutions for limiting them so poor that it was morally impossible to maintain support for the project.

Thus, while the public debate helped to clarify many questions and showed that it was not only a matter of choosing a route and improving its features, it was difficult to really progress in a negotiation of governance.

The Revelation of Divergences Among Local Stakeholders

While local stakeholders appeared very close at the beginning of the debate and while COPRA184 seemed to play a strong federative role, gathering together most elected officials of the area and many lay citizens, divergences among local stakeholders arose during the debate. This is partly because, historically, COPRA184 was more bound to people concerned by the red line. This is also because the former president of COPRA184 advised the public meetings that the association would agree on the blue line, though he did not seem to have been mandated to defend such a position. This is above all because local stakeholders became more aware of their diverging interests. Tensions among elected officials also appeared or were strengthened, because of local political rivalry that did not concern the debate itself. All these divergences made a debate about a possible solution still more difficult.

A Still Uncertain Solution Despite the Making of a Decision

After the public debate, the Minister of Transportation made his decision and chose the green line. This decision did not satisfy the local stakeholders, who then began their fight again. Some of them tried to obtain measures of protection for their city. Others lobbied to have the white line more seriously examined. The financing of the project remains an unsolved problem in a difficult economic context, which severely challenges the likelihood of public funding. Many stakeholders hope that a solution will be found after the passing of the new Master Plan of the Parisian area, which is being submitted to a public inquiry at the time of writing. The document plans the organization of a concerted process between the planner and local elected people by the president of the Ile-de-France Region 'to re-examine the opportunity of making' a new highway between Cergy-Pontoise and Poissy-Orgeval.

Conclusions

While deliberative practices, which have developed in planning in many countries, are expected to avoid stalemates, little attention has been paid to the way deliberation handles conflicting situations in practice. Such an undertaking requires articulating the concepts of conflict and deliberation better at the theoretical level. I have suggested that negotiation may play such a role and I have more precisely explained how it can be used as an interpretive tool.

The application of this approach to an empirical study shows that deliberation may indeed help to transform a severe conflict and progress toward a negotiation of governance. The public debate has actually been a real tool of inquiry in this perspective; more specifically, it has provided the possibility of revealing the plurality of the interests involved, while a project is often designed only to meet economic objectives. It has also led to investigating issues that had seemed definitively settled, and it has let new solutions appear. At the end of the public debate, the governance situation was much better understood than at the beginning, and new directions to go on and move forward have been discovered (especially the idea of a white line), even if it was not examined further by the planner. These elements are part of what can be described as a cognitive agreement related to a governance negotiation.

This empirical study has, however, also shown that severe conflict remains hard to handle through deliberation. First, a deliberative regime is difficult to establish, and requires creating an atmosphere of trust, which takes time and which may also impede deeper analysis of the problems. It is indeed difficult to organize meetings fulfilling such different functions as primarily listening to local stakeholders on the one hand and encouraging the participants to develop their arguments on specific problematic issues on the other. Put a different way, paying attention to the relational dimensions of the conflict and the technical dimensions of the problem at the same time during the debate is very challenging. It is then difficult to expect a complete reframing of the project. Furthermore, the questions raised may also require reconsidering the whole deliberative framework in order to take other policies into account or to extend the scope of the territory considered. Finally, the progress made during such a debate cannot be taken for granted in the pursuit of the process, if new relationships between the planner and the local stakeholders are not recognized as a necessary condition to go on and progress.

Such findings may probably be generalized to any other deliberating experiences involving the public in planning, on condition that they address severe conflicts and only represent a temporary initiative in the process. They make a case for opening such deliberative forums much earlier in the process, when conflicts are not so intractable, and for thinking about the organization of the pursuit of the interactions beyond the debate.

Note

1. Found on the governmental documents website www.legifrance.gouv.fr.

References

Allain, S. (2007) "La conduite d'un débat public sur un projet d'infrastructure: une activité de médiation spécifique. Réflexions à partir du débat public 'Francilienne'," in M. Revel, C. Blatrix, L. Blondiaux, J.-M. Fourniau, B. Hériard-Dubreuil and R. Lefebvre (eds.), *Le débat public: une expérience française de démocratie participative*, Paris, France: La Découverte: 112–122.

Allain, S. (2009) "Décrypter l'activité délibérative dans la régulation territoriale par la négociation," *Négociations*, 12(2): 229–243.

Aragaki, H. N. (2009) "Deliberative Democracy as Dispute Resolution? Conflicts, Interests and Reasons," *Ohio State Journal on Dispute Resolution*, 24(3): 407–480.

Brownill, S. and Parker, G. (2010) "Why Bother with Good Works? The Relevance of Public Participation(s) in Planning in a Post-Collaborative Era," *Planning Practice & Research*, 25(3): 275–282.

Cohen, J. (1998) "Democracy and Liberty," in J. Elster (ed.), *Deliberative Democracy*, Cambridge, UK: Cambridge University Press: 185–231.

Coser, L. A. (1956) *The Functions of Social Conflict*, London, UK: Routledge.

De Carlo, L. (2006) "The French High-Speed Méditerranée Train Decision Process: A Large-Scale Public Decision Case Study," *Conflict Resolution Quarterly*, 24(1): 3–30.

Deutsch, M. (1973) *The Resolution of Conflict*, New Haven, CT: Yale University Press.

Dupont, C. (1994) *La négociation: conduite, théorie, applications*, Paris, France: Dalloz.

Elliott, M. (1988) "Conflict Resolution," in A. Catanese and J. Snyder (eds.), *Urban Planning*, New York, NY: McGraw-Hill: 159–183.

Fischer, F. and Forester, J. (1993a) "Introduction," in F. Fischer and J. Forester (eds.), *The Argumentative Turn in Policy Analysis and Planning*, Durham, NC: Duke University Press: 1–17.

Fischer, F. and Forester, J. (eds.) (1993b) *The Argumentative Turn in Policy Analysis and Planning*, Durham, NC: Duke University Press.

Fisher, R. and Ury, W. (1981) *Getting to Yes: Negotiating an Agreement Without Giving In*, Boston, MA: Houghton Mifflin.

Flyvbjerg, B. (1998) *Rationality and Power: Democracy in Practice*, Chicago, IL: University Press of Chicago.

Follett, M. P. (1942) "Constructive Conflict," in H. C. Metcalf and L. Urwick (eds.), *Dynamic Administration: The Collected Papers of Mary Parker Follett*, New York, NY: Harper: 30–49.

Forester, J. (1989) *Planning in the Face of Power*, Berkeley, CA: University of California Press.

Forester, J. (2009) *Dealing with Differences: Dramas of Mediating Public Disputes*, Oxford, UK: Oxford University Press.

Gutmann, A. and Thompson, D. (1996) *Democracy and Disagreement*, Cambridge, MA: The Belknap Press.

Habermas, J. (1984) *The Theory of Communicative Action. Volume 1: Reason and Rationalization of Society*, Boston, MA: Beacon Press.

Healey, P. (1993) "Planning Through Debate: The Communicative Turn in Planning Theory," in F. Fischer and J. Forester (eds.), *The Argumentative Turn in Policy Analysis and Planning*, Durham, NC: Duke University Press: 233–253.

Healey, P. (1997) *Collaborative Planning: Shaping Places in Fragmented Societies*, Basingstoke, UK: Macmillan.

Healey, P. (2003) "Collaborative Planning in Perspective," *Planning Theory*, 2(2): 101–123.

Huxley, M. (2000) "The Limits to Communicative Planning," *Journal of Planning Education and Research*, 19(4): 369–377.

Huxley, M. and Yiftachel, O. (2000) "New Paradigm or Old Myopia? Unsettling the Communicative Turn in Planning Theory," *Journal of Planning Education and Research*, 19(4): 333–342.

Innes, J. E. (1995) "Planning Theory's Emerging Paradigm: Communicative Action and Interactive Practice," *Journal of Planning Education and Research*, 14(4): 183–189.

Innes, J. E. (2003) "Collaborative Policymaking: Governance Through Dialogue," in M. A. Hajer and H. Wagenaar (eds.), *Deliberative Policy Analysis: Understanding Governance in the Network Society*, Cambridge, UK: Cambridge University Press: 33–59.

Innes, J. E. (2004) "Consensus-Building: Clarifications for the Critics," *Planning Theory*, 3(1): 5–20.

Innes, J. E. and Booher, D. E. (2010) *Planning with Complexity: An Introduction to Collaborative Rationality for Public Policy*, London, UK: Routledge.

Johnson, J. (1991) "Habermas on Strategic and Communicative Action," *Political Theory*, 19(2): 181–201.

Lauria, M. (2000) "The Limits to Communicative Planning Theory: A Brief Introduction," *Journal of Planning Education and Research*, 19(4): 331–332.

Lavelle, S. (2007) "La politique de la discussion: la dynamique du débat entre conversation et négociation," in M. Revel, C. Blatrix, L. Blondiaux, J.-M. Fourniau, B. Hériard-

Dubreuil and R. Lefebvre (eds.), *Le débat public: une expérience française de démocratie participative*, Paris, France: La Découverte: 353–366.

Mansbridge, J. (2006) "Conflict and Self-Interest in Deliberation," in S. Besson and J.-L. Marti (eds.), *Deliberative Democracy and Its Discontents*, Aldershot, UK: Ashgate: 107–132.

Menkel-Meadow, C. (2011) "Scaling Up Deliberative Democracy as Dispute Resolution in Healthcare Reform: A Work in Progress," *Law and Contemporary Problems*, 74(3): 1–30.

Rein, M. and Schön, D. (1993) "Reframing Policy Discourse," in F. Fischer and J. Forester (eds.), *The Argumentative Turn in Policy Analysis and Planning*, Durham, NC: Duke University Press: 145–166.

Remer, G. (2000) "Two Models of Deliberation: Oratory and Conversation in Ratifying the Constitution," *The Journal of Political Philosophy*, 8(1): 68–90.

Rubin, J. Z., Pruitt, D. G. and Kim, S. H. (1994) *Social Conflict: Escalation, Stalemate and Settlement*, New York, NY: McGraw-Hill.

Schelling, T. (1981 [1960]) *The Strategy of Conflict*, Boston, MA: Harvard University Press.

Simmel, G. (1955) *Conflict*, New York, NY: The Free Press.

Susskind, L. (2006) "Can Public Policy Dispute Resolution Meet the Challenges Set by Deliberative Democracy?" *Dispute Resolution Magazine*, 12(2): 5–6.

Susskind, L. (2009) "Deliberative Democracy and Dispute Resolution," *Ohio State Journal on Dispute Resolution*, 24(3): 1–12.

Urfalino, P. (2005) "La délibération n'est pas une conversation," *Négociations*, 4(2): 99–114.

Walton, R. E. and McKersie, R. B. (1965) *A Behavioral Theory of Labor Negotiations*, Ithaca, NY: ILR Press.

Wolsink, M. (1994) "Entanglement of Interests and Motives: Assumptions Behind the NIMBY-Theory on Facility Siting," *Urban Studies*, 1(6): 851–867.

Yiftachel, O., Little, J., Hedgcock, D. and Alexander, D. (2002) *The Power of Planning*, Dordrecht, Netherlands: Kluwer.

Zartman, I. W. (ed.) (1994) *International Multilateral Negotiation*, San Francisco, CA: Jossey-Bass.

11

Large Infrastructures and Conflicts: Searching for 'Boundary Objects'— Reflections from Italian Experiences

Paola Pucci

Contested Infrastructures: Two Asymmetries

Public participation in policy-making is a consolidated and tested tool, and there exist a variety of approaches and techniques able to influence decision-making as well as the quality of deliberation.[1] When 'the problem in question' is a large infrastructure project and controversies are about its implementation, however, additional problems arise with reference to traditional procedures of community consultation.[2]

Following Fung (2006: 66), who argues that "whether public institutions and decision-making processes should treat members of the public as consumers, clients, or citizens depends partly on the context and problem in question," our approach takes into account the peculiarity of the decision-making process for large infrastructures and its influences on consultation procedures for managing conflicts.

As participation without redistribution of power is an empty and frustrating process for those who do not have a real chance to influence decisions, this condition is particularly important in decision-making processes for large infrastructures where the public's lack of real influence is enhanced by a double asymmetry.

The first concerns the well-known distributive asymmetry regarding any infrastructure in relation to the irreversibility of works and unfair cost distribution (concentrated locally) and benefits (distributed on a large scale). By implying that people are willing to support restrictive interventions as long as they are not personally affected (Burningham 2000; Portney 2005), this asymmetry refers to how they relate different interests and positions not only among various groups of the local civic society and within each group, but also in reference to wider-scale players. In this case, two well-known concepts of social justice are compared (Davy 1996). On the one hand, the utilitarian matrix considers as fair those solutions that provide greater prosperity for the largest number of individuals (we accept the sacrifice of local communities for public good, or more generally, collective interests). On the other hand, the concept inspired by Rawls's (1971) theory of justice considers legitimate those solutions that provide lower costs to the most disadvantaged groups (favoring choices that minimize risks for the communities affected). Accepting one concept or the other has consequences for the forms of public consultations, in three important dimensions along which forms of direct participation vary. The first concerns who participates; the second, concerns how participants exchange information and make decisions; and the third describes the link between discussions and policy or public action (Fung 2006: 66).

In addition to this, the second type of asymmetry concerns the unbalanced roles in the decision-making process between national government, technical agencies and private companies (as general contractors) who plan and design the infrastructures, on the one hand, and local communities, on the other. Being the focus of many theoretical reflections (Pizzorno 1973; Fourniau 1996; Offner 2001; Bobbio 2004; Ponti 2007), this asymmetry poses problems especially with regard to the inclusiveness and influence of the public in infrastructure project design. That the equilibrium of planning power shifted in favor of national authorities is evident when the infrastructure project is 'the' solution in reference to a mobility demand for local communities, but also when the infrastructure project is part of territorial strategies and large-scale scenarios, such as Trans-European Transport Networks corridors (TEN-T).

When the infrastructure project is a mobility-demand solution, asymmetric roles are linked to the political dimension of mobility demand, which is "a political question because it is not the result of the needs of a society, in general, but only of those needs that can be satisfied by a government" (Pizzorno 1973: 40). In this way, the treatment for mobility demand is part of the state government and technical agencies that "are not limited to executive tasks, but redefine the issue in relation to how they treat them" (Crosta 1995: 99). Indeed, as a consequence of this process, infrastructure solutions often do not actually solve mobility problems; this is due also to the fact that the treatment of mobility issues is influenced by the nature of funding, directed more often toward the construction of large-scale interventions rather than minute upgrading.

When the infrastructure project is part of national and transnational strategic visions, the decision-making process, motivated by supply, can be described as a DEAD procedure ('Decide, Educate, Announce, Defend') (Mermet et al. 2004; Hartz-Karp 2007), implying that the public has no real influence on the procedure. This approach has also "strengthened and consolidated the rhetoric of large projects as a value itself, therefore not negotiable" (Ponti 2007: 49–50), with important consequences for justification instruments and legitimization of the project, which would exclude ex ante comparative evaluations of different technical solutions, since in this case the utility of evaluation is predetermined and coincides with its usability in the process of legitimization. Evaluations are oriented toward a process of presumptive legitimization of the project, often assigned to a technical team, which is essentially responsible for the analysis of the economic and technical feasibility of the infrastructure. This leads to the increase of the assertive nature, rather than the evaluative nature, of the analysis, which often takes only formal charge of alternatives and does not follow on from a debate with local communities. In this case, the stakeholders' limited involvement in decision-making, as a condition to ensure the stability of the process, favors compromises in negotiating the various competing interests that have often resulted in the provision of compensatory measures, not always evenly distributed.

Compensatory measures have often focused on incremental interventions 'juxtaposed' to the project and shared between various municipalities, without a fully transparent distribution.[3] These practices, aimed at improving the acceptability of large infrastructures at a local level, imply additional interventions and costs that, on the one hand, are not always capable of dealing with the negative externalities that a large project may produce for local contexts and, on the other hand, highlight the limits of direct negotiations influenced by private interests. This asymmetry increases the controversy on the legitimacy of established routine processes of expert-based policy-making and the distribution of decision-making power (Hajer 2003). There is no single definitive solution in terms of procedures of community consultation, because this asymmetry, rather than a procedural one, is indeed a structural problem. The resulting tensions in terms of contradictory logics of action and inadequate skills, methods and expertise result, on the one hand, in a crisis of legitimacy and, on the other hand, in a crisis of effectiveness of state decision-making and planning.

This *double asymmetry* in the decision-making process for infrastructure projects gives rise both to 'process-related claims' and 'contents-related claims'; the conflicts concern both the less inclusive way in which the infrastructure project is planned with reference to non-negotiable requirements, as well as the land use, social and economic impacts of the new infrastructure. If contents-related claims are emerging more strongly from public challenges because they are linked to a localized claim and directly touched by the works, which loudly demand rethinking the project, then claims are made up of requests and needs that go beyond over-simplified interpretations of the NIMBY (Not In My Backyard) syndrome.

Because 'NIMBY positions' tend to lock residents in an illegal position (Jobert 1998), local mobilizations, in order to widen the consensus around their positions, use arguments with a more general appeal; they become an exercise of active citizenship (Della Porta and Piazza 2008), supporting alternative models of development.[4] From the limited scope of demands and claims typical of NIMBY positions, they switch to protest campaigns that broaden the topic so as to include the adverse effects on the environment and health caused by the project, and thus challenge the development model proposed by the project in question.

Contents-related claims also highlight the fact that the supply of transportation facilities (i.e., the contested project) is primarily a social product, as well as being a social transformation tool (Klein 2001). Because of this, public policy for new infrastructures must originate from formulating the problem to be solved, rather than the solution itself.

This way, the idea of deliberative engagement goes beyond consultation and aims to empower the public in actual decision-making, and to facilitate a change in the point of view of participants from that of self-interested parties to that of citizens with a real ability to deeply transform the contested project. As demonstrated by recent reforms in consultation procedures for large infrastructures,[5] it has become more and more important to introduce and to consider three normative criteria in order to characterize the process (Hartz-Karp 2007): *influence*, *inclusiveness* and *deliberativeness*.

Although influence, inclusiveness and deliberativeness may be seen as criteria of general validity for consultation procedures, in infrastructure project consultations they bear distinctive features.

Influence, insofar as deliberation results have an impact on policy-making, must consider the possibility that the contested project can be fundamentally amended or even totally rejected through public consultation. Accordingly, the importance becomes apparent of involving—especially in the early stages—the right skills to rethink the mobility problem that needs to be solved by the contested project, of developing alternative solutions, and of comparing the opportunities and constraints and evaluating the conditions of feasibility of each option. This requires deliberative arenas (Bobbio 2002) in which to discuss the issue, assuring that the final decision-making will be in the hands of the public.

The *inclusiveness* and the representativeness of civic society[6]—which includes traditional decision-making elites as well as the 'voiceless'—can be hampered in consultation procedures for large infrastructures when the stakeholders' open methods are based on self-selection, resulting in an imbalance in the composition of the participants (Fung 2003); 'indirect participation tools' must therefore be introduced which protect the 'position in favor of the project,' often under-represented, as well as non-local interests. An alternative participant selection method, open to all who wish to attend, consists in selecting participants randomly from the general population, conceived as a 'mini-public'[7] (Fung 2006: 68). This device contrasts with a more inclusive participant selection, but at the same time can limit the bias of partisanship.[8]

Deliberativeness, as a communicative process in which participants are considered equal and open to having their preferences shaped and transformed through reflective public reasoning (Cohen 1989), implies in infrastructure projects a requisite condition for reconstructing the framework of clear reasons for the infrastructure and the opening of a process of debate between different viewpoints and preference shifts, as an opportunity to influence the decision-making process.

Discussions on the type of issue being deliberated rather than on the project, from a diversity of viewpoints, ensures that the issue is considered from various angles (Hendriks et al. 2007: 366) and, at the same time, that immovable positions against the project can contribute to the reformulation of the problem through mutual understanding. Openness to preference shift is crucial as deliberators need to be flexible enough to have their perspectives enlarged and even transformed (Gutmann and Thompson 1996: 174). An informed debate has two main characteristics: it creates a neutral space for discussion by employing independent and skilled facilitators, and it makes an appropriate use of expertise, that is to say it uses experts with an informing role rather than with a controlling and decision-making role (Gastil and Levine 2005).

Boundary Objects as Shared Problems from Different Perspectives

A neutral space for discussion, in infrastructure projects, should hence start from the identification of the shared aspects of the problem that the contested project should be addressing. The issue here is not an investigation of collaborative approaches to stakeholder dialogue as a catalyst for consensus-building, because consensus is not decisive in large contested infrastructure projects. The conflict is physiological and contains a localized component of claims, asking to rethink the issue and the project, and a political and cultural component that is always antagonistic. Rather, it is about ensuring a neutral space for cooperation where participants with different positions interact, even assuming that positions are and can remain in conflict. This space is a tool for making cooperation possible, even without consensus because "consensus is not necessary for cooperation nor for the successful conduct of work" (Star and Griesemer 1989: 388). Considering that the subject is a contested large infrastructure project and decisions often derive from a centralized decision-making process, a neutral space is delineated to include a diversity of viewpoints that, in an interactive process, can discuss the reasons for rather than the solution of the project itself (the infrastructure project proposed as a solution to a mobility problem).

Discussions about 'why' (the reasons for the project) and not only about 'how' (the project as a determined artifact) are the condition for constructing a shared space for debate among divided coalitions that form around a large infrastructure project unlikely to become 'the project of all concerned,' but that still may rather aspire to become part of the project and to be accepted by others.

During public discussions, the challenge consists in identifying those issues that permit cooperation between irreconcilable positions that, on the other hand are willing to interact on a few recognizable problems, raised by the contested project. From this perspective, reference to the notion of *boundary objects* proposed by Star and Griesemer (1989), intended as problems shared under 'different perspectives,' can become a heuristic device, useful to manage conflict.[9]

In Star and Griesemer's work, 'boundary objects' are defined as policy issues that are both plastic enough to adapt to the local needs and constraints of the several parties making reference to them, yet robust enough to maintain a common identity across different sites. They are weakly structured in their common use, and become strongly structured in individual-site use. They may be abstract or concrete. They have different meanings in different social worlds but their structure is common enough to more than one world as to make them recognizable means of translation (Star and Griesemer 1989: 393).

As means of translation shared by many different communities, but used differently by each one of them, boundary objects can be useful in reformulating issues (congestion, pollution, transportation demand and so forth) and in overcoming the often irreducible conflict tied to solutions imposed from above, because they allow coordination without consensus.

By describing the way actors achieve coordination in time and space while retaining their own positions, Star and Griesemer propose the notion of boundary objects as a tool with which different players can negotiate their positions, and create an updated agreement, despite their widely differing views. Boundary objects permit different groups to collaborate on a common task, from a local understanding of a problem that can be reformulated, because "the creation and management of boundary objects is key in developing and maintaining coherence across intersecting social worlds" and positions (Star and Griesemer 1989: 393). Using the notion of boundary objects to describe how actors maintain their differences within a cooperative space and how they manage and restrict the variety of possibilities, Star and Griesemer highlight the properties required to maximize both the autonomy of social worlds and of the communication between them, because boundary objects do not favor any viewpoint and, at the same time, take into account the coexistence of several translation processes whose crucial problem is their overall consistency.

As a translation tool between heterogeneous worlds, a boundary object can be used for descriptive, heuristic or regulatory purposes. Star and Griesemer (1989: 410) distinguish four types of boundary objects: *repertoires*, built to deal with problems of heterogeneity caused by differences in the unit of analysis etc.; *ideal types*, abstracted from specific domains and serving as a means of communicating and cooperating symbolically; *coincident boundaries*, as common objects that have the same boundaries but different internal contents; and *standardized forms*, devised as methods of common communication across dispersed work groups (what Latour calls 'immutable mobiles,' as objects that can be transported over a long distance and convey unchanging information) (Star and Griesemer 1989: 411). In different disciplines, the various and multiple uses of the concept (Trompette and Vinck 2009: 10–16) consider it a support of heterogeneous translations (relating to the notion of translation in Callon 1986), and as a device for the integration of knowledge, as a mediation in the process of coordination between experts and non-experts.

Etienne Wenger (2000), using the boundary object notion in relation to a problem of knowledge management, highlights four dimensions in which the notion is set out.

1. *Abstraction*: it facilitates a dialogue among 'different meanings' as a common point of reference for conversation.
2. *Versatility*: it must satisfy different concerns simultaneously, because it is sufficiently pliant as a working arrangement to adapt itself to changing needs, adjusted as needed.
3. *Modularity*: different parts of the object can serve as the basis for dialogue between stakeholders.
4. *Standardization* of the information embedded in the object: it makes the information interpretable, as a means of translation, and used as a means of coordination and alignment.

With respect to the topics we are addressing, the interest in the concept lies in the nature of the 'knowledge infrastructure' that deals with the complexity of the interaction between different positions. As a heuristic device, linked to issues of shared and interpretive meaning, a boundary object becomes the neutral space that stems from the ability to recognize shared problems and issues, even in the presence of strong conflict about the object of the dispute.

If working on boundary objects can be useful for achieving partial convergence and for looking for innovative solutions, amenable to influencing the content and the feasibility of the project itself, then searching for boundary objects has implications for consultation procedures.

In fact, during the process of public consultation, the possibility of identifying boundary objects must be guaranteed as a condition for:

- working on defining the problem (e.g., the 'treatment of the problem of mobility') at the basis of the challenged infrastructure project; and
- proposing alternative solutions amenable to substantially transforming the project, by influencing the content as well as the feasibility of the project itself.

Facing the Problem: Consultation Procedures for Large Infrastructure Projects

In dealing with conflicts related to large infrastructure projects, institutional responses have led to different public consultation procedures. These are characterized by different degrees of institutionalization and equally diversified methods of community involvement and participation, as well as a different capacity to influence the decision-making process.

The devices proposed and tested can be traced to three main models: consultation, integrative negotiation and deliberation.

Consultation has a good example in the procedure of the *Débat public*[10] experienced in France and Quebec. The French procedure is the device with the highest degree of institutionalization; the debate, organized by a local committee (the CPDP), appointed by a national committee (the CNDP), takes place according to a detailed program on time and within outcomes. The self-selection of the public guarantees the participation of everyone wishing to debate. The possibility of non-realization of the project, as well as of changes to it, is admitted, although the final decision remains in the hands of elected politicians.[11]

The critical aspects of this procedure are well-known (Fourniau 2001; Zémor 2003; Rui 2004; Revel at al. 2007; Charbonneau 2010) and include the political impact and the influence on the decision-making process, since the French *Débat public* procedure does not imply formal decision-making and has no legal effect. However, it can bring out the main themes and topics (Fourniau 1996). The outcome of the debate is a report by the committee that evaluates the positions and themes that emerged during the process.

A further critical aspect is that, despite the opportunity to discuss the usefulness of the project, the French procedure does not provide an adequate temporal framework for detailed discussion of alternative solutions; in most cases, the *Débat public* confirms the initial project. This "ambivalent feature" of the *Débat public* (Charbonneau 2010: 278) is also reflected in the selection of participants, with involvement lacking from non-partisan players and often with the neglect of forms of protest that may develop in parallel to those that have been channeled into the debate.

The *integrative negotiation* approach (Fisher et al. 1981), unlike the distributive one, is based more on the confrontation of opposing interests rather than on different positions. By taking into account the interests of the different parties (not necessarily opposed), this approach stimulates the construction of alternative solutions that meet those interests, taking advantage of their differences. In this case, both parties are engaged in a process of creating alternatives in order to achieve a mutual gain. An extensive literature (Susskind and Cruikshank 1987; Susskind et al. 1999; Healey 2006; Forester 2009) insists on an approach based on the direct and creative debate between the different parties involved, and on the presence of mediators or facilitators who are entrusted with the task of managing the negotiations in a neutral and impartial way. Following Forester (2006: 447), "moving from facilitating dialogue and moderating debate to mediating negotiations," participation techniques can redirect conflict into joint inquiry, explore options rather than escalate demands and, ultimately, achieve practical results.

As known, this approach is particularly effective in the case of disputes between private citizens or between individuals involved in legal disputes within practices defined as 'alternative dispute resolution,' where the conflict is polarized (two 'positions' or opposed interests). The basic idea is that it is preferable that the parties themselves find a solution, rather than relying on the legal decision of a third-party authority (Bobbio 2004: 101). At the same time, the negotiation is possible only if both parties are willing to cooperate and question. These conditions—in addition to the mentioned specificity of the decision-making process for infrastructures—make this approach unsuited to conflict resolution for large infrastructures, which provide a more extensive range of conflicting positions and interests and require the involvement of multiple stakeholders, where controversy is high and goals and interests are in conflict. Confidence in the ability to employ skillful mediation practices in transforming real antagonism into working relationships and practical agreement by using sustained and creative effort (Forester 2006: 448) in the case of irreducible conflict poses some problems in terms of effectiveness and practicability.

In the *deliberative* approach, participants offer proposals and justifications to support collective decisions. The decision must be reached through the consensus generated by a dialogic process, based on rational arguments that change the reasons and initial preferences of the parties and oriented toward the common good (or common norms of fairness). This is the conceptual node of deliberative democracy that distinguishes it from decision-making based on polling or negotiation. Decisions resulting from deliberation may be more fair and legitimate, because they result from reasons rather than arbitrary advantages (Fung 2003: 344). Among tools and methodologies that can be traced to this third approach, the most common practice is the device of 'mini-publics,' as presented and argued by Fung (2003).

If a discussion, at a general level, may help individual participants to clarify their own views and modify their preconceived opinions, in the case of strong conflicts between irreconcilable positions the lack of mutual understanding and agreement represents an obstacle to deliberative approaches that must be addressed through a specific structure of discussion. This is the challenge for consultation procedures for large infrastructures.

Conditions of discussion conceive the boundary object concept as a translation tool for exchanging opinions and information between stakeholders with a non-consensual system of meaning and values, recognizing a few shared issues for cooperation, despite a lack of agreement or consensus. If the kind of issue under deliberation—e.g., large infrastructure projects—influences the effectiveness of consultation approaches, contextual factors such as the socio-political landscape play an equally important role.

In this framework, the Italian case study may be an interesting field of investigation to analyze how consultation procedures for disputed infrastructures can be rethought, looking for boundary objects with the aim of recomposing and refocusing the conflict. Interest in the Italian experiences derives from the experimentation of consultation approaches to address many ongoing disputes for large infrastructure projects,[12] outside institutionalized frameworks, characterized, on the contrary, by strong centralized procedures in the decision-making process.

Reflections on Italian Experiences

The problem of the political feasibility of new infrastructures in Italy is confirmed by the number of contested infrastructure projects,[13] unrealized for a long time, and partly related to the ineffectiveness of national laws, modified in 2001 with the *Legge Obiettivo*,[14] which redefines stakeholders' involvement, shifting the equilibrium of planning powers in favor of the national authority.

Moving from a decentralized legal context to a more centralized one, national procedures have wiped out discussions at a local government level and also with local communities, leaving the consultation procedures on project information without real influence in the decision-making process and in the technical and physical layout of the project, thus causing effects opposite to their intended goals (i.e., simplifying and accelerating the realization of infrastructures).

The institutional reform of the decision-making process for large infrastructure projects promoted in 2001 not only failed to solve the existing conflicts, requiring as it did the use of special procedures such as the appointment of a commissioner with special powers to supervise the challenges for the new high-speed railway in Val di Susa, but it also consolidated some problems that affect the political feasibility of infrastructure projects, including:

- a decision-making process in which the new infrastructure is interpreted as a strategic tool in itself, therefore not negotiable, for which ex ante evaluations about the mobility demand and the territorial impact, or the congruence with strategic territorial programs, play a minor part;
- less importance given to the ex ante evaluations, in comparison with the alternative hypotheses that are also useful for knowing the distribution of the negative and positive externalities created by the infrastructure project and that clearly define devices, recover all the surplus values and reach out toward all the positive externalities created by public investments;
- the weakness of direct communication among a plurality of institutional and non-institutional players involved in all the different steps of the project (idea, design, assessment and management), putting the available tools and procedures to the test;
- the gap between the institutional view of the relationship among all the institutions that have competency in planning and designing the infra-structures, and the real interconnection of skills and links between national institutions, planners, infrastructure designers, technical authorities and local communities; and
- complexity in administrative procedures that lengthen the time of design and construction of the infrastructures, combined with an excessive variability of regulatory systems and fragmented groups of objectives.

The reactions to the ineffectiveness of national procedure led to experiments with:

- special powers assigned by extraordinary procedures, to a mediator as in the case of the *Osservatorio per la Val di Susa*, involving only institutional players and established in 2006 by the prime minister following the important disputes for the Turin–Lyon high-speed railway line project (Bobbio and Dansero 2008; Della Porta and Piazza 2008);
- new institutionalized consultation procedures, proposed with regional laws in the Liguria and Tuscany regions, to enable effective integration of pre-assessments of the infrastructure project from local authorities and stakeholders; and
- foreign procedures adopted in a very different socio-political environment such as the French *Débat public* in the contested new highway project in Genoa.

Institutionalized Consultation Procedures in Liguria and Tuscany

The institutionalization of planning procedures for large infrastructures in the regions of Tuscany and Liguria, which modified the national institutional framework for the building of consensus in infrastructure projects, represents an interesting perspective on the problem of the feasibility of large infrastructures in Italy.

Although characterized by common purposes such as the rules for the guarantee of transparency and participation in complex territorial transformation processes, nonetheless these initiatives have substantial differences.

The Liguria region (with Regional Law n. 39, 2007) has in fact promoted an instrument for an integrated strategic program coordinated by the region

> with the concerned local authorities and with the contracting of the works, and their implementation, with the upgrading of the related territorial contexts by ensuring the sustainability of choices and offsetting any inconvenience through solving the problems of the local communities involved. (Article 3)

The Tuscany region (with Regional Law n. 69, 2007) proposes a new participatory institution as an ordinary form of government (Article 1), namely:

- the public regional debate (Chapter II, Art. 7–10) on large transformation projects and public works of significant environmental and social impact on the everyday life of the whole regional community, which lasts for six months and is organized and conducted "under the responsibility of a third monocratic" independent and neutral subject, such as the Regional Authority for Participation;
- strategic actions to support local processes of participation which are promoted both by public institutions and citizens and other players who may propose a participatory process on a specific subject and which may last up to six months, indicating methods and tools and ensuring inclusiveness; and
- the strengthening of participation, in given instances, in regional policies and planning procedures in the region of Tuscany.

Despite the innovations of the Act, which included not only new special procedures for public debate on important regional projects with remarkable socio-territorial impacts in the preliminary draft but more generally a reorganization of the inter-governmental and inter-sectorial decision-making system, it produced few effects on contested infrastructure projects under dispute.

Boundary Objects in the Public Debate on the
Gronda Di Ponente Highway in Genoa

In a framework characterized by obvious problems for the feasibility of large infrastructures in Italy, some reflections on the effectiveness of the application of foreign procedures may derive from the first public debate for a new highway in Genoa, as a non-institutionalized deliberative process in which some shared principles, referring to the French procedure of *Débat public*, may be accompanied by a relative openness to the priorities of the issues to be dealt with, to the sources of technical knowledge necessary for its activation and to the actors involved.

The public debate over the Gronda di Ponente highway[15] in Genoa was promoted in December 2008 with grassroots action by the mayor of Genoa, in agreement with the general contractor (Autostrade per l'Italia—ASPI), in a local situation of conflict as a consequence of the decision, taken by the State, the region of Liguria and the city of Genoa, to construct a new highway.

Conflicts concerned both the uninclusive way in which the Gronda di Ponente project was planned by ASPI and the non-negotiable requirements within the public debate, as well as the negative externals of the new highway, in an urban context increasingly subject to subtractive processes. As the consultation process was a bottom-up initiative promoted by the municipality, without any legal framework, the role of the national authorities in the process was marginal; only ANAS, the national technical and regulatory agency responsible for the management of large infrastructures, had participated as an observer in the public debate, without any active role. From a procedural point of view, the French model of *Débat public* was respected;[16] however, in terms of content, in the case of Genoa, the basic approach of French *Débat public* was partly contradicted.

The organization of the debate was entrusted to a committee—consisting of three experts supported by a technical team[17]—appointed by the mayor of Genoa and the town council, that is, by players involved in the process who were not neutral in reference to the contested project. In addition, the initial procedure of the committee only included the discussion of the five alternatives for the new highway project in the Valpolcevera area (Figure 11.1), rather than the public interest in the new project, as in the French procedure.

However, during the debate—which took place in Genoa from February to May 2009—the reasons for the infrastructure project were at the center of the discussions, opening with opposing positions on the efficacy of the Gronda di Ponente project in solving the congestion for the Genoa road network (Pucci 2010).

Table 11.1 describes the arguments used by different actors involved in the debate, highlighting traffic congestion as a shared issue and consequent views of the highway project in dealing with the congestion problems. Because traffic

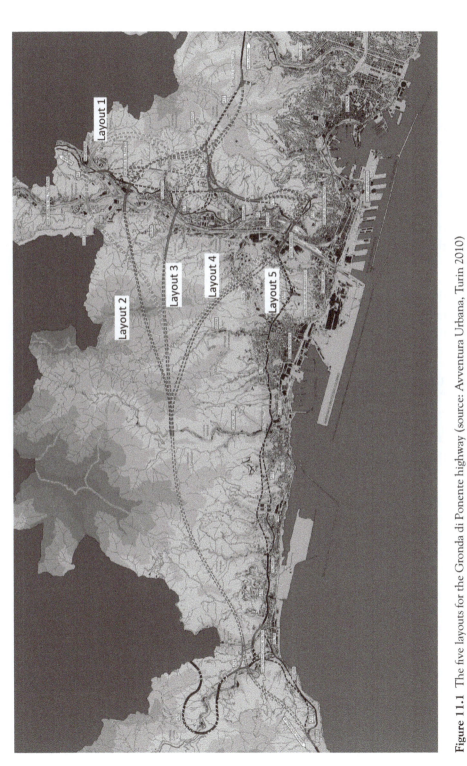

Figure 11.1 The five layouts for the Gronda di Ponente highway (source: Avventura Urbana, Turin 2010)

congestion was the only topic on which the different parties involved shared opinions, even if without shared solutions, it played an important role in facilitating the debate of very conflicting positions and in broadening participation of non-partisan players.

An open discussion on the traffic congestion with different groups (for and against the project) would therefore have represented the opportunity to focus on the reasons for the project and to evaluate alternative solutions that could solve this problem in the Genoa metropolitan area.

During the public debate, the opportunity to work on traffic congestion was found within the 'traffic and mobility' workshop. Even if this workshop did not create a change in the positions—also because the time available was too short (four meetings)—all the same it helped to introduce a critical dimension to the project.

The justifications about the utility of a new highway to solve the traffic congestion of the existing A10 motorway (supported by the general contractor, the Genoa municipality, the chamber of commerce, the port authority, managers of industries and trade unions), were compared with alternative hypotheses, including a new transport program, finalized to rethink the mobility policies and governance in Genoa and the Liguria region.

Table 11.1 If congestion is the problem ... the solution is not always the Gronda di Ponente highway

The Congestion Descriptions	The Gronda Project Role	For Whom
It is a **safety and efficiency problem** of the motorway system of Genoa with negative effects on the motorway networks in northwestern Italy.	**An infrastructure that cannot be postponed** for the sake of good traffic, circulation and safety in the motorway network.	General contractor (ASPI)
It creates problems for the functionality of mobility and has a **negative impact on the environment and livability.**	**A necessary link** in a planned scenario for reorganization of the road, railroad and public transport network in Genoa.	Municipality of Genoa, province of Genoa, Liguria region
It is a **problem for economic growth.**	**A necessary infrastructure,** given new resources for growth of the Genoese economy.	Industrial associations, port authority, trade unions
It is a **problem in terms of health, standards of living and livability.**	The **wrong solution** for an unmanaged problem (congestion).	Coordination committees, environmental associations
It is a **resource.**		Committee for peaceful decrease in population density

As a problem viewed from different perspectives, traffic congestion in the Genoa public debate represented a boundary object, because it was a 'recognizable means of translation,' around which the antagonistic positions found neutral space for discussion.

In reference to the four types of boundary objects proposed by Star and Griesemer (1989), traffic congestion was a 'coincident boundary,' intended as a "common object having the same boundaries but different internal contents" (Star and Griesemer 1989: 410).

Traffic congestion permitted different groups to collaborate from a local understanding of the problem, translated into different variations matching to different systems of meaning, which correspond to different judgments on the role of the highway project.

Working on these different systems of meaning, starting with access to each other's opinions, would allow a wider participation in the debate (by partisan and non-partisan players) and the opportunity for innovative solutions to emerge from a contested project.

Because there are different stages, from those least likely to produce collaboration to those most likely, it is necessary to have time to build collaboration around a boundary object and propose a shared solution. Despite an achievable level of mutual understanding being reached, the procedural conditions did not allow alternative solutions to the initial project, other than adjustments to the road layouts, offered at the beginning of the debate.

At the end of the public debate, the general contractor submitted a new road layout, partially redesigned according to the issues that emerged during the debate and aimed at reducing the impact on housing. In February 2010 the municipality of Genoa, the province of Genoa, the Liguria region and the general contractor signed the agreement for the new project for the Gronda di Ponente highway which was an outcome of a political decision, taken after the public debate.

In the Gronda di Ponente case study, a clear reference to the French procedure of *Débat public* provided some advantages, such as assuring the conditions for organizing an open debate with public access and information, the neutrality of the committee and a clear structure regarding time and products. All the same, even if the model tested in Genoa was an effective tool, some problems emerged clearly in terms both of lack of a legal agreement and a real chance to work on the construction of alternative solutions with respect to the time-frame of the procedure (Bobbio 2010).

The lack of a legal agreement caused some problems,[18] such as: the order of the debate with only about five alternatives for the highway route considered rather than public interest in the new project with the aim of resolving the congestion problems of central Genoa; the appointment of the chairman of the board by the local administration with repercussions for the position of neutrality of the board that the legitimatization process began; and the lack of involvement in public meetings by the subjects in favor of the project and by financial players (chamber of commerce, trade and industrial associations), who made use of other arenas to communicate their position (advertisements in newspapers and local television).

In terms of the real chance to work on the construction of alternative solutions, the implications for participation procedures led to ensure a space-time for identifying and then working on and around shared issues, which become a condition for the treatment of mobility problems at the origin of the contested project.

The Genoa public debate had, as its starting point, the objective of discussing 'which path to choose' between five preselected alternatives for the project, and not the usefulness of a new highway in terms of the effectiveness of the technical performances of a new infrastructure with regard to mobility demand. Discussing only the contested project, however, does not help to transform real antagonisms into working relationships.

Compared with the aim of public debate, working on the shared problems that the contested project should be addressing, rather than on the single contested solution, may be useful for partial convergences, searching for innovative alternatives, which are able to influence the content, and also the feasibility of the project itself.

Notes

1. See Fung (2006), Hartz-Karp (2007) and Brodie et al. (2009) for an overview of common techniques of public participation in policy-making.
2. Following Lowi (1964) and Wilson (1973) in the critical interpretation offered by Gustavsson (1980), our hypothesis is that the content of the policy affects the nature of the conflict and public participation procedures depend on the problem under deliberation and on the contextual factors such as the socio-political scenario (Newman et al. 2004).
3. Some interesting case studies are compensatory measures for the high-speed railway lines in Italy (i.e., Turin–Milan and Milan–Rome HSL) where funding for the clearing devices, incurred by national authorities, are given to each municipality involved in the project, toward a negotiation process, fragmented at the local scale and often ineffective in term of reducing the negative impacts of the infrastructure project. The funds, calculated as a percentage of the cost of infrastructure (not to exceed 5 percent) and conferred to each municipality, represent new financial resources, acquired from the government. In this way, municipalities are mostly in favor of large-scale projects. This is a condition that often leads to conflicts between them and the local community.
4. Examples for this are social movements inspired by 'de-growth' theory proposed by Nicholas Georgescu-Roegen and Serge Latouche (e.g. Georgescu-Roegen 1995; Latouche 2009), such as the *Movimento per la decrescita felice* in Italy.

5. For instance, the reformulation of contents through the *Débat public* procedure in France (with the law Démocratie de proximité 2002-297 and the law Grenelle II 2010-788), or the new Code of Practice in consultation in the UK.

6. As recalled by Baumann and White (2010), civil society can be defined as "formal and informal associations and networks in society, which exist outside of the state" (Hendriks 2002: 3) and differentiates between the different sectors according to "the degree to which they seek to influence the activities of the State" (ibid.: 4). It is important to note that there are differing interpretations of the idea of representation. Renn (2008: 303) discusses the theoretical foundations of six basic concepts of public participation, making apparent that they define representation in various ways, or do not require representation at all.

7. The 'mini-publics' that intentionally gather citizens in discrete bodies to discuss or decide matters of public concern are arenas or discussion groups, built around specific themes and sizes to select participants in a fully random selection. Participants are identified by extraction from a sample of the reference population (Fung 2003).

8. For the merits of partisan (such as key stakeholders) and non-partisan (such as lay citizens) forums in deliberative practices, see Hendriks et al. (2007).

9. The concept of boundary objects is closely related to the concept of the 'trading zone' coined by Galison (1997, 1999) in which knowledge and resources are exchanged in a restricted zone where coordination is good enough (Galison 2010). This notion has been taken up by Mäntysalo et al. (2011).

10. The French *Débat public* is an institutionalized open preventive public debate on a large infrastructure issue before projects are defined. It was introduced by Circulaire Bianco in 1992 and modified with laws in 1995 (loi Barnier), 2002 (Démocratie de proximité) and 2010 (Grenelle II).

11. At the end of the debate, the committee is restricted to making public a final report that presents the positions, arguments and proposals that emerged during the debate. After that, the general contractor, within a specified period, says whether he will proceed with the design project and, if so, how he intends to take into account the arguments arising from the debate and presented in the final report of the committee.

12. Among the best known cases: High-Speed Line (HSL) Lyon–Turin in Val di Susa, new highway in Genoa, bridge over the Strait of Messina, and highway Livorno–Civitavecchia.

13. According to Nimby Forum's research project, in Italy 320 infrastructures and large-scale plants are being challenged by the local population (www.nimbyforum.it) accessed November 20, 2014.

14. The *Legge Obiettivo* (n.l. 431/2001), as part of an institutional reform of decision-making process for large infrastructure projects, is aimed at guaranteeing the feasibility of programmed strategic infrastructures with simplification of the procedures that increase the power of the national government over that of local government.

15. The contested motorway project was designed in 1980 to solve traffic congestion on the A10 motorway (Genoa–Ventimiglia) that runs through the dense urban settlement of Genoa. Over the years, various project layouts have sought to reduce negative impacts and follow the demand of local requirements. The new highway project—proposed by Autostrade per l'Italia and approved by the Liguria region, the municipality of Genoa and the province of Genoa in 2006—crossed the Valpolcevera area, which is located in a densely urbanized district, with very important industries and also a high-density residential area, wedged between factories, oil depots, abandoned refineries and large infrastructures.

16. The debate comprised: a preparatory phase with useful information on the project; an information phase in which a website was set up and a timetable of meetings prepared for public presentation of the project; and a thematic in-depth phase on relevant issues arising from the project (issues relating to traffic and mobility, work sites, the impact on households and businesses, compensation measures, and the study and disposal of excavated materials). The top-down (from the advisers to the citizens), the bottom-up (from the citizens to the advisers) and the horizontal (between the citizens) communication by the website was also assured.

17. The town council of Genoa designated Luigi Bobbio as a chairman of the board (expert in deliberative and participatory processes, University of Torino) as well as Andrea Mariotto (expert in participatory processes, IUAV), Paola Pucci (expert in mobility and infrastructure policies, Milan Polytechnic) and Jean-Michel Fourniau (expert in transport policies, INRETS).

18. The French procedure, chosen by the mayor of Genoa, allowed the process to be managed without preliminary agreement with the Liguria region and the province of Genoa, of which the previous mayor of Genoa was not in favor. This non-institutionalized tool did not entail prescriptions on the acquisition of the results emerged from the public debate by local administrations.

References

Baumann, C. and White, S. (2010) "Enhanced Dialogue in Transport Policy Making: Enabling Change Towards Sustainability Through Deliberative Public Engagement," *Proceedings of 12th WCTR World Conference on Transport Research*, Lisbon, Portugal: WCTR: 11–15.

Bobbio, L. (2002) "Le arene deliberative," *Rivista Italiana di Politiche Pubbliche*, 32(3): 5–29.

Bobbio, L. (2004) *La democrazia non abita a Gordio*, Milan, Italy: Franco Angeli.

Bobbio, L. (2010) "La specificità del dibattito pubblico sulle grandi infrastrutture: il caso della variante autostradale di Genova," in U. Allegretti (ed.), *Democrazia partecipativa*, Firenze, Italy: Firenze University Press: 285–297.

Bobbio, L. and Dansero, E. (2008) *The TAV and the Valle di Susa: Competing Geographies*, Turin, Italy: Allemandi.

Brodie, E., Cowling, E. and Nissen, N. (2009) *Understanding Participation: A Literature Review*, available at: http://pathwaysthroughparticipation.org.uk/wp-content/uploads/2009/09/Pathways-literature-review-final-version.pdf (accessed May 25, 2010).

Burningham, K. (2000) "Using the Language of NIMBY: A Topic for Research, Not an Activity for Researchers," *Local Environment*, 5(1): 55–67.

Callon, M. (1986) "Éléments pour une sociologie de la traduction: la domestication des coquilles Saint-Jacques et des marins-pêcheurs dans la baie de Saint-Brieuc," *L'année sociologique*, 36: 169–208.

Charbonneau, S. (2010) "Les expériences françaises à des différentes échelles: de l'ambivalence de la participation," in U. Allegretti (ed.), *Democrazia partecipativa*, Firenze, Italy: Firenze University Press: 277–283.

Cohen, J. (1989) "Deliberation and Democratic Legitimacy," in A. Hamlin and P. Pettit (eds.), *The Good Polity*, New York, NY: Blackwell: 17–34.

Crosta, P. L. (1995) *La politica del piano*, Milan, Italy: Franco Angeli.

Davy, B. (1996) "Fairness as Compassion: Toward a Less Unfair Facility Siting Policy," *Risk: Health, Safety & Environment*, 7(2): 99–108.

Della Porta, D. and Piazza, G. (2008) *Le ragioni del no: le campagne contro la Tav in val di Susa e il Ponte sullo Stretto*, Milan, Italy: Feltrinelli.

Fisher, R., Ury, W. and Patton, B. (1981) *Getting to Yes: Negotiating Agreement Without Giving In*, London, UK: Random House.

Forester, J. (2006) "Making Participation Work When Interests Conflict: Moving from Facilitating Dialogue and Moderating Debate to Mediating Negotiations," *Journal of the American Planning Association*, 72(4): 447–456.

Forester, J. (2009) *Dealing with Differences: Dramas of Mediating Public Disputes*, Oxford, UK: Oxford University Press.

Fourniau, J.-M. (1996) "Transparence des décisions et participation des citoyens," *Techniques, Territoires et Société*, 31: 9–47.

Fourniau, J.-M. (2001) "Information, Access to Decision-Making and Public Debate in France: The Growing Demand for Deliberative Democracy," *Science and Public Policy*, 28(6): 441–445.

Fung, A. (2003) "Recipes for Public Spheres: Eight Institutional Design Choices and Their Consequences," *The Journal of Political Philosophy*, 11(3): 338–367.

Fung, A. (2006) "Varieties of Participation in Complex Governance," *Public Administration Review*, 66(Suppl.1): 66–75.

Galison, P. (1997) "Material Culture, Theoretical Culture and Delocalization," in J. Krige and D. Pestre (eds.), *Science in the Twentieth Century*, Paris, France: Harwood: 669–682.

Galison, P. (1999) "Trading Zone: Coordinating Action and Belief," in M. Biagioli (ed.), *The Science Studies Reader*, New York, NY: Routledge: 137–160.

Galison, P. (2010) "Trading with the Enemy," in M. E. Gorman (ed.), *Trading Zones and Interactional Expertise: Creating New Kinds of Collaboration*, Cambridge, MA: MIT Press.

Gastil, J. and Levine, P. (eds.) (2005) *The Deliberative Democracy Handbook: Strategies for Effective Civic Engagement in the Twenty-First Century*, San Francisco, CA: Jossey-Bass.

Georgescu-Roegen, N. (1995) *La décroissance. Entropie – Écologie – Économie*. Nouvelle édition. Paris: Éditions Sang de la Terre.

Gustavsson, S. (1980) "Types of Policy and Types of Politics," *Scandinavian Political Studies*, 3(2): 123–142.

Gutmann, A. and Thompson, D. (1996) *Democracy and Disagreement: Why Moral Conflict Cannot Be Avoided in Politics*, Cambridge, MA: Harvard University Press.

Hajer, M. (2003) "Policy Without Polity? Policy Analysis and the Institutional Void," *Policy Sciences*, 36(2): 175–195.

Hartz-Karp, J. (2007) "Understanding Deliberativeness: Bridging Theory and Practice," *The International Journal of Public Participation*, 1(2): 1–23.

Healey, P. (2006) *Collaborative Planning: Shaping Places in Fragmented Societies*, second edition, Basingstoke, UK: Palgrave Macmillan.

Hendriks, C. (2002) "The Ambiguous Role of Civil Society in Deliberative Democracy," paper delivered at the Australian Political Studies Association, Canberra, Australian National University, available at: http://web.iaincirebon.ac.id/ebook/moon/Civil Society/ambiguous%20role%20of%20civil%20society.pdf (accessed October 3, 2014).

Hendriks, C. M., Dryzek, J. S. and Hunold, C. (2007) "Turning Up the Heat: Partisanship in Deliberative Innovation," *Political Studies*, 55(2): 362–383.

Jobert, A. (1998) "L'aménagement en politique—ou ce que la syndrome Nimby nous dit de l'intérêt général," *Politix*, 11(42): 67–92.

Klein, O. (2001) *Les horizons de la grande vitesse: le TGV, une innovation lue à travers les mutations de son époque*, doctorat en Sciences Economiques, spécialité économie des transports, thèse soutenue le 9 novembre à l'Université Lumière-Lyon 2, available at:

http://theses.univ-lyon2.fr/documents/lyon2/2001/klein_o#p=0&a=top (accessed March 27, 2013).

Latouche, S. (2009) *Farewell to Growth*. New York: John Wiley & Sons.

Lowi, T. J. (1964) "American Business, Public Policy, Case Studies, and Political Theory," *World Politics*, 16(4): 677–715.

Mäntysalo, R., Balducci, A. and Kangasoja, J. (2011) "Planning as Agonistic Communication in a Trading Zone: Re-Examining Lindblom's Partisan Mutual Adjustment," *Planning Theory*, 10(3): 257–272.

Mermet, L., Dubien, I., Emerit, A. and Laurans, Y. (2004) "Les porteurs de projets face à leurs opposants: six critères pour évaluer la concertation en aménagement," *Revue Politiques et Management Public*, 22(1): 1–22.

Newman, J., Barnes, M. and Sullivan, H. (2004) "Public Participation and Collaborative Governance," *Journal of Social Policy*, 33(2): 203–223.

Offner, J. M. (2001) "Raisons politiques et grands projets," *Annales des Ponts et Chaussées*, 100: 55–59.

Pizzorno, A. (1973) "Per un'analisi teorica dei partiti politici in Italia," in A. Pizzorno (1980) *I soggetti del pluralismo: classi, partiti e sindacati*, Bologna, Italy: il Mulino: 39–42.

Ponti, M. (2007) *Una politica per i trasporti italiani*, Rome, Italy: Editori Laterza.

Portney, K. (2005) "Civic Engagement and Sustainable Cities in the United States," *Public Administration Review*, 65(5): 579–591.

Pucci, P. (2010) "The Public Debate on Gronda di Ponente in Genova. If Congestion Is the Problem: Acquisitions and Limits in the Treatment of Traffic and Mobility Topics," *Urbanistica*, 142: 67–69.

Rawls, J. (1971) *A Theory of Justice*, Cambridge, MA: Belknap Press of Harvard University Press.

Renn, O. (2008) "Essay 9: Integrating Deliberation and Expertise: Concepts, Features and Conditions of Science-Based Participation Processes," in *Risk Governance: Coping with Uncertainty in a Complex World*, London, UK: Earthscan: 284–331.

Revel, M., Blatrix, C., Blondiaux, L., Fourniau, J.-M., Dubreuil, B. H. and Lefebvre, R. (eds.) (2007) *Le débat public: une expérience française de démocratie participative*, Paris, France: La Découverte.

Rui, S. (2004) *La démocratie en débat: les citoyens face à l'action publique*, Paris, France: Armand Collin.

Star, S. L. and Griesemer, J. R. (1989) "Institutional Ecology, 'Translations' and Boundary Objects: Amateurs and Professionals in Berkeley's Museum of Vertebrate Zoology, 1907–39," *Social Studies of Sciences*, 19(3): 387–420.

Susskind, L. and Cruikshank, J. (1987) *Breaking the Impasse: Consensual Approaches to Resolving Public Disputes*, New York, NY: Basic Books.

Susskind, L., McKearnan, S. and Larmer, J. (eds.) (1999) *The Consensus Building Handbook: A Comprehensive Guide to Reaching Agreement*, Thousand Oaks, CA: Sage.

Trompette, P. and Vinck, D. (2009) "Retour sur la notion d'objet-frontière," *Revue d'Anthropologie des Connaissances*, 3(1): 5–27.

Wenger, E. (2000) "Communities of Practice and Social Learning Systems," *Organization*, 7(2): 225–246.

Wilson, J. Q. (1973) *Political Organizations*, New York, NY: Basic Books.

Zémor, P. (2003) *Pour un meilleur débat public*, Paris, France: Presses de Sciences Po.

12

Planning Through Emotions: Political Lessons from the Controversy Between 'Fat Cats' and 'Stupid Activists' over Rebuilding Brno Railroad Station

Anna Durnová

Introduction

Emotions that run high enough for each side to describe the other as 'fat cats' or as 'stupid activists' are an analyst's dream. Studying a relatively mundane issue such as the two sides that coalesced for and against a new main railroad station in the city of Brno presented the opportunity to address this issue, and the highly emotional language employed by both sides, augmented by extensive interviews, allowed for close analysis of the two discourses. Interpretive studies on planning have stated the heuristic potential of discourses for explaining policies and related conflicts (e.g., Bevir and Rhodes 2003; Griggs and Howarth 2004; Feindt and Oals 2005; Hajer 2005; Gualini and Majoor 2007; Fischer 2009a; Huxley 2010). This chapter advances the interpretive argument and suggests that we need to develop a deeper understanding of emotions that are part of these discourses and that, as such, enter the planning process. Emotions are neither side-effects nor faults of planning processes, but rather they have a governing role in such processes because they steer the identification of actors, explain any opposition to discourse and lay the ground for mediation when the policy becomes controversial.

The chapter sets the stage with the case of a prominent Czech planning controversy over the rebuilding of Brno railroad station, and reveals, through the highly charged language that the actors employ in the case, that emotions drive the very organization of both discourses. The discussion about moving Brno railroad station outside the city center has alienated both city residents and experts; on one side of the conflict stand those who want a railroad station at a new location outside the city center, and on the other side are those who want the station rebuilt at its current location. The first group recalls a 'modernizing discourse,' painting a picture of a fancy modern city, whereas the other group builds on a 'sustainability discourse,' claiming the relocation to be unnecessary and not user-friendly. The controversy over the location of the railroad station has developed into one over the participation of citizens in the decision-making process (as shown in Durnová 2013). The analysis looks closely at the process of escalation of both discourses to the negative labeling of 'stupid activists,' whom the 'modernizing' side sees as delaying the rebuilding process, and of 'fat cats,' whom the 'sustainability' side sees as resenting citizens' participation in the decision-making process. In June 2014, after activists scored numerous successes, public officials finally opened negotiations with them, and issued a joint press release about the result of an evaluation study that has compared both suggestions on the position of the railroad station. The city planning office released funding in order to prepare the complete documentation for the railroad station in the center so that both suggestions could be fully evaluated. This was a crucial step because the city planning office admitted that two equivalent suggestions might compete in the expert debate. Although the controversy continues, and will continue throughout 2015, a dialogue on how to unlock the conflict now seems possible, as at the time of writing.

In the Brno case, the chapter mediates between the interpretive tradition of policy analysis (Yanow 2003; Griggs and Howarth 2004; Hajer 2005; Fischer 2009a; Howarth 2010) and the psychosocial theorizing of emotions in the recent literature on public acknowledgment and participation (such as Thompson and Hoggett 2001; Newman et al. 2004; Barnes 2008; Blakeley and Evans 2009; Newman 2012), working toward a notion of *emotional experiences of discourses* (EED). EED is a conceptual framework that systematizes the interactions of actors inside and between discourses in order for us to understand the relationship among different discourses.

Supported by both the interpretive tradition and the psychosocial theorizing of emotions, the chapter investigates emotions through discourses. Therefore, the EED concept does not endeavor to solve the dilemmas between cognitive and representational nature of emotions (as mentioned for example by: Barbalet 1998; Jasper 2011) nor to study emotions as causal factors (Jasper 2006) or as urges and bodily sensation (Ticineto-Clough 2007; Stavrakakis 2008). Instead, it advances a notion of emotions in which they are inherent to discourses and yet also have the potential to transform them (see also Hochschild 1990; Glynos 2008; Kleres 2011). In that sense, 'emotional experiences of discourses' build, to certain extent, on the interactive dimension of emotions (as stated also by: Barbalet 1998; Reddy 2001; Collins 2004) but focus on the discursive context created by these interactions (as for example in the studies on social movement and participation: Krause 2008; Krinsky and Barker 2009).

Materials and Methods

The analysis is based on a wide-ranging and extensive set of sources: interviews, focus groups, correspondence between actors, participant observations, notes from public debates, policy documents and newspaper articles. The discourses of both sides of the Brno railroad station issue were meticulously examined and analyzed in policy documents and newspaper articles. Twenty qualitative semi-structured interviews were conducted between 2009 and 2012 with actors of both discourses. On the side of Brno public officials, I interviewed the former mayor of Brno, under whom the controversy started; a public official from the construction office of Brno, 'Brno South Center'; four public officials from the city planning office; the author of the 'Moving Project'; the two vice-mayors between 2006 and 2010—one from the Green Party and the other from the Social Democrats; and a politician (Social Democrat) from the urban quarter Brno-Židenice through which one part of the new railroad is supposed to go as at the time of writing. On the side of the activists, I interviewed four actors from the coalition 'Railroad Station in the Center'; two Green Party members who have been cooperating with them; one activist from the association 'Židenice for Its Citizens'; one independent urbanist; and two independent architects, one of whom is at the same time active in the civic association 'Brno on the Bike.' These key actors were identified via strategic sampling of policy documents and newspaper articles. Issues of the national daily and weekly newspapers as well as the local press published from 2003 through December 2012 were analyzed for this project. Additionally, I organized two focus groups in 2010. The first focus group included three participants: one public official and one lay person in favor of relocation, and one lay participant against relocation. The second focus group assembled five participants: one public official and one lay person in favor of relocation, and one civic activist and two lay people against relocation. In 2012, actors from both sides organized three debates in order to mediate between the groups, and I analyzed these debates as I followed them through participant observation and through the correspondence among the organizers. The first debate was organized by public officials and experts from the 'modernizing discourse,' and the last two debates were organized by the activists and experts connected with the 'sustainability discourse.' The analysis of focus groups and mediation debates illustrates the dynamic of the escalation, as it provides a validity check on the interaction practices that were articulated by the interviewees and in the policy papers and newspaper articles.

The interactions among actors are operationalized by following which actors speak to which communities, in what context they do so and what language, or rhetorical devices, they deploy. The analysis thus teases out the emotions as these appear in the textual data (Maingueneau 1998; Kerbrat-Orecchioni

1999; Charaudeau 2008; Rinn 2008; Durnová 2011; see also the narrative approach by Kleres 2011). The analysis examines how actors of one discourse are gathered around 'trust' and how they are opposed to actors from the other discourse through expressions of 'disdain.'

Brno 2003–2013: As the Train Goes Back and Forth

The idea to move the main railroad station in Brno to a new location approximately 800 meters south of the center goes back to the beginning of the twentieth century. The political controversy traced here was launched in 2003 with the mayor's office's unilateral decision to move the railroad station. This decision was the catalyst for a group of experts, environmental activists and civic associations to coalesce around the 'Railroad Station in the Center' (RSC) civic initiative that argued that modernization of the railroad station is possible in its current location and that the relocation project is therefore unnecessary. With this, the lines were drawn between the 'modernizing discourse' and the 'sustainability discourse,' leading to a local referendum in 2004. A clear majority, 85.78 percent, of voters were against the relocation, but as only 24.9 percent of Brno citizens voted on the issue, the mayor was not legally bound to the referendum decision. With that, a virtual tug of war between supporters of the 'Moving Project' and RSC members persisted from 2006 until 2009. In December 2009, the High Court of Administration, the State's highest court for affairs of local government, canceled the current version of Brno's zoning plan by finding in favor of an activist initiative against the new railroad station. As a result of the court decision, in early 2010 the mayor was forced to interrupt planning and construction negotiations of the relocation project. The court decision also ushered in a round of mediations between the groups that culminated in February 2013, when the Ministry of Transport issued the order that, in its new zoning plan, the city consider both possibilities of renovation. The ministry further charged Brno public officials with setting aside funds that could be directed to prepare proper planning documentation for the option of renovating in the current location.

The reciprocal expressive identification of both groups—either as 'fat cats' or as 'stupid activists'—aptly illustrates the dynamic of the conflict that moves from (1) the identification period (2003–2006), during which both the modernization and sustainability discourses were consolidated around specific groups of actors; over (2) the escalation period (2006–2010), in which both discourses promoted a policy setting including, or excluding, participation by citizens; to the (3) mediation period (2010–2013), which began when the Brno city planning office was forced by the court to reconsider the entire project and seek ways to work with activists in order to prevent future protests.

Identification Period (2003–2006)

The 2003 plan of the local government of Brno had long roots; since the nineteenth century, the city has been the industrial and commercial link between Vienna and Prague, and architects and planners are on record as stating that the proximity of Brno railroad station to its historical center prevents the city's further development (Flodrová 2003). Experts from the Brno city planning office advocated for a new railroad system. Constructing this system would include abandoning some lines that currently run through the city center and constructing a new railroad system, which would in turn require a new station. Many experts supported the idea of relocating the railroad station, because, as the former mayor points out, "the city center could then grow naturally." Both the author of the project interviewed in 2009 and 2012 and a former public official from the city planning office confirmed that. Opposing them stood other planners and engineers who warned that such a move would be too technically and financially demanding, contending that the renovation could indeed be accomplished without relocating the railroad station (as planners from RSC interviewed in 2009 and one independent architect interviewed in 2011 explained to me). The architect also added that the current station's convenient location near the city center has made it accessible for tourists and business travelers as well as for commuters in the region. Finally, Green Party members pointed out that renovating the railroad lines to the current railroad station would be less of an encumbrance on the environment (interviews in 2009).

In 2004, planners, Green Party members and independent political activists from environmental movements (Tůma 2008) were among those who formed and joined the RSC initiative, which came together rather quickly after the mayor's surprise announcement. RSC efforts coalesced around what it identified as four significant problems with the relocation project: its ecological encumbrance; its financial encumbrance; the necessity of rebuilding the entire Brno public transport system of tramways to adapt it to the new railroad station site; and the loss of pedestrian accessibility to the main station (RSC 2013).

Along with launching a flyer campaign that included "There Is No Rational Reason to Move the Railroad Station" and "The Decision Is Not Final Yet," RSC assembled experts from various areas who issued a joint public statement supporting the renovation of the railroad while retaining the station in its current city-center location. They were adamant that relocating the station was not only unnecessary but also financially demanding and environmentally unfriendly. They directed their statement to all of the involved local and national public administration offices, including the Brno City Hall, the Ministries of Environment, Transport, Finances and Regional Development, the Department of Czech Railroads, the National Fund of Transport

Infrastructure, the Regional Council of Brno and the Department of the Administration of Railroad Transport.

Later that year, RSC ran a successful drive to obtain sufficient petition signatures (*Rovnost* 2004a) to put forward a local referendum about whether or not to move the railroad station outside of the city center. The only legal instrument available to reverse a mayoral decision, a local referendum is valid only if at least 50 percent of the eligible voters participate. The referendum was announced for October 9, 2004. As already seen, although 85.78 percent of the votes were against the plan to move the railroad station away from the center, as only 24.9 percent of Brno voters had participated in the referendum, the city was not legally bound to the result (*Rovnost* 2004b).

At that point, the struggle developed into a conflict over public acknowledgment and citizen participation in the planning project. RSC exhorted the city administration to respect the voters' decision, to open discussion among experts from both camps and to establish an alternative planning study for the modernization of the railroad in the location of the current railroad station. For its part, the city administration was unwilling to engage RSC's experts in discussion because, as members of the city planning office told me in the interviews, it viewed its decision as a strategic issue for both the mayor's office and the city planning office. Inherent in this response was the administration's perception that it was legitimate to rely on institutionally established experts (which was emphasized especially by the former mayor, the current vice-mayor and the author of the project). As the former mayor put it, these actors are also "morally bound to what they have subscribed to" and, therefore, can be seen as "the acknowledged experts." For that reason, the city considered the issue to be one that neither the referendum voters nor independent experts were qualified to decide, added the Social Democrat vice-mayor. Indeed, the activists from RSC explained that the city succeeded in avoiding negotiating with RSC and in ignoring RSC's expert studies until 2006.

Escalation Period (2006–2010)

RSC pushed its agenda now more in the direction of criticizing how the project was communicated and how the role of citizens' participation was systematically circumvented. In 2006, the controversy came to a head because the city's negotiations with EU (European Union) officials had become bogged down (Ministry of Transport 2006). Two Green Party members I interviewed in 2009 revealed to me that RSC had played a direct role in this impasse by alerting EU actors to the fact that the project was controversial, presenting them with the result of the local referendum. This prolonged the city's negotiations on the application within the EU Structural Fund, which the city was counting on for a relocation subvention. The mayor of Brno I interviewed in 2009 therefore accused the adversarial actors of attempting to "shape the city" and the author of the 'Moving Project' was upset that Brno people were not able to "pull together" (interviewed in 2010 and 2012). Many of these accusations were regularly published by the local press.

In fall the same year, 2006, the Brno Green Party scored a historic victory in the local election (11.92 percent of the vote) and secured the position of vice-mayor. The Green Party then demanded that an impartial panel of experts perform an external review of both planning studies. It was successful in making this demand because, as the Green vice-mayor explained to me in 2009, two of its coalition partners—the Social Democrats and political movement Brno 2006—also favored rebuilding the railroad station in its current location. An external review, performed in 2007 by the Technical University in Prague, rated rebuilding the railroad station in the current location as more sustainable because it would burden the environment less and have lower financial costs. It also determined that modernizing the railroad with the station in its current location was indeed technically possible and could comply with current quality standards (Cityplan 2007).

However, in 2007, the Social Democrats changed their position (Czech Press Agency 2007). Both Social Democrats I interviewed in 2010 told me that the reason was that a new railroad station would provide investment opportunities for the city. They took the position that not building a new station would be "a step backward," a metaphor that was employed by the public official from the city builder's office, and it was also mentioned by other public officials. They argued that Brno instead needs a "modern face." The result of this about-face was that the city planning office had meanwhile continued its negotiations with investors willing to fund the relocation project and a further result was that the RSC coalition undertook contingency plans to determine a course of action should the relocation of the railroad station go ahead (Strategy Office 2009).

The controversy took on a new dynamic in December 2009, when the High Court of Administration, the nation's highest court for affairs of local government, found against the City of Brno and in favor of Židenice for Its Citizens, a Brno neighborhood civic association that opposed one segment of the new railroad because it would disturb a residential neighborhood (as was explained to me by one of their members). As a result of this decision, the Brno city planning office was forced to reconsider the entire project. Although the city builder's office did not foresee substantial changes to the new station location (their public official repeated to me that that the neighborhood would not be affected by that segment of the railroad), the authors of the relocation project lost confidence that the project would succeed (as stated in interviews with both the former mayor of Brno and the author of the 'Moving Project').

Mediation Period (2010–2013)

After the 2009 decision by the High Court of Administration, the mayor's office found itself in a tricky situation. On the one hand, without an official zoning plan, the investors had no assurance that the relocation project would be realized, so the planning was partly stopped. On the other hand, in order to advance the new zoning plan agenda, the mayor's office had to demonstrate that the alternative of relocating the railroad station was both still possible and advantageous, so some of the planning continued. The mayor's office initiated a campaign titled 'We're Stepping It Up!' that it conducted through the Brno information center. This situation was reinforced after the election in fall 2010, when the Green Party left the vice-mayorship, and the Conservatives built a large coalition with the Social Democrats, which gave them a comfortable majority for the relocation project.

The ambiguous behavior of the mayor's office toward the continuation of the project nourished an escalation of the conflict on the part of RSC. The group publicized that the city planning office was spending public funds on a risky project that had no legal basis for its realization (MF Dnes 2012). The critique of the mayor's office was supported by public polls (Rovnost 2012) in favor of renovating the current location and, more importantly, by statements of other civic initiatives that arose between 2009 and 2012 (Brnění 2013; Brno Cultural 2013; Brno on the Bike 2013; Žít Brno 2013), which shared RSC's concerns about the unsatisfactory communications from both the city planning office and the mayor's office. Not only did their members state this in the interviews in 2012 but they expressed the same in the last mediation debate where the debate turned into a general critique of the way city planning office communicates with independent experts. The critique also asked the question of whether corruption and lobbying had roles in the decision to continue with the relocation project. This aspect was raised by interviewed activists who criticized the Social Democrats' about-face, but they could offer no firm evidence of corruption or lobbying, and I was also unable to independently confirm either accusation. However, as the controversy continued, these suspicions were mentioned regularly in the debates by activists and they become powerful themes in the mediation debate in early 2012 where the activists accused their opponents openly.

In spring 2011, the new zoning plan of Brno was in preparation (Brno Website 2010). Activists—and also other experts—provided public comment, which the city planning office was legally bound to consider. As activists were working on the comment, their concerns around the citizens' participation had become more important than the sole issue of the railroad station (as they explained in the interviews in spring 2012). Some of the new initiatives were not against the relocation project per se, explained the independent urbanist, but objected to the way the city planning office communicated.

On the side of the modernizing discourse, experts on the one hand blamed the mayor's office for not having dealt with the activists' obstructions in a way that the project could be accomplished (interview with the author of the 'Moving Project' in 2012). On the other hand, the project's realization had become less certain once the Ministry of Culture opposed to the relocation because of concerns about preserving cultural heritage (City Planning Office 2013). At the same time, the relocation project was considerably challenged by the group of young architects Ruller, Rudiš and Chybík (according to the independent architect interviewed in 2012). The three architects presented a redesign for the current location (RSC 2012).

The incumbent vice-mayor stated in his interview in late 2012 that all these new aspects led public officials to change their strategy. It was also emphasized by one of the public officials. They invited activists to negotiations, in early 2012, and both the mayor's office and the activists organized public mediation debates, with both sides of the issue invited to the podium. In January 2012, the young architects made a public presentation of their project, which was followed by a public debate to which both the city planning office and the RSC members were invited. In April 2012, the author of the relocation project organized a 'Railroad Station Hurts' panel debate together with the Faculty of Architecture, and the Green Party organized a 'Don't Get Bogged Down by the Zoning Plan' panel discussion in November 2012. Independent of those endeavors, RSC was successful in bringing its case before the Ministry of Transport, which in early 2013 charged the city government with developing a zoning plan that allowed for the future realization of both possibilities—the relocation and the renovation in the existing location. At the same time, the ministry charged the city planning office to set aside financial means in order to accurately document the renovation in the existing location. Activists from RSC wrote me in our correspondence that they took the decision as a victory because they could now hope for a change in the opposition logic, which previously ignored them as equal negotiation partners. They also made a similar post on the RSC Facebook page in February 2013.

From Discourses to Emotional Experiences of Discourses

The Brno case is scarcely the only one to show that a clash of discourses results in planning becoming controversial (Schön and Rein 1994; Griggs and Howarth 2004; Gualini and Majoor 2007; Huxley 2010). However, the way in which the struggle about the future of Brno railroad station has been carried out by the actors invites us to devote more attention to how those discourses are emotionally experienced by the actors. The struggle goes beyond the opposition between 'modernizing discourse' and 'sustainability discourse' to reveal a conflict over whether the planning process should or should not involve citizens' participation (see also: Griggs and Howarth 2004; Mathur and Skelcher 2007) and how public officials and citizens should interact (see also: Fischer 2009a, 2009b; Healey 2010).

Emotions have been rather implicit in recent interpretive works (as shown by e.g., Newman 2012). The interactions of actors are studied by examining the particular networks of actors who fill policy fields with discourse, and showing how they formulate or criticize policy agendas (see e.g., Hajer 2005; Rhodes 2005; Zittoun 2007; Fischer 2009a; Sørensen and Torfing 2009). On issues of public acknowledgment and citizen participation, especially (e.g., Mathur and Skelcher 2007), these works have recognized specific problems in the interactions among actors.

First, as a result of the complex character of current policy issues, there is ambivalence in the knowledge about a policy issue that shapes the communication (issues having to do with scientific knowledge: Irwin and Wynne 2003; Braun et al. 2010; Healey 2007 for planning controversies). Second, actors are characterized by institutional ambiguity; governance has relaxed institutional rules, and actors now establish their positions through argumentation and communication (Fischer and Gottweis 2012), or through performance (Hajer and Versteeg 2005), in order to be acknowledged as actors. Third, although publics seek the advice of experts and institutions (see: Pierre and Peters 2000; Bevir and Rhodes 2003), they do not necessarily trust them (Fischer 2009b; Healey 2010).

In order for us to develop a deeper understanding of those ambiguities in the interactions between public officials and citizens, we have to consider the role of emotions in those interactions. That role has been a focus of the recent studies of social movements, which examine the historical, cultural and social dimensions in which emotions are experienced (see: Jasper 2011). Blakeley and Evans suggest, for example, that a social and cultural explanation of participation should be privileged (Blakeley and Evans 2009: 29) over an explanation based solely on rationality approaches. For them, emotions are experienced in these cultural or societal contexts, underpin actors' motivations to participate, and structure their positions in the policy process. A similar view is advanced by Jasper (2003, 2006). In his approach, emotions are elements that initiate actions, but they are also formative elements of our identities as actors (Jasper 2003: 154). Barnes too suggests taking note of the emotionally charged nature of values because the latter creates identities (Barnes 2008). Such a view is also at the core of Honneth's idea of mutual recognition of actors (Honneth 1995).

From such a viewpoint, of particular interest for interpretive studies are the political or social spaces where emotions can be expressed and shared. Interactions among actors build such spaces, which are shaped by discourses. Discourses, as interpretive works in turn have shown, are both the tools of construction for an issue and the ways of predetermining how the issue will be constructed (see: Hajer 2005; Howarth 2010). In the context of emotions, 'discourse' refers to the social and cultural spaces in which emotions are experienced. Nevertheless, this relationship is not one-sided; at the same time, emotions shape the discourses to which particular actors subscribe. Jasper speaks of 'reflexive emotions' (Jasper 2006) that arise from interaction practices (see also: Krinsky and Barker 2009).

Therefore, I propose framing the 'emotional experiences of discourse' (EED) in the interactions to denude the organization of a discourse. This phrase reveals the discursive nature of emotions (studied also in terms of culture and practices, see: Ahmed 2004; Gould 2009) without advancing a one-sided explanation of emotions that would stem from discourses. Instead, it focuses on the interactive dimensions that emotions add, so to speak, to discourse (as stated also by: Reddy 2001). The interaction is manifested through 'trust' that holds together one group of actors and directs 'disdain' toward the other group of actors. This opposition, I argue, can be revealed through the way the respective discourse is emotionally experienced by the actors. EED examines the rhetorical devices that actors employ during interviews, in policy papers and in media articles when justifying their position, or when distinguishing themselves from the opposing actors. By showing which discourses are shared and how these discourses consolidate actors into groups, EED can explain what might impede or reinforce the interaction in this particular context.

Analysis: Explaining the Fight between 'Fat Cats' and 'Stupid Activists'

The conflict becomes materialized for the 'modernization' side as between those who are in favor of the 'modernization of Brno' and those 'stupid activists' who want to stem it. Public officials used this expression during the interviews in 2009 while blaming activists for the current situation. RSC and its supporters, who took part in both focus groups, view the conflict, conversely, as one between 'critical citizens' who want to defend sustainability over the irrational spending of public money on 'megalomaniac projects' and those 'fat cats' who do not care what ordinary people think. The term 'fat cat' also appeared in interviews with Green Party members and came out during the mediation debates. The respective emotionally loaded caricatures of each discourse—'fat cats' and 'stupid activists'—lay the ground for identifying the emotional experiences of discourses in the interaction among actors. They help, in the final section, to explain the grounds on which mediation between both camps has been started.

The following analysis addresses, first, the ambivalence of knowledge, by considering rhetorical devices that actors use when describing their positions and that also appear in related newspaper articles or policy papers. Second, the analysis contends with the institutional ambiguity of actors by analyzing how actors describe the opposing group and what language they use in order to distinguish themselves from that group. Third, the analysis engages with the role of citizens' trust in public officials by attending to actors' expressions of 'disdain' and 'trust' toward each other.

Ambivalence of Knowledge

Both the 'modernizing discourse' and the 'sustainability discourse' are consolidated through actors who struggle over their conviction that theirs is the legitimate knowledge (technical, social, expert knowledge, everyday knowledge of users etc.) and that theirs is the legitimate way to proceed in planning. In that context, the former mayor of Brno highlighted the necessity of the project by claiming that the existing railroad system "*suffocates* the development of the town" (interview with the former mayor of Brno, emphasis added). Similarly, activists insist that "it is possible to modernize the railroad station there where it is" (interview with RSC activist). In order to promote their way of conceiving the issue, both discourses promote a specific image of the city. The modern high-tech city becomes the opposite of a sustainable city.

Interviewees favoring relocation therefore set the positive adjectives 'new,' 'modern' and 'revitalized' in opposition to the negative adjectives 'old' and 'insufficient.' They use also other means to highlight the modern aspect. One interviewee stated, for example, that technical parameters of the existing railroad station do not correspond "with the *exigencies of the railroad in the twenty-first century*" (interview with vice-mayor 2006–2010, emphasis added). Modernization incorporates "new" (positive adjective), "strategically important for the future" (rationalization), and the "hope for the city" (metaphor) (interviews with public officials in 2009, 2010 and 2012). The modernizing side employs these rhetorical devices to paint a picture of a "Brno building a new city," as stated in the strategic document of the same name.

Moreover, these 'modernizing discourse' interviewees described the existing Brno railroad station as "ugly and old" (interview with the former mayor, 2009), "embarrassingly odd" (interview with the vice-mayor, 2010), "simply shabby" (interview with a public official 2009), a "historical building having fulfilled its role, which is now over" (interview with a former public official) or in similar language. A review of the local press revealed that these comments were repeated in, and even supported by, the press. The city planning office warned against "a construction site in the middle of the city" (implied by the renovation option: Strategy Office 2009). It points, again, to the 'old': as the mayor asked in the policy document Strategy for Brno, "Do Brno citizens realize that the whole transportation system of the city is located on its medieval grounding?" (Strategy for Brno 2006). The adjective 'medieval' is the pejorative inverse or opposite of 'modern,' and the rhetorical question used here reinforces the urgency of a change.

Interviewees opposed to the relocation highlighted the same antiquated aspect of the current railroad station building but criticized primarily the financial encumbrance: "Yes, the building is old, odd, and embarrassingly insufficient, but we do not need some megalomaniac project outside of the town" (interview with RSC activist). Along the same lines, these 'sustainability discourse' interviewees criticized what they considered to be an overestimation of the importance of cars to the new station (interviews with Green Party members). This violated the sustainability concept inherent in mass transportation, including rail: "in all their strategic materials [in favor of a relocation], they highlight the large number of parking places, instead of supporting public transportation as the main access to the new rail station" (interview with RSC activist). The interviewees who opposed relocation valued public transportation over the use of personal cars, using adjectives such as "handy" and "agreeable" to refer to the former (interviews with member of the civic association Židenice for Its Citizens and RSC activist).

The 'sustainability discourse' interviewees also reinforced the role of pedestrians by describing the project as 'megalomaniacal' or 'encumbering.' As RSC underscored with its own rhetorical question in its strategic papers, since the modernization "is possible and even better" (RSC 2013) in the current location, "why spend so much money on building new when we can rely on the existing?" (interview with RSC activist). Some on the sustainability side sum up their position this way: "We want a railroad station accessible by pedestrians" (interview with RSC activists). "They don't build a city for people but for cars," complained one independent expert.

Actors' Status

The image that each side evoked of the city—whether as a shining new place of the future or as a medieval rat-trap—is related to the way planning is conceived and who the legitimate actor is in such planning. On the 'modernizing' side, official representatives, policy experts and city planners comprised the network of actors, whereas on the 'sustainability' side were assembled members from smaller political parties, civic activists and city planning experts from independent research institutions. That fundamentally different actors who constituted these two sides spoke to the general question of how to proceed in planning.

The modernizing side characterized citizens who were against the relocation project as 'ordinary,' 'peculiar,' as comprising only a 'small part' of the population, and as 'not having a clue.' As one interviewee put it: "You know, the problem is that these ordinary people think that they can decide on such a complex thing" (interview with the former mayor in 2009). They emphasized the legitimacy of their own actions: "We want the best for this town" (interview with the author of the project). They therefore saw voter input through the referendum as the major obstacle for the project, by using the pejorative term 'thing' ("this referendum thing, you know," interview with a public official in 2010) or by picturing the referendum as 'tragic' ("the tragic fact that we live in a State where some small activist movement can stop a large project like this because of some peculiar environmentalism," pointed out the Social Democratic vice-mayor, interviewed in 2006). In their view, all those "stupid activists" who "stem the hope for the city" (interview with a public official) had neither the knowledge nor the status to speak about urban planning issues; "It is a strategic issue, you know" (interview with the former mayor of Brno) or "planning is an expert issue, I tell you" (interview with the incumbent vice-mayor in 2012). The rhetorical device 'you know' or 'I tell you' in all these responses underscore the self-evidence that all interviewees attribute to their view.

In that context, RSC's people spoke of the city planners as "fat cats who want to carve their names in stone" (interview with a Green Party member in 2009), and they connected the relocation project to 'depersonalization' (interviews with an RSC activist and with the architect involved in the association Brno on the Bike). This was exemplified in the 'Mayor's Mile' campaign of 2004, in which RSC organized a procession to the proposed new location of the railroad station. Participants joined the walk with prams and bikes, and were accompanied also by seniors and disabled people to reinforce RSC's point that the new railroad station would be inaccessible to "ordinary citizens" (interview with the Green Party vice-mayor in 2009). The depersonalization theme appeared also in a powerful, pithy statement by one of the RSC experts in the group's publicity materials: "Rails should be adapted to people, not the other way around." This also explains the mistrust expressed by a focus group participant: "I would [be satisfied to] leave it to the experts [to decide], if those experts would sometimes travel by public transportation with luggage, or take a pram with them [...]—if they would [only] see what it means to travel when you are just an ordinary citizen!"

A similar opposition dynamic could be seen regarding citizens' participation. Interviews from 2009 into 2010 showed public officials to be opposed to citizen participation, which was apparent through their use of pejorative adjectives to describe the opposition, their negativity toward the referendum and their justifications for how they proceeded. Activists, for their part, had a fear of potential betrayal—as indicated through their justifications of their perspective and through their critique of public officials.

Whereas the modernizing discourse adhered to the vision that "experts along with public officials want the best" (as underscored by interviews with public officials) and should be trusted "because they carry the burden of responsibility" (interview with the author of the 'Moving Project'), for its part, the sustainability discourse took the view that "there are always controversial issues when you plan something like this. You have to negotiate that, and you cannot forget the everyday life of a town" (interview with a Green Party member). In the view of the latter interviewee, the legitimacy of the public official goes beyond an electoral setting and is formed through constant interaction with citizens. An architect opposed to relocation put it this way: "You have to establish fair rules of the game" (interview with an independent expert in 2012).

RSC was frustrated with the way the city administration treated the group about the referendum, as they explained to me both in interviews and in our correspondence. The mayor's office did not allow piggybacking the referendum on the same day as a candidate election, which generally produces higher voter turnout, thus raising the likelihood of achieving the necessary 50 percent participation for the referendum. As one RSC member said: "And tell me one reason why they [the mayor's office] did it [held the referendum vote] just one week before the [senatorial] election, on a Saturday afternoon, when everybody is out [of town] for the weekend?" Repeated fatalistic complaints on the modernizing side, such as "I fear we are already lost, and we cannot become an important European city" (interview with a public official), or that "if those activists would just be silent, we would have been on our best way to becoming a fancy European town" (interview with the author of the 'Moving Project') validated RSC's concerns.

Trust-Building

The Brno controversy came to a head because the modernizing side disregarded activists' concerns; this perspective was voiced from 2012 onward by both sides (interviews with the incumbent vice-mayor, the new interview with the author of the project, and interviews with independent experts in 2012). As one urbanist explained: "I do think that the relocation is a step forward and should be done. But I understand why the coalition [RSC] fights with the city." The vice-mayor observed that there were some "faults of communication" that should be now repaired. Also, the authors of the modernization project softened their language toward the sustainability group: "The debate was correct," commented one of them on the public debates organized to "get the issue solved" (as the author of the 'Moving Project' put it).

Until 2010, communication had been confrontational, but it since moved up to the main agenda. An interviewee from the modernizing side criticized the Brno city planning office: "I thought I would explode when I read in the newspaper the announcement that they would move the railroad station just like that, without any preparatory and explanatory campaign" (interview with a former public official from the Strategy Office). The sarcastic response from a member of the city planning office in one of the mediation debates articulated the disdain that the office had toward such campaigns: "If you ask people what they want, they tell you they want a wristwatch with a fountain on it."

'Trust' became crucial no matter where the railroad stands. During all three debates, participants asked at every opportunity, "How can a citizen trust you?" and "What tools of certainty do we have?" "This struggle shows in principle how this town despises people's opinion," summarized an interviewee from the Green Party. Another interviewee, although in favor of relocation, criticized the communication: "They don't care about people. You always knock on a door that is shut." "I am unhappy that my institution has such a reputation," complained a member of the city planning office in our correspondence.

Emotional experiences are not side-effects produced by a particular dynamic of the conflict, but they accompany the issue from the very beginning, as we can see through both the images of the city and the struggle over who are admitted as legitimate actors. As such, they also lay the ground for those debates. This shows repeated misbehavior in correspondence with the activists, as well as invectives during the public debates, such as "It is you to whom we owe this terrible status quo," shouted by one of the debates' participants, which characterized all three debates. The debates, while opening the floor to all voices, consequently enabled a space for both positive and negative interactions.

Conclusions

The main argument presented here is that emotions are neither the side-effects nor the faults of planning processes. Various rhetorical devices are presented in the case study to show how both groups emotionally experienced the events. Through the emotional experiences of their discourses, the chapter illustrates that emotions first steer the identification of actors, which is apparent in the way both groups gathered around a particular image of the city. Second, emotions explain oppositions of discourses, which was visible in the reciprocal invectives that elucidated what drives disdain or trust in actors. Third, emotions lay the ground for mediation, which was visible in interviewees' reactions to the earlier invectives and their call for trust.

The case study suggests extending the interpretive studies on planning by placing an explicit methodological focus on the ways that discourses are emotionally experienced by the actors, because the latter elucidates how discourses develop and in what way they differ from each other.

References

Ahmed, S. (2004) *The Cultural Politics of Emotion*, New York, NY: Routledge.

Barbalet, J. M. (1998) *Emotion, Social Theory, and Social Structure: A Macrosociological Approach*, Cambridge, UK: Cambridge University Press.

Barnes, M. (2008) "Passionate Participation: Emotional Experiences and Expressions in Deliberative Forums," *Critical Social Policy*, 28(4): 461–481.

Bevir, M. and Rhodes, R. A. W. (2003) *Interpreting British Governance*, London, UK: Routledge.

Blakeley, G. and Evans, B. (2009) "Who Participates, How and Why in Urban Regeneration Projects? The Case of the New 'City' of East Manchester," *Social Policy & Administration*, 43(1): 15–32.

Braun, K., Moore, A., Herrmann, S. L. and Könninger, S. (2010) "Science Governance and the Politics of Proper Talk: Governmental Bioethics as a New Technology of Reflexive Government," *Economy and Society*, 39(4): 510–533.

Brnění (2013) "Documents of the Civic Association 'Brnění'," available at: www.osbrneni.cz (accessed March 30, 2013).

Brno Cultural (2013) "Documents of the Civic Association 'Brno Cultural'," available at: www.brnokulturni.cz (accessed March 30, 2013).

Brno on the Bike (2013) "Documents of the Civic Association 'Brno on the Bike'," available at: www.brnonakole.cz (accessed March 30, 2013).

Brno Website (2010) "Presentation of Brno Zoning Plan," November 18, 2010, available at: www.brno.cz (accessed March 30, 2013).

Charaudeau, P. (2008) "Pathos et discours politique," in M. Rinn (ed.), *Emotions et discours: l'usage des passions dans la langue*, Rennes, France: Presses Universitaires de Rennes: 49–58.

Cityplan (2007) *Comparative Multi-Criterion Analysis of Conceptions to Renovate Railroad in Brno, Cityplan s.r.o. (Technical University Prague) 2007*, available at: www.europointbrno.cz/index.php?nav01=6299&nav02=8067&nav03=8089&nav04=9883 (accessed October 31, 2011).

City Planning Office (2013) "Correspondence of the Ministry of Culture with the Brno City Planning Office," available at: www.osbrneni.cz/novy-uzemni-plan-brna/vyjadreni-dotcenych-organu/vyjadreni-ministerstva-kultury (accessed March 30, 2013).

Collins, R. (2004) *Interaction Ritual Chains*, Princeton, NJ: Princeton University Press.

Czech Press Agency (2007) "Přesun nádraží v Brně je zřejmě definitivní; souhlasí i ČSSD," press release of the Czech Press Agency, September 7.

Durnová, A. (2011) "Feldforschung Intim: Von Erlebnissen, Bedeutungen und Interpretationspraxis in der Politikfeldanalyse," *Österreichische Zeitschrift für Politikwissenschaft*, 40(4): 417–432.

Durnová, A. (2013) "A Tale of 'Fat Cats' and 'Stupid Activists': Contested Values, Governance and Reflexivity in the Brno Railway Station Controversy," *Journal of Environmental Policy & Planning*, in advance of print, doi: 10.1080/1523908X.2013.829749.

Feindt, P. H. and Oals, A. (2005) "Does Discourse Matter? Discourse Analysis in Environmental Policy Making," *Journal of Environmental Policy & Planning*, 7(3): 161–173.

Fischer, F. (2009a) *Democracy and Expertise: Reorienting Policy Inquiry*, Oxford, UK: Oxford University Press.

Fischer, F. (2009b) "Policy Deliberation: Confronting Subjectivity and Emotional Expression," *Critical Policy Studies*, 3(3): 407–420.

Fischer, F. and Gottweis, H. (eds.) (2012) *The Argumentative Turn Revisited: Public Policy as Communicative Practice*, Durham, NC: Duke University Press.

Flodrová, M. (2003) *Brno v Proměnách Času*, Brno, Czech Republic: Šimon Ryšavý.

Glynos, J. (2008) "Ideological Fantasy at Work," *Journal of Political Ideologies*, 13(3): 275–296.

Gould, D. (2009) *Moving Politics: Emotion and ACT UP's Fight Against AIDS*, Chicago, IL: University of Chicago Press.

Griggs, S. and Howarth, D. (2004) "A Transformative Political Campaign? The New Rhetoric of Protest Against Airport Expansion in the UK," *Journal of Political Ideologies*, 9(2): 181–201.

Gualini, E. and Majoor, S. (2007) "Innovative Practices in Large Urban Development Projects: Conflicting Frames in the Quest for 'New Urbanity'," *Planning Theory and Practice*, 8(3): 297–318.

Hajer, M. (2005) "Rebuilding Ground Zero: The Politics of Performance," *Planning Theory and Practice*, 6(4): 445–464.

Hajer, M. and Versteeg, W. (2005) "Performing Governance Through Networks," *European Political Science*, 4(3): 340–347.

Healey, P. (2007) "The 'Collaborative Planning' Project in an Institutionalist and Relational Perspective: A Note," *Critical Policy Studies*, 1(1): 123–130.

Healey, P. (2010) *Making Better Places: The Planning Project in the 21st Century*, Basingstoke, UK: Palgrave Macmillan.

Hochschild, A. R. (1990) "Ideology and Emotion Management: A Perspective and Path for Future Research," in T. D. Kemper (ed.), *Research Agendas in the Sociology of Emotions*, New York, NY: State University of New York Press: 117–142.

Honneth, A. (1995) *The Struggle for Recognition: The Moral Grammar of Social Conflicts*, Cambridge, MA: MIT Press.

Howarth, D. (2010) "Power, Discourse, and Policy: Articulating a Hegemony Approach to Critical Policy Studies," *Critical Policy Studies*, 3(3/4): 309–335.

Huxley, M. (2010) "Problematising Planning: Critical and Effective Genealogies," in P. Healey and J. Hiller (eds.), *The Ashgate Research Companion to Planning Theory: Conceptual Challenges for Spatial Planning*, Farnham, UK: Ashgate: 135–158.

Irwin, A. and Wynne, B. (2003) *Misunderstanding Science? The Public Reconstruction of Science and Technology*, Cambridge, UK: Cambridge University Press.

Jasper, J. M. (2003) "The Emotions of Protest," in J. Goodwin and J. M. Jasper (eds.), *The Social Movements Reader*, Oxford, UK: Blackwell: 153–162.

Jasper, J. M. (2006) "Emotions and the Microfoundations of Politics: Rethinking Ends and Means," in S. Clarke, P. Hoggett and S. Thompson (eds.), *Emotion, Politics and Society*, Basingstoke, UK: Palgrave Macmillan: 14–30.

Jasper, J. M. (2011) "Emotions and Social Movements: Twenty Years of Theory and Research," *Annual Review of Sociology*, 37(1): 285–303.

Kerbrat-Orecchioni, C. (1999) *L'énonciation*, Paris, France: Armand Colin.

Kleres, J. (2011) "Emotions and Narrative Analysis: A Methodological Approach," *Journal for the Theory of Social Behaviour*, 41(2): 182–202.

Krause, S. (2008) *Civil Passions: Moral Sentiment and Democratic Deliberation*, Princeton, NJ: Princeton University Press.

Krinsky, J. and Barker, C. (2009) "Movement Strategizing a Developmental Learning: Perspectives from Cultural-Historical Activity Theory," in H. Johnston (ed.), *Culture, Social Movements, and Protest*, Farnham, UK: Ashgate: 209–228.

Maingueneau, D. (1998) *Analyser les textes de communication*, Paris, France: Dunod.

Mathur, N. and Skelcher, C. (2007) "Evaluating Democratic Performance: Methodologies for Assessing the Relationship Between Network Governance and Citizens," *Public Administration Review*, 67(2): 228–237.

Ministry of Transport (2006) "Minutes of the Meeting Between the European Commission and Ministry of Transport," Ministry of Finances and Department of the Administration of Railroad Transport, September 20.

Newman, J. (2012) "Beyond the Deliberative Subject? Problems of Theory, Method and Critique in the Turn to Emotion and Affect," *Critical Policy Studies*, 6(4): 465–479.

Newman, J., Barnes, M., Sullivan, H. and Knops, A. (2004) "Public Participation and Collaborative Governance," *Journal of Social Policy*, 33(2): 203–223.

Pierre, J. and Peters, B. G. (2000) "Perspective on Governance," in *Governance, Politics and the State*, New York, NY: Routledge: 12–27.

Reddy, W. (2001) *The Navigation of Feeling: A Framework for the History of Emotions*, Cambridge, UK: Cambridge University Press.

Rhodes, R. A. W. (2005) "Everyday Life in a Ministry: Public Administration as Anthropology," *American Review of Public Administration*, 35(1): 3–26.

Rinn, M. (2008) *Emotions et discours: l'usage des passions dans la langue*, Rennes, France: Presses Universitaires de Rennes.

Rovnost (2004a) "Zvláštní vydání k referendu o přesunu nádraží," October 10.

Rovnost (2004b) "Jaký je vlastně názor většiny?" October 18.

Rovnost (2012) "Průzkum Rovnosti: většina Brňanů chce vlakové nádraží v centru," available at: http://brnensky.denik.cz/zpravy_region/presun-nadrazi-chybi-podpora-brnanu-i-penize-20120821.html (accessed December 12, 2012).

RSC (2012) "Ruller, Rudiš, Chybík: modernizace brněnského nádraží je možná jen v centru," press release of RSC, June 13.

RSC (2013) "Documents of the Coalition 'Railroad Station in the Center' (RSC)," ("There Is No Rational Reason to Move the Railroad Station," "The Decision Is Not Final Yet"), available at: www.nadrazivcentru.cz/index.php (accessed March 30, 2013).

Schön, D. A. and Rein, M. (1994) *Frame Reflection: Toward the Resolution of Intractable Policy Controversies*, New York, NY: Basic Books.

Sørensen, E. and Torfing, J. (2009) "Making Governance Networks Effective and Democratic Through Metagovernance," *Public Administration*, 87(2): 234–258.

Stavrakakis, Y. (2008) "Subjectivity and the Organized Other: Between Symbolic Authority and Fantasmatic Enjoyment," *Organization Studies*, 29(7): 1037–1059.

Strategy for Brno (2006) "Policy Document of the Brno Town Hall's Strategy Office," December.

Strategy Office (2009) "Brno Building a New City," "10 Reasons for Rebuilding the Railroad Station," "We're Stepping It Up!" Policy Documents of the Brno Town Hall's Strategy Office, December.

Thompson, S. and Hoggett, P. (2001) "The Emotional Dynamics of Deliberative Democracy," *Policy & Politics*, 29(3): 351–364.

Ticineto-Clough, P. (ed.) (2007) *The Affective Turn: Theorizing the Social*, Durham, NC: Duke University Press.

Tůma, V. (2008) "The Railroad Station in the Center Coalition: Case Study of Social Political Actor on Municipal Level," doctoral thesis, Masarykova Univerzita, Brno.

Yanow, D. (2003) "Interpretive Empirical Political Science: What Makes This Not a Subfield of Qualitative Methods," *Qualitative Methods*, Fall, 1(2): 9–13.

Žít Brno/Living Brno (2013) Blog postings, available at: www.zitbrno.cz (accessed March 30, 2013).

Zittoun, P. (2007) "La carte parisienne du bruit, la fabrique d'un nouvel énoncé de politique publique," *Politix*, 20(78): 157–178.

13

Develop Stories, Develop Communities: Narrative Practice to Analyze and Engage in Urban Conflict

Nanke Verloo

Introduction

[To be a practitioner in conflict is not only to listen] but to receive their emotions, too. You not only have to give back their words but you also give back their emotions—the intention of what they are saying. If you can do that, then they feel that you can really understand them. [I show them that I understand] by changing the words [...], sometimes it's your body language but also by using different words, by showing that [...] you understand the story behind the words. It is a big mistake [to assume that professionalism is to put away all the emotions]. The most important thing [...] of the professional attitudes of people all over the world is [to not be] afraid of your own emotions. If you are not afraid of your emotions, for example anger, then you can listen very well to the emotion of the other person. Because, if [...] someone is very angry or emotional, if you [as a professional] are afraid of your own emotions, then you can't hear it. (transcript of a local practitioner working in the city of The Hague, spring 2009)

When conflicts arise, emotions come into play. Planning is change, and in that process it is inevitable that not everyone agrees about future plans. A chapter on using narrative to understand and deal with planning conflicts must therefore start by recognizing the importance of emotions. The professional in the above quote explains that he had to face the fear of his own emotions in order to allow himself to listen and really hear the stories of people he worked with. The account of his practice during a long-lasting controversy in the city of The Hague, Netherlands reveals how emotions run through our ability to understand the story of the 'other' in moments of urban conflict. However, this quote also shows how difficult it is to describe how to deal with emotions. Emotions are tacit and intuitive, hence a good response demands sensitivity.

But how can we critically reflect on tacit sensitivity? The practitioner explains that he gives back his emotional understanding of 'the story behind the words' through body language, but he is not able to make his embodied performance tangible. He says something about giving back 'words,' but is not able to reveal how he uses words to show his understanding. This chapter discusses a *narrative practice* approach to conflict and contentious planning processes that engages emotions through a bottom-up understanding of the stories of different parties.

The residents who convey their emotions to the practitioner are part of a group that was systematically marginalized in the context of a new town development. Coming from a so-called 'folk neighborhood' in The Hague, they had tried to reconstruct the effervescent community life they were used to in the past. In the new town, however, they shared their street with people who had a very different lifestyle and who were not in favor of spontaneous parties in the front yard, nor were they happy with a self-organized community center. Soon after the new town development was finished, the group had to close their self-organized, self-managed and self-regulated community center to make way for a professional facility. Ever since they lost their 'club,' they tried to recapture their role as community organizers, but failed to do so in a long-lasting controversy that included professional welfare workers, police officers and policy practitioners who limited the involvement of the group in the professional center. At the point the practitioner who is quoted above came into play, the parties had experienced seven years of escalating contention and frustration.

This case, and every other process of change, reveals that change consists of an element of grieving, letting go of what was in the past. In this case that meant letting go of nostalgic memories of a youth in the old neighborhood and weekly parties in the 'club.' In the field of planning, we often focus our attention on the process of change and the anticipated future, thereby tending to ignore feelings of grief and loss. We frame a bright future of what is yet to be, a future with limited space for the memories of a woman's first kiss behind the corner of that remote playground. The local and tacit stories of people whose communities are changing are usually difficult to engage in speaking about city planning or neighborhood development. They may seem too mundane and everyday to be taken into account, or do not fit the language of development on a larger scale. Despite the ambition of policy practitioners and planners to engage a diverse set of people in the decision-making process, many urban conflicts occur out of a failure to do so. Particular groups are excluded from taking part in the deliberative process because they do not speak the language of policy nor apply the usual repertoire of political action. In those cases conflict results in a deepening of the experience of marginality and tensions tend to escalate. A narrative practice therefore seeks to engage a variety of speech-acts, repertoires of participation, stories and emotions.

The practitioner, whose work is of great inspiration to the narrative practice proposed in this chapter, argues for an approach that engages everyday stories of people and their tacit emotions. Therefore it is first necessary to rethink an approach to emotions that allows for engaging groups on the basis of their distinct and tacit story. However, how do we understand and include stories in the process of planning? Stories reveal how people make sense of the situation at hand. Thus to understand the dynamics of conflict, we need insights into the way stories divert and overlap, where we see contradictions and space for deliberation. Are there stories that are not told in the process, and how could we engage with these stories? What would it mean for the field of conflict and planning if we allow emotions to become part of the planning process? And how do stories allow for that to happen? How can planners reflect on unintended processes of exclusion? In other words, to develop stories is to develop communities, but how do we engage in stories that allow for a community of change?

Engaging Emotions

To talk about the role of emotions in an academic discussion is difficult, but our linguistic repertoire also falls short in practice. Sociologists have tackled this problem by theorizing emotions in several ways. Arlie Hochschild offers the insight that emotions are not only tacit and uncontrollable but that people seek to manage emotions through 'feeling rules' that are embedded in or deviate from a social structure (Hochschild 1979). James Jasper (2011) re-thinks social movement theory and offers a typology of emotional processes. He concludes that emotions are a core part of actions and decisions that should be taken into account to understand how they shape interactions and choices (Jasper 2011: 14). These studies provide insights into the way societies shape appropriate emotions in certain circumstances and what the results or risks of emotions are in processes of change. These are very valuable insights for sociologists who seek to analyze social interactions, but in a narrative practice, evaluating the moral, appropriate or effective meaning of emotions is tricky.

The quote from the practitioner reveals how important acknowledgment is in a process of conflict management and resolution. The practitioner recognizes that emotions run through conflict and offer insights into people's experiences, but instead of problematizing them he proposes that they demand recognition. Instead of theorizing, his practice is to repeat the exact language of parties to "make them feel you truly understand." Through the repetition of language and the embodiments of his own emotions, he includes emotions in the story of planning without giving a normative evaluation. At the same time his repetition and embodiment is a sensitive response.

Since the mid-2000s, planning analysts have paid more attention to the role of emotions in the planning process. As they argue, the planning process is more influenced by cognitive relationships; and emotional ideas shape people's beliefs and judgments about future plans (Hoch 2006). The field of planning has overlooked how emotions and feelings shape the plans people make individually as urban dwellers or urban planners (LeBaron in Hoch 2006: 380). Hoch suggests that planners should look at the way emotions shape communication that informs and persuades people about proposed plans, and how emotions shape the expectations and criteria for future planning methods (Hoch 2006). From this perspective, however, emotions are once again evaluated. This time the evaluation is to allow planners to organize a better process of planning. The story of planning and the planning process remains at the heart of the analysis. The quote from the practitioner suggests an opposite perspective. He makes the tacit emotions of residents central to the process of acknowledging each distinct story.

Thus, a narrative perspective allows for a discussion about emotions without making them an abstraction. Without making emotions into abstract analytic tools, they allow for an insight into interests and judgments (Nussbaum 2003). Emotions then simply surface in the stories of people and reveal much about their intentions, grievances and worries. At the same time emotions can serve as a tool to engage people in a deliberative process simply because if we care, we act. Like scholars of planning and sociology, narrative practice requires us to make sense of stories through analyzing emotions, but it is also responsive to the emotions of people as practitioners try to engage and embody them, and most importantly acknowledge them by making them part of the future story of planning.

Narratives and Planning

Before moving to consider the use of stories in planning theory, we need to discuss how to understand the notions of 'story' and 'narrative.' As with many analytic tools, there is no agreed-upon definition of narrative in the social sciences. The use of narratives to understand social life has moved from more structuralist analysis (Labov and Waletzky 1967) that focused on a linguistic perspective and allowed for an evaluation of temporal and syntactic clauses, to a more constructivist understanding. Nowadays most narrative scholars use the latter perspective, which understands narrative as a sequence of events with a beginning, a middle and an end that have internal coherence which unfolds in time and space and features characters that are related to one another (Polkinghorne 1987; MacIntyre 1990; Bruner 1991, 2004; Porter Abbott 2008; Czarniawska 2010). Most of these scholars make a distinction between story and narrative. Porter Abbott explains that stories are sequences of events in action and the descriptions thereof, while narratives are the distinct way of conveying these stories into an analytic representation (Porter Abbott 2008: 19). The stories that people share about their experiences of conflict are often descriptions of sequences of events. Narrative scholars would argue that they turn into a narrative when these stories become 'emplotted,' when they become analytical reflections on the stories. This distinction is useful for our analytic vocabulary. When we speak of stories, we speak of the different storylines parties in conflict use to make sense of the situation. When we speak of a narrative, it is the reconstruction of these storylines into a narrative in which we add meaning; for example, the narrative of planning adds meaning as it brings many stories together into a shared whole and an emplotted future. As we will see later, the construction of one all-encompassing narrative is problematic in the narrative practice I propose.

Stories are understood as enacted (MacIntyre 1990), which makes them rich sources of insight into experiences and social interactions. Furthermore, stories are understood as forms of communication (Fisher 1984, 1987) as people tell stories to share thoughts, reveal emotions and convince others of ideas. Stories, however, do more than display emotions, ideas and interests; the stories people construct to make sense of a situation guide their future behavior and judgments. Stories in themselves have the ability to not only describe what is, but also to guide what ought to be (Rein and Schön 1977). Thus both stories and narratives shape meaning and provide insights into what the narrator finds important and unimportant. Bruner therefore argued that there is a mimesis between life and narrative; "the mimesis between life and narrative is a two way affair, narratives imitate life and vice versa" (Bruner 2004: 692). Thus the construction of a narrative of planning based on stories of experience taps back into social reality as it creates meaning, excludes other meanings and, as we will see in the account of the practitioner, excludes or includes people from taking part in the process of change. It would not come as a surprise to say that we must therefore be very careful with the meanings we want our narratives about planning to convey.

Since the 'narrative turn,' planners have moved to using stories about planning processes to describe emotions, feelings and contention in groups and individuals (Forester 1989, 1999; Fischer and Forester 1993; Mandelbaum 1991; Throgmorton 1996, 2003; Marris 1997; Sandercock 2011). These studies give interesting perspectives on how storytelling is part of the planning process and analyze emotions as they play a role in contention about future plans. In the field of planning we can roughly identify two ways in which planners have used a narrative approach. The first uses storytelling as a means to engage people in the deliberative process. Forester (2006, 2009) and Sandercock (2011) argue that storytelling is a democratic and inclusive practice that enhances the process of planning. Here storytelling is understood as a tool to engage different people in community participation and facilitate a space for people to share their stories and listen to others. Forester argues that ritualized storytelling and listening could be used as a means to reconcile deep conflicts and can offer hope where hope had seemed lost (Forester 1999: 78). He gives an account of talking circles where people were encouraged to share what places, neighborhoods or sites mean to them. In this approach storytelling is an important part of planning practice that seeks to engage different parties and people. Merlijn van Hulst clarified this approach as a model *for* planning (2012), in which storytelling is explicitly used as a method for the planning process.

The second approach uses narrative to construct a persuasive story of planning itself. According to Van Hulst this is a process *of* planning in which planning practice itself is much like storytelling (Van Hulst 2012: 302). This second approach is developed in the work of Throgmorton (1996, 2003) who argues that planning is persuasive storytelling about the future. He argues that planners are authors of a text that can be read and interpreted in diverse and conflicting ways (Throgmorton 2003: 127). The planning text has to emplot a possible flow of future actions that will be filled with believable characters who act within a setting. In order to shape the reader's attention and move the key antagonists around, the narrative should envelop conflict, crisis and resolution (ibid.). Moreover, Throgmorton recognizes that the persuasive story is constitutive of communities, characters and culture. Thus the narrative of planning shapes meaning by telling the readers and listeners what is important and what is not (ibid.: 128). Consequently, planning narratives shape the possibility for the engagement of specific groups and guide the repertoire of deliberation, as well as providing for including emotions. Throgmorton argues that we must therefore expand the language of planning and include the language of emotions (ibid.).

One could see how the two approaches reinforce one another. The former suggests a practice that allows people to participate in planning; the latter reflects on that process and allows the text of planning to become a narrative with an agreeable emplotment about the future. Both approaches, however, keep the planner in a central position. Let us move back to the case of the new town to grasp how storytelling and narrative are used there. The practitioner started out with storytelling as a way to engage the different experiences of people in the neighborhood. In line with Sandercock's argument, storytelling was his way to start the process of conflict resolution. He met with each separate group to get an insight into their distinct story of the controversy. He explained:

[It was important] to hear the different stories from different people about what was going on in their opinion so I could develop an idea about what was going on, what the intention was, what the inside people thought. I didn't know the policemen, I didn't know the youth workers, I didn't know the management, it was a completely new situation for me. The first weeks were spent making new contacts, talking about the situation, the incidents. (transcript of a local practitioner working in the city of The Hague, spring 2009)

These conversations enabled the practitioner to grasp the stories of different parties, as Forester and Sandercock argue. However, these conversations also revealed that not all stories are of equal value to the story of planning. The practitioner was confronted with the emotional story of residents who felt as if they were excluded from the process of decision-making between the welfare organization and the local authorities. The story of the residents coming from the old neighborhood revealed emotions like anger, frustration and sadness about the loss of their club. These emotions, however, did not surface in the more formal story of welfare practitioners. Their repertoire to engage in deliberation about the community activities was embedded in a formal language that would frame community organizing as a 'pedagogical responsi-bility' with an 'accountable organization' and a structure for 'voluntary workers' who wanted to help. On the other hand, the story of residents described the practical activities they used to organize. Their stories recalled the 'fun they had during Friday night bingo and karaoke in the club.' They understood their role not as 'volunteers' but as 'organizers,' and organizing activities was dependent on everyone who had a good idea and wanted to 'just go for it.' Over the course of the conflict, the different stories that parties used to make sense of the situation, the self and others came into interaction with one another. For example, during conversations with professionals, residents would raise their voices and portray their anger. The professionals were willing to discuss the matter but only in a way they called 'civil;' as a result they started avoiding having discussions with residents. One can see how the meaning of community organizing is different in each account and how the contradicting stories shape different behavioral patterns that deepen the contradiction and eventually result in the exclusion of the group of residents.

The language of welfare workers excluded informal descriptions of activities as their role and their word choices emphasize their formal responsibility. When we assume that saying something is doing something (Austin 1962: 12), we can see how the use of formal language to communicate with the residents did something to the relationship. Austin would call this speech act an 'illocutionary force' because the use of formal language is a conventional speech act that has an effect on the feelings, thoughts or actions of the audience and the speaker (Austin 1962: 115). In this case the effect is an experience of exclusion from the decision-making process in the center. The storyline of the residents that showed emotions of mourning about the loss of their activities did not get acknowledged in the storyline of the professionals. When the practitioner spoke with the residents, in hindsight he recalls their anger: "[They were] angry about the way they were treated, they were angry about the way that the children were treated" (transcript of a local practitioner working in the city of The Hague, spring 2009). He explains that the residents used sarcasm, humor and emotional outbursts to counter the formal story of the professionals, but that these elements of their story only reinvigorated their informal and thereby 'voluntary' and 'unprofessional' status in the community. As he explained in the quote at the beginning of this chapter, his purpose was not to only be responsive to these emotions: "Only when I gave back their emotion and crossed the line of formal communication, was I able to make a connection with them" (transcript of a local practitioner working in the city of The Hague, spring 2009). Furthermore he suggests embodying emotions and acknowledging them in the way he makes them part of his account of the narrative of conflict.

The account of the new town reveals how some stories do not find a way into the deliberation process because they convey a different language, plot or repertoire of communication. It suggests that the intention of narrative scholars like Throgmorton, Sandercock and Forester to give room to emotions during meetings does not mean that these emotions always get acknowledged, nor that they become part of the narrative of planning in conflict. A response to this problem is Jane Mansbridge's proposition to include everyday talk in the deliberative system (Mansbridge 1999). She rethinks the Habermasian perfect speech-acts of deliberation and argues that personal, not public, everyday talk should also be understood as political (ibid.: 214). Her argument provides an interesting insight into the use of every language in the deliberative process that, in her account, acknowledges structural power relations that influence any interaction, but allows for a sense of the agency of actors in deliberation (ibid.: 224). She argues that "the criterion of equality in deliberation should be modified to mandate equal opportunity to affect the outcome; mutual respect; and equal power only when threats of sanction and the use of force come into play" (ibid.: 225). Thus including everyday talk in the deliberative process could provide a way to engage in the language of residents and give way to their emotions. However, what remains after this powerful pursuit is the translation of everyday talk into a planning document, not engagement of emotions in the practice of planning. Scholars have convincingly shown how policy or other bureaucratic documents squeeze out the life juice and thereby position themselves as authoritarian (Finnegan 1998; Sandercock 2011). In such cases the policy or planning document only partially reflects the process of storytelling that residents and practitioners were engaged in.

Emery Roe (1989, 1994) proposed an alternative to this discrepancy. He argued that policy narratives should entail a meta-narrative that includes the stories of different parties. His meta-narrative does not focus on the facts but on the divergent stories people tell. Roe's theory on narrative in public policy is very valuable for the study of conflict because it recognizes that all policies are in themselves moral stories. Roe speaks about the necessity of a meta-narrative in highly polarized policy narratives where, as in cases of planning conflict, values and interests are fundamentally divided so that they paralyze decision-making (Roe 1994: 4). He argues that in such cases "the best alternative is to forgo searching for consensus and common ground in favor of a meta-narrative that turns this polarization in another story altogether" (ibid: 4). Although Roe is attentive to "objectively weaker arguments" that are the result of an unequal distribution of power relations that "work themselves out through stories, through their asymmetries, and through getting people to change their story" (Roe 1989: 266), the meta-narrative he proposes could be understood as a 'shared' narrative with which all parties can identify and—as he argues—find common ground.

It is exactly in that 'shared' approach where the approach to narrative practice opposes a meta-narrative. A meta-narrative implies a summary of the narratives of different parties. A summary means that one narrative reveals common grounds and differences, but the way differences and power relations are constructed remains unclear. The case study reveals that when people utter specific words or show their emotions, they position themselves through an interaction. Power relations are thus constructed in a discursive and often unconscious way. At the same time, decisions about where to organize public meetings, in the city hall or in a neighborhood center, also influence the power relations between parties in conflict. In the case of the new town, the use of formal language in interaction with the residents created a gap that deepened the experience of marginality for the group and strengthened the role of the professionals. To understand these power dynamics in processes of conflict, a meta-narrative is not sufficient because it summarizes events and does not allow for insights into the communication between parties. To acknowledge each distinct story that brings to the surface distinct emotions in moments of conflict, we must turn to an approach that keeps every storyline intact—like a braid that is not supposed to turn into a ponytail.

In sum, during episodes of conflict each party narrates the story in a particular way, values different events, uses particular language and gives meaning to events, places, identities and relationships. To understand the relationship between parties, the practitioner suggested staying close to the distinct language and performance displayed by each party. These cannot be revealed in a meta-narrative because a summary of stories tends to exclude thick descriptions of the discursive practices and emotions that reveal the marginal stories in conflict. Consequently, emotions do not find their way into the political discussion about planning. A narrative practice aims to engage in and acknowledge each particular storyline so that people in each storyline are empowered to speak their own language and repertoire to influence the outcome of a planning process. This approach to story and emotions seeks to move away from an authoritarian position of the planner that demands that he be evaluative of emotions. Instead, the planner moves toward a position that makes the stories of parties (residents and any other party in conflict) as much a part of the interdependent network of stories as his own story of planning. Dealing with conflict from this perspective demands that the practitioner engage in the stories of the 'other' and make them part of the story of 'self.' However, as Jane Mansbridge argues, that does not take place in a power vacuum. To understand power dynamics between storylines, we must understand the relationships between them. That way, policy makers, planners and conflict analysts can see where stories contradict and overlap, how they tap back into our understanding of conflict—for that more structural understanding we move to the concept of 'master' and 'counter' plots.

Master and Counter Plots

We have established that stories are means to make sense of conflict, but that these understandings also shape our ability to act in the process of dealing with conflict. Our repertoire to deal with conflict stems from power dynamics that allow certain storylines to become dominant and others marginal. When a party's storyline picks up on elements of the master plot, that story is more likely to be accepted as the 'real' or 'true' story and becomes the dominant interpretation of conflict. A master plot in the case of the new town was the story of the necessity of a professional community center. This is an ideal that refers to a broader story about the Netherlands as a well-functioning welfare state that offers everyone the same chances and is accountable in its organization. The storyline of welfare workers refers to this plot by using terms like 'pedagogical responsibility,' 'accountable organizing,' and 'activities for everyone.' By referring to a dominant story about the Netherlands, professionals legitimized their formal position as community organizers. On the other hand there was a counter plot that missed these strong rhetorical elements. Groups that form minorities usually shape these plots on the periphery, outside the realm of the dominant plot. Members of the group from the old neighborhood constructed their story in private gatherings where they commemorated their old club. The story that resulted out of these meetings revealed emotions and nostalgic memories that did not appeal to the dominant plot about a well-organized neighborhood. In fact, the informal and nostalgic memories about the old club revealed a private story that in its turn strengthened the dominant plot, the need for professional organizing.

A counter plot is usually understood as a less appropriate interpretation of conflict; therefore these counter plots become marginalized and cannot find their way into the public debate. In order to grasp the power relations that are in place in conflict, we must analyze the types of plot—master or counter— these stories refer to. Master and counter plots help us to become aware of what Mansbridge suggested, to understand the ability of different stories to affect the outcome of a planning process. This also allows us to get an insight into the ways people who identify with these stories get more easily included in or excluded from the deliberative process.

However, such a master–counter plot dichotomy could easily suggest that there is no way out of power relations. To allow for a sense of agency within the power dynamics of conflict, Bamberg convincingly complicates the distinction between master and counter plots. He speaks about master narratives and argues that they are apparent in every social interaction where they set up sequences of actions and events as routines, therefore one could say they delineate agency and reduce the repertoire of action (Bamberg 2004: 360). He continues, however, by saying that without that guidance and sense of direction we would be lost (ibid.). In other words, we are dependent on these dominant narratives and one could wonder how conscious we are about the way dominant narrative occupy our existence. Thus our complicity with them does not automatically result in being complicit with or supportive of hegemonic-knowledge complexes (ibid.). Bamberg seeks to understand the fabric of master narratives in order to understand the social and individual forces to change them. His argument is that master narratives guide and structure our understanding of positioning in society, but that "people have room for improvisation and careful management of perspectives that is sensitive to possible counters from the audience" (ibid.: 363). He calls that management "juggling several storylines simultaneously" and he concludes that "counter narratives always operate on the edge of disputability and require a good amount of interactional subtlety and rhetorical finessing on the part of the speaker" (ibid.).

The approach to narrative practice that I propose is attentive to the discursive performances that people develop to "juggle several storylines." Conflict starts out with one party feeling delegitimated as they disagree with the proposed process, plan or ascribed position. The power structure that is invoked by master plots entitles groups to certain roles and guides the repertoire of action. As a response, people attempt to regain legitimacy through the construction of a counter plot, or other discursive practices that reveal a counter plot in action. If we allow these discursive and maybe informal responses to become part of the narrative of planning, we open the possibility for engagement and renegotiation. Planning conflicts take place exactly at that intersection of dominant and counter plots. The challenge of narrative practice is not to be responsive to or summarize different stories, but instead braid them through the storytelling of decision-making. The next section will discuss how practitioners as well as analysts can engage in contradicting stories without losing sight of their own story and remain within the boundaries of what is pragmatically possible in a planning process.

Narrative Practice

A narrative practice starts from the assumption that there is a reciprocal relationship between the stories we construct to make sense of conflict and our future practices and behavior. Therefore, a narrative perspective bridges the gap between theory and practice. Both analysts and practitioners are responsible for the mimesis between life and narrative. In other words, whoever deals with parties in conflict becomes part of the dynamic relationships between different stories. Furthermore, the practice of the practitioner shows that only by understanding each story and the dynamics between them was he able to negotiate. As he said, his understanding of each story and how stories were embedded in the power context informed his responsiveness to and acknowledgment of emotions. Consequently, narrative practitioners need to be able to 'learn-in-action' (Schön 1983). To learn in the moment of action means to simultaneously understand the meaning of stories in relation to the conflict and to develop a practical response. Narrative practitioners are able to acknowledge dominant as well as marginal stories, so that they can start an inclusive process of decision-making. They need to understand as well as to respond to emotional outbursts. Therefore a narrative practice approach is an effort to bridge theory and practice as it allows for analyzing the meaning of diverse stories in interaction and provides means to engage them in the process of deliberate decision-making.

The narrative practice that I want to propose draws an ongoing discussion with scholar of narrative Sara Cobb. In the context of research we worked on together, she framed this narrative practice as 'braiding,' as in making a hair braid where at least three different strands are folded around each other. The idea of braiding sets out an argument for planners and policy practitioners to take up their responsibility to pay equal attention to each storyline (Cobb 2013). A simple sequence of events that the residents shared about their beloved bingo night in their old club is as important to the planning story as the dominant story of policy makers who sought to develop a lively community in the new town. The braiding analogy allows each story to be a strand that is folded around the other strands. As each story does not have to become part of a bigger whole or tale, the language of each party remains identical to their utterance, emotions stay within their context and memories shape the story people want to convey.

The first step in narrative practice as a braiding exercise would be what the practitioner had done in his very first quote: to listen to the diverse stories in place. The practitioner soon gets an insight into the dynamics between storylines as one story turns out to be dominant and others marginal. The challenge for the practitioner is to engage in each storyline so that he understands how each of them constitutes a morally appropriate story about the self. The moral values that the residents applied to their role as organizers were tied to their understanding of self during the days that they were organizing their club. That story got delegitimated in the story of welfare workers whose moral value was focused on the accountable organizing of such a club; their story of the history of these residents tied them to unprofessional events that were not attractive to everyone in the neighborhood. Narrative practice is not to condemn the story of professionals, but to understand how it delegitimates the story of the residents in this case, how people juggle several storylines and what the effect of that is. The narrative practitioner seeks to uphold the legitimacy of all stories and weave them together. Holding the narrative strands, the public official's role, in this practice of braiding, is to function as the 'holder' of the stories, and the one who helps the community to witness the legitimacy of all the stories that are present in the community (Cobb and Verloo 2011: 45). That is necessary because, as we have seen, the parties themselves are anchored in their own stories and often these stories have a centrifugal force that keeps those who tell them in their grip, as when the story of residents was supposed to counter the story of practitioners, and it ironically strengthened the dominant story of the need for professionalism in the neighborhood. Thus the narrative practice I propose keeps each narrative intact as a strand of a braid; that way, each story is given equal opportunity to affect the planning outcome. However, how can we make this braid if some strands are thicker or thinner than others?

When we look at the case, it seems that not every story is as thick, some references work better than others and not all stories have an emplotment about the future. To deal with that dilemma, we have to turn to what Sluzki (1994) and Cobb (2003) call 'better-formed stories.' Sluzki and Cobb argue that some stories are better than others and that the characters of 'not-so-great stories' cause conflicts to deepen and extend. According to Cobb, a not-so-great story of conflict reveals a time pattern that is focused on the past, whereby the description of the past is more vivid than that of the future; characters in these stories are usually flat and are often portrayed as victims; these stories have a linear logic that externalizes responsibility in the acts of the other, leading to passive, reactive positions for the speaker; and themes reveal hopelessness, suffering and vengeance (Cobb 2003: 10). A better-formed story, on the other hand, beholds the past, present and future; there are diverse characters in play and the boundaries between victims and victimizers are fuzzy; there is no determined causality between events; values circle around hope, development and participation (ibid.: 12). If we look at the case study, all the elements of a not-so-great story are present in the storylines. The residents focused on the past and described their memories vividly; in their description they were the victims of a system that discriminated against them, which left them suffering without any real role or agency. The storyline of the professionals was less focused on the past, but their presentation of the future portrayed a very flat description of the residents as being unprofessional and aggressive, which made the professionals the victim of a group of 'folk' people with whom they could not cooperate.

The second step in a narrative practice would be to recognize these stories as strands and develop them into better-formed stories without losing their specific characteristics. In the case of the new town, the practitioner did not stop with the simple accounts of parties that externalized agency. He continued his practice with storytelling and 'repeating': "I repeated their words very often, every word, every sentence, 'Do I really understand you well?'" (transcript of a local practitioner working in the city of The Hague, spring 2009). Using their exact words allowed him to construct the story in the distinct terms of each party. As the quote at the beginning of this chapter suggested, repeating words is not all; the practitioner also tried to embody the emotions of others without being afraid of his own emotions. That way, he was able to engage in the stories of people, instead of remaining in an outside and evaluative role. Embodying stories goes hand in hand with understanding how the characters, time, values and causality are interlinked within each story. That internal development allowed him to form better-formed stories together with each party, but it also helped parties to develop the 'critical intelligence' they needed in order to understand the other.

In the case of the new town, the practitioner was able to turn the stories of each party into better-formed stories that formed strong narrative strands. One could say the practitioner functioned as a 'narrative mediator' between the different stories that he embodied. In each group he was able to listen and engage in the story of self, but also counter that story by the embodied story of the other. He recalls how he embodied stories, but also how he countered them by revealing the story of the others while keeping to the distinct language and emotional values in each storyline:

You take time to listen to the neighbors and you also make time to go to the professionals. [They] asked me "What's your opinion?" How you react to that is very important. With that knowledge [and their response to my opinion] I could go back to the next meeting and talk [...] about it to the government. So it has to do with listening well to the people and listening well to the professionals. [...] So I would say personally, I always gave my opinion, it was important because I had that [personal] relationship with the people. (transcript of a local practitioner working in the city of The Hague, spring 2009)

Here the practitioner shows that he was not afraid to share his opinion with the group; he used their request for his opinion to make sure he embodied their story. Giving his opinion was in line with not being afraid of his own emotions and therefore becoming part of the network of stories and thereby the process of deliberation himself.

The residents of the old neighborhood were given a memorial of their club in the new center. That way, their story found acknowledgment and they were challenged to develop it into a narrative about their future role in the center in cooperation with the welfare workers. The welfare practitioners were challenged to think about their position in relation to the 'volunteers' and what such a title could mean from the perspective of residents. The practitioner was able to legitimate the role of the professionals within the narrative strand of the residents, and thereby their formal responsibility was acknowledged. Professionals became able to engage in the story of the residents, which enabled them to understand and recognize their grievances and give them responsibilities in the center without losing their own sense of self. Of course, cooperation was still problematic in practice as each group had different ideas and repertoires of action. However, now that they were able to communicate their distinct storylines and recognize how each of their stories overlapped and contradicted, they experienced interdependence and were also able to acknowledge each other as a legitimate party in deliberation. Their stories did not merge together as a common narrative; instead the narrative practice developed the agency of each party in the way they constructed their better-formed strand and affected the outcome of the deliberation about community organizing.

Conclusions

In this chapter I have set out an approach to narrative practice that seeks to engage and acknowledge each distinct storyline in the process of conflict. Planning conflicts were framed as inherently emotional as they propose a change and leave an old situation behind. Emotions are intuitive and intangible and therefore difficult to engage in the planning process. Nevertheless, narrative practice allows for engaging in diverse emotions by preserving the language in which they get communicated and acknowledged through an embodied performance. Stories are a tool to bring emotions to the surface without evaluating their appropriateness, because in episodes of conflict emotions provide an opportunity to engage diverse actors in the process of decision-making.

Two approaches to narrative in planning are developed into an approach that crosscuts theory and practice as it includes storytelling as a tool to analyze and embody the stories of actors in conflict. The narrative practice approach recognizes that planning in itself is a story about the future, but seeks to overcome the power relations that one such encompassing story prevails. The narrative practitioner becomes part of an interdependent network of stories, in which he or she is responsible for upholding all narrative strands in the process of deliberation. That way, a narrative practitioner can learn-in-action as he or she develops an eye for the relationships between dominant and counter plots. This approach suggests that each storyline has to remain intact as strands of a braid so that the distinct characters of each storyline become part of the deliberation. Narrative strands are challenged to develop into 'better-formed stories' so that each storyline can affect the possible outcomes of a planning process by describing a past, present and future with diverse characters and moral values.

The account of the narrative practitioner provided in this chapter reveals the interdependent relationship between the practitioner and conflicting parties as his purpose is to not only understand but also embody the stories so that he can inform and counter the stories of others and thereby juggle between master and counter plots. Narrative practice is therefore a means to acknowledge the parties who usually have trouble finding their way into the deliberation process. Multiple forms of communication are necessary to be taken into account; emotions, informal memories and embodied gestures reveal people's experiences as much as planning documents and strategic policy formulations, or formal repertoires of participation. In other words, if we seek to learn from and deal with planning, we need to elaborate the deliberative process and engage parties that lack the dominant language of policy. Narrative practice suggests taking all stories into account and developing them into storylines that acknowledge each other's legitimacy.

Acknowledgments

I would like to thank Tonie Boxman for allowing me to participate in and observe his practice for a period of almost two years. Furthermore I would like to thank David Laws and Sara Cobb for the many inspiring conversations we had about narrative, and Imrat Verhoeven for his insights into emotions. The case study in this chapter is part of my PhD research that was undertaken at the University of Amsterdam between 2008 and 2012. For further references about the case, please contact the author.

References

Austin, J. L. (1962) *How to Do Things with Words*, Oxford, UK: Oxford University Press.

Bamberg, M. (2004) "Considering Counter Narratives," in M. Bamberg and M. Andrews (eds.), *Considering Counter-Narratives: Narrative, Resisting, Making Sense*, Amsterdam, Netherlands: John Benjamins Publishing Company: 351–371.

Bruner, J. (1991) "The Narrative Construction of Reality," *Critical Inquiry*, 18(1): 1–21.

Bruner, J. (2004) "Life as Narrative," *Social Research*, 71(3): 691–710.

Cobb, S. (2003) "Fostering Coexistence within Identity-Based Conflicts: Towards a Narrative Approach," in A. Chayes and M. L. Minow (eds.), *Imagine Coexistence: Restoring Humanity After Violent Ethnic Conflict*, Harvard MA: Harvard Law School Program on Negotiation: 294–311.

Cobb, S. (2013) "Narrative 'Braiding' and the Role of Public Officials in Transforming the Public's Conflicts," *Narrative and Conflict: Explorations of Theory and Practice*, 1(1): 4–30.

Cobb, S. and Verloo, N. (2011) "Appendix II; Sara Cobb and Nanke Verloo on Narrative Braiding," in N. Verloo (ed.), *Rethinking Maakbaarheid: Van Maken Voor naar Maken Met*, Amsterdam, Netherlands: University of Amsterdam, Amsterdam Centre for Conflict Studies: 43–45.

Czarniawska, B. (2010) "The Uses of Narratology in Social and Policy Studies," *Critical Policy Studies*, 4(1): 58–76.

Finnegan, R. (1998) *Tales of the City: A Study of Narrative and Urban Life*, Cambridge, UK: Cambridge University Press.

Fischer, F. and Forester, J. (eds.) (1993) *The Argumentative Turn in Policy Analysis and Planning*, Durham, NC: Duke University Press.

Fisher, W. (1984) "Narration as a Human Communication Paradigm: The Case of Public Moral Argument," *Communication Monographs*, 51(1): 1–22.

Fisher, W. R. (1987) *Human Communication as Narration*, Columbia, SC: University of South Carolina Press.

Forester, J. (1989) *Planning in the Face of Power*, Berkeley, CA: University of California Press.

Forester, J. (1999) *The Deliberative Practitioner: Encouraging Participatory Planning Processes*, Cambridge, MA: MIT Press.

Forester, J. (2006) "Exploring Urban Practice in a Democratising Society: Opportunities, Techniques and Challenges," *Development South Africa*, 23(5): 569–586.

Forester, J. (2009) *Dealing with Differences: Dramas of Mediating Public Disputes*, Oxford, UK: Oxford University Press.

Hoch, C. (2006) "Emotions and Planning," *Planning Theory and Practice*, 7(4): 367–382.

Hochschild, A. R. (1979) "Emotion Work, Feeling Rules, and Social Structure," *American Journal of Sociology*, 85(3): 551–575.

Jasper, J. M. (2011) "Emotions and Social Movements: Twenty Years of Theory and Research," *Annual Review of Sociology*, 37(14): 14–19.

Labov, W. and Waletzky, J. (1967) "Narrative Analysis: Oral Versions of Personal Experience," *Journal of Narrative and Life History*, 7(1/4): 3–38.

MacIntyre, A. (1990 [1981]) *After Virtue*, London, UK: Duckworth Press.

Mandelbaum, S. J. (1991) "Telling Stories," *Journal of Planning Education and Research*, 10(3): 209–214.

Mansbridge, J. (1999) "Everyday Talk in the Deliberative System," in M. Macedo (ed.) *Deliberative Politics: Essays on Democracy and Disagreement*, Oxford, UK: Oxford University Press: 212–239.

Marris, P. (1997) *Witnesses, Engineers, and Storytellers: Using Research for Social Policy and Action*, College Park, MD: University of Maryland Urban Studies and Planning Program.

Nussbaum, M. (2003) *Upheavals of Thought: The Intelligence of Emotions*, Cambridge, UK: Cambridge University Press.

Polkinghorne, D. (1987) *Narrative Knowing and the Human Sciences*, Albany, NY: SUNY Press.

Porter Abbott, H. (2008) *The Cambridge Introduction to Narrative*, second edition, Cambridge, UK: Cambridge University Press.

Rein, M. and Schön, D. A. (1977) "Problem Setting in Policy Research," in C. H. Weiss (ed.), *Using Social Research in Public Policy Making*, Lexington, IN: Lexington Books.

Roe, E. (1989) "Narrative Analysis for the Policy Analyst: A Case Study of the 1980–1982 Medfly Controversy in California," *Journal of Policy Analysis and Management*, 8(2): 251–273.

Roe, E. (1994) *Narrative Policy Analysis: Theory and Practice*, Durham, NC: Duke University Press.

Sandercock, L. (2011) "Out of the Closet: The Importance of Stories and Storytelling in Planning Practice," *Planning Theory & Practice*, 4(1): 11–28.

Schön, D. A. (1983) *The Reflective Practitioner: How Professionals Think in Action*, New York, NY: Basic Books.

Sluzki, C. (1994) "The Better-Formed Story," unpublished manuscript (on file with author).

Throgmorton, J. A. (1996) *Planning as Persuasive Storytelling: The Rhetorical Construction of Chicago's Electric Future*, Chicago, IL: University of Chicago Press.

Throgmorton, J. A. (2003) "Planning as Persuasive Storytelling in a Global-Scale Web of Relations," *Planning Theory*, 2(2): 125–151.

Van Hulst, M. (2012) "Storytelling, a Model of and a Model for Planning," *Planning Theory*, 11(3): 299–318.

Afterword

Patsy Healey

Conflict and Urban Life

The focus of this book is on the interaction between conflicts that break out in urban areas, particularly over major development projects, and the institutions and practices of planning interventions. The particular concern is with the kinds of transformations in political practices and governance institutions that might promote more environmentally and socially progressive outcomes. The chapters are rich in ideas on how to move in such a direction, as well as in how to analyze such conflicts. In my reflections on these chapters, I comment very generally on the interaction between urban conflicts and planning institutions, and on the relationship of analysis to action.

Urban areas, like societies more generally, are always filled with the potential for conflict—over resources, over values, over ways of life, over memories and meanings, and over what really 'counts' to different people who share a place. However, these fractures are often not evident in the flow of life, existing instead as part of the taken-for-granted texture of the world we find ourselves living in. They surface and get reinforced or reformed when something arrives that disturbs and challenges this flow. Such disturbances are again regular phenomena in urban life, through both public and private initiatives, from projects to refurbish a valued park to schemes to redevelop whole segments of a city, or insert a new piece of infrastructure through the urban landscape. Conflicts may also arise over proposals to change how a public resource is managed and used, or residents may begin to notice that the character of where they live is changing around them as new people move in—perhaps younger, or richer, or just culturally 'different.'

The institutions of urban governance establish both formal and informal arenas that provide platforms for the playing out of routine conflicts. The systems of political control of formal government are one such arena. The dimension of planning systems that focuses on the regulation of physical development provides another. The formal organization of such systems is then brought to various kinds of life by the discourses and practices that develop in, around, through and over the formal arrangements. These systems and the practices that develop around them serve to channel conflicts into established norms and practices. However, such channeling may over time become disconnected from the issues at stake and the parties involved in the political momentum that sets the systems and practices in motion. They thereby lose legitimacy in the eyes of those involved in conflicts, and are sometimes captured by powerful interests with a direct intention to suppress the values and concerns of other groups cohabiting an urban area. Where a consolidated hegemonic urban regime prevails, many fractures and value differences become invisible, so that some people's concerns and need for resources and attention become seriously neglected. As Mössner and Del Romero Renau point out (Chapter 3 this volume), not all conflicts surface, being suppressed by prevailing power dynamics expressed in established discourses and practices. The effort to challenge such embedded mentalities of government regimes is the subject of several of the chapters (for example, Gribat and Huxley, Chapter 8 this volume; Allegra and Rokem, Chapter 7 this volume). In such cases, urban conflicts scale up from an issue or area focus to a system focus. Where major urban development projects are involved, this often means mobilizing through multiple scales, and reaching political communities linked to these different scales. There are echoes in some of the chapters of the transformative urban conflicts of the late 1960s and 1970s, when struggles against redevelopment and transport projects brought down political regimes in many cities in Europe and North America. Mössner and Del Romero Renau suggest that one reason why some potential urban conflicts are suppressed is because the activists of this previous generation are now those who dominate urban governance.

Along with Mössner and Del Romero Renau, I agree that urban conflict is not an aberration from an otherwise harmonious urban polity. Urban governance processes thus cannot avoid being drawn in to what Leffers (Chapter 6 this volume: 137) calls "messy engagement" with urban polities. There is no stable consensual position toward which urban political communities should strive, where the benefit of all can be secured. Instead, governance institutions and practices are better seen as temporary accommodations to the complex interplay of forces within a political community (see Dewey 1991 [1927]; Healey 2009; Pløger 2015). In the West in the mid-twentieth century, the ideal of a harmonious balance between otherwise conflicting forces seemed very attractive, as an alternative to war, oppression and violent revolution, which had been the raw experience in Europe in previous decades. Even in the urban struggles of the 1970s, some retained the hope that victory over narrowly based hegemonies could be replaced by a new stable regime committed to the concerns of the many, in which conflict would no longer be needed because the new political class and public administration would be committed to pursuing agendas focused on enhancing universal public welfare. However, experience and struggles over the rights and voice of neglected groups has since taught us that urban politics and administration is a complex amalgam of diverse agencies often caught up in the flux of reorganization, while urban societies are themselves made up of complex webs and threads of relations. Urban governance institutions may at times fall into temporary stabilities, which some urban scholars then identify as 'regimes,' but these stabilities are challenged by continual pressures from the interplay of contextual forces and internal evolutions. Pacchi and Pasqui (Chapter 4 this volume) note how Italian political communities are fragmenting, now that political parties are no longer the key arenas for articulating different positions about urban futures. As Pizzo and Di Salvo argue (Chapter 5 this volume), maybe hegemonies are never as all-pervasive as some analysts suggest.

The starting point for examining the relation between urban conflict and planning systems and practices must therefore be a recognition that urban areas are inherently full of potential conflicts. These are not just over materialities but over discourses and practices, that is, over ways of thinking and acting. Ways of addressing these conflicts will always have the potential to fall into habits and practices that fail to surface inequities in the way resources are distributed, regulations imposed and framing discourses arrived at. This leads to the argument, made here by Mössner and Del Romero Renau, following Mouffe and others, that we should judge the quality of urban political life by the vibrancy and range of the conflicts that surface into public attention. Durnová's case of conflicting discourses played out over multiple scales in relation to the future location of a major train station (Chapter 12 this volume) illustrates well the way in which vigorous 'agonism' brings dividends. However, we cannot neglect attention to the practices through which such conflicts are played out. The boundary between a lively 'agonistic' political culture and a violently 'antagonistic' urban life is by no means clear-cut. Experiences in places where there are deep conflicts between social groups, ethnic groups and age groups, between classes and political allegiances, indicate that real violence or the fear of it is part of daily life. Without some respect for laws and the institutions of governance and some connection between these and the norms and habits that govern daily street life, it becomes difficult to prevent conflicts turning into violent aggression. This prospect was an important motivation for Habermas's intellectual project (Specter 2010). Without some culture of respect for others who share urban life, that life can become destructively stressful. While entrenched institutions may benefit from energetic challenges, political communities need to find ways of legitimizing at least some institutional mechanisms for addressing urban conflicts. So the struggle to arrive at temporary accommodations should not be neglected. Our concern as analysts undertaking critique and informing initiatives is to explore when challenging and transforming established practices should be the target of action, to provide space and time for an alternative temporary accommodation, and when it might be more effective to work out how to make better use of the formal procedures and practices already available (Healey 2007).

Planning Systems and Practices

Spatial planning systems are an important element of the institutions of formal government. As is evident in several of the chapters in this collection, such systems are both generators of conflict, through the developments that are promoted through them, while also providing arenas and procedures for resolving the many ways in which conflicts arise over land and development projects. In the mid-twentieth century, the idea of urban planning was focused on building the urban dimension of 'modern' societies. In places such as Israel (and also India), the planned development of urban areas was seen as a key part of building a modern, socialist nation state (see: Allegra and Rokem, Chapter 7 this volume; Vidyarthi 2010). However, except in political systems with a strong socialist ideology committed to the role of the state as the main development agent on behalf of 'the people,' it soon became clear that much development occurred by private initiative. In rich Western countries, how this happened depended on the way in which a land and property development emerged. Planning systems evolved an expanding role in regulating such development. These systems, where they have been pursued effectively and not bypassed by so-called 'informal development,' thus became increasingly embedded in the institutions of formal government, shaping the evolution of both the property market and the politics surrounding urban land and property development (for the British case, see Healey 1998; Adams and Tiesdell 2013).

In the 1970s, the critique of such systems as tools of an oppressive capitalist state gathered impetus (Castells 1977; Scott and Roweis 1977). It was often argued in the 1970s that planners, far from being the vanguard of an inclusive public interest, in practice promoted the kinds of values and environments of their own professional training, as Gribat and Huxley show in their example from eastern Germany. By the 2000s, this interpretation was reinforced as the development industry became increasingly intertwined with the financial investment nexus, and a form of capitalism driven by financial capital (Harvey 1982). Other critiques highlighted how planning system instruments could be used for socially exclusionary purposes (Ritzdorf 1985), and for reinforcing ethnic or sectarian divisions (Yiftachel 1998). Allegra and Rokem examine the very disturbing case of recent ways in which the Israeli planning system has been used to strengthen the position of one ethnic group against another. Elsewhere, in a curious alliance, by the 1980s, left-wing critics of capitalist-focused planning systems joined forces with right-wing arguments seeking freedom from planning regulation for those initiating development projects. By the end of the twentieth century, it is these latter arguments that had gained most leverage in the popular imagination in countries such as the US and the UK, vigorously promoted by the agents of the property development industry. Land-use regulation was attacked as a bureaucratic procedure, allegedly holding back economic initiative, rather than as a tool for shaping markets in order to safeguard environmental resources and moderate the adverse externalities of market behavior. Political programs have increasingly called for the 'reform' of planning systems, to reduce the perceived 'heavy hand' of regulation.

Yet in practice the regulatory procedures of planning systems provide much-used arenas and practices through which all kinds of conflicts over land and property development proposals are enacted. As Pizzo and Di Salvo argue, these systems create an institutional chessboard over which conflicts can be played out, with an array of process steps that provide opportunities for different groups to express views, structure arguments and negotiate outcomes. However, it is a structured chessboard. Several of the chapters in this volume analyze the evolution of a conflict over some part of a specific institutional chessboard, to reveal the biases in play. Pucci and Allain (Chapters 11 and 10 this volume) both look at the ways inquiry processes have been used. Gualini (Chapter 9 this volume) probes the biases of an individual mediator. Pizzo and Di Salvo show how an apparently successful citizen protest failed to appreciate the impact of their success on another part of the city. These analyses illustrate well when planning institutions contain and structure a conflict, and when the structure of the chessboard and the rules of the game get in the way. Then the pressure builds up to 'crease up the board,' change the rules or even move to another arena altogether.

These analyses underline the importance of understanding just how a particular planning system is structured and how that structuring biases the power dynamics of urban conflicts. The literature on planning systems and practices is littered with generalizations about the role and impact of planning systems and about what 'planners' do. There is also an abundance of examples of how conflicts are played out in relation to procedures for consultation, participation and challenge. Yet these procedures are not autonomous bits of urban government structure, which can be slotted in to provide predictable effects. Their norms and practices are deeply embedded in the way governance practices and discourses have evolved in particular national and local cultures, and how they work out depends significantly on what get to be identified in a particular situation as the issues at stake. For this reason, the analysis of the discourses and discursive struggles that play out through planning systems in particular times and places is an important focus of analytical attention. Gribat and Huxley show how a planning issue was redefined not by changing the chessboard but by turning pawns into kings and queens; in other words, mobilizing against a professional discourse about historic urban structure to revalue a 'shrinking' working-class neighborhood. In these interactions between formal systems and civil society action, discursive innovations help to shape conceptions of what is at stake and who is affected, calling up and shaping the 'public' related to a proposal or project (Dewey 1991 [1927]). But such initiatives do not necessarily need to change the structure of a planning system. Their focus is more often on changing content and practices, so that other voices and values are given greater weight. Proposals to reform planning systems therefore need to be scrutinized to see how far the reasons for reform arise from the design of the chessboard, and how far this affects who gets to play, from what position, and according to what rules. This suggests that our case analyses need to emphasize the multi-scalar institutional trajectory through which a particular conflict has evolved and within which what is at stake for whom is embedded. As Allegra and Rokem (Chapter 7 this volume: 157) argue, planning practices need to be seen as embedded in a "bundle of institutional and individual networks, ideology and expertise" within a particular political environment.

In such analyses, we perhaps need to pay more attention to the dimensions of planning systems. It is well-established that how planning systems are used and the practices that have evolved vary between countries and cities. As Allain shows, urban governance practices and struggles have their own particular trajectories and evolutionary potentials. They are all differently situated in wider relational dynamics, which create a particular configuration of opportunities and limitations. For analysts, activists and reformers of planning systems and practices, it is important to develop ways of grasping how the relation between the particularities of planning system chessboards and the habits and practices of 'play' interact. Without this, transformative initiatives are likely to subside into impotence or achieve as many adverse effects as positive gains.

The Relationship Between Analysis and Action

I have argued so far that urban life is inherently generative of conflict and that governance institutions, from the formal to the most informal of civil society practices, provide a range of ways of drawing back from physically violent ways of settling disputes and fights. Planning systems are one such institution. However, as with all governance institutions, how they work and for whose benefit is deeply embedded in specific political, economic and cultural histories and geographies. So any analysis needs sensitive tools to probe what is at stake, for whom and how. The chapters make use of several different conceptual frameworks. But what actually is our analytical work for, and to what 'project' do we hope to make a contribution?

All the chapters share a progressive concern, however implicit. They develop analytical probes through which to explore the extent to which, in particular situations, conflicts arise through attempts to realize more socially just and environmentally sustainable outcomes, or they explore how the resolution of a conflict advances or inhibits such possibilities. They show how the power dynamics in a situation can both subvert the procedures of a planning system (Allegra and Rokem) and generate new force to challenge dominant interests (Pizzo and Di Salvo; Gribat and Huxley). But what is the purpose of our analyses and what contribution to the flow of action do we expect them to make?

We find ourselves—as citizens, practical experts, academic researchers and educators—approaching the discussion of urban conflicts from multiple positions. Some of the chapters stay at the level of research inquiry, revealing the dimensions of situations, exploring the relevance of theoretical concepts and challenging hypotheses available in the literature. Thus Pucci looks at the conceptual leverage of boundary objects as a way of both identifying what is at stake and helping parties locked in conflict to move beyond their divisions. Pizzo and Di Salvo challenge interpretations that assume that conflicts are structured by a pervasive 'neoliberal hegemony,' arguing that much more is going on. Allegra and Rokem aim to move beyond some of the critiques of communicative planning theory, while Gualini shows clearly that conflict mediation practices can take many forms.

Yet where does this analytical interest come from? Surely we hope that our analyses will help to contribute to the social action of citizens, as part of sustaining and expanding the 'agonistic' qualities of political communities in urban areas. Through critical analysis, researchers hope to enrich the understanding of activists in challenging and changing governance practices and systems as they struggle for more progressive outcomes. In this analytical mode, we hope to encourage people to think about alternative trajectories into the future, and to give voice to those currently suppressed by the weight of dominant discourses and practices. Gribat and Huxley provide ideas on how to develop alternative discourses through their analysis of how residents in a neighborhood of a shrinking eastern German town came to challenge outsider descriptions of their neighborhood, and through this develop an alternative vision with which to challenge dominant discourses. Durnová describes how an activist coalition used emotive concepts to mobilize momentum while they also searched for multi-scalar network support and found out how to use formal procedures to challenge the dominant approach to station location. Through her analysis of the limitations of a formal public discussion process, Pucci provides insights into when, where and how to mobilize to get alternative voices heard. Pizzo and Di Salvo, in their study of struggles over the content of Rome's spatial plan, show the importance of understanding what institutional arenas to target and the importance of paying attention to multi-scalar impacts. Gualini's account of a mediation practice in Stuttgart encourages activists to consider carefully the way the issues and 'objects' in dispute get focused.

These analyses suggest it would be helpful for activists if more attention were given in analyses of urban conflicts to the framing of what is at issue in conflicts. There are complex interactions here between actual experience, the discourses through which these experiences are channeled and what is seen to be at stake. Successful political challenge, and successful development of an urban governance strategy, depend a great deal on the formation of a 'public' around a particular interpretive discourse, which appears to 'make sense' of people's actual experiences. Our role as analysts contributing to the vibrancy and progressive potential of our political communities lies in the analytical skill with which we puncture the rhetoric of dominant discourses, and create some kind of movement of ideas and some kind of public, in the Deweyan sense, behind alternatives. Narrative skill, as Verloo argues (Chapter 13 this volume), is a very important resource here, for both analysts and for activists.

However, there is a third position that gives relevance to our analyses. All the contributors are analytical researchers, as well as citizens of some political community or other. Allain tells us that she is also an activist and an expert practitioner. Several of the contributors to this book have worked in planning systems and others of us are interested in how to think about the design of the planning system chessboard, the way the chess pieces are shaped and the moves available to them. What moves can a progressive planner make when a planning system has become so distorted that there are no options within the system through which to redress the deep ethnic divisions in a society and the resultant severe conflicts over land and access to parts of cities? What kind of consideration is needed where what appears to be a local conflict actually draws in stakeholders operating through very different scales? Is there any way of shaping the principles and ethics that planning experts in a progressive planning chess game should be expected to use, and any moves that they should be encouraged to make skillfully? One of the implications of the accounts and analyses from these chapters is that those involved in non-routine urban conflicts need access to expertise with a particular kind of orientation and skill. Such experts need to know when it is helpful to make use of a technical vocabulary of facts and procedures; when to provide space for the outpouring of anger and lamentation about loss and disrespect; when to use technical accounts of the process through which a decision has been reached, often needed for legal reasons; and when to adopt a narrative style, to which participants and those affected by a serious community conflict can relate. It is here that Forester's accounts of how planners exercise their expertise has relevance (Forester 1989, 1999).

There is a further important position from which our analyses are put to use—through the role many of us have (or have had, in my case) as educators. From this position, we use our research experiences as cases in our teaching, and our interpretations as concepts in the theories and ideas we impart to students. Many of those we teach go on to be expert actors in urban governance situations. Some will also be or become activists, and all will be citizens of somewhere, and maybe of several communities at once. In addition to the conflicts discussed in this book, studies of planners at work show how often the experts we start to train become conflicted themselves as the values they have developed at university, which often led them to study planning or urban studies in the first place, are challenged by the conflicting pressures on how they are expected to behave (Sager 2012; Clifford and Tewdwr-Jones 2013). Back in the 1990s, I argued that those involved in strategic planning work had an ethical responsibility to adopt an inclusionary sensibility, enlarging awareness of the range of issues and stakeholders affected by an issue or strategy, and counteracting tendencies to narrow the focus of attention to those of dominant parties (Healey 2006 [1997]). However, this is a hard challenge for an expert. Time and space needs to be found to take up the knowledge challenge that this involves. Experts are also often frustrated when their advice is not understood or appreciated. Only when a well-developed public and framing discourse come into being does a transformative idea begin to accumulate transformative power.

Finally

These chapters underline the value of an analytical focus on the interaction between urban conflict and planning systems and practices. The analyses warn against oversimplified assumptions and interpretations, and emphasize the importance of understanding the detailed dynamics and trajectories of particular experiences. They show a variety of ways in which planning systems and practices engender and provide 'resolutions' to urban conflicts, and direct attention to struggles between more regressive and more progressive outcomes. They also identify some critical moments in the way urban conflicts develop and suggest practical strategies for acting in these moments to move toward more progressive outcomes. It is perhaps here that more conceptual and analytical attention is needed, following the lead given by Gualini and by Pacchi and Pasqui in their discussion of types and trajectories of conflict. The social movement literature could indeed be very helpful here.

More attention is also needed by researchers to the institutional design of planning systems and how these shape the practices that may both generate conflicts and provide the arenas where they come to resolution. These designs typically transcend individual episodes of conflict, but may entrench long-standing divisions in a political community. They carry forward these biases from one situation to another and thus have significant structuring effects. Typically they are designed for a national or regional territory, but play out in localities, often in different ways. This means that assessing the consequences of any particular innovation in institutional design in terms of structuring the terrain of urban conflict is a challenging evaluative task. This is made more complex as those involved in making use of system procedures will always interpret them in particular ways. Yet if our analyses are to provide resources for activists and for those in government positions of one kind of another, then surely we should offer research studies that help those engaged in urban governance with a progressive purpose to grasp what to campaign for and what to resist.

References

Adams, D. and Tiesdell, S. (2013) *Shaping Places: Urban Planning, Design and Development*, London, UK: Routledge.

Castells, M. (1977) *The Urban Question*, London, UK: Arnold.

Clifford, B. and Tewdwr-Jones, M. (2013) *The Collaborative Planner? Practitioners in the Neoliberal Age*, Bristol, UK: Policy Press.

Dewey, J. (1991 [1927]) *The Public and Its Problems*, Athens, OH: Swallow Press/Ohio University Press.

Forester, J. (1989) *Planning in the Face of Power*, Berkeley, CA: University of California Press.

Forester, J. (1999) *The Deliberative Practitioner: Encouraging Participatory Planning Processes*, Cambridge, MA: MIT Press.

Harvey, D. (1982) *The Limits to Capital*, Oxford, UK: Blackwell.

Healey, P. (1998) "Regulating Property Development and the Capacity of the Development Industry," *Journal of Property Research*, 15(3): 211–228.

Healey, P. (2006 [1997]) *Collaborative Planning: Shaping Places in Fragmented Societies*, Basingstoke, UK: Macmillan.

Healey, P. (2007) *Urban Complexity and Spatial Strategies: Towards a Relational Planning for Our Times*, London, UK: Routledge.

Healey, P. (2009) "The Pragmatist Tradition in Planning Thought," *Journal of Planning Education and Research*, 28(3): 277–292.

Pløger, J. (2015) "Impossible Common Ground: Planning and Reconciliation," in J. Metzger, P. Allmendinger and S. Oosterlynck (eds.), *Planning Against the Political: Democratic Deficits in Contemporary European Territorial Governance*, London, UK: Routledge: 107–128.

Ritzdorf, M. (1985) "Challenging the Exclusionary Impact of Family Definitions in American Municipal Zoning Ordinances," *Journal of Urban Affairs*, 7(1): 15–26.

Sager, T. (2012) *Reviving Critical Planning Theory: Dealing with Pressure, Neo-Liberalism and Responsibility in Communicative Planning*, London, UK: Routledge.

Scott, A. J. and Roweis, S. T. (1977) "Urban Planning in Theory and Practice: A Reappraisal," *Environment and Planning A*, 9(10): 1097–1119.

Specter, M. G. (2010) *Habermas: An Intellectual Biography*, Cambridge, UK: Cambridge University Press.

Vidyarthi, S. (2010) "Re-Imagining the Neighbourhood Unit for India," in P. Healey and R. Upton (eds.), *Crossing Borders: International Exchange and Planning Practices*, London, UK: Routledge: 73–93.

Yiftachel, O. (1998) "Planning and Social Control: Exploring the Dark Side," *Journal of Planning Literature*, 12(4): 396–406.

Index